shows us why it deserves that honor. **It's taken almost seventy-five years for a sufficiently gifted writer to re-create the magnificence of that event, but it's been worth every moment of the wait."**

—PETER BODO, senior editor and chief columnist, *Tennis* magazine

"For those of us who believe that tennis is a metaphor for life, here at last in this **marvelous** narrative is proof, served up on the rackets of Budge and von Cramm. *A Terrible Splendor* is **a wonderful account of a time of great historical drama, with the world on the brink of war, and everything resting, or so it would seem, on getting the ball back over the net just one more time."**

—ABRAHAM VERGHESE, author of *My Own Country* and *Cutting for Stone*

"Through the prism of one of the greatest tennis matches ever played, Marshall Jon Fisher **throws open a window on the terrifying world of the thirties** in Europe, illuminating in vivid detail the persecution of Baron Gottfried von Cramm, the pitiful kowtowing to Hitler by the tennis authorities, and, rising above it all, the innate sportsmanship of the two friends and rivals, von Cramm and Donald Budge. **Between every Budge backhand and von Cramm volley, history rears up in all its 'terrible splendor.' "**

—RICHARD EVANS, correspondent, *The Observer* (London)

# A TERRIBLE SPLENDOR

THREE EXTRAORDINARY MEN,

A WORLD POISED FOR WAR,

AND THE GREATEST

TENNIS MATCH EVER PLAYED

## MARSHALL JON FISHER

CROWN PUBLISHERS · NEW YORK

Copyright © 2009 by Marshall Jon Fisher

Published in the United States by Crown Publishers, an imprint of the
Crown Publishing Group, a division of Random House, Inc., New York.
www.crownpublishing.com

CROWN and the Crown colophon are registered trademarks of
Random House, Inc.

Library of Congress Cataloging-in-Publication Data

Fisher, Marshall.
A terrible splendor / Marshall Jon Fisher.—1st ed.
    p. cm.
Includes bibliographical references and index.
1. Davis Cup—History.   2. Tennis—Tournaments—History.   3. Cramm,
Gottfried von, 1909–1976.   4. Tennis players—Germany—Biography.
    5. Gay men—Germany—Biography.   6. Gays—Nazi persecution.
7. National socialism.   8. Budge, Don, 1915–2000   9. Tennis players—
United States—Biography.   I. Title.

GV999.T47 2009
796.342—dc22         2008050527

ISBN 978-0-307-39394-4

Printed in the United States of America

*Design by Lauren Dong*

10   9   8   7   6   5   4   3   2   1

First Edition

*For Mom and Dad*

Fate . . . envelops and overshadows the whole; and under its lowering influence, the fiercest efforts of human will appear but like flashes that illuminate the wild scene with a brief and terrible splendor, and are lost forever in the darkness.

—Thomas Carlyle, *on the work of Friedrich Schiller*

# CONTENTS

## Author's Note

READERS MAY WONDER how I came up with actual dialogue and internal thoughts. Speech that is in quotation marks, and thoughts that are italicized, in conventional fashion, are directly from primary sources and are credited as such. At other times, however, I felt a need to dramatize a moment, without knowing for certain exactly what was said or thought. At these times I drew inspiration from Rachel Cohen's *A Chance Meeting*, stories of relationships between writers and artists from the nineteenth and twentieth centuries, in which she often imagines conversations that might have taken place. (She in turn acknowledges an indebtedness for this method of biographical nonfiction to writers such as Leon Edel, Justin Kaplan, Louis Menand, and a number of others.) To make evident where I have deduced or pieced together dialogue, interior and exterior, from other sources, these lines have no italics or quotation marks. Also, like Cohen, I have tried to make things even more clear by using words like *perhaps*, *must have*, or *likely*. However, it is important to note that none of these passages is fanciful: each is based firmly on my research (as referenced in the notes).

# A TERRIBLE SPLENDOR

# The GENTLEMAN of WIMBLEDON

J ULY THE TWENTIETH, 1937, AND Baron Gottfried von Cramm tosses a new white Slazenger tennis ball three feet above his head. It seems to hang there suspended for the slightest of moments, a distant frozen moon, before his wooden racket plucks it out of the electrified air of Wimbledon's Centre Court, rocketing a service winner past J. Donald Budge. The deciding match of the Davis Cup competition between the United States and Germany has begun, a contest that will long be called "the greatest tennis match ever." Fourteen thousand onlookers—aristocrats out to be seen, sportswriters, any tennis fans who could take off work on a Tuesday; Queen Mary, her entourage, several members of Parliament, and foreign diplomats in the Royal Box—shift in their seats as von Cramm's serve finally splits the fine membrane between anticipation and fulfillment. The thud of tight "catgut" strings against ball marks the moment: it is 4:57 P.M.

I T WAS ANOTHER UNUSUALLY GLORIOUS SUMMER DAY FOR LONDON. In fact, hardly a drop of rain had fallen all month, and today was cloudless again, the midsummer sun still high, the mercury steadfast in the mid-seventies, just as *The Times* had promised. The weather report, however, was the most uplifting part of the newspaper that morning—and

even the weather had to share its page with the obituary of Amelia
Earhart. She had been missing for a fortnight, ever since taking off
from Lae, Papua New Guinea, for Howland Island, some 2,500 miles
off in the Pacific. She'd made it three-quarters of the way through what
was to be the first around-the-world flight at the earth's full circumfer-
ence. Encountering unexpected headwinds, however, Earhart and her
navigator Fred Noonan flew for over twenty hours, exhausting their
fuel supply, without quite reaching the island. President Roosevelt had
authorized a $4 million search effort by nine naval ships and sixty-six
aircraft, but on July 18 the search was finally abandoned.

The front page was no more heartening. Londoners propping their
morning *Times* up against their teacups were presented with a palette of
ominous headlines: BITTER FIGHTING NEAR MADRID. Almost exactly a year
ago, the fascist General Francisco Franco had led a makeshift rebel army
of Moors and foreign legionnaires from Morocco across the Strait of
Gibraltar to revolt against the five-year-old Republican Spanish government. A gruesome civil war had ensued, and a year later there seemed no
end in sight.

The day's other headlines—CHINA AT BAY: ACUTE STATE OF TENSION
and COST OF AIR RAID PRECAUTIONS—reminded readers of Japan's ongo-
ing undeclared war against China, a dangerous harbinger of the threat
to come from the East, and of the growing recognition that the shock
waves of war could soon rattle the home isle.

Foreign Secretary Anthony Eden had given a major speech in the
House of Commons yesterday, commenting on all these situations. But
although he admitted to the "inherently dangerous" aspect of certain
current configurations, he assured the House that peace would prevail.
Putting aside objections to German involvement in the Spanish war,
along with Winston Churchill's outrage that "huge guns had been
mounted outside Gibraltar," Eden praised the Soviet and Nazi governments' new naval treaty, as well as the French government's "sincere"
desire for "appeasement both with Germany and in Europe." Rather
than bring Europe closer to another cataclysmic war, he reasoned, the
Spanish war "had shown all responsible people how much more horrible
war has become."

Winston Churchill sneered, and Labour MP Hugh Dalton "considered the Government a set of idiotic ostriches . . . blind to the new

technique of aggression practised by the Fascist Powers in Spain." If such techniques proved successful there, he argued, they would no doubt soon be applied in Central Europe.

Punch drunk from the long-building threat of war, along with eight months of royal scandal and political battles, London was relieved to turn back to that most reliable of diversions: tennis at Wimbledon.

In 1937 the world's most famous and perfectly groomed grass courts, site of the All England Lawn Tennis and Croquet Club, were to host a full month of world-class tennis. First, of course, there were the Championships: the tournament known simply as "Wimbledon." Then the All England Club would host the Davis Cup, the team competition formally known as the International Lawn Tennis Championships. The preliminary rounds, to determine the winners of the American Zone and the European Zone, had taken place in the spring, in Budapest and Berlin, Stockholm and Belgrade, San Francisco and Mexico City, and other cities. The two zone winners, Germany and the United States, were to face off in the Interzone Final, at Wimbledon, to decide who would take on the defending champion. Finally, in the Challenge Round, the British team would defend the Cup against the winning challenger. Great Britain had held the trophy for three years; this year, however, it was common knowledge that without three-time Wimbledon champ Fred Perry, who had turned professional and was thus ineligible, Britain stood little chance. The real championship was being contested in the Interzone Final and, as it turned out, in its fifth and deciding match, between Budge and von Cramm.

In an era when most world-class tennis, including the Davis Cup, Wimbledon, and the other major tournaments, was amateur, and players played for glory, not money, the Davis Cup was the most important trophy in tennis and one of the biggest competitions in world sports.

It all began in 1900, when a Harvard student named Dwight Davis placed an order at Shreve, Crump, & Low Co. in Boston for a trophy bowl made of 217 ounces of sterling silver and lined with gold. Davis and his classmates Holcombe Ward and Malcolm Whitman were lawn tennis fanatics and had decided to instigate an international team competition. That first year they invited only Great Britain; no other country had enough serious tennis players. The English team, which included future three-time Wimbledon champion Arthur Gore, sailed across the ocean only to fall prey to oppressive hundred-degree temperatures at the Longwood Cricket Club near Boston, as well as the Harvard boys' "American Twist" serve, recently invented by Ward.

Davis himself played in only one subsequent Cup competition before moving on in life. Despite horrific grades at Harvard (he was far more interested in tennis than in his studies), he became secretary of war in 1925 and later governor-general of the Philippines. But the Cup he donated became the most coveted trophy in tennis. Even late in the century, in the era of big-money professional tennis, superstars like John McEnroe and Arthur Ashe said that winning the Davis Cup was the highlight of their careers.

By the 1920s, in Europe, the Americas, and Australia, Davis Cup matches drew huge crowds, front-page headlines, and the attention of heads of state. "I sometimes wonder if the Davis Cup was a good thing," said Davis around this time. "It has become too big." Sometimes the pressure of playing for one's country and hearing "Advantage, United States," instead of their own name was too much for players. In 1932 the American world champion Ellsworth Vines crushed Bunny Austin in the Wimbledon final, losing only six games in three sets. But in the next year's Davis Cup he lost to Austin on the same court by almost the same score. Britain's normally unflappable Fred Perry got the jitters on the brink of victory against Germany's Daniel Prenn in 1932 and lost after leading five-two in the fifth set. Even the great Bill Tilden, avatar of lawn tennis in the 1920s, felt the pressure. "Tournament tennis is a wonderful game," he said, "but Davis Cup matches are mental torture. Every time I played against those Frenchmen in Davis Cup matches I suffered hell for weeks."

Tilden, the imperious world champion, almost single-handedly kept Dwight Davis's trophy in American hands from 1920 to 1927. But finally, slowed by age, he fell to "those Frenchmen," and the Cup rested in Paris for six years. Then Fred Perry and his British teammates captured it and successfully defended it at Wimbledon for four years. Now, for the first time in a decade, the Americans had a chance to bring it home. And Tilden was there, sitting ringside and cheering like the sport's biggest fan. But not for the side one would think. After having his offers to coach the American team repeatedly refused, Tilden had for the past couple years been helping to train the German Davis Cuppers. And over the past decade Tilden had become close friends with Gottfried von Cramm.

Von Cramm's game would not have been as strong were it not for Tilden—"Tilden effected startling changes in [his] backhand" at a crucial point in his development, von Cramm once said. But then tennis itself would not have been what it was in 1937 were it not for Tilden. No player before or since had anything near his influence on the game. He had taken a polite gentry pastime and transformed it into an arena for world-class athletes. To be fair, Maurice "Red Mac" McLoughlin, "the California Comet," had made inroads along these lines, thrilling crowds with his new aggressive "serve and volley" style as he won the U.S. Championships of 1912 and 1913. But his career was shortened—he was never the same after service in the Great War—and by 1926, near the end of Tilden's six-year reign as undisputed king of the sport, Tilden was "admitted by all to be the perfecter, almost the inventor of the modern nerve-racking sport so curiously camouflaged under its mild misnomer—'lawn' tennis. . . . Big Bill added bewildering change of pace, the stroke lob, half-volley passing shots, and all manner of over, under, and lateral spin. Under Tilden's transforming touch, tennis has become a smashing, dynamic test of speed and power where stamina and quickness of brain, courage and the closest psychological probing for the weaknesses of opponents must all be fused into the mental and physical makeup of a champion."

He had also been, since 1931, the prime attraction, chief promoter, and circus master of the still burgeoning (and not wholly respectable) enterprise of professional tennis. Tilden himself, before he finally turned pro at thirty-seven, considered professionals somewhere between household servants and prostitutes. But his outlook changed completely when he made a killing as one. Before Tilden, tennis players had remained amateurs and moved on to other careers when their tennis skills faded. Tilden was so great that he was able to have a long and illustrious amateur career and then, at the age when even the best players retired, turn pro and make big bucks for ten more years. But his example convinced the top players after him to leave the amateur game early. In recent years both Vines and Perry had turned pro at the peak of their games. Already, just after his first major championship, the rumors were flying about Budge. In a few months the young man would be tempted by a dizzying offer from promoter C. C. "Cash and Carry" Pyle.

There had been calls in some quarters for "open tennis," with the major tournaments open to pros and amateurs alike, but that would not happen for over thirty years. For the moment professionals were still barred from all the major tournaments, and the glory remained with the amateurs. And today's match would attain an instant luster that would only shine brighter with the passing decades. The young American superstar, on the verge of garnering all the riches that his talent would afford, against the ultimate amateur: the European aristocrat who would never turn pro, who played for the sheer beauty of the sport.

It was a tense afternoon for Tilden, von Cramm, and Budge. Both Tilden and von Cramm knew that this match could be critical for the German, who had run afoul of Germany's Nazi government. He had reason to think, he confided in Tilden recently, that he was being watched, and that only bringing the Davis Cup home to Germany could guarantee his safety.

And as little love lost as there was between Tilden and the powers that be in American tennis, he must have been somewhat uncomfortable sitting "in the other camp" at such a big Davis Cup match, after all those years of being the U.S. team's anchor. He was still playing professionally, at the age of forty-four, and would for years, but his best days were behind him. He was almost out of money, almost out of friends. He must have had some vague recognition in the back of his mind, as he watched this match, which he would consider the apotheosis of the sport he once ruled, that his own life was beginning a slow but irreversible unraveling.

For Don Budge, it was merely the biggest match of his life. This skinny red-headed kid, son of an Oakland truck driver, could not have presented a greater contrast with the dashing aristocratic German, or with the overbearing blueblood Tilden, sitting conspicuously up there in the grandstand. At twenty-two, he had just reached the peak of his game, crushing von Cramm two weeks before to win Wimbledon and become the unofficial champion of the world. But as they walked on court this day, it still felt like the baron was the focus of the crowd's adulation, the true tennis royalty. And Wimbledon champion or not, in 1937 the Davis Cup was still the crown jewel of tennis for any player.

It was a major event for all sports fans. In the United States that summer the Yankees and Giants were cruising toward an autumn World Series showdown. Seabiscuit had come east for the first time and was sweeping the horse races there, spurring talk of a Race of the Century with the unbeatable War Admiral. On June 22 Joe Louis, who the summer before had suffered a shocking upset at the hands of the German fighter Max Schmeling, captured the heavyweight crown he would wear for twelve years with an eighth-round knockout of James J. Braddock in Chicago. But no sporting event was bigger in mid-July than the Budge–von Cramm match.

As for Germany, it was trying to reach the Challenge Round for the first time. The Germans' first great chance had come back in July 1914. With world war imminent, Otto Froitzheim and Oskar Kreuzer had stayed behind in Pittsburgh to finish the semifinal round against Australia, while the rest of the squad sailed for home. War was the topic of every conversation; the international camaraderie characteristic of most Davis Cup competitions was absent, as the teams kept to themselves off the court. The Germans announced that they would leave the country the moment war broke out, whether or not the matches were finished. As it happened, the WAR DECLARED telegrams electrified the transatlantic cables during the final match, but the men in the press box couldn't bring themselves to shout out the news to the crowd until the match was over. The Australians, who were to win the Cup back from the Americans the next week, celebrated while Froitzheim and Kreuzer headed straight for their ship. Their boat was sunk off the coast of Gibraltar, and they were taken prisoner by the British. They spent the war years in an English prisoner-of-war camp.

After the war Germany was barred from international competition by the International Lawn Tennis Federation. It was reinstated in 1927, and made it to the Interzone Final a tantalizing four times in ten years, but was never quite able to attain the next level. In 1937, with von Cramm and the powerful Henner Henkel, the Germans figured they had their best chance ever.

The opening two days' matches had gone as expected. Budge and von Cramm, the top two amateur players in the world, had won their singles matches easily against Henkel and Bitsy Grant. In the doubles, Budge and Gene Mako had beaten von Cramm and Henkel in a tight match, just as they had a few weeks earlier in the Wimbledon tournament. Then, earlier today, Henkel had beaten Grant to knot the score at two-all. Now the world's best two players would play the fifth and deciding match. With only a relatively weak British squad waiting in the Challenge Round, the Budge–von Cramm contest was sure to decide who would win the Cup.

American tennis fans had reason to be nervous. Although Budge was a big favorite to win, nothing could be taken for granted in a competition that had come down to one match against the world's number-two player. "Budge versus von Cramm was a cinch, a sure thing, a pretty sure thing, a strong probability, a possibility, a forlorn hope," intoned *American Lawn Tennis*, the tennis player's weekly bible. In the United States thousands of fans stayed home from work to listen to the match on the radio. Countless others listened in while at the office. Still more "depended on the ticker, newspaper offices, or friends in Wall Street houses for updates." So many people took time off from their Tuesday to listen to the radio broadcast, it was said, that there was a noticeable lull in activity on the New York Stock Exchange.

And in London, on this bright English summer day, thousands of tennis enthusiasts, after reading of the brutal fighting in Spain and China and tossing the paper aside with a sigh, made their way out to Wimbledon by tube, bus, taxi, chauffeured Bentley, or royal motorcade to enjoy international competition of a more civilized sort.

Shortly after noon they began arriving, walking or busing it from the Southfields tube station a half-mile away or dropped off by their drivers in front of the All England Club, making their way onto the grounds, congregating along the two-hundred-yard-long promenade that led past the tea lawn to the tennis courts. To the left, behind a thick ten-foot-high hedge, the fifteen outer courts lay in peace, perfect green rectangles separated by similar hedges and manicured brick walkways, with simple garden benches for spectators. Ahead on the right loomed the Centre Court stadium.

Before 1937, whenever Davis Cup matches had been contested at Wimbledon, it had been the custom to save Centre Court for the

Challenge Round, playing earlier rounds on Court Number One. The five thousand seats of that adjoining arena were generally more than enough even for the Interzone Final, and the tender lawn of Centre Court needed to recover after the two-week stampede of the Championships. This year, however, the prospect of Budge, von Cramm, and their countrymen meeting in what everyone expected was the true Davis Cup championship clearly merited the sport's grandest theater. For the first time, Centre Court was prepared for use in the Interzone Final.

The people filed into the great structure, entering the dimly lit maze of corridors, negotiating this "bewildering rabbit warren of a place" and finding their way to the appropriate gangway for their seats. Helping them along was a regiment of crisply uniformed ushers, comprising members of the armed forces on leave.

The spectators emerging from the darkened passageways squinted at the sudden reappearance of sunlight and gazed down at the focal point of this modern coliseum: the most famous tennis court in the world, "green and taut as a billiard table." As the seats filled and two o'clock approached, the umpire, linesmen, and ball boys (of which Wimbledon employed a regular staff) entered the court and took their positions around the perimeter like security agents. Then, just before two, a door opened in the dark green wall at the back of the court, just under and to the left of the Royal Box. Out walked five men: the two nonplaying captains, Walter Pate and Heinrich Kleinschroth; twenty-seven-year-old Ted Tinling, a former player, budding dress designer, and Wimbledon's "player liaison"; and the contestants of the day's first match, Bitsy Grant and Henner Henkel. Expectant applause rose from the stands.

Many seats remained empty at two o'clock, for this first match was not the main attraction. It was expected that Henkel would have little trouble disposing of Grant and forging a two-two tie. Almost everyone, except the most ardent American fans, was looking forward to a showdown between Budge and von Cramm, the two greatest amateur players in the world, to break the stalemate.

Sure enough, when those two great champions emerged with Tinling and their captains from the same green door at 4:50 p.m., the score was United States 2, Germany 2, and the applause pulsed with excitement. The contingent turned and bowed to the Royal Box, which was quite full today. Remarkably, Queen Mary herself was now there, an unprecedented appearance for a mere interzone playoff in which the British team was not involved. In fact, every seat in the stadium was filled, as well as every inch of space in the standing room area, to which all twelve hundred tickets had been sold. Those recipients were the lucky front guard of a queue of some three to five thousand, many of whom had camped out there the previous night with stools, rugs, books, and kerosene stoves to cook their meals. Thousands more fans who had showed up too late even for the standing room had paid two shillings apiece for entrance to the grounds. They waited outside the stadium to follow the match's progress on the electric scoreboard there, a replica of the one inside. Both, remarked an impressed reporter, were controlled by a set of buttons at the umpire's chair.

The two players walked ahead of the others toward their courtside seats more like doubles partners than combatants in the most important tennis match of the year. Von Cramm, the impeccably groomed German aristocrat, wore his usual long cream-colored flannel trousers with the red and white belt, the colors of his home club, the famous Rot-Weiss Tennis Club in Berlin, and an immaculate white blazer. Budge, six years von Cramm's junior, still "a slim, freckled youngster out of Booth Tarkington," as he had been described two years earlier, was no sartorial slouch himself. As always, he wore a tightly fit polo shirt, today of course the U.S. Davis Cup team shirt with shield and initials over the left breast. And although a number of players had already begun to wear shorts on court, Budge never appeared in anything but his tailored gabardine white slacks. He must have worn them well, for one journalist, apparently unaware that Simpson's of London made the same pants for Perry, von Cramm, Budge, and presumably others, wrote: "Budge not only wears long pants, but the snappiest, whitest, best-fitting cricket-cloth affairs yet seen on the courts." In damp weather he might wear black spiked shoes for better traction on the grass, but on a fair day like today his outfit was unadulterated white, right down to his spotless sneakers. Shoulder to shoulder, the young men trod across the turf with their rackets, smiling and chatting.

As they strolled, von Cramm took one of his Dunlop Maxply rackets in his right hand and tossed it onto the ground ahead of them, as casually as if it were a Sunday club match. "Rough or smooth?" he asked. Budge chose rough. They reached the racket, and von Cramm retrieved it and carefully held it up for Budge to see. Together they examined the strings, commonly called "catgut" but actually made from the serosa, or outer lining, of sheep intestines. Near the bottom, a strand of red nylon was woven through, looped around the vertical strings; on one side you could feel the loops, on the other, not. The racket had landed with the smooth side up.

Budge grinned. Gottfried, he may have been saying, I still don't see how you can play with such a small grip. Von Cramm would have laughed back: If you had half a finger, you'd use a small grip too. When he was ten years old, one of the many horses on the family estate at Schloss Brüggen had bit him as he was feeding it by hand. The upper joint of his right index finger had to be amputated. As the accident occurred just before Gottfried took up tennis, though, it didn't put a damper on his game. He merely learned to play with the hand he was dealt. And always used a small grip.

They reached the net and arranged their rackets near the umpire's chair. Von Cramm carefully folded his white jacket and laid it down. Having won the toss, he elected to serve, and his friend chose to begin play on the north side. Budge took one of his rackets in his right hand and gave it a few swings. His weapon couldn't have contrasted more with von Cramm's. Whereas the German's British-made Dunlop, with a minimum of paint and markings, really looked like the piece of sculpted wood it was, Budge's Wilson "Ghost" was as white as his shirt. And although leather grips had been introduced several years before, Budge was one of the last players to favor a bare wooden handle: the sanded ash was almost as white as the painted wood above. Also in contrast to von Cramm, who used a light "bat" with a small grip just like Tilden, Budge used an extra-large handle—4⅞" around—and the heaviest racket of any of the players: a sixteen-ounce bludgeon. Swung with Budge's expertise, it produced what tennis players call "a heavy ball." As one opponent put it, "It's no use when Budge turns on the heat. That ball comes to you like a great piece of lead. It just about breaks your arm." Another player said that if you dared to approach the net against Budge's famous backhand, "you'd swear you were volleying a piano."

The captains, Pate and Kleinschroth, took their seats in wide wicker chairs on either side of the umpire. Budge and von Cramm posed for photographs together at the net and then began warming up, their deceptively relaxed swings knocking the ball back and forth with effortless power. Budge must have noted again with satisfaction, as he had the first two days, the same condition the BBC commentator was describing on the radio at that moment—that due to all the play of the previous few weeks, and the dry weather, "the surface of the court has become very fast, rather fast indeed. The ball skids a bit before hopping up. The grass seems to actually increase the speed of the shot." This was characteristic of grass courts, but particularly when they were dry and well worn. And this could only help Budge, the harder hitter of the two. Von Cramm had grown up on Germany's slow red-clay courts; it was no coincidence that his two greatest victories had occurred on the famous clay courts of Paris.

By now the stands were filled to capacity, excited murmurs echoing under the roof as though it were the home team defending the Cup today. Around the stadium the tiers of seats rose so steeply that the spectators felt themselves hovering over the players, cloistered together with them in an intimate shelter from the threatening world outside. The sharp thwack of ball against catgut alternated with the softer thud of ball on grass, a familiar percussive prelude. Finally, after exactly five minutes of warm-up, the fans still milling about outside could hear the electrically amplified voice of the umpire: "Quiet, please, ladies and gentlemen. Linesmen ready? Players ready? Play."

"The German's hair flashed," noted the young radio journalist Alistair Cooke, "he let loose a cannonball, and it was an ace for Germany." If there had been any doubt as to whom the crowd would be backing, it was instantly dispelled. The staccato crack of von Cramm's service ace was echoed by an explosion of applause.

The English audience had good reason to pull for von Cramm today. Their boys had little hope to defend the Cup in the next round, but they figured they had a better outlook against Germany than against the United States. Don Budge, after all, was the world's best, and the American team looked to be far superior to the Germans, despite the fact that this round had come down to the final match. Budge had demolished von Cramm in the Wimbledon final, and few experts gave the German much of a chance today. Yesterday, according to *The Times*, von Cramm had actually been the weaker member of the German doubles team. Perhaps the British team of the experienced but often outgunned

Bunny Austin and the untested lefty Charlie Hare could somehow manage to hang on to the Cup for one more year if they could only face the Germans.

VON CRAMM FOLLOWS HIS OPENING POINT WITH THREE MORE UN-returnable serves, and the first game is his "at love." As the players change sides, Budge feels an insistent throbbing in his right shoulder. Yesterday he and his buddy Gene Mako gave the United States a two-one advantage by prevailing in a marathon doubles match against von Cramm and Henkel, the winner of the French Championships in May. After winning the first set, the Germans were ahead five-three in the second set, had two set points in the third, and were up four-one in the fourth; yet the Americans prevailed 4-6, 7-5, 8-6, 6-4. From the beginning it had been clear to aficionados that Budge was nursing a sore shoulder. He rubbed it between points, and he hit none of his famous cannonball serves—the flat power ones, as opposed to slices or American Twists—until the final game of the match, when he finally let loose the cannon to secure the victory. "Budge, like Tilden in his prime," *The Times* declared yesterday, "can score an ace by service almost at will." But today even Budge has to be wondering if he might have fired his last ammunition in the doubles.

Even more troubling than Budge's shoulder, though, is the fact that this is obviously a very different von Cramm than the man he beat easily in the Wimbledon final a few weeks ago. The German seems determined to make up for that disappointment, as well as for the two Wimbledons before that, which he lost in the finals to Fred Perry. It appears to be one of those days that von Cramm's friend, the British player John Olliff, was referring to when he wrote that Gottfried "could, at times, play the most brilliant tennis imaginable. He could raise his game a little above what you and I always thought was perfect. For short spasms he could make Budge look like a qualifier."

Still, Budge is able to hold him off on his own serve, and then in the fifth game of the match, with the score tied at two-all, he thinks he has his first chance to take control. Von Cramm, who has been serving extraordinarily well from the first point, goes up forty-love on his service, but Budge battles back to deuce and twice gets to break point. In a match between two great servers like this, one break of serve usually means winning the set. But on each break point, von Cramm pulls out a great serve to get back to deuce. And now it is advantage Germany again. Von Cramm has a famous second serve, maybe even better than his first. He likes to toss the ball a bit to his left, almost behind him, and arch his back as he swings to create a rounded motion, catching the ball from left to right as well as back to forward, creating enormous topspin. It's Holcombe Ward's old American Twist serve, but this German has perfected it to the point that it perhaps should be renamed. On clay it has a particularly ferocious high bounce, since spin has more effect on clay, but even on the grass he is able to win points outright with his second serve. And in fact, on his fourth game point in this fifth game, he rears back and delivers a second serve that Budge chases almost into the first row of spectators, in vain. Three-two for Germany.

THE PACKED HOUSE ROARED AGAIN IN APPROVAL, AND NOT JUST IN hopes of an easier opponent for England. It was not unusual for spectators anywhere to cheer for the charismatic German. Von Cramm was the most popular tennis player around the globe. At five foot eleven, quite tall for the time, classically handsome, with "a personal magnetism that dominated any scene he was a part of," he was not only the greatest German player ever and the number-two player in the world for the past four years, he was also the very embodiment of style, grace, and sportsmanship. "Every player could take a lesson in etiquette and unostentatious good manners from the Baron," wrote *The New Yorker* that year. "He never bangs the ball back between points; he never makes an opponent wait, nor does he ever hurry one." He would never glare at a linesman, as the great Tilden was wont to do; von Cramm gave a bad call neither a second glance nor a second thought. Once when called for a foot fault—stepping on the baseline while serving before making contact with the ball—he even turned to the linesman and apologized for his error.

Most in the audience would remember what he had done over on Court Number One two years before in 1935, also in the Interzone Final against the Americans. In the crucial doubles match von Cramm had to hold up a far weaker partner, Kai Lund, against the experienced

American team of Wilmer Allison and John van Ryn. Playing what Allison afterward called "the greatest one-man doubles match" he had ever seen, von Cramm managed to bring his team to match point five times. On the last of these points, he delivered a thunderous first serve that Allison barely was able to block back. Lund, given the easiest setup of the day, fell to the pressure and dumped his volley into the net. He smashed his racket onto the grass in frustration, but "Cramm's expression did not change. No annoyance, no disappointment; by the serenity of his temperament he inspired his tired teammate." And then, on the very next point, Lund appeared to hit a winning shot to give Germany a sixth match point. But von Cramm, "the soul of chivalry," as one observer put it, walked over to the umpire and calmly informed him that the ball had grazed his racket before Lund had hit it. Neither the umpire nor any of the other players had noticed. It was the Americans' point, and they went on to defeat the Germans and advance to the Challenge Round.

In the locker room afterward, a German tennis official was beside himself. Never before, he reminded von Cramm, had the Germans come so close to the world championship. Froitzheim and Kreuzer became POWs in the 1914 effort. Twenty-one years later Germany had had another golden opportunity to reach the Challenge Round, all but winning the crucial doubles match to go up two-one, with von Cramm certain to provide the winning point in singles the next day—and he had given it away of his own accord! He had let down his teammates and his nation.

Von Cramm, with characteristic elegance and composure, stared calmly back. "Tennis is a gentleman's game," he said, "and that's the way I've played it ever since I picked up my first racket. Do you think that I would sleep tonight knowing that the ball had touched my racket without my saying so? Never, because I would be violating every principle I think this game stands for. On the contrary, I don't think I'm letting the German people down. I think I'm doing them credit."

He introduced himself as "Gottfried Cramm," preferring to drop the "Baron" and the "von" whenever possible. But his lineage was apparent from the first handshake, in his posture, his accent, his manners. His mother, Jutta von Steinberg, belonged to one of the great German dynasties; and since for the first time in a thousand years there had been no male heir to the Steinberg fortune, young Jutta became known as "The Great Prize of Hanover." The winner of this prize was Burghard von Cramm, a young man from another prominent local family. Von Cramm nobility had lived in the area since 1296.

Gottfried Alexander Maximilian Walter Kurt von Cramm was born July 7, 1909, at the family manor in Nettlingen, about thirty miles southeast of Hanover. When Gottfried was two, he moved with his parents and three brothers to yet another castle, Schloss Brüggen, the von Steinberg estate that they had recently inherited after the death of Jutta's father. For the next twenty-eight years Brüggen would be the main von Cramm home. Nestled in a majestic river valley in the foothills of the Seven Mountains, Brüggen had been established in 965 as the royal seat of Otto the Great. In the early twentieth century, when Gottfried was growing up, the von Cramm estate in Brüggen was a world unto itself. Visitors would drive slowly through the humble little town until they came to the high walls of the compound. They then passed through the main gate into an enormous courtyard—and another existence. Looming across the circular drive was the mansion, built in 1693 by Jutta's ancestor, Friedrich II von Steinberg, and now presided over by Jutta, her mother, and a staff of maids and kitchen help. A grand living room and dining room were decorated with landscapes of centuries past and portraits of Cramm and Steinberg ancestors. An ornate sitting room overlooking the rear grounds became a playroom for the boys, where they would read by the fireplace or play charades and chess.

But outside was the true glory of Schloss Brüggen. By 1917 there were seven von Cramm boys in the Seven Mountains, and the estate boasted acres and acres of farmland and fields to play on, with stables where the boys learned to ride the farm horses, coach horses, and even racehorses.

When war broke out in 1914, their father, a reserve officer, left for service; but other than that the Great War had little effect on the idyllic, insular life at Brüggen. The maids still taught the boys table manners at the great kitchen table. Private tutors still home-schooled them: the pastor from Oelber rode over to teach Latin and religion; teachers from the schools in Hanover and Braunschweig were hired to teach various other subjects; and then there was Fräulein Marggraff. Already an elderly woman when she first came to Brüggen, she had been governess and tutor at the royal courts of Spain and England. One of her students at Buckingham Palace had been Prince Edward, the future King Edward VIII, who would abdicate his throne to marry Mrs. Simpson. When hostilities commenced, Fräulein Marggraff, like the German Davis Cuppers in Pittsburgh, immediately sailed for home. She was more fortunate, though, and ended up living at the posh von Cramm estate as governess and instructor of modern foreign languages. From her the boys learned their faultless Oxbridge English, as well as how to behave like English gentlemen at teatime, a ceremony observed scrupulously at Schloss Brüggen under Fräulein Marggraff's watchful eye even while Germans and Englishmen slaughtered each other on the battlefield.

Just before the turn of the century, Gottfried's father had returned from studying law at Oxford, enamored of English manners and infused with the English love of sports. At that time in Germany sports were not considered proper activity. "Sport at this time was considered dangerous," one writer remembered. "You were thought crazy to mess with the pommel horse and horizontal bar. Soccer was thought of as about the same as card games or forbidden love." In England, however, Burghard von Cramm had been impressed by the prominence of organized sports in public-school and university life. Students pursued track and field, crew, cricket, rugby, soccer, and tennis with competitive zeal, but always, above all, emphasizing the ideals of sportsmanship, fair play, and honor.

Burghard encouraged his sons to pursue sports, sometimes even at the expense of their studies. Off at war he wrote home to Gottfried, "You shouldn't study so much in the summer. Tell your teacher in my name: in the German climate the winter months are for mental work, the summer for strengthening the body." So for breaks between classes, the boys ran races out in the fields. And their life after school and on weekends embodied the recent popularity of sports in German life— for by 1914 the English enthusiasm for the sporting life had finally spread to the Continent. The boys formed a soccer team, augmented by two workers from the estate and two village boys, and forever remembered their hard-fought victory over a team from the nearby town of Alfeld. And with the stables so available, the boys all learned to ride well; Gottfried's younger brother Erne even became a celebrated jockey.

Shortly after the family had moved to Brüggen, Burghard had had a beautiful red-clay tennis court built, along with a wall to practice against. During the war years the court got only sporadic use, but after Burghard came home for good, he encouraged his sons in this sport and also built clay courts at their other estates at Oelber and Bodenburg. Tennis was beginning to soar in popularity in Germany, spurred on by the successes of Otto Froitzheim, Robert and Heinrich Kleinschroth, and others. The von Cramms' summer home was Schloss Oelber, the primary von Cramm castle since the sixteenth century, and when the guest rooms were full, as they invariably were, the tennis court became the social center of the estate. And in 1919, when he turned ten, and shortly after recovering from the loss of part of his finger, Gottfried von Cramm began playing tennis in earnest.

He learned on one of the most magnificent spots on earth to play tennis. Adorning a leveled section of hillside overlooking the round stone castle, the Oelber court afforded players a sweeping view of the von Cramm gardens and farm fields stretching for acres off into the distance. Uphill was the family-owned church, built in 1585, which served the entire town, and the red-brick von Cramm mausoleum and graveyard. After tennis guests would leisurely follow the von Cramm boys, who ran down the hill on a path through the daffodils, over a small creek, and down to the gazebo, where everyone was served tea with a view of the grandiose, circular castle, its tower rising from the central courtyard.

Long after the family and guests had returned to the castle for cocktails and hors d'oeuvres, Gottfried would remain on the court, practicing his serve. Something about the game had grabbed him, never to let go. When a family friend asked him what he wanted to be when he grew up, Gottfried answered in his typically serious manner, "World Tennis Champion."

His father, who had watched the famed Doherty brothers and other English champions at Wimbledon, taught him everything he could. But soon Gottfried was learning from the best German players of all time. The von Cramms spent a good part of their summer days at their friends the von Dobenecks' estate in nearby Burgdorf. Burgdorf surpassed even Oelber, with two beautiful clay tennis courts, a golf course, and a crab-filled pond to complement the stalls full of riding horses and the mansion full of guest rooms and staff. There were two pretty daughters to boot—Victoria, the same age as Gottfried, and the younger Elisabeth, or Lisa—who rode and fished and played tennis right alongside the von Cramm boys.

Frequently among those guests at Burgdorf were the living legends of German tennis. There was Froitzheim, *der Altmeister* (Old Master) at age forty, seven-time winner of the German Championships and top-ranked from 1905 to 1928. Roman Najuch, the longtime coach at Berlin's Rot-Weiss Club, the capital of German tennis. And the Kleinschroth brothers. It had been said at one time that Robert, the elder, could beat anyone in the world on a given day. Heinrich, the younger brother, played Davis Cup for his country from 1913 to 1931 and for many years after that led the team as captain. A lifelong bachelor, he also became something of a second-father figure to Gottfried, and they remained close friends for life. Kleinschroth had earned a medical degree but never got around to practicing medicine. Instead, he made a life as a player, coach, and organizer and was the most familiar face in German tennis for decades.

At Burgdorf, Gottfried watched Germany's greatest players and listened to their stories of life on the international tennis circuit. Winter on the Riviera, the tournaments at Cannes and Nice. Then Paris in the spring for the French Championships. To England for the grass-court tournaments, culminating in the pomp and perfection of Wimbledon. Traveling around the world chasing the Davis Cup. Of course, all that was before August 1914. The Great War interrupted all international sports, and since the armistice Germans had been barred from international tournaments. But that couldn't last much longer. Soon, they were sure, German players would be reinstated in the world of international tennis.

The boy was entranced and vowed to himself he would someday join that world. When he was eighteen, in 1927, the ban on German players was lifted. The next year he finished his private schooling and was determined to devote himself to tennis. Otto Froitzheim had taken a particular interest in him, coaching him a bit each year on his visits. And in the spring of 1928 Froitzheim brought with him to Burgdorf none other than the most famous tennis player in the world, the greatest of all time, Big Bill Tilden.

It was Tilden's second visit to Germany, and it came just as the first chinks in the champion's armor were beginning to show. Eight years earlier, after working all winter to develop an offensive topspin back-hand, Tilden had won his first Wimbledon and U.S. championships at the advanced age of twenty-seven. Over the next six years he didn't lose a single match of consequence. He was the primary force in wrest-ing the Davis Cup from Australian hands in 1920 and keeping it in the United States for seven years. But in 1926 the thirty-three-year-old began to stumble. Hobbled by a knee injury, he lost his first Davis Cup match ever. It was a meaningless match to René Lacoste, as the United States had already clinched the Cup the day before. But to the French team, it was like the day Bleriot flew across the English Channel. Once someone did it, everyone thought they could do it too.

The next week Tilden played the U.S. Championships (also called the nationals) at Forest Hills and missed reaching the finals for the first time in nine years (although he only went out eight-six in the fifth set of the quarterfinals against eventual champion Henri Cochet). And in 1927, although still playing brilliantly, he would lose in all three of the major championships (the French, Wimbledon, and the U.S.—at that time, few players were willing to make the long sea journey to play the Australian Championships) and finally relinquish the Davis Cup. In fact, Tilden would make only two more major finals in his am-ateur career, though he would win both for his last big titles: the 1929 U.S. Championship and the 1930 Wimbledon crown.

But in May 1928, although dinged up a bit and not currently hold-ing any of the major championships, Big Bill Tilden was still the univer-sally acknowledged monarch of the game. In the words of his biographer Frank Deford, "Tilden simply *was* tennis in the public mind: Tilden and tennis, it was said, in that order." Upon his arrival in Berlin for the first time the year before, his train was greeted by a crowd of fans, and he was honored at a special dinner at the Rot-Weiss Tennis

Club. Standing ovations greeted him wherever he played—and even when he served as honorary umpire.

The Rot-Weiss Club soon became one of his favorite locales. The clubhouse, with its aging photographs and atmospheric scent of cigars and coffee, seemed to evoke the very history of tennis in Europe. He pronounced the Center Court, with its finely manicured clay and bucolic view of the Hundekehle Lake behind the south baseline, "an inspiration to any tennis player." He played a series of exhibitions against both pros and amateurs, and the next year, 1928, after once again trouncing the best that Berlin had to offer, Tilden accepted Froitzheim's offer to join him visiting the beautiful country estate in Burgdorf before continuing on his tour of Belgium, the Netherlands, and finally Paris and London. There, on and around the pristine clay courts, Tilden had his first glimpse of eighteen-year-old Gottfried von Cramm.

"Every year that von Cramm steps onto the Centre Court at Wimbledon," it would be said a few years later, "a few hundred young women sit a little straighter and forget about their escorts." Slender and good-looking, with gray-green eyes and dark blond hair, Gottfried could not have helped but arouse Tilden's attention. For one of sport's biggest secrets in the 1920s and 1930s was that Big Bill Tilden was a homosexual. What's more, he was a homosexual with a decided preference for teenage boys, preferably blonds. Everyone in the tennis world knew of Tilden's predilections, but few outside it did. For years the United States Lawn Tennis Association, for whom Tilden was a cash cow—or more like a cash mammoth—had been on tenterhooks, worried that at any moment Big Bill would say the wrong thing or touch the wrong boy. The year before, at the French Championships, some European journalists following the tennis circuit tried to expose him. At the Paris hotel where all the tennis players were staying, they bribed a bellboy to try to seduce Tilden. The bellboy was closer to thirty than thirteen, but blond and baby-faced. They slipped him some francs and sent him up to Tilden's room. To the newspapermen's chagrin, however, the young man was back in the lobby in a few minutes. The most he could get Tilden to do was to fondle him a bit.

Throughout the 1920s, a time so homophobic that homosexuality was rarely even discussed in public, Tilden, like many gay men, remained securely in the closet. In fact, as long as he stayed on top of the tennis world, he seems to have derived enough fulfillment from tennis to sublimate his sexual urges almost completely. Frank Hunter, Tilden's close friend and doubles partner, traveled with him extensively and often barged in on Tilden's hotel room for one reason or another, yet he never saw him with any sort of romantic partner. "I thought he was sexless," he said.

"He is as famous as Babe Ruth in his own country," wrote the leading newspaper columnist Westbrook Pegler around this time, "and just as famous in other countries where nobody ever heard of Babe Ruth, but the mysterious Mr. Tilden, though he glories in his celebrity . . . nevertheless is a stranger to the public. . . . His temperament has withstood description in a thousand attempts and defied popular understanding, and the people know him only as a figure, a celebrity, not as a person."

In what might have been an attempt to hint at the barrier to an open understanding of Tilden's character, Pegler, later to become infamous for his racial bigotry and anti-Semitism, mentioned, "Mr. Tilden also fancies himself as a patron of young boys who wish to play tennis."

Indeed, through the years Tilden developed close relationships with a number of young tennis players whom he referred to as his "heirs" or "successors." Although he apparently never made sexual advances toward these surrogate sons, it was always the same sort of young, "cute" boy who attracted Tilden's attention. First there was Frederick Staunton, the future newspaper publisher, who met Tilden as a teenager when Tilden was stationed in Pittsburgh in the army in 1918. Tilden took to coaching him on the tennis court every day and "soon began to speak grandiosely of tennis as the boy's life's work." Then in the early 1920s there was Sandy Wiener, a favorite from his home neighborhood of Germantown, in Philadelphia. In 1928 he became enamored of fifteen-year-old "Junior" Coen, a young player out of Kansas, and even managed to get him onto the Davis Cup team. (He's still the youngest player ever to play in a Davis Cup match.) In each case, however, the protégé decided that tennis was not in fact his "life's work" and turned to other endeavors; Tilden dropped him instantly and moved on.

In the spring of 1928, when he met Gottfried, he must have been attracted to the handsome young aristocrat. On the other hand, once he saw the boy hit a tennis ball his thoughts would have become strictly tutelary. Tilden never made passes at his prodigies; tennis was too important for that. Gottfried had the youth and good looks, the bright mind, and the athletic talent to set off all the bells in Tilden's mind. What's more, he already considered tennis his "life's work"; he was determined to be a champion. And as if to cement the relationship, elder and younger shared what seemed almost like a divine marking: a surgically shortened digit on the right hand. (Tilden had torn his finger on a tennis fence in 1922; the wound had become infected, and part of the finger had been amputated.) You too? Bill must have said, noticing the boy's deformity, so much like his own. They would have compared hands, each showing how he gripped the racket to compensate for the lost fingertip. Well, the older man may have joked, if I can win eight Wimbledon and U.S. championships with half a finger, I suppose you can do all right too.

Cramm would have been thrilled with the attention. Growing up in such a proper, structured environment in a society at least as reticent as Tilden's regarding sexual eccentricity (the Brüggen estate was only two hundred miles away, but a world apart, from the excesses of Weimar Berlin), Gottfried might hardly have noticed slowly emerging instincts that would mark him as different from what he was supposed to be. But here was one of the most famous athletes in the world, by far the most important figure in Gottfried's chosen field of endeavor, taking such an interest in him. And though he may have lost a few tough matches, Bill Tilden was still in his prime—thirty-five years old, still one of the greatest players on earth, and a physical presence to match. Although his face was not a handsome one—"apish, but attractive" was the best compliment one player's wife could manage—the total package was striking. "A tall, gaunt figure with hulking shoulders and the leanest of shanks," six foot one and 175 pounds, Big Bill always gave the impression of being an even larger man. Years later, contemporaries couldn't believe it when told he had been only six one. He seemed larger than life, dominating every room and every conversation. Even George Lott, a fellow player who always disliked Tilden, had to admit, "When he came into the room it was like a bolt of electricity hit the place. Immediately, there was a feeling of awe, as though you were in the presence of royalty. You knew you were in contact with greatness."

Tilden immediately identified Cramm as a potential successor to his throne. But the boy's game was far from ready. One crucial piece was missing—the same piece Tilden had needed to add to his own arsenal in 1919 in order to conquer the world. Cramm's backhand was a weak, defensive slice. With the Continental grip he was using, he was unable to hit through and over the ball with an offensive topspin.

Tilden had spent the winter of 1919 holed up in Providence, Rhode Island, chopping wood to strengthen his right arm and teaching himself the offensive backhand drive on a friend's indoor tennis court. Now he told Cramm that he must learn the same shot if he wanted to realize his potential. Tilden taught him to turn his grip more and hit through the ball rather than slicing down on it. Gottfried took the advice like sacred gospel, and before long he had mastered the new backhand. Within months he was able to attack with his backhand as well as his forehand, and his game was transformed.

The summer of Tilden's visit, 1928, Cramm had finished his schooling and yearned to move to Berlin and the Rot-Weiss Tennis Club, that enclave of sixteen red-clay courts on the edge of the sylvan Grunewald that was the epicenter of German tennis. For their part, Froitzheim, Najuch, and Heinrich Kleinschroth had been urging Gottfried's parents to send him to Berlin so they could coach him full time. Burghard and Jutta, however, felt that Gottfried should pursue a career in international diplomacy. Finally an agreement was reached: he would move into the apartment of good friends on Rauchstrasse, located in the Diplomats' Quarter right on the southern border of the Tiergarten. He would begin law studies at the university, and in his spare time he could play tennis.

The Rot-Weiss (Red-White) Club, formally the Lawn Tennis Turnier (Tournament) Club but always better known by its colors, was founded in 1897 and by 1906 had moved from its original central Berlin location to its permanent home, a quiet corner of the affluent southwestern suburb of Grunewald, on the edge of the vast forest of the same name. By the 1920s Rot-Weiss was the sporting and social home to almost all of the country's top players. And in turn they represented their club whenever they played. Even in international tournaments, players would show up wearing the red-and-white-striped blazers that marked them as "Rot-Weissers."

In contrast to the rival "Blau-Weiss" club a mile away, whose membership was generally conservative and included many top military personnel, the Rot-Weiss members were more in keeping with the world's image of Weimar Berlin. Many were artists, musicians, and writers; half of them were Jews. In general it was a liberal crowd, passionate about sports, culture, and high living. The young aristocrat from the countryside fit right in. Shortly after Cramm arrived in Berlin, a well-known graphologist analyzed his handwriting: "This script, though still not completely developed, shows already an unusual harmony and musical gift, and it would not surprise me if the [subject] developed into a great artist."

When Gottfried first showed up at Rot-Weiss, apparently not without some reputation for his efflorescing game, one female member remarked to another, "If he plays tennis as well as he looks, he'll be world champion." Whenever the handsome newcomer with the elegant strokes took to the court, he drew a crowd. At first, though, the toughness of his game may have lagged a bit behind his physical presence. Soon after his arrival Paula von Reznicek, a top player who would win the women's German Championships the next year, challenged him to a friendly match for three bottles of good wine. By attacking the boy's weak sliced backhand (he was still working on the new backhand Tilden had recently showed him), she embarrassed him by winning, seven-five in the third set. Six months later they made the same bet, and she told a friend, "I'll just take advantage of his weak backhand again." But this time he beat her in two quick sets for, as the friend understated, "Gottfried von Cramm no longer had a weak backhand."

He had told his parents he was moving to Berlin to study law, but they must have known where his true ambitions lay. Tennis soon filled not only all of his spare time but also much of his study time. He practically lived at the Rot-Weiss Club, spending most of the money sent from Oelber on lessons with Najuch and Kleinschroth. Although his game had become impressive, they were handling him with kid gloves. They felt that the pressure of competition at this point would stunt his development. And so that first year Cramm played no big tournaments, just worked out as a sparring partner for all the club's top players. Considering the club, though, this was no mean apprenticeship; it meant getting to play with all of Germany's greatest players. Cramm got to test his game against veterans like Kleinschroth and Friedrich-Wilhelm Rahe and also against current champions Daniel Prenn and Hans Moldenhauer. These two were only a few years his senior and, along with Froitzheim, made up the top three German players.

Cramm had arrived in Berlin at the beginning of a golden age for German tennis. The previous year, 1927, when Germany had finally been reinstated into the International Lawn Tennis Federation and allowed to play in the Davis Cup, international stars began coming back to Berlin to play in the German Championships at Rot-Weiss. Tennis was suddenly a mass-spectator sport, as it had never been before in Germany. Thousands packed the stands to watch Prenn, Moldenhauer, and Froitzheim take on Tilden, the French "Musketeers," and other stars.

In 1929 the German tennis craze turned to near hysteria as the Davis Cup team, in only their third attempt since reinstatement, won the European Zone, defeating Italy, Spain, and England along the way. For two weeks in July the Rot-Weiss Club was the hottest spot in Berlin. First the German team took out one of the Cup's perennial powers, Great Britain, led by two victories by Prenn, a Jewish engineer who had fled the Russian Revolution with his family as a teenager and finally settled, like so many other Russian émigrés, in Berlin. His unexpected five-set victory over Bunny Austin in the deciding fifth match made him a national hero. For a few days German fans allowed themselves the feverish fantasy of the German team playing in the Challenge Round against the French at Roland Garros stadium. But then Big Bill Tilden came to town.

He hadn't played in the three rounds of the American Zone. In fact, the USLTA had suspended him from all amateur competition the previous August for the crime of sportswriting. (In the hypocritical modus operandi of the day, star players were paid extravagant "expense" money, as well as under-the-table payoffs, but were not allowed to earn any income from tennis-related employment, including journalism.) He was reinstated in February 1929, his missing the U.S. Championships at Forest Hills being deemed enough of a slap on the wrist. But he was conspicuously absent from the Davis Cup team in its wins over Canada, Japan, and Cuba. Perhaps, German tennis fans mused wishfully, Tilden was sitting out Davis Cup play in retaliation for his suspension.

With the United States facing a surprisingly tough German team, however, and with the chance to play in Germany, a country he had grown fond of, Tilden showed up in Berlin as, once again, the savior of American tennis. "The Germans," as one journalist wrote, "quietly allowed their hopes, strong as they were, to die." Indeed, Tilden arrived in his usual grand manner, renewed his friendships with various Germans, including Cramm, and trounced Moldenhauer and Prenn in straight sets. The other matches were closer, but the Americans won, five matches to none.

This expected loss did nothing to dampen the enthusiasm of the Germans, who had finally gotten back to the highest level of international tennis. "Tennis fever" raged all over Berlin; every day the stadium was sold out, even after the Americans had clinched victory. Cramm had to be satisfied with a good seat in the stands, but he knew that his time was not far off.

That summer Cramm's coaches finally unleashed their star greyhound, and he won the German Student Championships in Münster. One observer remembered a "very slender, very blond, very nervous" youngster who was obviously agitated at having to compete in front of so many onlookers. "If looks could kill, he would have murdered all of us who were disturbing him by our mere presence." Yet he overcame his nerves and upset the highly ranked Fritz Kuhlmann in the final. "Never have I been so thrilled with a victory," he recalled years later.

Cramm may have looked like a movie star and played like The Natural—"Gottfried was the most fluent and best looking stroke maker I have seen in my fifty years of international tennis," said the legendary Australian coach Harry Hopman—but as usual such natural ease was deceiving. Cramm had achieved such a fluid game by "practicing like a professor of mathematics for five hours a day," as the Czech star Roderich Menzel put it. "His rising from a junior to world star was accomplished with the help of a well-judged plan as the staff of an army would work out in case of mobilization." Each morning he would work with a masseur to limber up his body and jump rope endlessly until a five-set match would feel like a warm-up. In the afternoon he would meet Najuch or, more and more frequently, Kleinschroth at Rot-Weiss to practice. Hour after hour they worked methodically on each stroke, until there were no weaknesses in his game.

And even when his coaches were through with him, Gottfried wasn't. Kuhlmann, his tough opponent in the student championships, was a member at the rival Blau-Weiss Club, but they would often travel to each other's clubs to practice together. "It was a tough assignment to train with him," said Kuhlmann. "He had his own system and could practice various shots for hours, that were in his view still in need of improvement. Nothing could bring him to end his training program, where I often would rather have played him a set for a Berliner Weisse [beer]. But on that he remained hard as iron."

Even if Gottfried had played for a Weissbier, he wouldn't have drunk it. For he had forsworn alcohol, tobacco, and late nights while training toward his ultimate goal. He would go out at night with friends but would refrain from the champagne and cigarettes they enjoyed, and when the clock struck midnight, he would suddenly rise like Cinderella and bid his companions goodnight many hours before their festivities ended. One of his favorite nightspots was the Roxy Sportsbar on Rankeplatz, just off the Ku'damm, a well-known meeting place for athletes and their circle, where "no one expected that you drink a lot." Famous jockeys, race-car drivers, and hockey players met here, as well as their more well-heeled fans. Here, in 1928, Cramm first met Max Schmeling, Germany's young boxing champion, who was preparing for his first tour of the United States.

Cramm played his first international tournament that summer of 1929, held at the Blau-Weiss Club, and although the great René Lacoste took the title, Gottfried beat several notable opponents, including Tilden's own protégé Junior Coen. Already his trademark shot, that wicked American Twist serve, was in place. The ball would bounce high to a right-hander's backhand, and on the heavy European red clay the effect was particularly potent. One opponent of that year remembered that he almost hated to see Cramm miss his powerful first serve, for then "a second serve followed, with such a strong spin that after bouncing it would spring up two meters, a loathsome thing."

The tall, dashing twenty-year-old with the bearing and manners of a prince had become a popular character at the Rot-Weiss Club. He cut quite a figure in his long white flannel pants, dashing about the court like no one else, reaching seemingly impossible balls, afterward bowing to kiss a lady's hand upon introduction. Women especially, whether thinking of him for themselves or for their daughters, were dazzled by his well-schooled dancing at club functions and by the way he would gallantly offer his arm. They fell over themselves trying to get him seated at their table.

Don Budge himself said that "no matter how proud and confident you might feel—and I was, believe me—whenever you walked onto a court with Cramm, it was difficult not to feel that you were walking in his shadow." And on this July day in London, eight years after Gottfried's international debut, the young Californian feels it more than ever. True, he is the newly crowned Wimbledon champion, the number-one player in the world. But Cramm is a great champion as well, twice having won the French Championships at Roland Garros. And the German has lost gallantly in three Wimbledon finals in a row, making fans of the English crowd with his brilliant play and pristine sportsmanship and drawing their sympathy for his failure to quite bring off the championship.

If Budge thought Cramm looked a bit nervous in the warm-up, that proved an illusion from the first game. The German is back in his usual form: relaxed, elegant, and masterful. The only thing unusual is just how well he is playing. The Wimbledon final of three weeks ago is ancient history. "Today a different Cramm stood on the grass," noted Menzel, the Czech champion, "as concentrated as a Yogi and as full of playful joy as a coltish youth. As hard as Budge hit, as daunting as his smashes were and as aggressively as he stormed the net, it was in fact Cramm who set the tone and tempo and answered the pace with even greater pace, precision with artful placements, and the gleaming attacks of his rival with unsurpassable penetrating power." The transformation isn't lost on Budge. "Good God," he tells himself, "I'm going to have to find a way to raise my game again."

It is one thing to think it, another to do it. Aside from his aching shoulder, he is feeling in his legs the tremendous amount of tennis he's played over the last month. Did yesterday's doubles match finally do him in? To many in the crowd, he seems lethargic, failing even to run for some of Cramm's deft drop shots. He does manage to break serve in the ninth game, finally converting his fifth break point to lead five-four. But as if even that struggle, so early in the match, has tapped the last of his strength, he quickly misses two easy forehands in the next game. And Cramm responds with a small surge of his own, cracking two return-of-serve winners to break right back for five-all. A vocal wave of restrained excitement ripples through the stands. The locals came out to Wimbledon today not really thinking Cramm could pull off a victory. And when Budge broke him, they figured he would serve it out for six-four. But Cramm has stood up to the Budge cannonball and sent it right back. The German has a chance!

I⊤ HAD BEEN A ROUGH YEAR IN ENGLAND. THE PREVIOUS DECEMBER, the populace was shocked suddenly to read of the king's decision to abdicate his throne in order to marry his lover, the twice-divorced American, Mrs. Wallis Simpson. Edward VIII had worn the crown only for eleven months and as king had proved as popular a figure as he'd been for years as the Prince of Wales. But Prime Minister Stanley Baldwin and his Cabinet demanded that Edward part with either his love or his crown. Even before this news broke, the scandal had been the dominant gossip of the past two years. "Though nothing about Mrs. Simpson appears in the English papers," wrote Cecil Beaton, "her name seems never to be off people's lips. As a topic she has become a mania, so much so that her name is banned in many houses to allow breathing space for other topics." When Baldwin's ultimatum became known, large crowds protested in the king's favor outside Buckingham Palace, but in general public opinion was with the government's sense of propriety. Edward chose his lady over his kingdom, announcing his abdication on December 10, 1936.

This domestic drama capped off a year of rising international tension. In March 1936 a supposedly disarmed Germany had marched without warning into the Rhineland, the large area west of the Rhine River that had been declared a demilitarized buffer zone by the Treaty of Versailles. France and England could easily have stopped them; in fact, the still-weak German army had orders to retreat immediately if the French resisted. But eighteen years had done little to calm the frayed nerves of war-torn Europe. Citizens and governments alike would do almost anything to keep the peace. After all, the French and British both reasoned, this was nothing like Mussolini's barbaric recent invasion of Ethiopia; Hitler was merely going "into his own back-garden." They believed—or wanted so much to believe—his announcement that he had "no territorial demands to make in Europe." Conscience-stricken over the punitive Treaty of Versailles, they acquiesced in this virtual nullification of it.

That summer, while King Edward was vacationing with his mistress on a yacht in the Mediterranean, civil war was breaking out in Spain. Hitler and Mussolini, viewing the Spanish battleground as a training field for the larger war to come, supported the fascist Franco with aircraft, weapons, and soldiers. By May 1937 there were 80,000 Italian and 30,000 German soldiers fighting in Spain. Holding them off were the Spanish militia, bolstered by the International Brigade—foreign volunteers who swarmed in from around the world to fight fascism—and Russian planes, tanks, and arms.

Throughout, war-shy Britain stuck to a policy of nonintervention. In the meantime, innocent citizens on both sides of the Spanish lines were being massacred. The republican government army—a ragtag militia of socialists, communists, anarchists, and Basque nationalists—burned churches, murdered priests and nuns, and executed anyone suspected of harboring sympathies for Franco's "nationalists." The nationalists, supported by the upper classes, the church, and the monarchists, were even worse. In every town they captured, hundreds or even thousands of people with the slightest suspicion of being nonfascist were forced to dig their own mass graves and then were mowed into them with machine guns. As news of fascist atrocities filtered in, the British people began to cry for intervention on the side of the republicans, but Parliament stood firm. The Spanish Civil War fostered political class warfare in England as never before: "open support of the Spanish nationalists was certainly confined to the upper classes and to Conservatives."

In December, still desperate to avoid war, the British government "warned" Germany to stop aiding Franco, offering rewards for compliance with the nonintervention agreement that the Germans had signed but ignored. Little did the British know that Hermann Göring, in a secret speech to German industrialists and officials that very month, had proclaimed that "the final battle is in sight . . . we are on the threshold of mobilization, and we are already at war."

In April 1937 Belgium declared its neutrality, making France—and therefore England—particularly vulnerable to attack. That same month the Luftwaffe's elite Condor Legion, supporting Franco's drive through the Basque Country, bombed the undefended Spanish town of Guernica, and its six thousand peaceful inhabitants, into oblivion. The public mood in England passed from tenuous hope for peace to resignation or even to what *The New Statesman* called "a terrified waiting for war."

Still, Londoners clung to what good cheer they could. In May, as they read of the wedding in France of their former king and his paramour, they celebrated "with a brave show of pomp" the coronation of his successor, King George VI. "The town was decorated until it resembled one huge carnival," the American scholar Ralph Bunche, who was living in London that spring, wrote to a friend at home. "The government was exerting itself to the utmost to put on the greatest show ever . . . because of the desperate necessity for rekindling reverence for the monarchy . . . and because a great display of empire unity and magnificent force and spirit would undoubtedly be the occasion for deep reflection by the high-riding Fascist dictators." The coronation was also a mid-Depression boon for the tourist trade and small businesses, such as the fashion-design concern of tennis personality Teddy Tinling. Socialites stopped buying new dresses for months after the king's abdication, but the coronation, he said, "happily put everything back in place."

And then there was always Wimbledon.

The stadium and grounds were fifteen years old, but the world's tennis championships had been held in this rather plain suburb of London since 1877. That was only four years after a British army officer, Major Walter Wingfield, had invented the game, which he called Sphairistiké, Greek for "playing at ball," adapting it from court tennis and squash. The great champions of old—Ernest and Willie Renshaw, Reginald and Laurie Doherty, Arthur Gore and Tony Wilding—had waged the early battles of the sport at the old grounds, "a little sandbox of a stadium" at 21 Worple Road. Early in the new century the very word *Wimbledon* already denoted not only the tournament held at the All England Club but also the unofficial championship of the world.

Then in 1919 Suzanne Lenglen came to play. Only twenty years old, "La Lenglen" or "La Divine," as the French press would come to call her, conquered Wimbledon for the first of six times. Playing the estimable British champion Dorothea Douglass Chambers, who wore the traditional ground-length dress with stays, petticoats, and a high-necked shirtwaist, Lenglen shocked the British by appearing on court revealing her ankles, her calves, and almost her entire arms! She showed off her ballet training, leaping back and forth across the court in an epic duel with the forty-year-old Chambers. Her 10-8, 4-6, 9-7 victory, aided by her trademark sips of brandy between games, made her a celebrity, France's greatest sports star yet.

She lost only one match from 1919 to the end of her career in 1926, and that was when she was ill. A passionate player who pouted, argued, and wept openly during matches, she and Tilden became tennis's first idols and were by far the sport's biggest drawing cards. "She became the rage, almost a cult," wrote one sportswriter. "Businessmen canceled appointments, and internationally famous hostesses postponed parties that conflicted with Suzanne's appearances because they knew no one would attend." She created such an unprecedented demand for tickets at that 1919 Wimbledon that masses of people were turned away. Immediately plans were made to construct a new venue, plans made even more urgent the next year, when Big Bill Tilden made his initial Wimbledon appearance, won the title, and created almost as much of a stir as Lenglen. In 1922 the new grounds were ready, complete with a fourteen-thousand-seat Centre Court stadium, and the big-time spectator sport of international tennis had arrived.

Inside that twelve-sided concrete building, which reminded some of a palace, some of an Elizabethan theater, and others of an aircraft hangar, was the finest tennis court in the world, "a piece of land that is revered in the game." Eighty-four hundred square feet of lawn, about a fifth of an acre—a mix of *Poa pratensis*, or long-stalked meadow grass, Chewings fescue, and American browntop—was emblazoned with the standard seventy-eight-by-twenty-seven-foot rectangle of pulverized chalk known as whiting.

The lines were laid down personally by groundsman Robert Twynam, who had grown up within a mile of the All England Club and started out there in the early 1920s as a ball boy for Tilden, Lenglen, and others. "It's not everyone can line a court out—get it really spot on," he would say. "If the lines are dead straight and the corners are true, it's a picture." No power machines were ever employed on Centre Court. Every day in the spring Twynam got between the shafts, designed for a workhorse, of a twenty-hundredweight (2,240-pound) lawn roller. Four other men then pushed as he pulled what they called the Old Horse Roller, and they rolled the Centre Court. "What the roller does is put a polish on," said Twynam. "The court is firm enough as it is, but the roller makes a nice gloss on the top of the grass." Also every day they mowed the court with a manual lawn mower to exactly three-sixteenths of an inch. The daily cuttings amounted to a couple of handfuls of botanical dust. They mowed lateral rows in early spring and diagonals in May, and as the Championships approached in June they mowed lengthwise, creating the familiar columns of dark and light green, parallel to the sidelines. The same lawn that was laid down when the stadium was built in 1922 would grow there for more than a half century to come.

By 1937 the Wimbledon championship was "the greatest title in modern sport," and this lawn had become the altar, this building the holy temple, of tennis. Every great champion—Tilden, Lenglen, Vines, Perry, and most recently Budge—had bowed his head there.

THIS IS THE PLACE WHERE LESSER PLAYERS FALTER, THEIR STROKES stiffening autonomically from the awe of playing on Centre Court. There have been players who might ride a streak of brilliant upsets into the Wimbledon final but come crashing back to earth when facing a Tilden, a Perry, or a Budge on Centre Court. But Gottfried von Cramm, who three years in a row has succumbed to a clearly greater force in the finals, looks as comfortable as on his backyard court at Oelber. Even now, late in a tight first set in the biggest match of his life, the Gentleman of Wimbledon strides the manicured lawn like a garden party host: calm, respectful, proprietary. As they change sides, with Cramm leading six-five, Budge sips some tea at the courtside table, wondering when Gottfried will give him an opening. In the last game Cramm rushed the net with unflappable sangfroid to hold serve easily. Now he nods at the young American, pops a sugar cube into his mouth, and saunters on to the other side of the court.

If Budge seemed sore-shouldered and lethargic early on, he has long since healed and been Earl Grey–caffeinated. It's clear that a merely workmanlike effort won't suffice today. Don Budge reached the heights of his greatness only this spring, and if the United States is going to win back the Cup after eleven years and keep it out of Nazi hands, he is going to need all of that greatness today. Serving at five-six, a juncture at which many players might spring a leak, Budge is air-tight. He fires two of his cannonball first serves for aces and ties the set at six-all.

But the German is relentless. Point after point, after his "loathsome" hopping serve forces a weak return, he attacks the net with deep, penetrating approach shots. "Budge's backhand pulled back balls that seemed already to have whizzed into the stands but von Cramm was there, swift, accurate, and smooth as a whippet" to volley the ball back to Budge's forehand corner for a winner. He holds serve for seven-six and calmly changes courts to face the Budge cannonball yet again.

And this time Budge does falter. He hits no aces, and in fact misses a couple of first serves, allowing Cramm to hit deep returns and follow them to net for winning volleys. And at thirty-all, a familiar demon comes back to haunt him. Most players are weaker on the backhand side, but for Budge the backhand has always been the more natural stroke—and the best backhand the world has ever seen. Up until 1936, though, his forehand was a bit of a liability. Intense workouts that winter with his coach in Berkeley, Tom Stow, ironed out the forehand, and although it would never equal his backhand, it was strong enough to make him world champion. But now, at six-seven, thirty-all, Cramm attacks that forehand. And as the U.S. captain Walter Pate, who had been sitting impassively in his seat in the shadow of the umpire's chair, "begins to stroke his chin and cross and re-cross his legs," Budge's forehand misfires twice in a row.

There is a moment of stunned silence. With both players holding serve so fiercely, one almost expected it to go on forever. But Budge has suddenly been the first to blink, and the first set is over, eight-six for Germany. The stands shake with wild applause.

Certainly the British public cannot know of the Nazi government's war ambitions. Not even the German people were aware of the "top secret" memo sent to the chiefs of their armed forces just one month ago: "Preparations of the armed forces for a possible war in the mobilization period 1937–38 must be made. . . ." Still, despite its fear of renewed hostilities and consequent policy of appeasement, the British government recently passed a $1.5 billion rearmament bill. As one historian will write, "A new era had begun: one in which the British people began to face the imminence of war." And it is becoming hard to ignore the fascists' blatant disdain for human rights. Already the Nuremburg Laws have reduced the Jews of Germany to the legal status of nonhuman pests.

Yet on this still-peaceful English summer day, the Swastika is flying high over Centre Court, along with the Union Jack and the Stars and Stripes. Nazi officials are sipping tea with the queen in the Royal Box. And from the very first point of this tennis match, there has been no question where the crowd's sympathy lies: the English are rooting for Hitler's man.

# APPEASEMENT

I N THE ROYAL BOX, NAZI REICHS-sportführer (Reich sports leader) Hans von Tschammer und Osten, who had just flown in that morning to witness the big match, may have turned stiffly toward the queen to accept a congratulatory nod. For the first time ever the Nazi flag was waving over the famous stadium. On Saturday Ambassador Joachim von Ribbentrop had attended the first day's matches, enjoying Cramm's regal destruction of overmatched Bitsy Grant. The German officials must have been pleased to sense the pro-German sentiment of the spectators, even if they knew it was partly a longing for a more vulnerable opponent for the British champions.

Indeed, aside from such interest and Cramm's personal magnetism, a palpable pro-German sentiment was running through the crowd. Presumably it emanated from that faction of the Wimbledon audience representing the upper crust of English society, for in 1937 the English aristocracy was decidedly Teutonophilic. Ribbentrop, the new German ambassador to England—though "incompetent and lazy, vain as a peacock, arrogant and without humor," as one foreign journalist put it—had achieved the post due to his influential friends among the British aristocracy. ("When I criticized Ribbentrop's qualifications to handle British problems," Göring said, "the Führer pointed out to me that Ribbentrop knew 'Lord So and So' and 'Minister So and So.' To which I replied, 'Yes, but the difficulty is that they know Ribbentrop.'") Soon the German Embassy in London was the scene of extravagant parties where the British upper class either developed or confirmed a "snobbish pro-Germanism." One political cartoon that year showed Lady Astor and her cohorts dancing to Goebbels's baton.

Lord Londonderry, a cousin of Winston Churchill and confidant of King Edward VIII, had been head of the Air Ministry from 1931 to 1935 and openly expressed his enthusiasm for Hitler and the Nazi cause. Invited by Ribbentrop, Lord and Lady Londonderry had had a marvelous time at the 1936 Winter Olympics in Garmisch, Germany, hobnobbing with Göring and thrilling at meeting the Führer himself. "I beheld a man of arresting personality," wrote Lady Londonderry afterward. "I felt I was in the presence of someone truly great. He is simple, dignified, humble. He is a leader of men." Sir Nevile Henderson, the new ambassador to Germany, had announced before leaving for Berlin in May, "Guarantee us peace [as Hitler was happy to do] . . . and Germany will find that she has no more sincere, and, I believe, more useful friend in the world than Great Britain." And Lady Diana Guinness, the daughter of the right-wing Baron Redesdale, had recently married Sir Oswald Mosley, the leader of the British Union of Fascists, in the admiring presence of Hitler and Goebbels in Berlin.

Mosley had begun political life in the 1920s as a Conservative MP, then become a prominent member of the Labour Party before breaking off to start his own New Party in 1931. When this failed, Mosley visited Mussolini in Rome and returned home to found, with the financial support of publisher Lord Rothermere, the British Union of Fascists. These "blackshirts," modeled after Hitler's brownshirts, reached their peak of popularity in 1934, with twenty thousand members in four hundred branches around the country. Their rallies were marked by fervid anti-Semitic, anti-Communist tirades by Mosley, punctuated by violent attacks on protesters in the crowd. Spotlights would be turned on the hecklers, who were savagely kicked and beaten as they were ejected.

Just nine months before, in the fall of 1936, Mosley had announced that five thousand of his blackshirts would march through the Jewish Quarter of London. Early that Sunday morning a defiant and outraged crowd of a hundred thousand protesters showed up and lined the planned route of the march. Ten thousand London police headed to the Jewish Quarter, prepared for the worst, before the commissioner of police finally forced Mosley to call off the march at the eleventh hour.

The upper class, however, was not alone in harboring delusions about Nazi Germany. Although the BUF was on the wane by 1937, and many English were paying attention to Spain and Ethiopia and fast becoming wary of fascism's dangers, most of Mosley's blackshirts were working-class and middle-class young men, left jobless and hopeless in the wake of the Depression. David Lloyd George, the son of a schoolmaster who became a leader of the Liberal Party and prime minister during and after the Great War, and who had championed the cause of the Jews, had recently visited Ribbentrop and Hitler in Berchtesgaden. Utterly smitten with the Führer's personality, he reported back to the British people: "[Hitler] is a born leader of men [with] a magnetic dynamic personality.... The Germans have no longer the desire themselves to invade any other land.... They have definitely made up their minds never to quarrel with us again." (Lloyd George was soon enough undeceived, but his misjudgment would remain a blemish on his career.)

In fact, Hitler had been preparing his war machine for years. Tschammer and Ribbentrop, sitting in the Royal Box at Wimbledon, may not have known about the top-secret German directive of just four weeks ago, calling the armed forces into preparation for war. But surely they knew that Hitler intended more than one Swastika to wave over London.

They also knew, as most of the crowd did not, that Gottfried von Cramm was not quite what he appeared to be. Tall, blond, and athletic, "handsome to a fault," he was serving their purpose as a model of the superior Aryan race. But in private, and more recently in public, he had been far from a spokesman for the Nazis. Time and again, in his travels around the world, he had ignored their requests to speak in praise and defense of Hitler. In Australia recently he'd complained to one reporter about the Davis Cup team "losing the services" of the great Jewish player Daniel Prenn. To another he'd lamented that Hitler's new mandatory military service was robbing young athletes of the most crucial years of athletic development. And despite Göring's repeated personal requests, he had refused to join the Nazi Party. He could not help, with his natural elegance, well-bred sophistication, and unsurpassed sportsmanship, but reflect well on the German people. But he would not directly defend a government he loathed.

No matter. For the moment, on the verge of bringing Germany its first Davis Cup, von Cramm was useful. As long as he kept winning, and wasn't too overtly critical of the regime, it was best to leave him be. The Gestapo had an ever-growing file on von Cramm and his public and private activities—there were ways other than political in which the tennis champion was no ideal Aryan. And when the right time came, the file would still be there.

GOTTFRIED HAD ARRIVED IN BERLIN IN THE SUMMER OF 1928, AT the height of Weimar art, culture, and decadent nightlife. Only a few years earlier Berlin had been a capital of abject misery.

The Weimar Republic had seemed doomed from the start, rising as it did from the ashes of war, the November 1918 revolution that overthrew the kaiser, and festering resentment over the humiliating Treaty of Versailles. The Left resented the old imperial order for having dragged Germany into the bloodiest, most gruesome war in history for no good reason at all. The Right created a myth that lasted for decades, which told of the treachery of "Jews and Bolsheviks," who had capitulated to the Allies just as the great German army was nearing victory. It was a lie that Hitler didn't invent, but which he seized upon and rode to power.

The "bloodless" revolution of November 1918, which put the liberal Social Democrats in power, was followed in early 1919 by a violent revolt by the Communists, which the government was able to suppress only through a devil's bargain with the right-wing Freikorps, a group of paramilitary organizations that eventually melded into the Nazi SA (Sturmabteilung, or "assault detachment," commonly called "storm troopers" or "brownshirts"). The moderate government stayed in power, but on the streets a brutal battle raged between the Left and Right. "Vigilante groups made up of unemployed ex-officers and criminals continued to occupy the capital, murdering at will, clubbing and beating people accused of 'unpatriotic' activities." The artist George Grosz said Berliners were "like boats lost in a storm, heading for disaster."

And then came the hyperinflation of 1923–24. Inflation had begun during the war, but afterward, when the German government was unable to pay back loans with reparations it had expected to extract from the defeated Allies, and in fact was saddled with astronomical reparation payments itself, inflation skyrocketed. When the government began printing more money as the only way to pay its debts, it fomented a hyperinflation unique in history.

The German mark, which had gone from four per dollar to seventy-five between 1914 and 1921, shot to 48,000 in February 1923. In October a dollar would buy 440 million marks, and the next month 4,200 billion. Paper money became worthless as soon as it was printed. A life savings of a hundred thousand marks suddenly wouldn't buy breakfast. Retired generals and ambassadors on fixed pensions could be seen scouring garbage cans for bits of food. There were reports of people withdrawing their entire savings to buy one last postage stamp for their suicide note.

On the other hand, those who had their money in foreign markets, or tourists with foreign currency, could live like billionaires. One hundred dollars could buy a lavish mansion or rent the Berlin Philharmonic for the night.

"No other nation has experienced anything comparable to the events of 1923 in Germany," wrote the young journalist Sebastian Haffner, who lived through them. "All nations went through the Great War, and most of them have also experienced revolutions, social crises, strikes, redistribution of wealth, and currency devaluation. None but Germany has undergone the fantastic, grotesque extreme of all these together; none has experienced the gigantic, carnival dance of death, the unending, bloody Saturnalia, in which not only money but all standards lost their value."

One immediate result was "an atmosphere of light-headed youthfulness, licentiousness, and carnival," according to Alexandra Richie. "Now, for once, the young had money and the old did not. Moreover, its nature had changed. Its value lasted only a few hours. It was spent as never before or since; and not on the things old people spend their money on." No sexual thirst was left unquenched. Reputable hotels hired male and female prostitutes to satisfy patrons in various permutations. "As things grew increasingly dire Berlin threw itself into an orgy of dancing, drinking, pornography and prostitution with *je m'en fous* being the order of the day. The higher prices rose the greater the abandon, the madder the nightclubs, the faster the dance steps, the louder the jazz bands, the more plentiful the cocaine. But this was not yet the joyful dancing of the so-called 'Golden Twenties'; it was an insane dance of forgetting, a dance of despair."

And then, seemingly as suddenly as it had started, the inflation was over. The government printed new "Rettenmarks," currency stabilized, and Berlin emerged into a new prosperity. The true apogee of Weimar Berlin commenced, when it was the destination for so many writers, artists, and musicians who epitomized the age, and for travelers who wanted to be at the center of cultural life. It was the Berlin of Bertolt Brecht and Kurt Weill, of Klee and Grosz and Gropius. There were eight or ten concerts every night, featuring greats from around the world like Louis Armstrong, Yehudi Menuhin, and Pablo Casals. Josephine Baker brought her famous "banana dance" and the Charleston. Marlene Dietrich was singing on stage and appearing in films. Theaters like the Deutsches Theater and the Kammerspiele rivaled any in the world.

Nightclubs grew to the size of department stores. Haus Vaterland occupied an entire city block and featured five floors and twelve different restaurant "environments" to accommodate six thousand patrons. In one of them, the Rhineland Wine Terrace, there was an artificial river and a seventy-foot-wide panorama of the Rhenish countryside. Each hour the band would stop playing for the "Storm on the Rhine": cloud cover darkened the room, simulated lightning flashed, thunder boomed, and artificial rain would sprinkle the room, followed by a mechanical sunburst and rainbow. Another club, the famously promiscuous Resi, had mechanical geysers, a hundred mirror balls, hundreds of tables with numbered telephones, and pneumatic tubes for chatting up other customers and sending special "gifts."

*Girlkultur* was all the rage: at clubs all over town, young women were dancing nude, stripping to all kinds of music. Each club tried to outdo the others with sheer quantity. "Ever since [*Girlkultur*] undressed the female body to the point of total nudity," wrote Walter Benjamin, "its only available mode of variation was quantity, and soon there will be more girls than spectators." There was *Boykultur* too, as clubs like Silhouette and Eldorado catered to a fashionable homosexual lifestyle. Everyone was talking about the *Berliner Luft*, the Berlin air—there was something in it, they said, like a drug that kept them going all night and brought out their most hidden sexual impulses.

Gottfried drank Weimar Berlin in like the champagne that he forwent. He loved the theater, the music, the nightlife; apparently there was plenty of fun to be had before midnight. Somewhere between tennis and the nightclubs, he squeezed in some study of the law. It wasn't that he wasn't intellectual; he had always been an avid student. It was just that both his tennis game and Berlin's attractions were too fine to ignore. "Gottfried was always [out with us at night]," said Paula von Reznicek. "But he didn't smoke, drank little, and required lots of sleep. He trained like iron. He wasn't a party pooper, but as soon as the festivities lasted past midnight, he would disappear." One night some French visitors kidded him as he made his apologies: "Everything comes so effortlessly for you, a little bar-hopping won't slow you down!" He just smiled: "Contrary to popular belief, champions don't fall from the heavens, and in any case they occasionally meet their match on earth."

His first six months in Berlin he lived, as agreed, at the home of family friends near the Tiergarten. But in the spring of 1929 he moved to the popular Pension von Saukken, on the Reichstagsufer, right by the seat of government. This afforded him more privacy, but even as he was able to delve deeper into Berlin life, he also enjoyed racing his Opel roadster across the two hundred kilometers of countryside back to Brüggen or Bodenburg to spend time with his family. And just as in his boyhood, he spent much time in the summer of '29 at the Dobeneck estate in Burgdorf. In particular, he was spending a great deal of time with Lisa von Dobeneck.

Raised like Gottfried on a lavish bucolic estate near Hanover, she was privately tutored at home, in horseback riding and tennis as well as the academic subjects. Her older sister, Victoria, was Gottfried's coeval. But Lisa, seventeen, became Gottfried's closer companion at Burgdorf that summer. Both girls reveled in the sporty, outdoor life, but Lisa more completely personified the new German female, who embraced sport as participant for the first time. She was a serious gymnast and almost as fervent a dancer. She swam, skied, and was a good tennis player and an even better field hockey player. She even looked the part of the archetypical modern German woman. Slim, athletic, and beautiful, she sported the

short "Eton" or *Bubikopf* pageboy haircut that was all the rage, just like
the flappers' bob cuts in New York. In fact, the model of the new, liberated young woman, in Berlin as well as Paris and New York, was nothing if not mannish. Women bound their breasts to fit the new image
and were perfectly comfortable for the first time driving cars, smoking
cigarettes, and drinking alcohol. Her eyes as black as her hair, Lisa was
like a darker-hued, female version of Gottfried. And as with Gottfried,
one could almost *see* her aching for Berlin.

By the time Gottfried was back in Berlin in the fall of 1929, Lisa
was writing to "her" Gottfried: "You have made me completely crazy.
I also can't sleep anymore, as I always hope that a miracle will happen,
and you will appear here in my room. I constantly play with the thought
of simply getting into the Chrysler and driving to you." In Burgdorf in
early December, with both families present, Gottfried raised his glass
and announced that he and Lisa hoped to be married before 1930 was
through.

In a few weeks Lisa turned eighteen and remained in Burgdorf to
start planning an autumn wedding, and Gottfried returned once again
to Berlin and tennis. At the end of the 1929 season he had been ranked
in Germany for the first time, tied for tenth in the nation with three
other players. But those others would soon fall way back in his wake.

In February the rising star made his first circuit of the French Riviera, the center of European tennis every late winter. Since the turn of
the century the tennis season had begun there, with tournaments at
Nice, Cannes, Beaulieu, Mentone, Monte Carlo, Bordighera, and An-
tibes. Cramm was not yet ready to win these tournaments, but the
twenty-year-old did make quite a splash with victories over the French
"Fifth Musketeer" Christian Boussus and the Hungarian champion Béla
von Kehrling. "Like a comet a new star fell from the tennis heavens,"
hailed the Riviera newspaper *Eclaireur de Nice.* "A 'youngster,' whom no
one knew yesterday, is on the way to becoming the world's best."

Aside from the big amateur tournaments, and a few for professionals, there were also the crowd favorites: the Handicap tournaments, in
which lesser players—club members and prominent guests—were
matched up with the top touring players in doubles competition. The
most popular participant, a beloved "permanent guest" in these tournaments, was referred to on the drawsheets only as "Mr. G." Known

more formally as King Gustav of Sweden, the seventy-one-year-old monarch was something of a tennis fanatic. After discovering the new game of lawn tennis as a twenty-year-old visiting England in 1878, he'd brought it back to Sweden and championed it ever since. He never missed the Riviera tennis circuit, just as he never passed up a good pickup doubles game at the Rot-Weiss Club on his diplomatic visits to Berlin.

In February 1930 the king, who generally was given the handicap doubles partner he wanted, was paired with the Austrian champion Wilhelm Matejka; but he couldn't help but notice the elegant play of the handsome young German. Jokingly, he remarked to Matejka, "I would probably take the trophy if this Gottfried von Cramm would choose me as his partner." The king and the baron did match up the next year, and it was the beginning of a close friendship for life.

Back in Berlin in the summertime, with the wedding all planned for September and the university closed, Gottfried was edging closer and closer to a career decision. Every day, it seemed, he made another improvement in his game; already the best players at the best club considered him the hottest prospect in Germany. "Gottfried's unspeakably gifted!" exclaimed Hans Moldenhauer, the number-one German player, one day at Rot-Weiss. "He doesn't even realize what he's doing out there." Daniel Prenn, the number-two man on the Davis Cup team, known as the mentally toughest player in Europe, agreed. "Combine his shots with my head . . . and Big Bill wouldn't be so big." He had been practicing daily with the boy, in his typically forceful way urging Cramm to take his tennis even more seriously. "Prenn spoke with me yesterday," Gottfried wrote his mother. "He wants, as I had predicted, to commandeer me for tennis." In less than a year Prenn and the Rot-Weiss coaches would have their way. For someone with this much talent on the tennis court, academics and the law could never compete with the lure of sport. Gottfried von Cramm was about to explode upon the European tennis scene.

In September Gottfried and Lisa were married in a lavish affair at Burgdorf. And then Lisa made her transformation from country aristocrat to Weimar Berlin maven, just as Gottfried had two years before. But first a honeymoon. They took the train to Venice and set up camp at the Hotel Excelsior Palace. "We are very happy here," he wrote home. "The sun is out, we're getting browner and browner. . . . Many family friends are here, but they respect our honeymoon." As was only fitting, they continued on to Territet and Meran to take part in the tennis tournaments there, but traveling with a bride was not quite the same as having a coach and practice partner. Remarking on his drop to a five-way tie for twelfth in the German rankings at the end of the year, the Rot-Weiss annual report noted, "Following his wedding, von Cramm played somewhat poorly. . . ." It was, however, to be but a brief slip before his ascent.

Early in the new year of 1931 the newlyweds found their first Berlin apartment together, at 35 Dernburgstrasse in Charlottenburg. With the help of a generous monthly allowance from Lisa's grandfather, they were able to set up a smaller, urban counterpart to their lavish upbringings, complete with maid, cook, butler, and chauffeur. Not surprisingly, their apartment became a focal point of their social circle. Lisa loved to entertain and was a popular figure at Rot-Weiss and elsewhere. She almost immediately became a leading figure of the women's number-one field hockey team at Rot-Weiss, and so the apartment on Dernburgstrasse became a secondary clubhouse not only for the tennis crowd but also for the hockey players. In turn, Gottfried and the other tennis players played field hockey in the winter to stay in shape, as there were at that time few indoor tennis courts in Berlin. After practices and games the tennis and hockey players would all congregate on Dernburgstrasse to unwind and launch the evening's entertainment. Other friends, including stars of the theater and film, such as the actress Zarah Leander, would join them. An impromptu cocktail party would invariably ensue, followed perhaps by an evening at the theater. When summer came, they often ended the night with an excursion to the Wannsee, a lake on the other end of the Grunewald, where they would top off the day's pleasures with a late-night swim.

The young von Cramms' life in Berlin was like a paradisiacal island in a turbulent sea of misery. For Berlin in 1931 was in the midst of a Depression as paralyzing as that in the United States, worsened by lingering war wounds and a government on the verge of collapse. Mere weeks after the New York Stock Exchange collapsed in October 1929, the first ripples of economic trouble rumbled through Berlin.

Weimar's "Golden Twenties" turned out to be an unsupported facade, and the sudden cutoff of U.S. capital brought it crashing to the ground. By the end of the year there were 31,800 unemployed in Berlin; two years later there were about 400,000. They spent what they could on boiled horse meat or else lined up in front of the soup kitchens. Many went to live in squalid tent camps on the outskirts of town, Berlin's version of Hooverville. Just as writer Emily Hahn was noticing in New York's Central Park "throngs of people standing around [the ornamental bridges] or sitting on the ground underneath, holding their places until nightfall," Erich Maria Remarque was watching Berlin's unemployed wandering through the art museums "in order not to fall into paralysis and despair. They were thinking of bread, always and only of bread and occupation; but they came here to escape from their thoughts for a few hours. . . . In a revolting way, life had shrunk to a miserable battle for bare existence. . . . Life had become too dirty for happiness, it couldn't last, one didn't believe in it any more; this was only a breathing space, not a harbour."

Out of this wretchedness, social unrest was boiling over once more. "Jewish Bolsheviks" were again being blamed for Versailles, economic woes, and anything else one could think of. Jews were banned from many nationalist organizations, and anti-Semitic novels were crowding the best-seller lists. On September 12, 1931, more than a thousand Nazis attacked Jews emerging from Rosh Hashanah services, screaming, "Kill the Jews!" and destroying a popular Jewish café. Embittered veterans drinking themselves numb in dark taverns were jolted out of their reverie by the noise of protesters—"grim, submerged-looking Communists"—marching past to the beat of "*L'Internationale,*" followed by violent brown-shirted youths shouting "*Deutschland Erwache!*" (Germany Awake!), and then once again the long, silent, ragged lines carrying signs demanding work and bread.

In this reckless and desperate climate, though, hedonism and sexual libertarianism continued to flourish, much as they had in the hyperinflation of 1923. And Berlin remained famous for public displays of sexuality of all types, as it had in the Golden Twenties.

Berlin had been accepting of homosexuals as far back as the 1750s, when Frederick the Great had forbidden his elite Praetorian Guard to marry, and homosexual relationships between soldiers became commonplace. The city became a haven for homosexuals, bisexuals, and cross-dressers in the nineteenth century, and by 1922 there were an estimated 100,000 homosexuals and 25,000 teenage male prostitutes in Berlin. By the end of the decade those numbers had tripled. Although homosexuality had been technically illegal, via the infamous Paragraph 175, since the consolidation of the second German Reich in 1871, the local police had long practiced a tradition of tolerance, and by 1914 there were some forty gay bars in the capital. Add to that the devil-may-care attitude fostered by the bloodiest war in history and a postwar economy that seemed to distort values of every kind, and you have the famed unfettered polysexual nightlife of Weimar Berlin.

"It's hard to imagine now how wild it was in Berlin," recalled one lesbian years later. More than six hundred nightclubs around the city offered sexual floor shows and services. Eighty-five clubs alone catered exclusively to lesbians who, unlike their counterparts, exhibited their lifestyle freely in broad daylight. And for gay men, as Christopher Isherwood, the young English writer who went to live in Berlin in 1929, put it, "Berlin means Boys." His friend W. H. Auden called it "a bugger's daydream." Venues ranged from the swanky Hollandaise, where the elegant couples on the dance floor appeared to be straight, with the "men" in tuxedos and the "women" in velvet dresses and pearls, to Isherwood's favorite dive, the Cosy Corner, featuring cheap beer and amateurish young prostitutes. In between there was a club to cater to any conceivable taste. At the Monte Casino, blue-collar husbands politely and openly left their wives to enjoy the transvestite review while they went into back rooms to pay for oral sex with the performers. Another place was frequented by chubby older men wearing schoolboy knickers or tight sailor suits. Yet another establishment supposedly "catered exclusively to balding stockbrokers, who spent their picturesque evenings dancing with 'elegant pansies.'" At every train station and hotel lobby there were guidebooks to this erotic Berlin underworld, such as *Führer durch das "Lasterhafte" Berlin* (Guide to Decadent Berlin) or *Was Nicht im Baedeker Steht* (What's Not in Baedeker). As the Russian writer Ilya Ehrenburg wrote in 1931, "Berlin has become the paradise of international homosexuals."

In early 1931 Gottfried was out one night at the Eldorado bar on

Lutherstrasse, with a group that probably included his brother Asch-winn. The Eldorado was one of Berlin's most popular night spots for the more liberal members of high society, adventurous tourists, and local artists, writers, transvestites, and homosexuals. Dozens of packed tables encircled a dance floor, where couples of ambiguous sexuality whirled by, as much as daring the onlookers to guess their true genders. The smell of French perfume pervaded the air, as the "diva" in front of the orchestra belted out risqué Parisian *chansons* in a haunting falsetto.

At a nearby table a group of actors was drinking and unwinding after their performance at the nearby Grosses Schauspielhaus. They were the cast of the popular new Austrian operetta *Im Weissen Rössel*, a particularly campy piece with plenty of room for sexual (and homosexual) innuendo. As the night wore on, the two groups began to mingle, and Gottfried found himself in deep conversation with one of the actors. Manasse Herbst was an eighteen-year-old Galician Jew whose family had been in Berlin for years. He had acted in a few films and stage roles and was living with his parents on Grenadierstrasse, in the Jewish neighborhood of Spandau.

The two young men may have left the bar together, or perhaps they merely exchanged phone numbers. Soon afterward Gottfried may have accompanied his brother Aschwinn and his own new homosexual acquaintance, Georg Heck, when they went to see Herbst in *Im Weissen Rössel*. Before long Gottfried was picking "Manny" up in his Opel after the show and taking him to various homosexual hangouts, such as the Silhouette, the Kleist-Kasino, or the Hollandaise—Heck's favorite place, where he gathered every week with a "round table" of friends. Often they went out in the company of Aschwinn and Heck.

If in fact Aschwinn was spending time on the town with a homosexual, it didn't mean he was gay. Homosexuality had become *à la mode* in Berlin. "It was a necessity of avant-garde fashion," wrote one historian, "to arrive at parties or go to the opera with a member of the same sex: it proved that one was 'modern' and that one had broken with the 'tired bourgeois morals' of the pre-war era." According to Heck, the other von Cramm brothers also explored the gay world a bit. But if they did, they were merely young men of their time and place; not to have done so would have left them out of the vanguard in Weimar Berlin.

However, for Gottfried it was more than a passing fashion. It was only a few months since he had married his young bride, but already he was beginning a double life, at the age of twenty-one. In public he was half of the dashing young athletic couple, hosting cocktail parties with Lisa, attending social dinners at the Rot-Weiss Club and elsewhere. But whenever he could get away he would meet Manny, and it was here, in the dark demimondain establishments of *Lasterhafte Berlin*, here parked in his sports car on a quiet side street, here in a room at the Petersburger Hof hotel, that he found the true object of his physical longing.

More accurately, it was a triple life, for his greatest and most demanding love remained tennis. No matter how madly his social and love lives raged, he was always jumping rope by ten A.M. after a full night's rest; each afternoon he still "practiced like a professor of mathematics for five hours."

Finally, in the spring of 1931, his time had come. In April Kleinschroth visited Gottfried and Lisa at Burgdorf with a surprise. "In three days," he told his star pupil, "we're going to Athens to play in the Greek Championships. And you and I are playing the doubles." Three days later Gottfried, Lisa, and Heinrich took a train to Trieste, where they boarded an Italian freighter bound for Athens. There they not only played the tennis tournament but also visited the Acropolis, the Parthenon, and other sights. "Heinrich bought a Baedeker," Gottfried wrote Aschwinn, "and now we're experts.

"The women in the stands are all dressed very chicly," he went on, "but Lisa was a great success. I love hearing all the praise heaped on her by the people of various nationalities. And on Saturday I play the finals against the Frenchman Berthet. If I pull myself together, I can be champion of the Mediterranean." On April 25 Gottfried von Cramm became just that, winning his first international titles, in singles and in the doubles with Kleinschroth.

If Gottfried returned to Berlin with hopes of being named to the German Davis Cup team, though, he was disappointed. The German Lawn Tennis Federation wasn't quite ready to put its trust in the young rising star. (And Germany promptly lost in an early round to

South Africa.) However, it did sponsor his travel about Europe that season, including trips to the French Championships and Wimbledon. And his Greek championship served another purpose as well. It allowed him finally to convince his parents to allow him to drop his legal studies. It was clear by this point that he was destined to be an international ambassador of a different sort.

He wasted no time building his reputation. In Paris he sent home a gentle rebuke to the federation by beating the number-one South African Vernon Kirby on his way to reaching the fourth round. The reigning U.S. and French doubles champion George Lott crushed him there, but even in a one-sided loss Cramm impressed the crowd. Tennis journalist Ned Potter wrote, "I seem to recall remarking a sense of pleasure in the stroke execution of George's victim, his earnest desire to play every ball for all it was worth, and that he showed no especial sign of discouragement although the beauty of his style and his effort was availing so little."

A few weeks later Gottfried made his debut at Wimbledon, and although his game had been molded on slow red clay, the same as they play on in Paris, he did just as well on the fast English grass, reaching the fourth round there as well, "hitting his ground strokes with delightful freedom."

At the end of the 1931 tennis season von Cramm was ranked number one in Germany, tied with Daniel Prenn. And there was no longer any doubt that the next year he would join his friend in leading the German Davis Cup team. Clearly he had made the right career choice.

His life had changed completely, seemingly within the course of a few months. Where before there had been tennis, school, and hockey in the winter, now there was only tennis. Indoor tennis courts had sprung up in Berlin, as they already had in the Scandinavian countries, so the German players could practice all winter long. They also played international team matches against Denmark and Sweden, in Copenhagen, Stockholm, and Berlin. Then early in the year everyone would head down to the Riviera; Gottfried also accepted invitations to visit Cairo and Alexandria to practice in the heat and play the tournaments there. After that, of course, he traveled the European circuit, including Paris and Wimbledon, as well as the Davis Cup.

The best hotels of Europe began to feel more like home than the apartment back on Dernburgstrasse. He entered more and more tournaments, and since he was winning more matches and progressing deep into the draws, he had at most a day or two between tournaments. Instead of returning home for a few days or a week, he would scarcely have time to pack and catch the train or ship to the next tournament. At first Lisa traveled with him, but she quickly tired of the tennis tour and began spending most of her time alone in Berlin.

When Gottfried was there with her, they put on a good show. Already in November 1930, when they were still engaged, they were posing for the cover of the popular *Berliner Illustrirte Zeitung* (*Berlin Illustrated Gazette*), as handsome as two movie stars, their faces in overlapping profile, dressed in tennis whites, her fingers lightly caressing a wooden racket. They appeared at the theater and club dinners as husband and wife. But if their marriage had ever felt real, even to them, that was already in the past. They continued to play their parts, and they remained good friends, but in reality they were no more than that.

Cramm could not have chosen a better time to burst upon the German sports scene. Just as Germany was rejoining the international tennis world, and the great tennis stars of the time returned to Germany to play the German Championships and the Davis Cup, sports in general were becoming an important part of cultural life in Germany. The Berlin "Six Days" bicycle race, in which teams of cyclists sped around an oval track for 144 hours, was one of the biggest events of the year. "Packed buses race through the streets headed for the Kaiserdamm," wrote famed literary journalist Joseph Roth. "At eight o'clock the megaphone announced that there were no more tickets. There are resigned people, turning back around, quiet, sad, their heads hanging. . . . Enough of those unhappy ones! Let's turn our attention instead to those prudent souls who four days ago locked up their homes and set off with backpacks, subtenants, grandchildren, dogs, parrots, and canaries to the Kaiserdamm, to set up house there. . . . Heads are mounted on bodies, and the bodies are glued—glued by excitement and sweat—to their seats. Ten thousand throats emit a wild cry. . . ."

"The youth of the country," noted *The New Yorker*, "has almost made a religion of physical fitness and games." Some saw an ominous side; Sebastian Haffner wrote, "It did not occur to [the Left] that through sport, the lure of the war game, the old thrilling magic of national rivalry was being exercised and maintained and that this was not some harmless venting of bellicose instincts. They failed to see any connection. They were blind to Germany's relapse." The Left must not have read *Mein Kampf*, written in prison in 1924, in which Hitler had promised: "Give the German nation six million bodies of flawless athletic training, all glowing with fanatical love of their country and inculcated with the highest aggressive spirit, and in less than two years if necessary a national state will have created an army."

But left-wing literary authors too were writing enthusiastically about sports for the first time, including Bertolt Brecht, who considered boxing as the symbol of two individuals struggling for survival and a metaphor for the class struggle. Boxing, which had been illegal under the kaiser, began to catch on in Germany only after the Great War, when German POWs, who had learned it from their English guards, brought the sport back home. Max Schmeling, the son of a Hamburg shipping navigator, whom Cramm knew from the Roxy Sportsbar, became Germany's first heavyweight champion of the world in 1930 and was painted by George Grosz and sculpted in bronze by Rudolf Belling. He defended his crown on July 3, 1931, just as Cramm was making his impressive Wimbledon debut.

The heroics of the 1929 Davis Cup team had helped make tennis one of the most popular sports in Germany, and as Cramm rose to the top, he became one of the most recognizable sports stars on the streets of Berlin—particularly after the "inconceivable" success of the 1932 Davis Cup campaign.

After winning the European Zone in 1929, in that feverish season when they defeated mighty England only to lose to Tilden and the Americans, the Germans had had two disappointing years. Former national champion Hans Moldenhauer had died in a car crash in Berlin in early 1930, and Daniel Prenn couldn't do it alone. In 1930 and 1931 the Germans quietly went down in early rounds. But in 1932, with the burgeoning Cramm finally on the team, and with Prenn considered Europe's number-one player, German tennis fever was rising again.

In the first round, against India at the Rot-Weiss Club, the German fans gave their twenty-two-year-old rookie rousing ovations as Cramm and Prenn won easily, five matches to none. In the next round, played in Vienna, they just squeaked past Austria, three-two. Cramm was clearly still a step behind Prenn; he sealed the victory, but just barely, eight-six in the fifth set against Matejka, whom Prenn had dispatched in straight sets. That was followed by another easy victory at home against Ireland, which set up a rematch of the 1929 miracle: Germany and England, on the red clay of Berlin.

England had every reason to be confident. Aside from the revenge incentive, it had the stronger team on paper. Henry Wilfred "Bunny" Austin (nicknamed after a comic-strip rabbit named Wilfred) had been a top player since his undergraduate days at Cambridge in the late 1920s, and he was fresh off his finest showing at Wimbledon, where he lost in the finals to Ellsworth Vines. In the 1929 Davis Cup Austin had lost the deciding match to Prenn, cramping up in the heat during a long clay-court battle and finally being forced to retire at five-one Prenn in the fifth set. Convinced that the long flannel pants of the day were keeping his legs humid and causing his cramps, Austin "invented" tennis shorts in 1931 when he finally cut off one of his pairs of pants just below the knee. In 1932 he was still the only player in shorts.

Teamed up with Austin was England's new star, Fred Perry. The son of a working-class MP from Cheshire, Perry was a world champion at table tennis at eighteen before he ever played serious tennis. The same age as Cramm, in 1932 he had already won the mixed doubles at the French Championships and was poised to take over the tennis world. In 1933 he would win his first major title, at Forest Hills, and from 1934 to 1936 he would be the world champion, winning Wimbledon three times in a row.

The stadium at Rot-Weiss was packed for the three days of the Germany-England tie (as Davis Cup competitions had come to be called, in the tradition of English horse racing, where a race for a cup trophy was called a "cup-tie" or just "tie"). Chancellor Franz von Papen and other dignitaries watched from the VIP box, while those not lucky enough to get a ticket climbed trees outside to get a glimpse of the matches. The news of each day's results flashed across the front pages of Berlin's newspapers.

On the first day things went much as expected; Perry crushed the newcomer Cramm 6-1, 6-2, 6-3, and Prenn beat Austin in four sets.

The English team of Perry and Hughes won the doubles, which meant that when Austin took care of Cramm on the third day, the English would move on to the Interzone Final. But after Austin took the first set seven-five, Cramm began to feel more comfortable on his home courts and started banging away at the ball, knocking it from corner to corner, rushing the net whenever possible. The home crowd could scarcely believe it, but their boy was taking apart this world top-ten player like an old pro. It was over quickly, 6-2, 6-3, 6-2 in the last three sets, and the competition was tied at two matches each. Now it was up to Prenn.

Daniel Prenn was as unlikely a candidate to become the hero of German tennis as one could imagine. Born a Jew in the Lithuanian city of Vilnius (then part of Russia) in 1904, he had grown up mostly in St. Petersburg. Czarist Russia was no paradise for Jews. Even in urbane, progressive Petersburg, Jews were subject to extreme restrictions. There were quotas on how many Jews could practice the law, how many could be admitted to the hospitals, and how many could be buried in city cemeteries. They could be expelled from the city at any moment on the slimmest of pretexts. And in the provinces millions of Jews perished in intermittent, bloody pogroms between 1821 and 1917.

Then things got worse. After the Russian Revolution in 1917, it was clear that the Communists were no saviors to the Jews. Pogroms broke out again during the revolution and ensuing civil war, killing another 70,000 to 250,000 civilian Jews. Along with the Russian aristocracy, who were being hunted down and executed by the Bolsheviks, many Jews chose to emigrate. Prenn fled with his family, along with thousands of others, down the well-worn escape route: south to the Crimea, of which the White Army still had control, by ship to the Balkans, and then northwest by rail to Berlin.

Berlin had long had a reputation of tolerance toward political refugees, and in 1920, when the Prenns arrived, it was also a very cheap place to live. Half a million Russians fleeing the revolution settled in the German capital, "imitat[ing]," as Nabokov wrote, "in foreign cities a dead civilization, the remote, almost legendary, almost Sumerian mirages of St. Petersburg and Moscow, 1900–1916 (which, even then . . . sounded like 1916–1900 BC)." The Russians in Berlin forged an émigré community that was an efflorescent world within a world. There were Russian hairdressers, grocers, pawnshops, and money exchanges. There were Russian orchestras and soccer teams. In 1923 Berlin, not Moscow, was the capital of Russian literature, with 150 Russian-language newspapers and journals and 86 Russian publishing houses. The thousands of Russian artists, writers, and other intellectuals who had been driven out of Soviet Russia convened around Berlin in Russian cafés, at literary soirées, and at charity events such as the masked ball where Vladimir and Véra Nabokov met in 1923. Véra, a Jew, and Vladimir, an aristocrat (though his father was a liberal reformist politician), had been part of that same exodus through the Crimea to Berlin.

Prenn and Nabokov might even have met at Rot-Weiss, which was probably the club that gave the impecunious literary genius playing privileges based on his skill level. Nabokov had learned an elegantly expert game as a child in Russia, and though he was not a tournament player, he did earn a part of his living at times in Berlin by giving tennis lessons, "like a slick automaton, under the slow-moving clouds of a long summer day, on dusty courts, [ladling] ball after ball over the net to [businessmen's] tanned, bob-haired daughters." But Prenn was not like Nabokov; he was not a literary man, not to be one of those refugees heartbroken over a world lost, those whom the poet Nina Berberova recalled as "all of us sleepless Russians wandering the streets until dawn," dreaming of a return one day to a Russia that had finally come to her senses. Instead, he assimilated into German society and remained in Berlin even when the hyperinflation of 1923–24 drove most of the Russian community to leave for Prague or Paris. Tough-minded and scientific, Daniel flourished at the Charlottenburg Technical High School and worked after school at a sports shop, as money was scarce. He was an enthusiastic boxer and soccer player and excelled at table tennis, but it was out on the tennis courts that he found his true métier. The red-clay rectangles turned out to be the perfect outlet for his innate combativeness, perhaps intensified by his obligatory role as an outsider. Though he never had the most graceful or powerful game, he was a clever strategist, "seemingly inexhaustible," and became known as "the most tenacious tennist in Europe." Roman Najuch, who had turned professional early and was one of the world's best players at the time, called him "the fiercest competitor I ever saw. . . . His iron will to win, combined with an astonishing power of concentration, was singular." By 1929 he had earned a graduate degree in engineering and the number-one ranking in German tennis. And that same year he led the German team to its unlikely victory over England.

Now, in 1932, he was being asked to do it again, in the deciding fifth match against Perry. And he came through with the match of his life. Perry took the first two sets 6-2, 6-4 without much trouble, but then Prenn dug into the clay and fought for the next two, 6-3, 6-0. That fourth set came so easily that the German crowd wondered whether Perry was merely "playing dead," as Tilden and Cochet used to do, saving himself for the fifth set. It certainly seemed so, as Perry unleashed a monstrous attack, which even on the slow red clay carried him to five-two and match point.

And then once again Danny Prenn would not give in. He ran down every ball, refused to make an error, and came all the way back seemingly on willpower alone. He won the last five games and the match, seven-five in the fifth, and Germany had beaten England again.

"This day, 10 July 1932, will never be forgotten by anyone who was part of the overflowing, roaring Center Court crowd," proclaimed a leading Berlin newspaper the next day. "[It was] one of the most inconceivable and most fascinating results of all time in the 'white sport.'"

Two weeks later, in Paris, Prenn and Cramm couldn't quite pull off another miracle against the Americans. They each beat the handsome, swashbuckling, hard-drinking Frank Shields, but they had no answer to the veteran American doubles team of Wilmer Allison and John van Ryn, nor to the current world champion Ellsworth Vines, and so they lost three-two. But this did little to dampen the enthusiasm back home for the stars who had brought Germany so close to the Davis Cup.

At the Rot-Weiss Club's annual Christmas gala that year, an unprecedented turnout of fifteen hundred crowded the great hall of the Esplanade, one of Berlin's most opulent hotels. The ambassadors of France, Spain, Italy, and other nations mingled in their finery, the Jack Hilton Orchestra kept the throng swinging on the dance floor, and Gottfried and Lisa and Danny and his wife Charlotte were the toasts of the evening. "The motion of the [shoulder-to-shoulder mass of people] was so great," read one society column the next day, "that the waves carried off tennis champion Prenn and his pretty blonde wife, who had been so near for a few seconds, before one could even call out good wishes on their one-year anniversary."

The festivities at Rot-Weiss belied the somber, threatening political landscape of that year. Already back in October 1929, with the American economy all set to implode, "there was something oppressive in the air" of Berlin, according to Sebastian Haffner. "Angry words on the poster columns; and on the streets for the first time, mud-brown uniforms and unpleasant physiognomies above them; the rat-tat-tat and piping of an unfamiliar, shrill, vulgar march music." A year later, in the Reichstag elections of September 14, 1930, the Nazi Party took many by surprise, expanding from 12 seats to 107, becoming the second-largest contingent in the parliament. Party leader Adolf Hitler "was still widely regarded as a somewhat embarrassing figure. . . . For ordinary Germans, his personal appearance was thoroughly repellent—the pimp's forelock, the hoodlum's elegance, the Viennese suburban accent. . . ." Yet amazingly, the notion that this failed artist and rabble-rouser, with his "interminable speechifying, epileptic behavior with [his] wild gesticulations and foaming at the mouth, and the alternately shifty and staring eyes," might come to power no longer seemed absurd.

Two years later it felt inevitable. The Nazis had steadily gained ground in election after election and were the leading party. Many felt Hitler might be rendered "harmless" by giving him "responsibility." Government leaders negotiated with him, offering him first the vice-chancellorship and then the chancellorship. In the summer and fall of 1932 the Weimar Republic disintegrated in front of the public's eyes. To Haffner, the second half of the year seemed a crazed nightmare of anarchy:

> The republic was liquidated, the constitution suspended, the Reichstag dissolved, reelected, dissolved again, and again reelected. Newspapers were banned . . . and all this took place in the almost cheerful atmosphere of a final supreme fling. . . . The Nazis already filled the streets with their uniforms, which they were at last officially permitted to wear, already hurled

bombs, already drew up their blacklists. There was no constitution anymore, no legal guarantees, no republic, nothing. . . .

The Christmas gala at the Esplanade was to be the last such spirited event for Rot-Weiss for many years, and for Daniel Prenn the final night of glory in Berlin. A month later, on January 30, 1933, senescent President Paul von Hindenburg appointed Hitler chancellor of Germany.

Four weeks later, on February 27, arsonists burned down the Reichstag. It is still not known whether Hitler's charge against the Communists was correct, or whether the Nazis started the fire in order to blame the Communists. In the end it didn't matter. That very night more than four thousand Communists, Social Democrats, and other political opponents were awakened in the middle of the night by SA fists pounding on their doors. Most were never seen again, and those who were were torture-ravaged shells. The first wave of midnight arrests and executions was sweeping over Berlin. Soon the prisons were so bursting with victims that concentration camps were set up to house, and hide, the overflow. The SA had taken over the Berlin prisons, as well as these camps, and were already devising inhuman new tortures to extract confessions and take revenge on former adversaries.

The very next day Hitler began his *Gleichschaltung*, or coordination of power—the process of legally securing absolute power. He got Hindenburg to sign an emergency decree suspending all constitutional rights and providing for more liberal use of the death penalty. With the SA and their trained dogs barring opposing delegates from entering, the Reichstag passed decrees "For the Protection of the People and the State" and "Against Treason against the German People and Seditious Actions," euphemistic new laws that allowed the SA and Gestapo to arrest anyone they liked without evidence or even charges. More political opponents, and the first few thousand bewildered Jews, began to disappear from Berlin.

Hitler also took the opportunity to abolish free speech, confidentiality of the mail and telephone, and the right of any other political parties to campaign. On March 23 what was left of the Reichstag voted for the Enabling Act, or "Law for Removing the Distress of the People and Nation," which handed over to Hitler all its own legislative powers, along with the power to "deviate from the constitution" when necessary.

The Third Reich had begun.

With total power finally theirs, the Nazis wasted no time turning their anti-Semitic rantings into national policy. The Enabling Act had been passed on a Friday; on Monday morning the newspapers announced that beginning that Saturday, April 1, all Jewish businesses would be officially boycotted. Aryan businesses, as well as Jewish ones, were ordered to fire all Jewish employees, and Jewish shops had to pay Aryan employees their full salaries even during the boycott. On Saturday morning SA troops were posted outside all Jewish shops, preventing anyone from entering. They also visited all Jewish doctor and lawyer offices to make sure the waiting rooms were empty.

The boycott was temporary, and Jews were later allowed to return to work for the time being, but it was a chilling prelude. Already pamphlets and posters were appearing everywhere informing the public that their Jewish friends, neighbors, and colleagues were a "subhuman" race that had been poisoning German society.

On April 7 the first new anti-Semitic law demanded the immediate firing of all Jews from the civil service. Soon afterward Jewish professors were dismissed from the universities. By August Jewish law students had been forbidden to take their exams, and all Jewish doctors were fired from city hospitals. Jews were forced to sell their businesses to "Aryan" buyers at ridiculously low prices.

The glorious new German sports culture, of course, could also no longer be infested with subhumans. "We need waste no words here," declared the Nazi weekly *Der Stürmer.* "Jews are Jews and there is no place for them in German sports." The new Reichssportführer, Hans von Tschammer und Osten, a fervent Nazi and enthusiastically brutal SA colonel, was right with the program. By the end of the year Jews were barred from every German boxing, rowing, gymnastic, skiing, and tennis club. Soon they were forbidden to swim in public pools and lakes or to ski at public resorts. Rudi Ball, a famous ice hockey star, defected to France, and Alex Natan, a member of Germany's world-record-tying 400-meter relay team, fled to England.

Tennis was no different. Already in April 1933 the German Lawn Tennis Federation announced, "Non-Aryan players can no longer take part in international matches." As if this weren't clear enough, the statement went on: "The player Dr. Prenn (a Jew) will not be selected for the Davis Cup team in 1933."

In one stroke Daniel Prenn's tennis career seemed to be over. Not only was he barred from the Davis Cup, but it was only a matter of time, he knew, before Jews were barred from all competition. Already the federation announced it was waiting for orders from above regarding whether it could enter Jewish players in individual tournaments, including the French and Wimbledon championships. A stunned Prenn did manage to win the Austrian Championship just a few weeks after the pronouncement, and a leading Viennese newspaper wrote:

> Last year, when Prenn beat Austin and Perry and won for Germany its great victory over England, there was no German newspaper that did not exalt "the Jew Prenn" in all possible ways. . . . Today these same papers write that Prenn can be no German, as he is Jewish. . . . When on Monday Prenn, the new champion of Austria, took the trophy from President Miklas and held it overhead, great applause fell on the scene. Prenn on Monday won the tennis championship of Austria, but Germany lost this and much more.

Daniel Prenn was Jewish by blood only. He was nonpracticing and nonreligious, and in fact his wife Charlotte was Christian. But this mattered little to the new regime. Dr. Theodor Lewald, the popular head of the German Olympic Committee, was forced to resign due to the fact that his father had been born Jewish and had been baptized only 110 years earlier. The many prominent Jewish members of Rot-Weiss were fast disappearing, and it was uncomfortable for Prenn even to appear at his beloved old club. When King Gustav of Sweden visited Berlin that spring, he made a point of playing a public doubles match with his old partner. But that gallant gesture helped little. Nor did the letter that Bunny Austin and Fred Perry, Prenn's victims at the Davis Cup triumph the previous year, wrote to the London *Times*:

*Sir,—We have read with considerable dismay the official statement which has appeared in the Press that Dr. D. D. Prenn is not to represent Germany in the Davis Cup on the grounds that he is of Jewish origin.*

*We cannot but recall the scene when, less than 12 months ago, Dr. Prenn before a large crowd at Berlin won for Germany against Great Britain the semi-final round of the European Zone of the Davis Cup, and was carried from the arena amidst spontaneous and tremendous enthusiasm. . . .*

*We view with great misgivings any action which may well undermine all that is most valuable in international competitions.*

*Yours faithfully,*

*H. W. Austin*

*Fred Perry*

It was notably the only protest from the international tennis community at all. Not only did the International Lawn Tennis Federation have no issue with member nations barring players due to race, but a few years later, when Nazi Germany took over Austria and Czechoslovakia, the ILTF bent over backward for them, voting in a new law allowing players from annexed countries to play for their conquerors.

Prenn had been uprooted by bloody revolution already once before in his life; perhaps for this reason he was one of the prescient Jews who left Germany while they were still able. By the end of the year he had made his decision. Already it was difficult; many countries had Jewish quotas, and the Nazis were not allowing anyone to take their money out of the country. But Prenn had a sponsor in London. Simon Marks, the millionaire head of the Marks & Spencer department stores and a big tennis fan, had befriended his fellow Jew on Prenn's visits to Wimbledon, and he made it possible for Prenn to emigrate. Leaving his family behind (his parents and younger sister were now living in Poland), Daniel Prenn fled yet another pogrom, and he and Charlotte sailed for England.

Gottfried von Cramm was suddenly in a very awkward position atop the German rankings. To be sure, he had won the German Championships in Hamburg in the summer of '32, beating Roderich Menzel handily in the final, after which he was the second athlete, and the only tennis player, ever to be granted a personal audience with President Hindenburg. Surely he felt, as many fans did, that in 1933 he would take over the undisputed number-one spot in Germany. But he wasn't there yet. That same summer the world rankings came out with Prenn at number six and Cramm number eight. Going into the 1933 Davis Cup season, he and Prenn were considered a symmetrical, powerful, two-barreled weapon that might finally bring Germany the trophy.

And now so suddenly, just two weeks before their first match against Egypt, Cramm had lost his partner. Stunned, he played through the season with a variety of far lesser players, beating the weak Egyptian and Dutch teams before bowing out quietly to Japan. Gustav Jaenecke, the hockey star and Lisa's close friend, played number-two singles and lost both his matches, while Gottfried lost the doubles with a little-known partner. The new regime was apparently happier to lose with Aryans than to win with Prenn.

Only twenty-three years old, the young baron, who had never shown much interest in politics, was suddenly forced to confront it. His close friend and partner had been thrown out of tennis, forced to emigrate. All around him, every day it seemed, his friends who were Jewish or otherwise despised by the Nazis were disappearing. Sebastian Haffner, who was the same age as Cramm, wrote:

> The world I had lived in dissolved and disappeared. . . . Every day one looked around and something else had gone and left no trace . . . it was as if the ground on which one stood was continually trickling away from under one's feet, or rather as if the air one breathed was steadily, inexorably being sucked away. . . .
>
> The men who had been the focus of attention, whose books one had read, whose speeches we had discussed, disappeared into exile or the concentration camps; occasionally one heard that one or another had "committed suicide while being arrested" or been "shot while attempting to escape." . . . The radio announcer whose voice one had heard every day, who had almost become an old acquaintance, had been sent to a concentration camp, and woe betide you if you mentioned his name. Charming [actress] Miss Carola Neher was suddenly a traitor to the people; brilliant

young [actor] Hans Otto . . . lay crumpled in the yard of an SS barracks: "thrown himself out of a fourth-floor window in a moment when the guards had been distracted," they said. Others just vanished. One did not know whether they were dead, incarcerated, or had gone abroad—they were just missing.

What was one to do? To speak out appeared to be suicide. Many Jews, like Prenn, were already emigrating. But most were hesitant to abandon their homeland, not to mention their livelihoods. The general feeling was that this regime, like the succession of Weimar governments, would pass. The people would stand for these outrageous acts for only so long.

The von Cramms had called Hanover home for eight hundred years. They weren't about to become Englishmen or Americans just because some maniacal Austrian had seized political power for a while. Emigration was a natural and wise choice for Daniel Prenn, but for Gottfried Cramm it wasn't even an option.

But how could he continue to play tennis for the glory of a criminal regime? Paula von Reznicek—who, like Gottfried's wife, had a Jewish grandfather—was also forced to retire from tennis. But her new husband was Hans Stuck, Germany's greatest race-car driver and a personal acquaintance of Hitler, and she was spared any further trouble. Lisa and her family also had yet to be harassed by the Nazis. Was it due to her marriage to Germany's rising tennis superstar? Gottfried had to wonder.

He must also have been wondering if that was why they hadn't come after him for his own suspect activities. For the Jews were not the only group on the Nazis' hit list. They had made no secret of their long-standing plans to rid Germany of its Communists, Gypsies, Jehovah's Witnesses, and nonconforming clergymen, not to mention the lame, the mute, and the epileptic. Furthermore, they boldly intended to "delouse" Germany by exterminating those responsible for the "epidemic" of "unnatural lechery between men."

In fact, they often combined their anti-Semitism and their homophobia. In 1930 Hitler's official newspaper wrote:

Among the many evil instincts that characterize the Jewish race, one that is especially pernicious has to do with sexual relationships. The Jews are forever trying to propagandize sexual relations between siblings, men and animals, and men and men. We National Socialists will soon unmask and condemn them by law. These efforts are nothing but vulgar, perverted crimes and we will punish them by banishment or hanging.

The Nazis' resolve to persecute homosexuals stemmed, at least publicly, from a belief that such perversion would "emasculate" the German people and weaken their fighting spirit. Life was a battle; only the strong would prevail. And all undisciplined free love, but especially homosexual love, would undermine the population. "Anyone who thinks of homosexual love," announced the party, "is our enemy."

Of course, there were those among the Nazis themselves who were thinking of homosexual love. Ernst Röhm, Hitler's right-hand man since 1919 and the leader of the terror-mongering brownshirts, the SA, was known to be gay, as were several of his SA lieutenants. But Hitler had always been tolerant of his friend's indiscretions. When other Nazis complained about Röhm's unapologetic cavorting, Hitler even went so far as to contradict party ideology, declaring that an SA officer's sex life "belongs purely to the private domain. . . . His private life cannot be an object of scrutiny."

Heinrich Himmler was not so tolerant. Himmler, the mousy pincenezed bureaucrat who looked like an accountant or elementary schoolteacher, would as head of the SS and Gestapo organize the mass slaughter of millions of innocent people. Like his Führer, he detested Jews, Communists, and a host of other declared "enemies." But Himmler "had a special horror of homosexuals." So rampant and maniacal was his homophobia that it would have been laughable had it not resulted in such astronomical human devastation. The ancient Teutons "knew what to do with homosexuals," he ranted, "they drowned them in bogs. No, it should not be called punishment. It was 'extermination of abnormal existence.'" He would perform the same extermination: "Otherwise, if we continue to have this vice predominant in Germany without being able to fight it, we'll see the end of Germany, the end of the Germanic world."

Upon taking power, the Nazis wasted no time commencing their campaign against homosexuals. On February 23, 1933, all homosexual-rights organizations were banned—and all pornography to boot. On May 6 hundreds of Nazis broke into the Institute for Sexual Research, a renowned (and reviled) institution founded by the Jewish homosexual Magnus Hirschfeld in 1919. Over the years, as he fought for the reform of sex laws and oversaw voluminous research into sexuality of all forms, Hirschfeld was often attacked and beaten after his speeches by fascist thugs and was constantly vilified in the rightwing press. Luckily, he was out of the country when they finally came to destroy his institute. The marauders stole and burned his priceless collection of tens of thousands of books and photographs. The chairman of his institute, Kurt Hiller, was arrested and sent to the new concentration camp at Oranienburg, where he was tortured repeatedly for months before being mysteriously released.

Throughout the summer of 1933, as the Nazis went on rampages, rounding up their enemies, real and potential, the SA raided gay bars all over Germany, closing most of them down. The Eldorado was closed as early as March and was turned into a Nazi Party election office. In the fall the first groups of homosexuals arrived at Dachau. Yet still, like the Jews, Germany's homosexuals for the most part couldn't believe that such an extreme government could last, or that Berlin—*their* Berlin, the homosexual's paradise—could turn from a haven to hell so quickly. Many actually joined the Nazi Party to try to blend in, or better yet enlisted in the Wehrmacht, the regular army, which the Nazis were never able to fully control. Most simply continued to live their lives, unharmed for the time being, with a constant eye over their shoulder.

Gottfried Cramm saw his nightspots go dark, noticed people disappearing from the nightlife and the tennis club, and had to wonder what the Gestapo might have on him. In Paris that May the German authorities chose to enter him only in the doubles, not the singles, even though Prenn of course had been left behind. Was it an ominous sign? They did let him play the singles at Wimbledon, where he won two matches before bowing out quietly against an obscure American, Cliff Sutter. Afterward S. Willis Merrihew, the publisher of *American Lawn Tennis*, congratulated him on a good showing and asked if he would be coming to New York for the U.S. Championships. Gottfried smiled and shrugged. "I would like to do that very much," he said. "But I don't think I am good enough yet." He may also have been wondering if he was good enough, without Prenn bolstering the Davis Cup team, to save his own skin.

But that very week Cramm and Hilda Krahwinkel ran through the mixed doubles draw without losing a set, quite by surprise bringing Germany its second Wimbledon trophy ever. (Cilly Aussem had beaten countrywoman Krahwinkel in the 1931 finals.) Though it didn't quite match beating England in the Davis Cup the year before, Cramm was once again the toast of German tennis circles. The Berlin papers heralded him as "our greatest Davis Cup weapon," and the foreign press praised him as "a sticker, and at his best in five-set matches."

He proved this again at the 1934 French Championships the following May. His years of training discipline paid off, as he won four five-set matches in a Parisian heat wave to win his first major title. In both the quarterfinal and semifinal, he was up two sets to one and then lost the fourth before taking the fifth set easily. When others were wilting in the heat and humidity, Cramm would look more refreshed than ever. He looked as if he would happily play ten sets on that slow red clay and then perhaps some doubles.

In the finals he faced the great Australian Jack Crawford. The twenty-six-year-old Crawford never talked much and was thought a grouch by the press but was well liked by his fellow players. A big man, at six feet and 185 pounds, he had great foot speed and was "a [tennis] genius with a sensitive touch and every stroke at his command." The previous year he had come within a whisker of winning all four major championships in one year—what would later be called the Grand Slam. Having already won the Australian, French, and Wimbledon championships, he came to Forest Hills, ran through to the finals, and met Fred Perry. After losing the first set 6-3, he won the second in a 13-11 marathon, and the third 6-4. But then, one set away from completing the season sweep, the asthmatic Crawford began to collapse in the muggy Queens weather. Some said it was the asthma, some said it was taking a bit too much brandy between games to help the asthma, but for whatever reason Crawford was finished and lost the last two sets 6-1, 6-0.

But Crawford had retained the number-one world ranking for 1933 and was still number one when he stepped onto the Court Central at Roland Garros to face Cramm. He couldn't have been happy with the weather, which felt just as oppressive as Long Island. On one of the hottest days anyone could remember at the French Championships, and after his grueling victories in the earlier rounds, Cramm came out as fresh as a young boxer in round one, hitting full strength on every point. His power and exuberance carried him to a 6-4 victory in the first set, but the world champ stayed calm and came back to win the next two 9-7, 6-3. And then in the fourth Crawford broke Cramm's serve in the seventh game and was serving at 5-4, ad-in: match point.

All day Cramm had been forcing his way to the net, only to see the Australian throw up lob after gorgeous lob, sending him back to the baseline like Sisyphus. "I had never seen a man make such perfect lobs," Cramm remembered later. But now, again, even down match point, after a long exchange of ground strokes from corner to corner, Cramm got a short ball and pounced on it, leaning into his forehand, knocking the ball deep to Crawford's backhand and rushing the net. Crawford's oddly distinctive flat-topped racket flashed through the sunlight, dipped under the ball, and sent up one more deep lob. Sensing that he had hit another "perfect" one and won his second straight French crown, Crawford followed his shot forward to take the net and cut off whatever weak return might come back. But this lob hadn't been quite as deep as the others, and instead of running back to retrieve it, Cramm had simply turned sideways, skipped back a few steps, leaped into the air, and crushed an overhead smash. The hardest-hit ball of the day shot just over the net, past a flabbergasted Crawford, and down the line to save match point.

If Crawford wasn't drinking brandy that afternoon, he should have been. Cramm won the next three games for the set and ran through the fifth for six-three and the championship. The French title was second in prestige only to Wimbledon, and this was Germany's first victory ever at Roland Garros.

The Paris crowd, which had been impartial in this final between two foreigners, rose and cheered, completely won over by the young German's style, demeanor, and fortitude. "Only two foreigners in my observation ever captured the Parisian crowd," wrote John Tunis in *Collier's*. "One was our own Bill Tilden. The other is the German nobleman." That very night a French reporter wrote that "if Germany had put all her children through a test, she could not have picked one worthier, or more French, to wear the title of champion of France."

A few days later in Berlin a member showed up at the Rot-Weiss Club in the early morning with her young son. All the courts were empty, the clay still damp with dew, except for one. On Center Court, alone save a young club employee he had recruited to pick up the balls, Gottfried Cramm was practicing his serve.

It seemed he was always practicing his serve. He would place a few of the cardboard boxes that balls came in as strategic targets in the service box, serve until he hit each one, and then set them up again. He was a perfectionist when it came to tennis. If his backhand had gone a bit off, he would wear out several practice partners working on that one stroke for four or five hours. But practicing the serve is a solitary activity and can become something of a meditation, the repetitive motion loosening the mind, providing escape from the tensions of everyday life. Ball after ball after ball he would toss up to the exact same spot. Then, arching his back and springing up, he would sweep each one out of the sky and send it like a bullet to the corners of the service boxes.

He had much to escape, for such a young man. A marriage that had become a charade. The stress of living under a terrorist government that threatened him and his friends, lovers, and family. Not to mention the pressures of his love life itself. Manasse Herbst had left Germany in February 1933, seeing immediately, as Daniel Prenn had, that he and his family needed to emigrate, the sooner the better. His parents and he had managed to get visas to Portugal, but how would they live there? The Nazis were already clamping down on currency; no one emigrating was allowed to take along more than seven percent of his property. Jews were monitored particularly closely. Any substantial withdrawal from their bank account was subject to investigation. At the border Jews faced far more scrupulous inspections than Aryans. One violation of any of the complex foreign-exchange laws, and they were thrown in jail while their precious visas—and hopes—expired.

A few days before the Herbsts' ship sailed, Manasse showed up ashen faced at Gottfried's apartment with a small satchel. The bag was bulging with Reichsmarks. It was his father's life savings, he said.

There was no question of their simply taking it on board with them; the authorities would find it immediately and arrest them all. But if anyone could smuggle it on board, it was Gottfried. Surely the irreproachable Aryan aristocrat, the great hope of German tennis, could walk on board a ship without being searched. The money was not too bulky to be concealed in numerous parcels about his person. Terrified and thrilled, Gottfried agreed.

But when he showed up at the steamer on that bitter winter day to bid Manasse farewell, the pockets of his overcoat were empty. Manasse was crestfallen, but Gottfried explained that it had been too risky; they were searching everyone these days, and it wasn't like he was world champion yet. The money was safe in his bank, he told him. And he would get it to them eventually, little by little. It was the only way. The steamer sailed, and Gottfried rode the boat train back to Berlin feeling the weight of all that money as though it were indeed strapped to his body.

And then came the Night of the Long Knives.

In late June 1934 Cramm, the new French champion, was in London playing Wimbledon. He was determined one day to conquer this tennis Everest, although the English grass courts really didn't suit his game. He had molded his strokes on red-clay courts, similar to those of Roland Garros. Clay-court specialists, used to a slower and surer bounce, developed longer strokes, enabling them to generate more power and topspin for the sluggish environment. But on grass the ball skidded low and quick and often erratically, so one needed a short backswing in order to react. "My backswing is too pronounced for grass," Cramm admitted. "Moreover, grass takes half the effect from a high-kicking service favored by many [clay-] court players like myself." Also, in the damp London air he had come down with a virus that afflicted more than sixty players. He got a bye and lasted a couple more rounds but fell in the fourth round to Vernon Kirby, the South African he had beaten handily in the past.

Much worse was the word from home. The news was just coming out about the execution of Ernst Röhm and the rest of the SA leaders. Hitler personally had never seemed to mind his friend's sexual predilection, or at least had been willing to overlook it. But lately it had become more than inconvenient, considering the party's hard line on homosexuality. And Röhm had become a thorn in the Führer's side in other ways.

Röhm, feeling a bit too secure in his position as Hitler's old friend, had been pressuring Hitler to dissolve the traditional Wehrmacht into the "brown flood" of Röhm's SA troops. After all, it was the SA that had provided the brute force, the street terror, that had carried the Nazis to power. And Röhm had grown its numbers from 300,000 men at the beginning of 1933 to nearly three million.

But Röhm had overestimated his own importance. His brown-shirted thugs, invaluable to Hitler in his early years as he tried to make his mark and frighten opponents, had recently become a bit of an embarrassment. Now a head of state and in absolute power, Hitler needed a more sophisticated force, one that could carry out its acts of torture and violence behind a facade of official order and correctness. Himmler had convinced him that it was his own elite guard, the black-uniformed SS (Schutzstaffel, or Protective Squadron), that should fulfill this role. Furthermore, Röhm had never grasped the importance of maintaining favor with the Wehrmacht; Hitler knew that even he needed the army behind him to assure the stability of his Thousand Year Reich. In fact, the Wehrmacht, behind President Hindenburg, was threatening to declare martial law and seize the government if Hitler did not suppress the SA.

Hitler knew what he had to do, and Himmler and Göring gave him the pretext for doing it. They fabricated a plot by Röhm and the SA to stage a putsch. "Reacting" to "news" of an uprising, Hitler flew to Munich at two A.M. on June 28. SA officials were being rounded up and arrested all over Munich and Berlin. At a hotel out in the Bavarian countryside, Röhm and a number of SA men on vacation were fast asleep, several in the arms of other young men. Just after dawn Hitler and his SS troops burst into the hotel and dragged them all out of bed. Edmund Heines, the SA Obergruppenführer of Silesia, a convicted murderer "with a girlish face on the brawny body of a piano mover," had been in bed with his young male chauffeur. They were brought outside and shot. Hitler personally arrested Röhm and sent him to a nearby prison. Hundreds of SA men were executed that night. And as they had after the Reichstag fire, the Nazi leadership seized on the opportunity to do away with all sorts of opponents. General Kurt von Schleicher, the last chancellor before Hitler, was shot dead by the SS as he answered his door in the middle of the night, as was another general, Kurt von Bredow. Gregor Strasser, a Nazi ally of Hitler's from the early days who had moved too far to the left and even joined Schleicher's government, was arrested and then gunned down in his prison cell. Even an old retired political opponent, Gustav von Kahr, who had helped suppress Hitler's Beer Hall Putsch in 1923, was hauled out to a swamp and hacked to death with pickaxes. Hundreds were tortured and murdered in this Night of the Long Knives, which Hindenburg called Hitler's "gallant personal intervention which nipped treason in the bud and rescued the German people from great danger."

As a courtesy to his old friend, Hitler ordered a revolver placed at Röhm's disposal in his prison cell. Röhm sneered. "Let Adolf do it himself. I won't do his job for him." Adolf declined, but soon afterward Röhm was shot down point-blank in his cell.

As long as Röhm, Hitler's trusted old friend, had been in good standing with the Führer, German homosexuals had had some reason, despite Himmler's ravings, to think they might be able to weather the storm. Now, as Himmler and Göring raged publicly against the "homosexual SA pigs" who had been justly slaughtered, gay Germans' last straw of refuge seemed to have caught fire. After the Röhm purge, Himmler, the murderous homophobe, was unquestionably Hitler's right-hand man.

GOTTFRIED CRAMM CALMLY WALKS BACK TO THE BASELINE ON Centre Court. He will serve to begin the second set. Three years have passed since the Night of the Long Knives. Friends and acquaintances have disappeared. He has been followed, watched—there is no doubt about that. What will they do with him? It is always on his mind. Except when he's on a tennis court. Here he knows he is doing exactly what he should be doing, what everyone, friend and enemy alike, wants him to be doing. It has become the only place where he is truly calm, at peace, even when thousands of eyes are watching his every move. Here the spotlight brings him privacy.

The first set is his, eight-six. He has been just as his fans imagine him: physically exquisite, mentally flawless. Even Gottfried has to wonder how long he can keep it up, how long the high will last. He accepts two balls from the ball boy—each thrown with one bounce, arriving chest high, always perfect at Wimbledon—and steps to the baseline to serve. A familiar wave of *Gemütlichkeit* flows through him. All those countless hours, alone on court, firing thousands of tennis balls at empty boxes. Swinging this thirteen-ounce piece of wood through its exact, never-altering curlicue down behind his back and then up into the air above him is like walking, breathing, eating. And as he tosses the first ball of the second set, even in the split second just before making contact with the ball, he knows that this new level of tennis he has reached is not going to fade away, not today.

The serve is perfect.

As the second set progresses, both players hold their serve, but Cramm is doing it more easily than Budge. Alternating cannonball flat serves down the middle with his famous "kicker" spin serves to the ad court, which pull Budge way out past the doubles alley, Cramm is either hitting service winners or else forcing weak returns that he can dispatch without trouble. And the German's returns of serve are so good that Budge is having trouble getting to the net. After forcing a baseline rally, Cramm is employing his favorite strategy, one he learned from Tilden. How did Bill put it? "A method I frequently prefer is perhaps dangerous, but it's exciting, and if successful it inflicts the most lasting of all defeats. It is to play your opponent's strength until you break it." Once a player realizes that he isn't going to win points even with his best shots, he's finished. And so whenever Cramm finally gets a short ball on his forehand side, he drives it deep to Budge's backhand—his famous, unassailable backhand—and rushes the net, setting up a volley winner to the other corner or, on one memorable occasion, "an astonishing stop-volley from the centre of the court." When the American does manage to get him on the defensive and rush the net as he loves to do, Cramm is coming up with "improbable passing shots" or winning lobs. All Budge can do as the ball sails by him is utter his crowd-pleasing gasps of admiration: "Oh baby!"

The English audience loves Budge's sportsmanlike reactions almost as much as Cramm's brilliant winners. An amused titter also runs through the stands as the players change ends, Cramm having held serve again for a five-four lead. After daintily sipping some tea from a china cup, Budge suddenly grabs the pitcher of ice water left out for the players and "douses his head like Jeeter Lester," the Georgia sharecropper in Erskine Caldwell's recent novel, *Tobacco Road*.

The young American shakes his head dry as though trying to throw off his frustration. Beneath his veneer of sportsmanlike conduct, he is simmering. "I'm supposedly number one in the world," he thinks, "and I'm playing as well as I ever have. Yet I'm down a set and struggling just to stay even in the second. The fewer mistakes I make, the fewer he makes."

DON BUDGE WAS INDEED THE UNOFFICIAL CHAMPION OF THE world. He was also, amazingly, only seven years removed from his first junior tournament. At twenty-two, he was still a skinny, freckled, working-class kid from Oakland, "conspicuously red-headed, even among red-headed men." "Despite his many triumphs," wrote one reporter, "Budge still comes to a tennis court looking a little like an awkward country lawyer about to pit his homely talents against the brilliance of metropolitan advocates. . . . Six feet one and only 160 pounds, of a gangling build, his naturally milk-pale skin reddened by sun and spattered with freckles, his chin receding to a thin neck and with a modest grin cracking his homely visage, Budge in repose has always seemed unpromising material for a world's champion. Among such figures as the perfect-featured Austin, the cocksure, swashbuckling Perry, and the chivalric von Cramm he is a kind of Airedale among human lions."

The Californian's background, in fact, could not have been more different from that of the baron across the net. His mother, Pearl Kincaid, was a Scottish American who grew up in San Francisco. His father, Jack, grew up in Wick, the northernmost town in Scotland. A top soccer prospect, by the time he was nineteen Jack was playing for the Glasgow Rangers, one of Scotland's top teams. But his career ended when he developed serious pneumonia and bronchitis one winter. His doctor ordered him to seek out a healthier climate for his lungs and suggested California.

Jack arrived in San Francisco in 1905 and got a job in the composing room of the *San Francisco Chronicle*. He left there soon for a job driving a laundry truck, as the atmosphere of the composing room was hard on his lungs, but his tenure there was consequential, as he had met the young linotype operator Miss Kincaid. When he met her, Pearl had the flaming head of red hair that she would bequeath to all her children, but according to family legend, the next year, in the great San Francisco earthquake of 1906, her hair turned permanently white from the terror of clinging to her bed as it was thrown violently from one end of the room to the other.

Jack and Pearl were soon married and had three children: Lloyd in 1909, Jean in 1913, and John Donald Budge on June 13, 1915, about a month after a German U-boat sunk the British passenger ship *Lusitania*, bringing America closer to entering the Great War. The Budge kids grew up on Sixtieth Street in Oakland, in a two-bath, three-bedroom wooden-frame house with a front porch—a far cry from the Philadelphia mansion in which Bill Tilden was reared, not to mention the von Cramm castles outside Hanover. But it was a comfortable middle-class existence, as Jack Budge rose in the laundry business to eventually become manager. Apparently his was one business affected little by the Great Depression, for even as wages around the nation fell by sixty percent, and the soup lines of the unemployed and homeless snaked around city blocks, life for Don and his siblings went on much as before.

Two blocks from the Budge home was Bushrod Park, a kids' paradise, with baseball and softball diamonds, basketball courts, swings and jungle gyms, and three gravel tennis courts with lime chalk lines. Don loved all sports from an early age, particularly baseball and basketball. Tennis was probably his least favorite, but his big brother Lloyd had gotten the tennis bug early and went on to become a good college player and a well-known teaching pro. And Bushrod Park didn't have a backboard, so when Don got to be thirteen, Lloyd would drag his little brother out to the courts, give him an old racket, and hit with him. Don learned to bat the ball back consistently, in fact became something of a human backboard, but still would rather be shagging fly balls.

Then a couple of years later Lloyd issued a challenge. At dinner he announced to the family that if Don weren't so lazy, he could probably win the upcoming state tennis championships in the fifteen-and-under division. But then, he continued, it would probably never happen, because his little brother wouldn't practice.

The kid took the challenge. Every day for the two weeks before the tournament, Don Budge was at Bushrod Park from early morning on, hitting balls against anyone he could drag out onto the courts. It was then that he developed the backhand, based on his left-handed baseball swing, that would always be his best shot. Aside from that, all he really had was fast feet and determination.

Budge showed up at the tournament in dirty old sneakers, a plain white T-shirt, and light tan corduroys—the closest thing to tennis whites his mother could find in the closet. In the first round, he simply ran down every ball he could, "like a golden retriever," as he put it, hitting everything back in the court, and won without too much trouble. Only afterward did he learn that he had just beaten the top seed. After that he ran through the rest of the draw and was the California fifteen-and-under champ.

Tennis immediately superseded baseball as Don Budge's sport, and he began traveling to play tournaments around the state. His humble background didn't deter his new ambitions to become a world-class player. After all, despite tennis's reputation as a country club sport, plenty of champions had already come from public courts. George Lott and Johnny Doeg, for instance, and above all Budge's fellow Californian Ellsworth Vines, who was on the brink of becoming world champion.

Three years later, in 1933, the Northern California Tennis Association paid Budge's way to the National Junior Championships in Culver, Indiana. At eighteen, he was still only five foot six and a half, still the red-headed retriever with little power. Unseeded and still fairly unknown, he scrambled all the way to the finals, where he met the number-one seed, his buddy Gene Mako.

Mako, the "golden boy of southern California tennis," though six months younger than Budge, was already over six feet tall and muscular. The son of a Hungarian artist, he had been born in Budapest in 1916. After the war his parents had moved to Italy, then to Argentina, and finally settled in Los Angeles when Gene was seven. "I played every game you could imagine from the time I could walk," he remembered ninety years later. He starting winning tennis tournaments when he was twelve, four months after hitting his first balls on a local public court. In his mid-teens he was a national table tennis champion, playing tournaments all over the country. After his great years of playing championship doubles with Budge were over, he would become a semi-pro basketball player. Right now, though, he was America's top junior tennis prospect.

Mako and Budge had met two years before, when they were sixteen, and had quickly become fast friends. They both loved jazz music and all sports and were soon as comfortable together as brothers. They began pairing up in doubles immediately. For the first few years Mako was the stronger player. The first time they played together, Mako pointed to the deuce (or "forehand" side) of the court. "You play there," he said, "and I don't care what you do, but don't miss a ball."

In 1933, at age eighteen, Budge was finally catching up. On their eastern tour Mako beat him in the Michigan State Championships, but when they got to Indiana for the national juniors, Budge beat his partner in the finals, 6-2, 6-2, 1-6, 0-6, 8-6. Mako had been up five-three in the fifth set and even in the end had won more games (24-21) and more points (160-150), but Don Budge was the new national junior champion. Still, the retriever got no respect: the champ was irritated to read a few weeks later the proclamation of Big Bill Tilden, lord and high priest of tennis: "The future of American tennis rests with Gene Mako, Frank Parker, and possibly Don Budge."

After winning the national juniors, Budge enrolled at the University of California, Berkeley, for the 1933–34 school year. But in the spring he was named to the United States Davis Cup auxiliary squad, and although he intended to return to college in the fall, tennis took over his life. That summer he finally got a chance to play the eastern grass-court circuit, the mecca for all American tennis players. He and Mako traveled together, staying mostly in private homes, where their hosts provided their meals. The USLTA gave them $1.50 a week for laundry and the same amount for spending money, and they thought they were on top of the world. They won two tournaments in doubles and reached the quarterfinals of the national doubles championships,

played each year at Longwood Cricket Club near Boston. And at Forest Hills, Budge reached the fourth round of the nationals, losing in
four sets to the South African Vernon Kirby, who had taken Cramm
out of Wimbledon a couple months earlier. Budge clearly had arrived,
although he still did not appear in the world top-twenty rankings for
1934.

In what turned out to be one of the best decisions he ever made,
Budge turned down an offer to be part of an American team touring
South America and the Riviera that winter and instead returned home
to Oakland to train with his coach, Tom Stow. Stow, a former national
intercollegiate champion in doubles for Berkeley, and now the pro at
a local country club, had offered his services to Don after he won the
national juniors. He knew Don couldn't pay him yet, but he thought
he had the makings of a champion and was willing to take a gamble
that could pay off later.

Stow was a firm, somewhat gruff man, an intense perfectionist who
turned a lot of people off. But if he believed in you, and you in him, you
couldn't ask for a better coach. And Stow devoted himself to Budge that
entire winter, working to change his forehand. Like many Californians,
who grew up on hard courts, Budge had a western grip, which was
great for hitting topspin off balls bouncing high off the cement. But on
grass—the surface of all the big eastern tournaments, including Forest
Hills, not to mention Wimbledon—the western grip was a liability. It
made it difficult to pick up balls skidding low off the grass, or to hit the
slice approach shots that were most effective on grass.

Stow was determined that Budge must change to an eastern grip if
he wanted to rise to the top of the tennis world. All that winter Stow
had other players hit to Budge's forehand day after day. "Tom had a
different kind of personality," recalled one of those sparring partners.
"You either learned the way he wanted you to play or not at all. . . . I
would rally by the hour with Budge, while Tom screamed at him on
the forehand."

By the spring of 1935 the transformation was complete. Don
Budge was no longer the pint-size retriever. His backhand had always
been his best shot, and Stow hadn't touched that. And now at six foot
one, 160 pounds, Budge had a powerful serve and forehand and a

dominant net game to go with it. Rushing the net at every opportunity, he would attack his opponent and never let up.

The previous fall Walter Pate had astounded reporters by declaring, "Budge's forehand needs work, but he's the fellow we need to bring back the Davis Cup." Budge was as surprised as anyone; when he'd been asked after his strong showing at Forest Hills whether he hoped to make the Davis Cup team next year, he'd coyly shot back: "I'd be lucky to get on the Canary Island team. . . . I'd rather play basketball than tennis anyway." But a few months later the popular fifty-seven-year-old Pate, a New York lawyer who had been a nationally ranked player in his youth and a USLTA official ever since, was made the new Davis Cup captain and promptly named Budge to the team, despite his low ranking of number nine in the United States. "We aren't going to win it overnight," he explained, "and that young man will be ready in a couple of years."

Budge and Mako got to play against China and Mexico in the preliminary rounds in Mexico City but were slated to be reserves for the Interzone Final against Germany, to be played at Wimbledon a few weeks after the Championships. Thrilled to be making their first European trip, the California boys packed up their phonograph and jazz records, along with their rackets and tennis whites, and set sail for England with the United States team.

They almost missed the boat, sprinting up the gangplank together "bare-headed and in shirt sleeves" at the last minute. They had been doing some last-minute shopping for jazz records. From then on the trip was five days of relaxation. One ship on the Atlantic route had a tennis court, and the great Helen Wills used to book it so she could practice on the way over, but the USLTA thought it a good idea for the players to have a few days away from tennis, and they all agreed. They did play a lot of Ping-Pong, though, "to the considerable amusement of their fellow passengers," wrote one tennis journalist on board. "Mako is a marvel at table tennis. He plays seven feet back of the table, and makes the most astounding shots, particularly a forehand slice which he hits with excessive spin *below* the table level, so that his baffled opponent remains unaware of what has happened to the ball until it suddenly floats back to him and spins off at right angles."

Just about to turn twenty, Budge wasted no time on his first overseas journey accruing a reputation for naïveté. His teammates loved to kid him about the time the customs officer knocked on his cabin door the morning of their arrival in England. Don had been asleep and stumbled to the door. "Pardon me, sir," said the man, "may I see your visa?" Thinking the man was referring to the eyeshades that he always slept in, Budge asked, "What on earth do you want to see my visor for?"

A more famous anecdote illustrates how the English public loved to see Budge as an American hayseed even when he didn't deserve it. It happened a few weeks later, in the quarterfinals at Wimbledon. The American kid, ranked only number nine in his own country, had astonished the fans with his new power game, which had carried him through the first four rounds. In fact, the only set he had lost so far was in the fourth round against the eighth seed, Christian Boussus.

Now, in the quarters, he was matched against Bunny Austin, the fourth seed and home crowd favorite, the handsome Cambridge man who had invented tennis shorts. Austin took the first set six-three, and it appeared that the young American's impressive debut would end suitably in the quarterfinals. But Budge hung on. The second set reached eight-all, and Austin had his chances to put the boy away, but finally it went to Budge ten-eight, and before the crowd could digest this development and assimilate the possibility that their man would actually fall to the newcomer, Budge had taken the third set six-four. Then, late in the fourth with the score tied, Austin desperately trying to force a fifth set and Budge trying to finish him off, Queen Mary arrived.

It was Budge's first glimpse of royalty, but he knew what to do. All the players had been carefully instructed that if the queen were to arrive during a match, they were to stop play immediately—even in the middle of a point—and stand at attention until she was seated in the Royal Box. As Al Laney of the *New York Herald Tribune* wrote around that time:

> The King and Queen go to other events and people stand as they enter or pass by, but nowhere else does it compare with the entrances and exits at Wimbledon. . . . The ball is traveling back and forth when suddenly, as though a command had been given to a well-drilled body of troops, the eighteen thousand spectators

rise as one, uncover and stand in silence. The noise they make in rising signals the players to stop. When their majesties have taken their seats, the crowd seems to breathe again. The players, standing stiffly at either end of the court, unbend. Play is resumed.

In this case the royal entourage had appeared between points—lucky for an American who wasn't used to abandoning points in the middle—and the entire stadium had instantly risen en masse and frozen in attention, as had Austin, facing the Royal Box.

Budge was the last to do so, but only by a few seconds. After wiping some sweat off his forehead with the sleeve of his shirt, as he did frequently on court, he dropped his arms to his sides. The queen and her entourage sat down, the players took their positions for the next point, and play resumed. Budge never thought twice about it, and no one said anything to him afterward.

One English journalist, however, had seen more than a wipe of the forehead. The next day he reported with great amusement that the brash American had actually waved to the queen. The story got told and retold, embellished with each reiteration. Years later a leading tennis expert wrote that it wasn't until Budge had switched sides that he realized what the disruption had been about, and then when he found himself right under the Royal Box, he had waved, a sheepish grin covering his suddenly crimson face. This version also has it taking place in the semifinal round, against the second-seeded Gottfried von Cramm, "all elegance, suave, completely at home, the perfect aristocrat, an old hand at center-court play." When the queen entered, "Cramm let a ball pass him, dropped his racket, turned, clicked his heels and stood at rigid attention. Budge looked all around, fumbled with his racket, shuffled his feet and wandered about the court. . . . At the end of the game they changed courts, and Budge said something to Cramm. Cramm replied, and Budge's face flamed red." Consequently the grin and the wave. This hyperbolic version doesn't stop there:

A gasp rose from the packed stands. An unthinkable breach of etiquette had taken place and surely the stars would fall. The thousands sat in horrified silence, awaiting the clap of doom. . . .

The Queen was shocked too. She sat rigidly upright for an instant. And then she smiled at Budge. She raised her hand a little as though to wave back—and then solemnly inclined her head in a bow until the gray hat with the pink flowers showed its top to the crowd.

The tension was broken. Far across the court, someone began to titter. From the standees came a voice, low, but clearly heard, saying, "God bless the Queen." Someone cheered, and the stands took it up. They cheered Budge, and they cheered what was one of the most gracious gestures ever to come from royalty.

In any case, after Budge finished off the fourth set against Austin, it was indeed the stately Cramm awaiting him in the semifinal round. Now the consensus number-two player in the world, Cramm had only just missed winning his second straight French championship, falling in a close final to Perry, who had finally risen to greatness. This would be Budge's most formidable test yet. Budge had only read of the exploits of the great German champion, for he had never visited the United States, and this was Budge's first foray abroad.

After his victory over Austin, Budge spoke with various reporters. "I was heady with new success," he said later, "and probably, naturally, a bit smug, though I was trying desperately to be properly modest and to create the right first impression." He bathed in the luxurious players' locker room, exulting privately in his victory, and dressed in suit and tie. He was preparing to join Mako and the other Americans for dinner, and just beginning to think about how he might do against Cramm in the semis, when a natty young man just a few years older, in a suit and tie that made Don feel shabby, approached him and said in clipped Oxbridge English with just a taste of a Continental accent, "Excuse me, Don, I'm Gottfried Cramm."

Budge had never even seen a good photograph of him, just some grainy action shots in the magazines. He jumped up and shook hands nervously, and Gottfried asked if he would like to chat a bit and "get to know each other." They walked out of the stadium and found an empty bench by an outside court, which wasn't being used this late in the tournament. Don was nervous, but Cramm seemed quite easygoing, and flush with victory, Don thought he could feign savoir faire chatting modestly about his great match.

But Cramm knocked him off his game with his first words. "You know, Don," he said, gazing evenly into Budge's eyes, "I watched your match today, and I must say I thought you were a very bad sport."

Budge couldn't even speak. He was dismayed, and also stunned: he could have sworn he had been the very paradigm of sportsmanship against Austin.

Cramm saw the younger man's face fall and began again. "Look, Don, we're going to play each other in two days, and I have the feeling that we're going to play each other a great deal more in the years ahead. I was perhaps too blunt, but I do think it is a good idea if we try to understand one another from the start."

Budge just nodded. He still couldn't imagine what Cramm was talking about. Then Cramm explained. It was in the third set, still a tight match at one set all. Budge had forced his way to net on a big point, and Austin had hit a strong passing shot right by him, landing close to the sideline. The linesman called it out, but Budge felt sure it had hit the line. It seemed that Austin had thought so too, though he had given it just a slight second look before walking dutifully back to the baseline to serve the next point.

Then Budge did what he thought was the proper thing when an error had gone in his favor. Austin served the ball, and Budge deliberately, obviously, hit it into the net. The crowd applauded appreciatively, and the match continued on.

"Yes, I remember," said Don. "It was a terrible call. I did the right thing, didn't I?"

"Absolutely not," said Gottfried. "You made a great show of giving away a point because you felt the call had wronged Bunny. But is that your right? You made yourself an official, which you are not, and in improperly assuming this duty so that you could correct things your way, you managed to embarrass that poor linesman in front of eighteen thousand people."

Don had never thought about it that way. He had been following the example of the great Tilden, the Barrymore of tennis, who never let a linesman's error go unrectified. First he would stride up to the offending judge, hands on his hips, with a glare that could only be described as withering, and ask, "Would you like to correct that error?" If penitence was unforthcoming, he would approach the umpire and loudly declare, "I won't accept that point." If even the umpire wouldn't overturn the call, Tilden would take matters into his own hands and theatrically throw the next point. On at least one occasion, when a linesman's incompetence was simply beyond the pale, Tilden threw an entire set before calmly finishing off his opponent—and this was in the Challenge Round of the Davis Cup. What's more, he expected everyone else to act accordingly. If you were playing Tilden, and a shot of his, which he thought was good, was called out on your side of the court, he expected you to throw the next point. It didn't matter if the linesman, umpire, you, and the entire crowd agreed that the ball was out. If you accepted the point, you faced the ire of Tilden.

Cramm had learned much about tennis from Tilden, but apparently he did not share his imperious views regarding etiquette. And Budge recognized that when it came to tennis etiquette, Cramm was the one to emulate. By the time their conversation ended, the young American was convinced that they should always "play the points the way they're called."

Two days later the new acquaintances met on Centre Court in the semifinals. As it happened, in the very first game a shot of Cramm's that appeared to clip the line was called out. Budge glanced up at him out of the corner of his eye, but Cramm was merely walking over to receive the next serve, apparently not giving the call a second thought. Budge played hard and won the game. As they switched ends of the court, Gottfried looked at him "with just the touch of a wry smile" and said, "I guess you do see things my way."

Budge went on to surprise Cramm in that first set, six-four, and the audience began to wonder if this kid was actually going to beat the number-two player and even challenge their own great Fred Perry. But Cramm, calm as ever, proceeded to follow his lesson in sportsmanship with a tutorial in controlled power and steadiness in match play. He took the second set 6-4 and dominated the last two, 6-3, 6-2. As the players left Centre Court, Gottfried noticed that the door that led to the locker room for some reason had not been opened yet by the attendant. So Gottfried, whom the English would soon be calling "the Gentleman of Wimbledon," skipped ahead of Budge, opened the door, and held it while his vanquished opponent passed through. Then he disappeared himself, to the cheers of the crowd.

Then the seasoned German was in new territory himself: the Wimbledon final. He had finally figured out how to adapt his leisurely clay-court game to the grass of England. The trick was to attack, attack, attack. When he was at the net he didn't have to worry about quick and sometimes unpredictable bounces upsetting his long smooth backswings. Of course, his opponent in the final, Fred Perry, was the master of grass-court aggression himself. But at least Cramm would have a chance to pay him back for last month in Paris.

In the French Championships Perry had taken Cramm's crown in the finals, beating the defending champ on his own surface in four sets. Now Cramm would try to take the dashing Englishman on his home court. But Cramm had the misfortune of rising to his first Wimbledon final just when Perry was at the peak of his athletic life. Probably the fastest tennis player who'd ever lived, he had relied on that speed plus a murderous wristy forehand to win the last two U.S. Championships, along with the Australian and Wimbledon titles in 1934. His only weakness had been on clay, and that had cost him the chance at tennis's first Grand Slam in 1934, as he lost in the quarterfinals of the French. Now, after showing he could win on clay as well, he was looking for his second straight Wimbledon. If the dashing Englishman, in his perfectly tailored whites, playing to the crowd and chatting with British VIPs in the gallery between games, was second only to Cramm in sophisticated élan, he was also the German's sole superior on a tennis court. And he had little trouble in the finals, beating Cramm 6-2, 6-4, 6-4.

Still, Cramm had to feel good about his chances of taking tennis's premier trophy in the near future. He had reached the finals fairly easily, and against Perry, as one American reporter wrote, "no score could be more deceptive than that by which Perry beat von Cramm.

For perfection of stroke, for sheer speed and daring, three such closely fought sets have rarely been played." And a veteran English tennis observer noted that "the game between Perry and von Cramm was such super-tennis that many people did not realize its quality. To all intents and purposes anything like an inferior stroke paid the penalty and neither man dared go to the net except on a super-shot."

After Wimbledon came the final rounds of the Davis Cup, and German tennis fans in 1935 had every reason to expect another strong charge toward the Challenge Round, as in '29 and '32. Their man Cramm had fully matured and on a given day could certainly beat anyone. And it seemed they might have finally found a worthy replacement for the departed Prenn. The son of a Berlin businessman, the nineteen-year-old Rot-Weisser Henner Henkel had a pugnacious face, carefully slicked-back blond hair, and a powerful first serve that turned heads. He had become Cramm's main protégé at Rot-Weiss, despite his languid attitude toward practice, and his Davis Cup counterpart in singles. The young Henkel had suffered the Germans' only loss against Italy in the second round, but against Australia in the next round he'd been a godsend. The Australians had two high-ranking players in Jack Crawford and Vivian McGrath, and although Cramm was able to beat them both on the red clay at Rot-Weiss, for some reason he didn't play the doubles, and the little-known team of Kai Lund and Hans Denker lost to Crawford and Adrian Quist. So Henkel had to win one of his matches or Germany was out. And the untested Berliner, who had gone out early at the French, went and beat them both. He topped McGrath, a quarterfinalist in Paris, in four sets on the first day. And on the final day, after Cramm had wrapped things up against McGrath, Henkel went ahead and took out the world number three, Crawford, six-four in the fifth set.

So when the German team beat Czechoslovakia in the European Zone final in Prague shortly after Wimbledon, they came back to London with high hopes of upsetting the Americans in the Interzone Final. After all, Cramm had run through Budge easily at Wimbledon and could expect to do the same to Wilmer Allison. Allison, the former University of Texas Longhorn who was currently the number-one American, had been seeded fifth at Wimbledon but had gone down in the first round to McGrath. If Henkel could conjure another surprise as he had against Australia, or if Cramm's mastery would be enough to pull off a one-manned doubles upset of the experienced team of Allison and Johnny van Ryn, perhaps the Germans could make their first visit to the Challenge Round.

Once again the papers back in Berlin were touting Cramm as the savior of German tennis. But of course, Germany was now a very different place than the last time Davis Cup fever had gripped the capital, back in 1932. Two and a half years of fascism had bolstered the economy but thrown prison chains, real and psychological, around much of the population.

For many in Germany, 1935 was the peak of good times. For those not in a targeted social group and able to turn a blind eye, jobs were plentiful, salaries high, and cultural life in full Weimar-era efflorescence. Economically, things had turned completely around since the dark early days of the Depression. Partly, Hitler had been lucky to come to power just as things couldn't get any worse and to some degree were getting better already. Also, his domestic program, based on foolhardy economics or sometimes no economics at all (he despised professional economists), just happened to work. Much as the Weimar governments had done, he had new money printed to pay for expensive building projects, such as the construction of a national Autobahn system. But in contrast to 1923, when war reparations and other factors had conspired to make the new money worthless, the economic recovery already occurring was great enough to support the new money, and in fact the national deficit shrank during Hitler's early years.

Another reason for the economic recovery, of course, was Nazi Germany's secret rearmament. In flagrant violation of the Treaty of Versailles, Hitler had been building his war machine, and in 1935 he decided secrecy was no longer necessary. He had Göring let a British representative know that Germany had a military air force and waited for the reaction from London. There was none. The next week, on March 16, he announced a new law establishing universal military service and a peacetime army of half a million men. London protested meekly but politely inquired whether Hitler would still receive the British foreign secretary on his upcoming visit. The Führer graciously agreed.

The next day was one of enormous celebrations all around Germany. The shame and humiliation of Versailles were history. Hitler had planned his announcement for the day before Germany's *Heldengedenktag* (Heroes' Memorial Day), and this year the parades were displays of militarism the like of which hadn't been seen since 1914. At a massive ceremony at the Berlin Opera House, thousands of "young officers stood like marble statues holding upright the nation's war flags."

On May 21, the same day that he had secretly made official the creation of the new Wehrmacht, with himself as Supreme Commander of the Armed Forces, Hitler gave one of his most cleverly specious speeches. War is senseless and useless, he told the Reichstag: "Our racial theory regards every war for the subjection and domination of an alien people as a proceeding which sooner or later changes and weakens the victor internally, and eventually brings about his defeat. . . . No! National Socialist Germany wants peace because of its fundamental convictions."

The democracies of the West ate it up. *The Times* of London wrote, "The speech turns out to be reasonable, straightforward, and comprehensive. . . . It is to be hoped that the speech will be taken everywhere as a sincere and well-considered utterance meaning precisely what it says."

The Führer was seen now as "the symbol of the indestructible life-force of the German nation, which has taken living shape in Adolf Hitler." Optimism was high, and people had confidence in the banks and the government and were investing their money again. For the average citizen, life was good.

For a sizable minority, though, life had become tenuous and threatening. Although Gottfried still loved Berlin, he hated the beast that occupied it, and for the most part he was happiest now to be out on the tennis tour, away from Germany. At home there was constant stress, much of it related to Manasse Herbst. Herbst was back in Berlin, trying once again to find a way to get his family's money. Gottfried had sent some to Lisbon from St. Moritz and Stockholm during trips to tournaments there, but he was worried about the danger and reluctant to risk larger amounts. In Berlin he was virtually supporting Manasse, a situation that neither man was comfortable with. Nor could they be comfortable with the cauldron of hatred their city had become.

Like others, they probably sought respite by walking into the Grunewald to disappear among the fir trees, the oddly displaced objects of refuse—an iron bedstead here, a dressmaker's dummy there—and the undressed bathers and lovers. They might well have crossed paths with the Nabokovs pushing their little boy in his stroller; perhaps Gottfried and Vladimir recognized each other from the Rot-Weiss Club. The Grunewald, wrote Nabokov, "was infested with human bodies in various stages of nudity and solarization . . . repulsive, seal-voiced males, in muddy swimming trunks, gamboled around; remarkably comely but poorly groomed girls, destined to bear a few years later—early in 1946, to be exact—a sudden crop of infants with Turkic or Mongol blood in their innocent veins, were chased and slapped on the rear . . . rows of young men, of a pronounced Nordic type, sat with closed eyes on benches and exposed their frontal and pectoral pimples to the nationally approved action of the sun." Gottfried and Manasse would stop and rest in a grassy area, as others did, but even there, in the peaceful glade under a gorgeous blue sky, they could not escape. Every ten minutes another group of schoolchildren would march by, accompanied by a pince-nezed teacher, cheerfully greeting everyone they saw with their new slogan, *"Juda verrecke!"* (Drop dead, Jew!)

From inside cafés they could hear the brass of marching bands. Walking outside, they would see column after column of troops gliding down the street, countless swastikas bobbing like menacing anemones in the brown sea. As the red and black flags passed by, pedestrians on either side raised their outstretched arms and shouted *"Heil Hitler!"* They had little choice; those who didn't were dragged aside and beaten. Like anyone whom the sea of Nazis nauseated rather than inspired, Gottfried and Manasse learned quickly to duck into an alley or building entrance whenever they heard the singing and music approaching. "The swastika flags were everywhere," wrote Sebastian Haffner, "the brown uniforms that one could not get away from; not in buses, cafes, in the streets, or even in the Tiergarten park. They were everywhere, like an army of occupation. . . . The red posters with the announcements of executions on the poster pillars almost every morning, next to the cinema programs and the posters for summer restaurants; I did not even notice them anymore."

Gottfried was glad to get back to London with the Davis Cup team. But even the London air was not free of the Nazi menace. No sooner had the confetti from the May celebrations of King George's silver jubilee settled than Londoners were reminded of the unstable international situation. Despite *The Times*'s belief in Hitler's claims of pacifism and its support for a policy of appeasement, many people felt war was inevitable, and this point was brought home when the Home Office began to distribute air raid precaution circulars. Still, most people felt sure that not even Hitler would dare revisit the horrors of the Great War. German visitors were still very welcome in London, and none more so than the popular Cramm.

Into this tense political scene of 1935 strode the young Americans, Budge and Mako, on their first trip abroad, looking for jazz music and good times. They made a smart pair, posing for photos in their white flannels, white shirts, and matching white tennis sweaters with black buttons, each with an arm around the other's shoulder. As they rose and shaved each morning, those in the neighboring rooms could hear Benny Goodman and Tommy Dorsey swinging through the walls.

"Budge's curly red hair, his bright red cheeks, and his sky-blue eyes gave him the look of a Modigliani portrait," wrote one observer. Others were not as flattering. The United States' chances in the Davis Cup, according to *Time* magazine, "depend[ed] largely on the newest, homeliest, and youngest member of the team . . . shambling, freckled, red-haired, 20-year-old Donald Budge."

> A phlegmatic, gentle youth, so homely that even his mother smiled when a friend [probably Mako] said that, if not the best tennis player in the world, her son was certainly the ugliest, young Budge is likeable but undistinguished off a tennis court. He barely graduated from high school a year ago, spends his spare time imitating Bing Crosby or the Mills Brothers, drinks nothing stronger than milk. On the court, the quality that

marks his game is the one in which he sometimes seems most lacking elsewhere—savoir-faire.

But good looks and sophistication counted for little on the tennis court, and all of a sudden, after one great Wimbledon, the young Californian was the hope of the U.S. team. Although he was officially still ranked only ninth in the United States, most people considered him number two after Allison, and in fact he had been beating both Allison and Sidney Wood in the team's practice matches. Wood himself went to the team captain and suggested he replace him with Budge. And with Budge's victory over Austin at Wimbledon, the Americans suddenly had hope of beating Perry and England and bringing the Cup home. But to get a chance in the Challenge Round, they would first have to get past Germany. Most experts felt that Cramm was a sure thing to win his two singles matches and that the United States would win the doubles and the match between Wilmer Allison and the young Henkel. So everything would probably depend on the opening match between Budge and Henkel.

Having made a far superior showing on the same Wimbledon courts a few weeks earlier, Budge was the favorite. But the pressure of playing for his country in his first Interzone Final seemed to hamper him, and after three sets he found himself in a tight battle, 7-5, 11-9, 6-8. In the fourth, though, Budge relaxed a bit and brought out his new power game, and the set and match were his, 6-1.

If the experts were right, the United States had all but clinched a visit to the Challenge Round. But the next day the celebrated American doubles team of Allison and van Ryn had their hands full with Cramm and Kai Lund. True, Lund was a weak link, but Cramm raised his game so majestically that it almost turned everything around for Germany. The match "was dominated throughout by [Cramm's] wizardry of execution and lightning-quick subtlety of stratagem," and he brought his team to match point five times. But they couldn't quite get that last point, and then came the famous moment when, after Lund had apparently hit a winner to give them a sixth match point, Cramm notified the umpire that the ball had grazed his racket. Gottfried von Cramm made a name for himself as the ultimate sportsman, but Allison and van Ryn won the match 3-6, 6-3, 5-7, 9-7, 8-6. And when Allison beat Henkel on the third day, as expected, the United States officially advanced.

After that Budge and Cramm came out to play the final match, as is always done in Davis Cup, even though it was now a meaningless match, known as a "dead rubber." In their Wimbledon semifinal Cramm had been more impressive with each set, winning 4-6, 6-4, 6-3, 6-2; now he picked up where he had left off, running through Budge in the first set six-love. He then had set points in the second set, at five-three, but after Budge fought back to five-all, Cramm "seemed to lose all interest in the proceedings," as Budge remembered later. It was still close, even with Budge playing at full tilt, but the American ran out the match 0-6, 9-7, 8-6, 6-3, and most observers agreed with the victor that Cramm's play had been halfhearted. Perhaps he was discouraged by yet another loss to the Americans in the Interzone Final. Or maybe he was thinking ahead to his imminent return to Berlin, the omnipresent Gestapo, and the problem of Manasse's money.

Whatever the case, the loss to Budge would come back to haunt him. For as Budge remembered it, "He had defeated me soundly at Wimbledon a short time before, and I had no faith at all that I could beat him. It was he who opened the door for my hope, because once you have beaten someone, no matter how tainted the win, it is a great deal easier to accomplish it the next time. . . . A match may be meaningless in one context but quite significant in others."

The next time they played was two years later, in the Wimbledon final of 1937. Not only was Budge a much stronger player by then, but he remembered having beaten Cramm even before this improvement. Playing what more than one person described as "perfect tennis," he dispatched the German in straight sets.

TWO WEEKS AFTER THAT, THOUGH, IN THE 1937 INTERZONE FINAL, Don Budge is thinking that it feels just like Wimbledon '35. He thought he'd finally passed Gottfried by when he beat him so soundly to become world champion, but today it's the German who's playing like the best player on earth. Budge must be asking himself, Was Wimbledon a fluke? Did I underestimate Gottfried? I figured he was peaking a couple of years ago at age twenty-six. Could he still be improving at twenty-eight?

Budge's cannonball serve and enough backhand winners are keeping him in the match, but Cramm clearly has the advantage. "He attacked incessantly," Budge will say later, "and kept me on the run and tried to exploit a bad patch of my forehand that showed up here." Still, the American keeps holding on. Five-all in the second. As the set reaches its twilight stages, a gloaming that theoretically could go on, agonizingly, forever, "the crowd passed from enthusiasm to something near hysteria." At the climax of a particularly protracted point, a woman's shriek pierces the taut atmosphere over the Centre Court. The conclusions of rallies spark men's yells, cheers, and groans.

At five-six, Budge walks to the baseline to serve with brand-new balls and holds up two of them to show Cramm, a standard courtesy. There is nothing a big server loves more than new tennis balls, and in less than a minute the American is up forty-love. Apparently this second set will go to "extra innings" just like the first. It seems only appropriate, given the extraordinary level of play from both sides. But then Budge begins to miss his first serves. Cramm attacks the second serves and twice comes to net and puts away inspired volleys. When Budge then attacks on his own after a long rally, the German calmly passes him to come back to deuce. Each player earns game points and loses them, until finally, on another break point, Budge again misses his first serve. Sensing his chance, Cramm inches forward and takes the second serve on the rise, slicing it deep toward the baseline and advancing to the net behind it. Budge hits a "dangerously deep passing shot," but Cramm moves to it "with a dancelike leap" and picks it off with a crisp, aggressive volley that hums by the advancing Budge and brings up a cloud of chalk from the left sideline.

Fourteen thousand voices erupt at once. "*Furor teutonicus!*" shouts Stanley Doust, a top Australian player from the 1910s, now doing radio commentary for the BBC. In the press box the pipe of the *Daily Telegraph*'s Wallis Myers falls from his mouth as he exclaims, "Gottfried is inimitable!" Irmgard Rost, a young German player who has been watching with clenched hands that at critical moments reach up to clutch at her heart, "jumps to her feet and literally screams with delight." "Game and second set, Germany," calls the umpire, but his next words, "Germany leads, two sets to none," are drowned out by the rising cheers, screams, and incredulous applause of the gallery.

One German fan in the stands remains calm and simply rises with a proud grin on his face. When an American sitting next to him compliments him by remarking that Cramm plays tennis like no other player, the man nods and quietly replies, "He plays just like God would play."

# An AMERICAN TWIST

THOUGH HE DOESN'T SHOW IT, Don Budge is steamed, "more mad than analytical," as he will put it later. I'm blowing everything at once, he thinks. Not only my chance to be the undisputed world number one, but the Davis Cup trophy for my teammates and everybody back home. If he could see the match statistics, he would be even more frustrated. Each man has won exactly eighty points. Each has hit fifty-eight winners. And yet he's down two sets, on the brink of defeat. The only statistical edge the German has is in errors: he has made only twenty-five, the American thirty.

Back in the States, tennis fans in their offices, living rooms, and neighborhood bars groan as Cramm hits his winning volley and the cheers of the Centre Court crowd suffuse their radio speakers. "When news of the second set loss came across three thousand miles of sea," Alistair Cooke will say, "men drinking highballs nearly choked. Walter Pate at this point did something more desperate than choke over a highball. He decided on the English form of suicide. He ordered himself some tea."

As for Cramm, he merely walks to the back of the court and turns to the ball boy for balls to serve with. As he does, though, he can't help but catch the eye of Henner Henkel, sitting in the stands, "his very wide mouth wide open in an admiring grin." All German tennis fans must be grinning. Cramm is making the biggest match of his life his greatest.

Budge, for his part, shows no sign of his inner turmoil. "In the face of such superlative play," notes one reporter, "Budge did not blow up. He maintained, at least outwardly, complete control of himself, had a few brief words with Captain Pate during the changeovers, and hewed grimly to the line." He knows that he is playing well, and if he is ever going to catch Gottfried off guard, now is the time. One of the most difficult things to do in a tennis match, he well knows, is to maintain your high peak of effort and aggression, your killer instinct, when you're already up by two sets. A spirited counterattack right now could bring him right back into the match.

Sure enough, Cramm does not continue his withering advances toward the net in the first game. Instead, he seems content to play from the baseline and even tries a couple of drop shots that fail to fool Budge at all. The American, meanwhile, throws off his lethargy and disappointment and takes the net every chance he gets. A trademark blistering crosscourt backhand goes for a winner to break Cramm's serve. Already the German's onslaught is stemmed.

On such a warm humid day this match could become exhausting. It is already over an hour old. In this era, before television and its commercial breaks have arrived, tennis matches are much briefer. Like this one, they are almost always best three out of five sets, but even without tiebreakers—still thirty years in the future—many three-set matches finish in less than an hour, and a two-hour contest is considered a great test of endurance. But if anything, five-setters in the 1930s are even more grueling than the four-hour marathons of the future, for there are no breaks. "Play shall be continuous," state the rules of tennis, and as the players change ends every two games, they are allowed no more than a wipe of the towel and perhaps a quick sip.

As Budge and Cramm change ends at one-love in the third set, however, they take some extra time toweling themselves off, almost as if they both realize a change of momentum is occurring. Pate's tea is delivered. In the stands there is an air of jubilation, not only because Germany seems on the doorstep of victory but simply in reaction to the quality of play. All around the stadium spectators turn to one another and remark how they have never seen tennis played this well.

Of course, not all of them are pulling for Cramm; far from it. In America, Budge "is in fair way to become the most popular tennis idol since [the early 1920s]." And he has also become quite a crowd favorite at Wimbledon over the past two years. First there was the apocryphal wave to the queen, and then, through another strong showing in 1936 and finally his title run in 1937, Budge has never failed to display his simple, homegrown sportsmanship and humbleness. "The Wimbledon crowd admires him," according to Alistair Cooke, "but they also like him, for the very silly but good reason that he has been nobody but himself. The Americans they have admired have been straight and undeniable Americans who said American things and pitched frankly and easily." Budge is as American as Mark Twain, Cooke avers, and has the potential to be as embraced by the English as was that Yankee superstar.

"Don Budge is a really nice kid on top of the world," *The Bystander* told London fans this month. "Jimmy Dorsey is his favorite tenor saxophonist, Ray Bauduc his idea of a real trap-drummer, Bob Crosby's his favorite band. He likes doubles better than singles and swing music better than either. He admires spaghetti, Errol Flynn, Olivia de Havilland, and Virginia Bruce," in that order. His voice has matured into a smooth drawl reminiscent of his favorite crooner. "Give me some Bing Crosby and Tommy Dorsey records," he coyly told the host of a radio show, "and I'll gladly lay off the tennis."

His public persona had begun to evolve shortly after his first trip to England in 1935. "Budge reached real greatness in his last-day triumph [the dead rubber in the Davis Cup] over a somewhat fatigued and dispirited von Cramm," wrote the poet Conrad Aiken, who lived in Rye and was relieving "boredom, isolation/insulation . . . loneliness," and an unraveling second marriage with occasional journalistic jaunts to London to pay the bills. "Once more it was clear that Budge must never allow himself to be lured into a softening of his game; to sacrifice his beautiful natural speed and the characteristic daring of his attack is to give too many hostages to fortune."

He came home a different player, tearing through the eastern grass-court tournaments with new aplomb. "It won't be long," noted *The New*

*Yorker*, "before the slim young redhead will dominate his American opponents in much the same way that Ellsworth Vines did." His newfound confidence was readily apparent in his "swift, easy-flowing, low-bouncing strokes to the corners" and also in his relaxed demeanor. At an important moment during Budge's five-set comeback win in the finals at Newport, the charismatic Frank Shields mistakenly hit back a Budge serve that had been several feet out. "Sorry, Don," called Shields, for this was a breach of etiquette that made the server wait for the court to be cleared before hitting his second serve. "Take two." Budge just grinned slightly as he raised his racket. "One's plenty," he said. And it was.

Though his confidence was rising, he was still a boy of twenty and not yet the tennis machine he would become. At Forest Hills the next month he was taken out in the quarterfinals by Bitsy Grant, the diminutive scrambler from Georgia who gave everyone fits and would be Budge's number-two man in the 1937 Davis Cup tie against Germany. On this occasion Grant dismantled Budge's power game with a barrage of slices, lobs, and steady returns, tearing up the grass with his "sprints, slides, and dives," according to James Thurber, "like the deer fly of tennis (the deer fly is an insect that is terribly hard to get away from once it begins to pester you)." Such a loss would be unthinkable within a short time. Nonetheless Budge ended 1935 ranked number two in the United States (behind Wilmer Allison) and six in the world (with Perry and Cramm the top two).

Don Budge had arrived. But still the papers had a field day with his Rockwellian visage, employing the word "homely" more often than "backhand." During the 1935 U.S. Championships *The New Yorker* ended one tennis column with this vignette:

> At one of the movie theatres in Forest Hills there was a picture called "The Raven," with Bela Lugosi and Boris Karloff. A mother had brought her small son as far as the lobby and then balked at taking him in. "I'm afraid those men would frighten you so you wouldn't sleep," she said. "Aw, gee whiz, Mom," he said. "They don't scare me any more'n Donald Budge does."

Forgoing a career in horror films, Budge returned home to Oakland shortly after the nationals to continue the postseason routine he had begun the year before. For six weeks, beginning in early October, he would not touch a tennis racket. After months of the tour, it was a relief not to have to step on a tennis court. A couple weeks later he would start dropping by the Berkeley Tennis Club to see friends, and just watching people play would make him itch to hit some balls. By the end of the forced vacation, he woke up every morning eager even for Tom Stow's exhausting practice drills. He would drive the four miles from his parents' house in Oakland to the Claremont Country Club for a three-hour workout with Stow. They worked on all aspects of his game, but again the emphasis was on the relative weakness ("How many masters of the game would love to have this weakness!" wrote Roderich Menzel)—it was forehand, forehand, forehand.

They also worked on conditioning, but Budge would soon learn that it was not enough. His first big matches of 1936 came in late May, when the United States played Australia in the Interzone Final at the Germantown Cricket Club in Philadelphia. The brutal Philadelphia summer had arrived early, and the temperature when Budge and Jack Crawford stepped onto the grass was over one hundred in the sun, with high humidity. No amount of training in northern California could prepare one for this. Still, Budge figured the weather was in his favor, as Crawford was asthmatic and well known to wilt under such conditions. Just such weather had prevented him from capturing tennis's first Grand Slam in 1933.

Budge came out strong in the heat and took a quick two-set lead over the great Australian. But then he made the mistake of becoming defensive in his play, and Crawford came on strong to take the third and fourth sets, and then a five-three lead in the fifth. He served for the match at five-four and got to thirty-all, but Budge managed to break his serve and knot the match. Then the war of attrition really began. Crawford appeared to be finished: he "staggered about the court, reeled and almost fell; yet he kept the battle alive." Budge didn't feel much better than Crawford looked. Throughout the match Crawford had maintained a strategy of patiently hitting slow deep slices that forced Budge to generate his own power. The burden had taken its toll. Slower and slower they both moved between points, less and less was Budge willing, or able, to expend the energy to attack as he had in the first two sets, and the fifth went agonizingly on serve to twelve-eleven. Then

Budge finally earned a break point, and match point, and went for a backhand crosscourt winner from the backcourt. Crawford reached it and went for a winner of his own down the line. The American made a desperate attempt to reach it and swung in vain; the ball went by him—and landed two inches out. The match was Budge's, thirteen-eleven in the fifth.

The victor was on the ground, though. His body had finally given in to the conditions, and he was wracked with leg cramps, unable to stand up. Walter Pate, who was back as team captain after having missed the overseas trip in 1935, came out and supported him as he rose and made his way toward the net to shake hands. But Crawford was not at the net. As his final errant shot had fallen, he had "wavered, swooned, and at last fallen flat out in a dead faint."

Budge recovered for his remaining matches, but the cramps were a bad omen, a lesson he would not learn for a few more months. His recovery also was not enough to allow the United States to return to the Challenge Round against England. Wilmer Allison, the defending U.S. champion and number four in the world but thirty-one years old and in the last few months of his tennis career, lost both his matches. And Budge and Mako, who were expected to win the doubles, suffered a rare mental hiccup. They won the first two sets easily against Crawford and Adrian Quist, and then just as Budge had done against Crawford, they quickly gave up the next two. This time, however, the Americans came on strong in the fifth and were leading four-one. But they never won another game, in fact scored only six more points as the Aussies took five straight games and the match. The memory of that loss would irritate Budge for the rest of his life, but it did teach him one thing, if he didn't know it already: a one-four deficit isn't as daunting as it sounds.

At Wimbledon a few weeks later, Budge made another strong showing but failed to improve on 1935. This time it was Perry who spotted him a set in the semifinals before taking him apart 5-7, 6-4, 6-3, 6-4. Compared to the artful elegance of Cramm and Austin in the other semi, this was "a battle royal, a masterpiece of savagery, and just about the only piece of genuinely masculine tennis in the tournament." The polished but hard-nosed Englishman then beat an injured Cramm in the finals to "retire" the Wimbledon trophy. (It was the custom in tennis, if someone won a tournament three times, to give him the original trophy, along with the duplicate the winner usually gets, and buy a new one for next year.)

Budge's loss did nothing to stem his growing confidence. When the American team returned to New York, a group of reporters met them on the dock. When asked about his match with Perry, Budge told them not to worry, he was going to knock off the world champ at Forest Hills. At this point team captain Walter Pate stepped in, perhaps worried that his young star was promising more than he could deliver: "I have no doubt that Don is going to catch up with Perry, but maybe not so fast. I think you'll see it happen in '37."

"Oh, no," Budge calmly replied. "It's going to be this year. Fred is probably at the peak of his form, and I almost had him at Wimbledon."

On a warm, muggy, drizzly day in Queens, Budge's brashness seemed justified. He and Perry had steamrolled to the Forest Hills finals without much trouble. Very few foreign players had taken the long ocean crossing to play the U.S. Championships; out of ninety participants, only nine were foreign, three of them from Canada and four from France. Perry was the lone Englishman, and not surprisingly, no one from the strong Australian team that had beaten the United States in Philadelphia ventured to make the three-week ship ride back for the American tournament. Once again, as had been the case since before the war, the German Lawn Tennis Federation sent no one to Forest Hills, and so Cramm was home in Berlin instead of seeking another shot at Perry. Still, no one could complain that the final match was not world class; the world champion was facing the man everyone expected sooner or later to assume that mantle.

For the two weeks of the tournament, Budge and Mako stayed as houseguests of Walter Pate and his wife in Glen Cove, Long Island, about twenty miles from the West Side Tennis Club, where the championships were held. "For wild excitement at night," Budge recalled, "we would usually play a few hands of cards." Then, around ten-thirty or eleven, Don and Gene would head to the local drugstore for some extra-thick chocolate milkshakes before turning in for the night.

The quiet routine seemed to work, as Budge, like Perry, lost only two sets in his first five matches. (And Mako, for his part, ran through to the fourth round before being crushed by Perry, no embarrassment that.) But Budge was starting to feel some ill effects from his diet even before the finals. One day, practicing on a side court with the current world champion pro, Ellsworth Vines (who, as a professional, was ineligible for the nationals), he started feeling sick and just made it to the locker room before vomiting. After beating Frank Parker in the semifinals in straight sets, he again was sick in the locker room. The milkshakes were just the beginning of it. "They tell me Budge sometimes goes in for hot dogs and soda pop before a big match, the way Vines used to," wrote James Thurber in *The New Yorker*. The rumors were accurate. There were also "all the other sweets I had refused to deny myself." By the time of the championship match, Don Budge was as fearful of his digestive system as he was of his great English opponent.

Saturday, September 12, arrived, dark and tempestuous. By midafternoon, when Perry and Budge took to the court, it felt like evening, with ominous clouds darkening all of New York City. With no lights in the stadium, the match was played in a dim, eerie, stormy atmosphere. The crowd seemed edgy from the threatening weather, moving around frequently even when the ball was in play. Perry, who had been "mildly pestered all week by galleries which somehow failed to be amused by his favorite mannerism—staring rigidly at the spot far beyond the line where an adversary's erring shot had landed until the linesman shouted 'Out!' "—seemed particularly distracted today. Budge came out stormlike himself and thundered through the first set six-two, but Perry managed to come alive, regain his Wimbledon form, and take the second by the same score, despite a half-hour rain delay at five-two.

In the third set both players produced "some of the greatest shot making of the season." Perry was trying to hit every ball with his famous forehand, and Budge was trying to do the same with his backhand. With both players trying to run around their weaker stroke, the result was some "remarkable maneuvering," as one spectator remembered, "and in fact many winners were hit from the baseline because the other guy was cheating." Finally it was Perry who broke the American in the fourteenth game to take the set eight-six. But when he got down in the fourth set, he seemed to lose all interest, seemingly annoyed by the partisan crowd, and made little effort. Budge took it six-one, and they headed to a fifth set.

While Perry was resting during the fourth set, however, Budge was working hard, and by the fifth he was feeling the same nausea and exhaustion he had had all week. He somehow managed to find a way to break Perry's serve, to go up five-three and serve for the match, causing "a Niagara of a roar in the crowd," but then his body began to give out. "I was so exhausted in reaching up to hit my serve," he recalled, "that I felt as if I were leaning on the ball." He double-faulted to lose his serve, and although he managed to hold serve three more times, he had no energy left to try to force a break. Finally Perry put him out of his misery. "Four beautiful drives from Perry's racquet," wrote the *New York Times*, "two of them passing shots, cost the groggy Budge his service game, and the champion ended the match with a service ace in the eighteenth." Perry had won his third U.S. title, holding off Budge one last time before turning pro, ten-eight in the fifth.

Actually, Budge did bag one victory over Perry a few weeks later, just before the Englishman left the amateur ranks, but it was at the Pacific Southwest tournament, on the hard courts at the Los Angeles Tennis Club, Budge's favorite surface and one on which no major tournaments were played. But the final major step in his evolution into a world champion came after that, back home in Oakland. On the long rail journey out west ("I think Gene Mako and I established a new sleep record on the train," he wisecracked to an L.A. radio show host), Budge had vowed to himself that he would never lose another match—much less a major championship—due to poor conditioning. And once he was back home, even before he began his training sessions with Stow, he started really getting in shape for the first time.

For starters, he immediately cut out all the chocolate and fried foods that he loved almost as much as jazz. He also began a regimen of exercises to improve his wind and his abdominal muscles—the ones that had given out on his serve at Forest Hills. Every morning he would perform a battery of sit-ups and deep knee bends, among other exercises. Then he would run.

For years Don had been receiving free rackets from the Wilson Sporting Goods company, and in the past few off-seasons he had been working for the company part time as a packing clerk. Since technically even the greatest players in the world, if they wanted to keep playing Wimbledon and the other top tennis events, could not be paid a dime for anything to do with tennis, it was typical for sporting-goods companies to put them on the payroll ostensibly for blue-collar positions like this. Having virtually no living expenses—on tour all the tabs were picked up by others, and in the off-season he lived with his parents— Budge had been able to save a thousand dollars, which he now transformed into a beautiful new Packard 120 sedan. Every morning, after doing his abdominal exercises, he would drive the Packard up into the Berkeley Hills. By eight o'clock he was parked in the foothills out along Tunnel Road. For the first few weeks he would walk up the hills and then run along the ridge, enjoying a spectacular view of Oakland and Berkeley, the bay, San Francisco, and some days all the way out past the Golden Gate to the Pacific. Then he'd run downhill at the other end and walk back to the car. Eventually he was running the entire route, uphill and down. For the next three years, well into his professional career, he didn't miss his exercise-and-running routine more than a half-dozen days.

At the end of 1936, as everyone had expected, Fred Perry turned professional, leaving Cramm and Budge as the top two amateurs in the world. Ellsworth Vines, Wimbledon and U.S. champ in 1932, had been the top pro since toppling Tilden in 1934. Now he had his strongest challenger yet in Perry, and when they played the third match of their nationwide one-on-one tour in the Chicago Arena on January 9, 1937, the promoters arranged for a guest umpire: twenty-one-year-old Don Budge.

As it turned out, Vines was coming down with the flu and offered little resistance to Perry that night, but that detracted little from Budge's delight. Watching Perry from the umpire's chair was completely different from playing him, and he experienced a revelation. He now realized why he so often had felt like a yo-yo dangling from the Englishman's hand.

When he was playing junior tournaments Budge had tried to pattern his game after that of Vines, who somehow, razor thin as he was, managed to crush the ball harder than anyone and never seemed to have to run very hard. "I liked his hard hitting," said Budge, "and his free, easy, rhythmic shots. I thought it wonderful to mope around the court like Ellsworth. I became obsessed with the idea that this was the thing to do."

He had expected Vines to blow Perry off the court with his powerful ground strokes, but instead it was Perry knocking the American from corner to corner, controlling the points. Suddenly Budge realized why. While Vines waited for the ball to reach a comfortable height, or even waited until it was coming down again, using his almost 360-degree windup to launch his colossal shots, Perry was *taking the ball on the rise*. Bounding about the court like a rabbit, he would let the ball bounce only six or eight inches off the floor before whisking it away with a beautifully compact stroke. As a result, Perry was able to transfer Vines's power into his own, take the ball early, get to net, and make his opponent run corner to corner, deep behind the baseline. "Before the match was even over," wrote Budge, "a new concept had begun to form in my mind: Suppose a man could hit the ball as hard as Vines and take it as early as Perry? Who could beat that man?"

Back in Oakland, his self-imposed six-week respite from tennis over, Don Budge began to channel the spirit of Fred Perry. In his daily workouts with Tom Stow, he worked constantly on scooting around the court with quick steps, taking the ball on the rise and getting to net. With the Perry style infusing his subconscious, he began walking faster between points. By the time he got to Wimbledon that year, he would even be wearing the same trousers as Perry—DAKS, made by Simpsons of London, which he had picked up at their retail store in Piccadilly. Beautiful white flannels, with just a tinge of yellow, they had the Simpsons-patented adjustable self-supporting waistband (no suspenders!) with buttons. Perry, Cramm, and Budge all wore DAKS and were noted for it.

But true to his Chicago insight, Budge did more than copy Perry. He adapted the Englishman's style to his own game, sacrificing none of his remarkable power. At first it was difficult to control the ball when combining these two elements, and for weeks he blasted away, "knocking down about every fence in Oakland." But with practice came accuracy, and in the end he owned an attack no one could withstand.

At least that was the thinking at the Claremont Country Club in late winter 1937. Stow and Budge's goal was clear: number one or bust. With Perry gone, Cramm was the only great obstacle, and Budge had already gotten over the mental hurdle of beating him in their 1935 Davis Cup match, meaningless though it was. Now, to further his psychological progress, Stow instructed Don to think of himself as number one at all times. Finally, at their last workout before

Budge headed east for Davis Cup matches and then overseas—as it turned out, their last workout ever—Stow told him, "I am convinced that you are the best player in the world. Now you go out and prove that I'm right."

The J. Donald Budge who stepped off the ship in England in June 1937 was a far cry from the hayseed who had arrived for the first time two years earlier. Walking on court in his new DAKS, together with his U.S. Davis Cup shirt and jacket, "he looked like Mr. Tennis," recalled one player. "He made you feel like you might be his ball boy." Even his rackets set him apart. He had always favored white rackets, and recently Wilson had designed one just for him. As he was an amateur, they couldn't put his name on it, so they called it the Ghost. And Budge's Ghost was a substantial weapon, heavier and with a bigger handle than anyone else's. What's more, this year he had decided to forgo the leather grip that most players had been using for a few years. To him, the new grip was a gimmick to allow companies to charge a dollar more for a racket, and it just absorbed sweat and grew slippery. The combed basswood handle that Tilden still used, he felt, gave a drier, more consistent grip. But to the other players it just added to his mystique. "He let me play with his racket once," said Sidney Wood. "After one set I couldn't hold it anymore; it fell out of my hand. Everything about that man was superhuman."

But Budge's new aura wasn't all show. The real source was his new game, the unassailable package of power and consistency that many would consider the finest ever even seven decades later. It all began with the serve, the best in the world. It was considered as fast as Tilden's great cannonball, and his accuracy was also Tildenesque; like the old master, he seemed to be able to produce an ace whenever he needed one. And though his spinning second serve was not as revered as Cramm's, it rarely faltered. "I always felt that if I served a couple of double faults in a five-set match I wasn't serving well," he said. "Even the most meticulous foot fault judge is obliged to admit that Don never transgresses," wrote one tennis reporter. "Yet he gets almost a flying start and reaches the net position with remarkable speed when he is going all out for the point."

Mostly, though, Budge preferred to stay on the baseline after his serve and wait to attack with his backhand. "No matter how you forced him," wrote one expert, "his backhand would turn offensive." This famous stroke "had that extra flair, that great freedom of motion," wrote another, "which made it the envy of every player who ever lived." Even on the return of the serve, the backhand shone. He would stand closer to the net than anyone when returning serve and pick it up on the rise just as he did with his ground strokes. The forehand return was no weakness either. Even Jack Kramer, possibly the greatest serve-and-volleyer of all time, was thrown off by Budge's returns when they played each other as professionals. "Nope, I couldn't serve and volley against Budge," he said. "I had to change my game."

Budge's thunderous attacking game, however, came off looking effortless. Like all the best athletes—or craftsmen of any sort—he made it look easy. "He was a marvelous athlete," said Mako, "smooth as could be. He never looked like he was doing anything." "At the end of a hot match," wrote a reporter, "Budge's short-sleeved shirt may be moist, but he can put his trousers right back in the bandbox." He was not a particularly fast runner, yet with great anticipation and quick opening steps he covered the court as deftly as anyone. No one appreciated this more than Robert Twynam, the Wimbledon groundsman who would later become head groundsman and watch over his Centre Court like the fussiest gardener in England. When players dragged their toes, digging divots into his beloved turf, he could hardly stand to watch. Twynam always rooted silently for the players who didn't drag or slide into their shots. He always rooted for Budge. "They all slide to a certain extent," he said, "but the *great* players don't slide much. I mean, they know where the ball is coming, don't they? Don Budge never slides."

"When in form," wrote Al Laney that summer, "Budge presents no weakness." And by the time of Wimbledon, Budge was in top form. He had run through the warm-up tournament at the Queen's Club without so much as a close set and won the doubles easily with Mako to boot. Officials of the All England Club were impressed and seeded him number one for Wimbledon, even though von Cramm was number one in most of the world rankings. Budge and Mako were seeded only second in the doubles, but they seemed ready to continue where they'd left off the previous September, when they won the U.S. doubles championship for their first major title. And Budge was also a heavy favorite and seeded first in the mixed doubles with Alice Marble.

Marble was making her London debut, three years late. A fellow northern Californian, two years older than Budge, she had grown up in San Francisco and also learned to play by hanging around public courts, in her case the cement courts at Golden Gate Park. Traumatized by being attacked and raped in the park on her way home at the age of fifteen, she overcame that ordeal and became one of America's most promising junior tennis players. But on her first trip abroad, with the U.S. Wightman Cup team, she collapsed during a match at Roland Garros and was sent home with a diagnosis of pleurisy and tuberculosis. She was told she would never play serious tennis again, but she moved in with legendary teaching pro Eleanor "Teach" Tennant, trained hard for two years, and won Forest Hills in 1936. Now she was finally making her way to Wimbledon. She would eventually take the hallowed championship in 1939, to go with four U.S. titles. Her personal life was no less dramatic, as she would have several affairs with both men and women and lose her first husband, a fighter pilot, in World War II just days after miscarrying their child following an auto accident. And according to her autobiography, the OSS recruited her as a spy during the war and sent her to Switzerland to rekindle an old affair with a millionaire banker who was helping Nazis hoard stolen riches. During the operation she was shot by a Nazi agent, rescued by the OSS, and recovered to live a long and relatively uneventful life (at last) in California.

An attractive but powerful-looking blonde, Marble was a phenomenal all-around athlete. In her teens she has been a ball girl and mascot for the minor-league baseball team the San Francisco Seals, and she'd often shag balls with the players. Joe DiMaggio, who was with the team then, said that she was the only girl he had ever seen who could throw a ball in from deep center field to home plate on one bounce. "It was really a lark playing with Alice," said Budge, who had played mixed with her in California tournaments as early as 1934. "There was no romance between us, it was all tennis. But she played more like a man than any woman. She could take overheads better than the best men. So we would just waltz through the other teams."

So after winning the singles and doubles at Queen's, Budge was looking for a triple crown at Wimbledon. Although he still had won no major titles and officially was ranked number two in the world behind von Cramm, expectations for the redhead ran high, and not just from himself. London's biggest bookmaker listed the "red-headed American Davis Cup star" as an even-money favorite to win the Championships. Next best was von Cramm, at 2-1 odds. After that it was a steep drop to Bunny Austin at 6-1 and Henkel at 7-1.

Budge and the oddsmaker's confidence were justified. He roared through the draw to the finals with the loss of only one set, to Frank Parker in the semifinals. His draw was not particularly easy either. He took out Ladislav Hecht, a Slovakian Jew who would become the top European player before fleeing the Nazis to the United States in 1939, 6-4, 6-2, 6-2. In the quarters he dismantled Vivian McGrath, the number-seven seed, 6-3, 6-1, 6-4. And after dropping a set to Parker, who had upset Henkel, he dispatched him 6-4, 6-4, 6-1. All that was left between Budge and his first Wimbledon crown was Gottfried von Cramm.

Cramm was by now a popular favorite at Wimbledon, not only for his elegance, sportsmanship, and sui generis shotmaking but also to some extent out of sympathy for his second-place finishes the last two years. Of course, the crowd has been all for Perry on those occasions, but now that no Englishman was in the finals (Cramm had taken care of that with a close four-set win over Bunny Austin in the semis), many a Wimbledon regular would have liked to see the charismatic German finally put his name on the winner's trophy.

As Cramm and Budge stepped onto the court for their first battle in two years, they presented the audience with a distinct contrast: the experienced, battle-tempered German, buoyed with the confidence of having won two French championships but also hardened with disappointing losses in two straight Wimbledon finals; and the rocketing young American, already considering himself the best and playing like it. The sophisticated European aristocrat and the callow red-headed working-class boy. For despite the strides Budge had made in his wardrobe and his bearing, he was still no baron. "Whereas Cramm is all elegance," Al Laney jotted in his notebook, "Budge presents an angular figure. It is strange that so great a player with so fine a game is yet so little graceful compared with the other great ones."

The two men walked on court chatting amicably, to the polite applause of the crowd, and carefully piled their spare rackets near the umpire's chair. As much as Budge felt that this was the moment he had worked for, when he would become world champion, Cramm must have felt the same. His one superior, Perry, had left the scene; he would feel as though the crown had been bequeathed to him. He had handled Budge easily in their only important meeting, two years earlier. Don's not the only one intent on winning this title, he may have thought. It has been my goal since I first started knocking the ball against the wall in Brüggen. He's only twenty-two, he'll have his chances. Today is mine.

When Budge said later that no matter how confident he felt, whenever he walked onto a court with Cramm, it was difficult not to feel he was walking in his shadow, he may have been thinking of this Wimbledon final. Gottfried was so perfectly turned out and so calm. The rising cheers were for him, the hopes and sentiment were for him, the women sitting straighter and neglecting their escorts were doing so for him.

"Budge seems always a bit the underdog as he stands by the umpire's seat and submits to the gymnastic cameramen," reported *The New York Times Magazine* the next week. "Then he takes the court and turns loose the magic of his racquet, long rapier thrusts or sudden explosions of dynamite." Today, however, there was, for Budge fans, a gut-wrenching time lag between "takes the court" and "turns loose the magic." After working so hard to perfect his game and unleashing it through six rounds to at last reach the pinnacle of his dreams, the Wimbledon final, Budge was nervous. He won the toss, elected to serve, and was promptly broken. His subconscious magnified the service break over and over. Despite Tom Stow's enjoinments, he couldn't help but visualize defeat as they changed ends.

Gottfried was off to the start he had dreamed of, "finding a perfect touch at once," and found himself serving at three-two, with a game point for a four-two lead. On his second serve he tossed, arched his back for his trademark American Twist, and sent it sizzling in to the backhand side. He could hardly believe it when the shout "Foot fault!" echoed through the stadium. On this occasion he did not apologize. But without the slightest protest or hesitation, or even a glance at the baseline judge, he stepped back to the line to serve the deuce point. And Budge broke back for three-all. "Thus was the cool, crisis-proof Budge revealed," wrote Wallis Myers.

The rest of the set was all Budge, six-three, as he "began to hit the ball harder and longer, to take it earlier, and von Cramm was forced to make his strokes on the run as his adversary followed in to volley." The American continued his assault in the second set, breaking to go up three-one. The only thing that slowed him down was his old friend Queen Mary, the queen mother since the death of her husband George V the year before, who arrived in the Royal Box at the beginning of the second set. The crowd, well aware of the American's supposed wave to the monarch two years before, stood at attention and looked to see what the young man would do now. "I have to report," wrote James Thurber, "that Budge's stance in the royal presence, like his game, is greatly improved. This time he stood with arms at his side and made a quite presentable, if wholly unaccustomed, bow to Queen Mary. Baron von Cramm, of course, made a much better bow." The queen mother was satisfied enough to stay for the entire rest of the match and even provided some comic relief. Three times she got up and moved deeper into the Royal Box in order to avoid the lowering sun. Each time audience, players, and officials ceased their activity and stood at attention. By the third time the crowd had a good laugh, and the queen mother smiled back good-naturedly.

Serving at three-two, though, the American's nerves began to creep back in. "All right, Budge," he told himself, "just remember, all you have to do is hold your serve three times and you're two full sets ahead in the finals of the championship of the world." He knew that was the worst thing any player could say to himself, but he couldn't help it. And sure enough Cramm broke him right back for three-all, and at four-all had a game point to go up five-four. But at this point Budge's power game took over once again. He broke, held for the set, and went way up in the third set. He was doing whatever he pleased: knocking Cramm corner to corner and coming to net at will, or bringing him to net with short balls and passing him left and right. *The Times*'s polymathic tennis correspondent (who of another match had written, "One would not cast Henkel in Iago's sinister part, but he might well have muttered, 'O! You are well tun'd now, but I'll set down the pegs that make this music'") now lamented that "von Cramm's stealth on the volley was to be as destructive in the end as the store of silver was to Nostromo."

Finally Don Budge was serving at five-two for the Wimbledon championship. "Now I was literally shaking," he said later, "drowning in my own sweat. The nearness of the possibility was beginning to overwhelm me." At forty-fifteen he allowed Cramm to take control, and the German came back to deuce with two brilliant winners, "one a low forehand volley that pitched just inside the line." Twice Cramm had break point, but finally Budge got to his fourth match point and worked his way to net. A crisp backhand volley made him the unofficial champion of the world.

"I practically had to crawl to the net to shake hands with Gottfried," he said. Afterward the two finalists were led up to the Royal Box and formally presented to Queen Mary. "You know, Mr. Budge," the queen mother addressed him, "I did not see you a few years ago when you waved to me, but had I, I want you to know that I would have waved back." The new champion was too dumbstruck to deny the story.

Don and Gottfried rested while one doubles semifinal played, and then they took back to Centre Court to play the other semi. It was to be a preview of the Davis Cup doubles match coming up in a couple weeks, provided Germany beat Czechoslovakia and came back to London for the Interzone Final. And just as Budge now had psychological advantage over Cramm, Walter Pate hoped that Budge and Mako would get a leg up on Cramm and Henkel.

His hopes seemed dashed after the first two sets, which the Germans took in only forty minutes, 6-4, 6-4. Both Cramm and Henkel, the new French champ and number-three seed, were serving so hard and consistently that the Americans simply had no chance to break. Mako, whose fortunes had been sinking since a debilitating shoulder injury the previous summer, was by now considered a very weak link in the American doubles team. He had had to default in the second round of the singles, and now he was wilting against the cannonball German serves, returning fewer than fifty percent of them. Budge had refused to play with anyone else, but when Mako went down fifteen-forty on his serve in the opening game of the third set, Pate had to be wondering how he could convince Budge to take a new partner for the Davis Cup.

And then Gene Mako drew the line. He simply refused to be pushed around any further. He and Budge brought the score back to deuce, and Mako hit two "resplendent" overhead smashes to hold serve. Budge got down love-thirty on his service game, but they came back in that one too, broke Henkel for three-one, and never looked back. They took the third six-two, the fourth six-four, and fought to four-three in the fifth. Then they broke Henkel on a gorgeous Mako lob winner, and Budge ended the match with an ace. It was their greatest win yet, and Walter Pate let out a sigh that was almost heard above the Centre Court applause.

The doubles final the next day was anticlimactic, as they rolled through the top British team of Pat Hughes and Raymond Tuckey in four quick sets. After a short rest Budge was back on Centre Court for the mixed doubles final and hardly worked up a sweat as he and Marble trounced the French team of Yvon Petra and Simone Mathieu, 6-4, 6-1. Budge had "come down like the wolf on the fold," as Thurber put it, and had become Wimbledon's first triple crown winner. He had also won over the English crowd, although by the time of "Budge's third Wimbledon championship in twenty-four hours, people began to move out. They had had enough of the red-headed American who had blasted the element of competition out of their championships." Walter Pate, however, couldn't get enough of it. And Tom Stow must have read the papers with a grin that week.

That night the Lawn Tennis Association hosted the Wimbledon Ball at Grosvenor House on Park Lane. The annual formal dinner dance traditionally kicked off with an opening dance between the men's and women's singles champions. Budge's luck held out, for he was able to spin around the floor with the relatively svelte Dorothy Round, who had only narrowly squeaked by the tanklike Polish star, Jadwiga Jedrzejowska, seven-five in the third set. Six hundred and fifty guests dined elegantly at a hundred tables in the ballroom, and then, in his victory speech, Budge was able to win back any fans who had been left cold by his onslaught. "I do appreciate this chance you give me," he intoned without apparent nervousness in his jejune but dulcet Bing

Crosby voice, "to pay a tribute to a great-hearted gentleman. For when it comes my turn to lose, I hope I may lose with half the gallantry, half the graciousness, and with something of the fine spirit of sportsmanship shown by Baron Gottfried von Cramm yesterday afternoon."

It brought down the house.

SEVENTEEN DAYS LATER THE TABLES HAVE BEEN TURNED, AND DON Budge is trying to set them right again. With the same gallantry and graciousness he displayed in losing Wimbledon, Gottfried has him down 8-6, 7-5 for the Davis Cup. But already Don has broken him to start the third set, and he holds his serve easily for two-love. He is close to breaking for a three-love lead, but Gottfried plays one of his miraculous drop shots ("What is he doing?!" Budge's incredulous look seems to say) and then holds with an ace. Two-one for Budge.

That's all right, he tells himself. I'm up a break, and I am *not* going to lose my serve. He stands resolutely at the baseline, tosses up the ball, and fires in one of his best first serves. Everything feels perfect, the energy rising up his arched back, up through his whiplashing arm and from racket to ball. A wave of satisfaction massages his nervous system as the ball shoots over the net and disturbs the corner of the service box—even as Cramm moves toward it like a raptor, hardly swinging at all, using Budge's power as he blocks it crisply back down the line for a winner. Don doesn't even have time to vocalize his "Oh baby!" Well, that can happen, even against my cannonball, he thinks. Moves over to the ad side and fires in another one. It feels just as good, and Cramm's return looks just as good. Budge doesn't touch it. Again at love-thirty, again at love-forty: perfect serves, perfect returns. His service toss is the only thing he is able to reach all game, and the third set is even, two-all.

GERMAN FANS, "SCREAMING IN DELIGHT," WERE NOT THE ONLY ones overcome by the tension, drama, and beauty of the play. At least one reporter was moved to forget all about journalistic dispassion. "That was me tearing my hair and pounding the knee of the English lady on my left," reported James Thurber of *The New Yorker*.

The great American humorist was forty-three years old and in his "golden years as man and artist," a fleeting period when he was able successfully to solve what he called life's "equation of perplexities . . . men, women, dogs, liquor, and party talk." Two years before he had ended the slow, painful deterioration of his first marriage in divorce and married his second wife, Helen Wismer, a magazine editor eight years his junior. Now they were two months into a yearlong sojourn in Europe, prompted by an exhibition of Thurber's drawings in London. Though he had begun his famous tenure with *The New Yorker* in 1927 as an editor and writer, he was by now just as well known for his wry line drawings depicting . . . men, women, dogs, liquor, and party talk.

Thurber was not at the Budge-Cramm match by whim. A full-fledged tennis fanatic, he had been writing the magazine's "The Tennis Courts" column intermittently since the previous year, under the pen name Foot Fault. His fascination with tennis had burst forth in 1926 at what everyone was calling the Match of the Century: the first (and last) meeting of the charismatic, melodramatic queen of tennis, Suzanne Lenglen, and the introverted, detached young American champion Helen Wills. Thurber was living in Nice that winter and went to Cannes to cover the big match (which Lenglen won, 6-3, 8-6) for the Riviera edition of the *Chicago Tribune*.

He came home smitten with the game and began playing any chance he could get, particularly at friends' private courts in the country during the summer, "nearly driving himself mad with frustration." For though he had excellent hand-eye coordination, the rest of his body, self-described as "six feet, one-and-a-half inches [and weighing] 154 pounds when fully dressed for winter," had trouble keeping up. "He was just good enough at tennis to get mad a lot of the time," said one friend. "If you hit the ball to his blind side [where he was missing an eye], he'd lose it, so we'd try to hit it to his right, but if he suspected you were catering to his handicap he'd get mad at that, too. . . . He was a pretty bad loser. It wasn't fun to beat Thurber at anything." He had fun with his own incompetence, though, writing from Bermuda in 1936: "Ada has a tennis court, on which we played ten sets in two days, me cursing every second stroke. . . . In making a backhand I look and act like a woman up under whose skirts a bee has climbed. I will get over this. I must get over it."

Abroad in the summer of 1937, Thurber and Helen were spending time with various London literati, including the much younger Alistair Cooke. Cooke, only twenty-eight, was a film critic for the BBC and also the London correspondent for America's NBC radio network. Once a week his erudite voice delivered his fifteen-minute *London Letter* to living rooms all over the United States. Cooke later became an American citizen, and his *American Letter* (later *Letter from America*) was a mainstay on BBC radio for fifty-eight years. His *London Letter* of August 4 would give his impressions of the heroic Budge-von Cramm Davis Cup struggle, around the same time his new friend Thurber's own dispatch appeared in *The New Yorker*. At their first meeting Thurber reminded Cooke "of a grasshopper finally come to earth. He had a spiderly stance . . . and glasses as thick as binoculars [that gave him] a Martian quality." Thurber and Helen were a hit with London's literary set and visited a group of several couples, "painters, writers, [and] editors," at their rented country estate in Hampshire where, on its lovely grass tennis court, he "won the only set of tennis he'd ever won in his life."

"Went to Wimbledon three days," he wrote to friends, "quarter finals, semi, and finals, and watched Budge knock 'em cold. . . . It cost the New Yorker 3 pounds a ticket for us." In fact, his seat for the Budge-Parker semifinal was twelve miles away, inside Alexandra Palace. The previous November the BBC had begun a two-year "test period" of the new technology of television. In 1937 the coronation and Wimbledon were highlights of the test broadcasts, and more than nine thousand receivers were sold in London. Thurber was invited to the BBC studio at Alexandra Palace to appear onscreen making his famous drawings of dogs and people on large sheets of paper with crayon. Then he settled down to watch the Budge-Parker match like a couch potato from the future. "It was a cloudy day," he reported,

> but the little miracle came off beautifully. Budge, the size of your index finger, against Parker, the size of your little finger, wielding match-stem racquets hitting a speck of white. You could hear the impact of the racquets, the judge's droning count, and the barking of the linesmen. You could see the tiny, tense faces in the stands, the tiny heads moving in unison, following

the infinitesimal ball. . . . It was like watching a photograph in an album come to life. Extremely interesting, but not entirely satisfactory, because you can't get a grasp or feeling of the match as a whole.

Ted Tinling remembered "the baseline on the primitive screens being arched like a rainbow so it seemed impossible for anyone to hit over the lines." Gottfried Cramm was probably too busy during the Championships to catch any of the broadcasts, but he may have had his first glimpse of television in Berlin the year before, as the Berlin Olympics had been televised to an audience of 150,000 watching in twenty-eight "television rooms" around the city. Goebbels declared it another great victory for his Olympics, and Germany not only the leader in gold medals but also the world leader in the new technology. (He didn't mention that they had used American-made television cameras.) During the 1937 Wimbledon the papers discussed the controversy over the very word *television*. "The word is half Greek and half Latin," intoned one editorial. "No good will come of it." Cramm may well have read this and thought of two other Greco-Latin hodgepodges—*automobile* and *homosexual*—and smiled: there you have it, the three great scourges of the twentieth century.

For Thurber, seeing the Centre Court shrink to a moving photograph must have felt like a metaphor of his waning vision. He had lost his left eye at the age of seven, when his brother accidentally shot him in the eye with a toy arrow. When he was thirty-four his other eye began to go bad, gradually clouding up with a growing cataract. Shortly after his return from Europe in 1938 the situation would grow critical; a year later he had his first eye operations and was left virtually blind. "Life is no good to me," he wrote his ophthalmologist, "unless I can read, type, and draw. I would sell out for 13 cents." He was given no such opportunity. His "punishment," as he once termed his condition, led to nervous breakdowns, alcoholism, and a long tenebrous purgatory finally truncated by a brain tumor at age sixty-six.

But a few weeks after experiencing television, sitting at Centre Court in July 1937 watching Budge and Cramm play what he later called "the greatest match in the history of the world," James Thurber was happy. Like the two younger men prancing on the grass below him, he was at the height of his powers. For Thurber, it was a halcyon moment before a slow surrender to the battering siege of time.

I'VE PLAYED TENNIS WITH PAUL LUKAS, AND CHARLIE CHAPLIN, and the four Marx brothers too." Don Budge was answering a radio host's question in early 1936, a year and a half before the big Cramm match. He had been spending part of his off-seasons in Los Angeles, which would soon enough become his home. For now he would stay at the Makos', and Don and Gene would often hang out with the Hollywood set, at one private court or another. Tennis was the hot sport of this crowd, who came out in droves to the annual Pacific Southwest tournament at the L.A. Tennis Club. Alice Marble was a regular at William Randolph Hearst's mansion and became close friends with Carole Lombard and Clark Gable through tennis, and Budge and Mako were familiar guests at the movie stars' homes.

"The movie people seemed to look up to us as much as we did to them," Budge remembered much later. "A guy like Errol Flynn, as an example—he was the best tennis player in the movie colony." Several top players of the day later reminisced about playing with Flynn, a superb athlete who spent almost as much time on the tennis court as he did in the studios and in actresses' beds. (Never mind that he was married almost continuously, three times, from 1935 on.)

Mako remembered playing an impromptu doubles match with Flynn against Budge and Frank Shields. Shields, a Davis Cup regular of the early 1930s, and a finalist at Forest Hills in 1930 and at Wimbledon in 1931 (as well as the future grandfather of Brooke Shields), had put tennis on the back burner at age twenty-six and moved out to Hollywood to pursue an acting career, which lasted for seven forgettable films between 1935 and 1938. He and Flynn, his best buddy in Hollywood, shared powerful and well-exercised attractiveness to women, flamboyance, a penchant for drunkenness, and what one reporter called "a reputation for night-club fistionics." In this friendly set of doubles, with perhaps a small bet on the line, Mako and Flynn managed to beat the best player in the world and a recent top-tenner. No wonder Mako remembered it vividly almost seventy years later.

"Flynn was a hell of an athlete, and I had a way of making my partner play better." He also knew when to quit. "They wanted to play another set, but I said no way, no chance."

Some of Budge and Mako's Hollywood crowd found their way to Centre Court, Wimbledon, for the 1937 Davis Cup. As Budge battled Cramm in the third set, no one was cheering louder than Jack Benny, Ed Sullivan, and Paul Lukas. Lukas, forty-two, had made a successful transition to Hollywood from his native Hungary in 1927 and was now a well-known movie actor. He would later win a Best Actor Oscar for the 1943 film *Watch on the Rhine*. A hugely enthusiastic tennis player and fan, Lukas "had just about become an unofficial member of our team" in the weeks before the Germany tie, according to Budge. And he had dragged along to the Davis Cup matches his friends Benny and Sullivan. Benny, forty-three, only a moderate success in New York vaudeville into his late thirties, had become an enormous national star with his *Jack Benny Program*, which began in 1932 on NBC radio. Sullivan at this time was still a newspaper columnist, but one of the most popular. He'd moved from sportswriting in New York (where he covered the big tennis events for the *Evening Mail*) to being a Broadway gossip columnist, and he'd just recently assumed a similar position in Hollywood. No one could have been better suited for the job; within weeks he was a regular golf partner of Fred Astaire and pals with just about everybody. And now he made the pilgrimage to Wimbledon with Lukas and Benny, whom he'd once written was "the sleepiest of all Broadway personalities. . . . He invites 20 people to 55 Central Park West, and then curls up on the living room couch and goes to sleep. . . . If he could learn to sleep standing up, he'd make a fine cop." But Benny wasn't nodding off at Centre Court today; he and Sullivan were cheering as hard as Lukas at every Budge ace and passing shot. Benny didn't know much about tennis, but the United States versus Germany was enough for him. He'd sat ringside the year before to see Joe Louis fall to Max Schmeling. Could he be watching another such inconceivable upset?

The stars' cheers melded into the civilized cacophony of applause around them. Tennis etiquette prevailed here more than anywhere on earth, and even a partisan crowd clapped for good shots from both players. There were certainly other Americans on hand to add to

Budge's support, and he was popular with the British as well. Nevertheless the general mood was jubilant. The underdog, the charismatic sentimental favorite, the only hope for the British team, was winning against all odds. Two sets to none for Cramm, and dead even in the third.

One voice in the crowd, however, cheering vigorously for the German, emanated from the most incongruous source. Big Bill Tilden, the most famous tennis player in the world and the greatest of all time, who'd almost single-handedly kept the Davis Cup in the United States for most of the 1920s, was vociferously cheering against his old team.

In some ways it was not surprising. The U.S. team was officially under the auspices of the United States Lawn Tennis Association, and Big Bill and the USLTA had been restless bedfellows for twenty years. The entire time Tilden had been world champion and angel of the American team, Mike Myrick, the omnipotent president of the USLTA, had been trying to clip his wings. And Tilden had been just as stubborn in pushing the limits of his freedom. Tennis was strictly an amateur sport (professionals were not allowed to play Wimbledon, Forest Hills, or the rest of the circuit until 1968; the Davis Cup held out until 1973), and in the 1920s the definition of amateurism was sometimes applied absurdly. Myrick repeatedly threatened to suspend Tilden for writing newspaper columns about tennis, Tilden repeatedly apologized and then went right on writing. Newspaper accounts by athletic stars were the "color commentary" of the day, and Tilden made about $25,000 a year (a luxurious sum in the 1920s) for his offerings. Journalism, in fact, was his stated profession before he became a tennis star, and his greatest loves of all were writing for the theater and acting.

But the USLTA couldn't afford to suspend him. The stadium at Forest Hills (used for the U.S. Open until 1978) was built in 1923 for a quarter of a million dollars specifically to accommodate the crowds clamoring to see Big Bill play. Tilden turned tennis from an upper-class diversion into a big-time spectator sport and, playing as an amateur, earned a fortune for the tennis establishment.

But though the USLTA depended on Tilden, it secretly wished he would disappear—and not just because he was a constant thorn in their sides. Myrick and his cronies feared that if Tilden's sexual proclivities became public knowledge, the scandal would bring "the House that Tilden Built" crashing to the ground.

Tilden, however, was not cheering on Germany in the 1937 Davis Cup simply out of spite. And he had nothing against Budge, in fact was on perfectly friendly terms with him and his partner Gene Mako. But Gottfried Cramm had become a good friend, certainly his closest companion whenever he visited Germany. And after he'd spent considerable time there every summer since 1927, the German Lawn Tennis Federation had asked him a couple of years ago to help out with its Davis Cup squad. He'd been only too happy to help train the German boys at the first-class Rot-Weiss Club. And by now he was an unofficial paid coach of the team.

THE GREATEST TENNIS PLAYER, PERHAPS THE GREATEST ATHLETE, of his age would never have been born were it not for the diphtheria epidemic of 1884. Tilden's father, William Tatem Tilden Sr., had worked his way up as a young man to a responsible position in a Philadelphia wool-importing business. He was impressive enough for the owner of the business to match him up with his daughter, and Tilden married Selina Hey in November 1879. The couple, and the business, prospered, and by 1883 there were two little girls and a boy running around the three-story brick house in the fashionable neighborhood of Germantown.

Then in late 1884 diphtheria swept through Philadelphia. The disease was a scourge in those days, and the first antitoxin would not be developed until the next decade. Within a period of two weeks all three Tilden children were dead.

The Tildens started over and had two more boys, Herbert in 1886 and William Tatem Tilden Jr., born February 10, 1893. But life was never the same in the Tilden house. The old sunny atmosphere of a happy family living a charmed life was gone. Overleigh, the enormous mansion on McKean Avenue where the Tildens now lived, was "a house where there was little expression of love and gaiety." "The impression of grief," said Big Bill's niece, "was conveyed by members of the family in fleeting glances, in sudden silent moments of despair that could not be controlled."

The Tildens were known as one of the most affluent families around, and one of the most extravagant. Overleigh had its own stables for horses to pull the Tilden carriages. (Little Herbert had his own horse and buggy.) When automobiles arrived in Philadelphia, Bill Sr. always had the flashiest one on the road. Both boys were spoiled, but "Junior," as Bill Jr. was called by everyone, was coddled and overprotected to extremes. Once when he awoke at the age of six or so in the middle of the night, crying for some toy he had seen in a store window, a servant was dispatched to wake the store owner and bring back the object of desire. Though there is no record of him suffering any unusual infirmities, his mother, unnerved by the memories of 1884, decided that he was too sickly to go to school and had him tutored at home until the age of thirteen. At the end of each afternoon the servants' cries of "Master Junior! Master Junior!" would echo through the neighborhood, as young Tilden was brought back into the house to avoid any exposure to the cool of evening. Decades after his death old childhood acquaintances would marvel at how such a "sickly" child turned into one of the world's greatest athletes.

A block away from the Tilden house was the Germantown Cricket Club, whose pristine lawn tennis courts became one of the early centers of the sport in America. From 1921 to 1923 the U.S. Championships would be held there, and Bill Tilden would successfully defend his crown practically across the street from home. Unlike Don Budge, Tilden learned his tennis here, at an exclusive country club; but like Budge after him, he was inspired by an older brother. Herbert, seven years his senior, was his idol. Tall and handsome, extroverted, so comfortable joking around the clubhouse with other young men—and with young women too—Herbert was also a superb tennis player, the number-one player at the club and later to win the national intercollegiate doubles championship.

Herbert—manly, a success in all ways at the University of Pennsylvania, engaged to a pretty young woman while still there—was clearly his father's favorite. Junior worshipped and was worshipped by his mother. In fact, his father pretty much left him completely under the care of his mother, who treated him like the daughters she had lost.

She dressed him in velvet suits, gave him "dolls and other girlish gifts" at Christmas instead of the baseball bats and footballs that Herbert got, and instilled in him a fear of the diseases that result from close contact with other people's bodies.

And then she left him. In 1908, when Junior was fifteen, his mother was stricken with kidney disease and was almost instantly transformed from a strong-willed vibrant woman running the vast household to a somber immobile figure sitting in her wheelchair on the porch, attended by a nurse. At the same time his father was consumed more than ever by business and political interests (he was considering running for mayor), and Herbert was about to graduate Penn, get married, and move back into Overleigh. Junior, as a result, not only was finally sent to school, the exclusive Germantown Academy, but was also sent to live nearby at his aunt Mary's house—just on the other side of the Cricket Club. Mary, whom he called Auntie, had never married and had always been a close presence in the Tilden household, helping her sister raise her youngest boy. She had also raised her niece Selena, who still lived with her, and whom Tilden knew as Twin, due to her having also been born on February 10 (fifteen years before him). Twin and Auntie soon became his closest family members, and their house was his primary home for most of the rest of his life.

Tilden was not popular in high school; he was considered odd due to his tendency to seek out younger boys as companions. He played for the tennis team but was not number one until his senior year. Five foot ten and only 128 pounds when he graduated, his stated ambition in the school yearbook was "to be a clown." He matriculated in the Wharton School of Business at Penn to please his father, but he had not the slightest interest in school. He was lonely and unhappy, and just a short time later few from the Class of '15 remembered that he had been there.

This was partly because he never graduated. Near the end of his freshman year, his mother suddenly suffered a massive stroke and lay on her deathbed. According to Frank Deford:

> At the end, May 2, 1911, he sat outside her door at Overleigh all through the night, crying uncontrollably—by his own account "utterly in shock." Her dying so shattered his soul that he

grew nervous, even physically jittery, shaking. The poor boy was floundering badly. Not only had he lost the anchor of his sacred mother, but he was trapped in a school discipline he could not stand; he was forced to live away from his own house; he understood, surely, by now, that he was a homosexual; he was nearly friendless and literally repelled some people; he was ravaged by nervousness; despondent, confused, lost.

He took a year off from college; it stretched into two, three, four years. He worked as a part-time reporter for the *Philadelphia Evening Ledger*. He coached the tennis team at his old academy. The pain gradually dulled, and on his twenty-first birthday his father granted him the unusual request of a dance in his honor at the Germantown Cricket Club. He considered resuming his college career. But then the roof caved in.

First, in the summer of 1915 his father was attacked with kidney problems and died on July 29, with his two sons at his side. Herbert was as decimated by this death as Junior had been by their mother's. He drank hard in a daze of mourning the rest of the summer. When he took his wife and two children to the seaside, he caught a cold which deepened into pneumonia. Just two months after watching his father die, Bill Tilden sat by his beloved older brother as he too slipped away. It was like the stories he had heard of 1884. Everyone was gone. He was twenty-two years old.

He retreated to his room at Auntie's, listening to his hundreds of phonograph records over and over. Months went by. Eventually it struck Bill Tilden what he must do. From some source deep inside him bubbled up to the surface a burning ambition. His brother had been a fine collegiate tennis player but had put the game aside when he got married and became a manager at his father's company. He himself had grown up on the courts at the Germantown Cricket Club. Tennis was where he could make his mark. Tennis would be his University, his Tilden Woolen Company, his family. "He suddenly was compelled," remembered a friend of the time, "to want to be supreme in the game of lawn tennis."

Others were bemused. Tilden was ranked seventeenth in the country. He had failed even to make the starting six on the Penn team. He had won the U.S. Mixed Doubles title at the Philadelphia Cricket Club in 1913 and 1914, but he had had the good fortune to play with the national women's singles champion of those years, Mary K. Browne, and in fact not too many teams competed. He was certainly not considered much of a prospect. Said the same friend, "If you had asked me around 1915–16 if I thought Bill Tilden would ever be national champion, I would have been stunned. I just would have replied, 'Whatever would make you ask me a foolish question like that?'"

Tilden began working on his game like an obsessed engineer. He analyzed every aspect and picked on it, worked at it, perfected it. He was constantly hitting tennis balls, in the countless small tournaments he entered all around the Northeast, on the practice courts at Germantown, alone against a backboard, even indoors on squash courts all winter. He was not just working at tennis, he was studying the game, beginning to develop the theories of spin, technique, and strategy that he would later publish. It was possible—and understandable, as there was no money to be made in the game—that no one had ever taken the game of tennis as seriously as Tilden now did. "Most tennis players look upon the ball that is used as merely something to hit," he wrote a few years later. "Let me suggest the ball for a moment as an individual. It is a third party in the match. Will this third party be on your side or against you? It is up to you."

The ball was at first a coy partner. In his first U.S. Nationals, being played in 1916 for the second year at the West Side Tennis Club in Forest Hills, Tilden lost in the first round in straight sets to one Harold Throckmorton. It was no upset either; some players were even calling him "one-round Tilden" behind his back. That didn't stop him from proselytizing other players to his new theories of tennis. When Vincent Richards first saw Tilden, "he was holding forth on the porch of the Merion Cricket Club. . . . It is hard to put your finger on what it is about Tilden that has always made him the center of attraction."

The next year he reached the quarterfinals, but by that time the United States had entered the Great War, the nationals were rechristened "the Patriotic Tournament," and most of the top players were away in the service. Tilden himself joined the Army Signal Corps, was diagnosed with flat feet, and was stationed in Pittsburgh, where a tennis-fan commanding officer gave him plenty of time to practice and even travel to tournaments. In the summer of 1918, with the country still at war, he won his first national title, the U.S. Clay Courts in Chicago, and he reached the finals at Forest Hills. He was a legitimate top player, if still not suspected of greatness.

In 1919 America's soldiers were back from the war, including the man everyone considered the nation's best tennis player, "the most popular tennist ever to step on a court," Bill Johnston. Another Northern Californian who learned the game on the public courts of San Francisco, Johnston had won the U.S. title in 1915, when he was twenty. Only five foot eight, Johnston's great weapon was his mighty forehand, hit with a severe western grip. This grip normally produces copious topspin, but Johnston liked to hit the ball way up at shoulder height, almost completely flat. He used this dominating stroke to advance forward, expertly volleying winners from near the service line—unusually far from net—due to his lack of height. Johnston had spent the war years in the navy, but now American tennis fans welcomed him back to reclaim his crown.

The finals of Forest Hills that year featured the first of many battles between the Bills. The contrast between them couldn't have been greater in physical stature, in style of play, and in personality and popularity. For Tilden's smugness and confidence had matured in advance of his game; as a result, he was suffering derision in the press and in the stands even before he had stockpiled any championships for people to resent. "In 1919," wrote Al Laney, "the feeling of the public, and among players too it was said, seemed to be 'Beat Tilden at any cost.'" Laney, a young reporter at the time, couldn't help but share the public's feeling when he had his first glimpse of Tilden. A day before the tournament Tilden had been practicing on a side court when some photographers showed up:

> Tilden was in charge, telling them exactly how they should do their work. He was not to be champion for another year but already was acting the part and a little more, and doing it in a particularly offensive way.... The lantern jaw and wide straight mouth above the long neck were familiar from pictures. They suggested great determination and it was a face on

which no expression of humility seemed possible. It was lit with enthusiasm when I first saw it, and there seemed to be a conscious feeling of superiority.

In the finals, the crowd, in love with Little Bill as much as they were aligned against Tilden, saw their fondest wish come true. Tilden had improved greatly in three years but was not yet a match for the diminutive Johnston. That bomb of a western forehand came raining down again and again deep to Tilden's backhand, which Tilden could hit only with a serviceable but unintimidating slice. For the second year in a row he had lost in the finals in straight sets. The lesson could not have been clearer.

Tilden only became more resolved. He had built up his game piece by piece, but obviously the job was not finished. Never again, he vowed, would anyone attack his backhand like that.

He had become friendly with a man named Jones, a tennis fan and owner of an insurance company in Providence, Rhode Island, as well as one of the country's few indoor courts. Tilden moved in with the Joneses for the winter of 1919–20 and ostensibly took a job selling insurance. What he really did was practice tennis eight hours a day on the Joneses' court, either with their son—one of the country's leading sixteen-year-old players—or against a wall. He changed his backhand grip to allow himself to hit a more offensive shot, driving through the ball instead of slicing under it, and then hit backhand after backhand after backhand, all winter long. On that cold, remote, lone court—which Frank Deford has called "the Valley Forge of American tennis"—Tilden perfected the final component of the arsenal that would dominate the tennis world for a decade.

A few months later Tilden went to Wimbledon for the first time to try out his new game. Using the power backhand, which *The Times* called "the shot that made it impossible to keep Tilden on the defensive for long . . . the one stroke that put him above the class of his contemporaries," he plowed through the draw and earned the right to play the defending champion, Gerald Patterson, in the Challenge Round (a system similar to that of the Davis Cup, which lasted at Wimbledon until 1922). Then, deploying "the soundest and brainiest tennis ever seen on English courts," he took apart the great Australian in four quick sets. Five years after his brother's death Bill Tilden was the unofficial champion of the world.

Had he had any intimates to tell of his ambition back in 1916, no one would have believed it. But now he had arrived, and it was as if destiny had been fulfilled. Even before he had won any big titles, he would stride onto the court like a monarch granting an audience. Now, returning home as Wimbledon champion, he completely usurped American tennis.

Bill Johnston had been at Wimbledon, but Tilden hadn't beaten him directly, and the majority of American tennis fans expected Johnston to exert his famous forehand on the Forest Hills courts and put the rangy upstart in his place. Big Bill and Little Bill, as they were now called, tore through the U.S. Nationals draw and met in the finals. On a gray day at the West Side Tennis Club, more than ten thousand fans filled the wooden stands around Center Court to see Little Bill give Big Bill another trouncing. But those days were over. Like von Cramm eight years later after benefiting from Tilden's tutelage, Tilden no longer had a weak backhand to attack—or anything else to attack, for that matter. Johnston used every ounce of his tenacity and experience and made it "the most nerve-racking battle that the courts have ever seen," in the hyperbole of the day. But Tilden's dominating serve (twenty aces) and impregnable ground strokes were too much for him. Big Bill won 6-1, 1-6, 7-5, 5-7, 6-3 and was now the undisputed master of the sport. Already the *New York Times* was calling him "perhaps the greatest of all time."

For the next six years Big Bill Tilden didn't lose a tennis match in any of the major tournaments or the Davis Cup. It was a period of dominance that may never be equaled. In 1924 there is no record of him losing a match at all. The next year he produced a feat now reminiscent of, and that will probably last even longer than, DiMaggio's fifty-six-game hitting streak. He won fifty-seven games in a row, against the top competition of the day. That's nine six-love sets in a row, plus a few. "He was the autocrat of the courts as no other player has been since," Allison Danzig, who began covering tennis for the *New York Times* in 1923, wrote in 1963, "an absolute monarch in a period when

American tennis was at its most resplendent and great players were developed in many lands."

Tilden and Johnston continued their rivalry throughout the 1920s, but from 1920 on it was mostly no more than a backdrop for historic Tilden performances. In 1921, after Tilden had successfully defended his Wimbledon title, they met in the quarterfinals of the U.S. Championships, held that year at Tilden's home club, the Germantown Cricket Club. (Seeding was not introduced until the following year.) Irritated by talk that he had beaten Johnston the year before only due to his unreturnable cannonball serve, Tilden decided to play without that weapon. Serving no aces at all, he beat Johnston soundly using only his ground strokes and went on to defend his title.

The next year, 1922, they met again in the final, again at Germantown. Though Tilden was the unquestioned number-one player in the world, the rivalry with Johnston still appeared to be a close one, as they each had five victories over the other. What's more, they had each now won the nationals twice, as had other masters through the years, such as Dick Williams and Maurice McLoughlin. Ever since champions had had to play through the entire tournament, no one had managed to earn a third victory and retire the trophy. Long before the tournament even began, the press was building up the projected Big Bill/Little Bill championship as the "match for the Greek gods," the battle for the most coveted prize in tennis history. The stands at Germantown were packed with twelve thousand fans, including four rows of standing room. And not many were rooting for the neighborhood boy. Everyone wanted their beloved Little Bill to finally slay the impertinent giant.

For two sets it looked as if he would—as Johnston played his game supremely well, winning 6-4, 6-3. Tilden took the third easily, six-two, but when Little Bill jumped out to a three-love lead in the fourth, it appeared he had merely been conserving his energy for an all-out assault, a common strategy at the time. As they changed ends, Tilden couldn't help but catch the eye of USLTA bigwig Mike Myrick. Myrick couldn't stand Tilden for his effeminate sissiness and his imperious demands, and the feeling was mutual. "Well, Bill," Myrick sneered at him, "it's been a great match."

"It's damn well gonna be one," Tilden shot back and stormed to the other side of the court. Johnston won six more points in the set and no more games. Tilden won the final set, six-four.

Big Bill Tilden was just entering his peak years, and nothing could stop him, not even the loss of part of a finger. Playing an exhibition in New Jersey in the fall of 1922, he cut his right middle finger on the fence while retrieving a deep lob. A staph infection set in, and a week later he was in Germantown Hospital, where the doctors wanted to amputate the entire finger. But this would have made tennis impossible, so he asked them to save as much of the finger as they could, and in the end they cut it down only to the second joint. "I will consider myself lucky to get into the top ten in 1923, and I mean it," he told reporters when he left the hospital. All the experts agreed; Tilden was finished.

But all that winter he practiced indoors, as he had done three years before. Surprisingly, he had to alter his grip only slightly. "My racket did slip after a few exchanges," he said later. "So I forced greater power and sharper angles into my shots in order to draw the other fellow more quickly out of position and end the rallies." By early 1923 it was clear that Tilden had lost little. If anything, he had gotten better. The only record of him losing at all that year was to the great Spaniard, Manuel Alonso, in the finals of the Illinois State Championships. That apparently didn't sit well with the resurgent Big Bill, who settled the score in the quarterfinals at Forest Hills, 6-0, 6-0, 6-2, "easing up a little" in the last set, according to one reporter. A new stadium had been built at the West Side Tennis Club for a quarter-million dollars specifically to meet the demand created by Tilden's superstardom. And in the first championship match played there, Tilden destroyed Little Bill in the finals in less than an hour.

Then he improved again in 1924, losing no matches at all, despite constant bickering with the USLTA about his right to write about tennis for newspapers. He was also devoting more and more time to writing and acting, using his inheritance to indulge a lifetime fascination with the theater. He always swore that given the chance he would gladly give up tennis for the stage, but luckily for tennis fans and theatergoers everywhere, he was never given the chance. He did, however, finance (and star in) several plays right in Germantown, and although his reviews were withering, he even managed to get onto Broadway occasionally in a benefit performance.

Despite the division of his energies, he remained supreme on the courts. After a tough semifinal win over the young Vinnie Richards at Forest Hills, there was talk once again that Tilden was devoting too much time to other endeavors, and that Johnston would take back the U.S. crown. Tilden responded by going "rampant" in the finals, rendering Little Bill "as helpless as an infant," 6-1, 9-7, 6-2. Tilden had beaten him once again with mostly baseline play, but in the final game, as ominous thunderclouds gathered above the new stadium, he figured he'd better not fool around. "Bill took one look at the weather," wrote Grantland Rice, "turned to Johnston and ripped across four service aces to close out the match and title just before the downpour." Afterward Gerald Patterson, whom Johnston had dominated in the semifinals, said, "Tilden is the only player in the world. . . . [The rest of us are] second graders." Almost fifty years later Laney would write, "That was Tilden at his absolute peak, and I have not since seen the like of it."

Tilden's rise coincided with that of the Roaring Twenties, a postwar decade characterized by world-weariness, irreverence for old social mores, and the keyword *ballyhoo*. Dance marathons, flagpole sitters, six-day bike races, mah-jongg, crossword puzzles, miniature golf, the Charleston: each new fad transfixed the nation until obliterated by the next fad. Prohibition, rather than making drinking obsolete, created a whole new culture of drinking, one that included young women imbibing hard liquor in speakeasies, instead of just the "old boys' club" downing beer at the pub. For the first time respectable girls were smoking cigarettes and getting "stewed" or "blotto" from fashionable hip flasks and then going joyriding in the middle of the night with young men in the new "closed" automobiles, which one conservative social critic called a "house of prostitution on wheels." F. Scott Fitzgerald stunned some readers with his report, in *This Side of Paradise*, on the new generation of young women "eating three o'clock, after-dance suppers in impossible cafés. . . . 'I've kissed dozens of men,'" muses one of his female characters in a particularly shocking line, "'I suppose I'll kiss dozens more.'"

Tilden, though he proselytized against liquor, eschewed the four-letter words that were becoming commonplace even in mixed company, and was really too old to be a part of this brash new generation, became one of the figureheads of the Twenties. The decade has long been considered a golden age in sports, and Tilden took his place alongside Bobby Jones, Babe Ruth, and Gene Tunney as emblems of their sports. But of all of them, Big Bill had the most complex and memorable personality. Tilden "was not only the supreme, the most complete player of all time," wrote Allison Danzig, "he was also one of the most colorful and controversial figures the world of sports has known." Even before his homosexuality was exposed, many fans reviled him for his haughty manner, his prissy insistence on everyone conforming to his particular idea of sportsmanship, and his abuse of ball boys, umpires, and linesmen.

In this respect he was truly ahead of his time. He demanded that ball boys throw him the ball so that it bounced once and would hit him in the heart if he didn't catch it. If one was off target, and Tilden was in a querulous mood, he would step aside, let it go, and wait for a proper offering. But linesmen had it worse; the official who called a ball out when Tilden thought it was in was truly to be pitied. Big Bill would walk slowly over to him, put his hands on his hips, and stare at him for a long minute. Or else he would throw his hands up in the air and gaze up at the heavens as if to invoke a higher judgment. "He elevated the procedure [of glaring at linesmen] to an art," wrote his friend and doubles partner Vincent Richards. "He transfixed the blundering official; he craned his neck at him, and sometimes he would merely smile and that hurt most of all." Most officials felt they had no choice but to suffer this abuse silently. But several refused to officiate at a Tilden match, and at least one "went for him with clenched fists." In this case, after the man had been restrained, Tilden deliberately threw the next point, successfully reclaiming the favor of the crowd.

He was not always so successful. He was often "carping, demanding and fault-finding to a point where the gallery turned against him," said Danzig. Indeed they were usually against him from the start, as his reputation preceded him. Tilden didn't mind. Like Ty Cobb, whom he got to know well (and who, on first seeing Tilden play, cried, "Who is this fruit?"), he loved to "ride" an antagonistic crowd. His colleagues each had a favorite Tilden story. John Olliff remembered Tilden often stopping play in the middle of a game in order to reprimand the crowd for applauding an undeserving stroke. Ted Tinling recalled him once stopping a match at Wimbledon to complain of a woman in the stands repairing her makeup with a compact mirror. He claimed the glare from the mirror was bothering him, but everyone could see the real reason: Bill Tilden did not suffer inattentive spectators.

Strangely, though, this maltreater of linesmen and ball boys, who never shrank from getting the psychological upper hand over his opponents, presented himself as the paragon of sportsmanship. And he was, in his own way. A winning shot by his opponent often drew the exclamation, "Peach!" When he did lose, he was as gracious as could be, giving full credit to his opponents. But for him it was more about justice than etiquette. "I never once saw him take a point that he believed did not belong to him," said George Lott, his Davis Cup teammate. If his glares and protestations couldn't convince the umpire to change the call, he would take matters into his own hands and throw a point or two, or sometimes even a whole set. (Some people admired this, but even his friend Gottfried Cramm realized—and convinced Budge—that Tilden was practicing a specious form of sportsmanship.) "I'm not throwing anything for the gallery," he once said, "I'm doing it for inside of me." "I feel I must compensate when there is an obvious error," he explained another time, then smiled. "Especially since I'm going to beat the guy anyway."

To be sure, though, Tilden considered himself a performer above all else, no less on a tennis court than in the theater. Even in the warm-up he would perform a review of all his famous shots, showing off the highlights of his repertoire while his opponent struggled to get in a little practice. Finally Big Bill would call out in his stage voice, "Ready when you're exhausted, partner!" From the moment he walked on court in his favorite woolly-bear sweater, or perhaps a polo coat and muffler covering his famous "Tilden" V-neck sweater, a dozen rackets under his arm, he was director, master of ceremonies, and star.

In fact, once he had attained his goals in tennis, Tilden longed more than anything to be an actor and playwright, and his antics on court often bore the hallmarks of the melodramas he would later pen. Often, to woo the favor of an audience that came out rooting for the underdog, he would "hippodrome": put himself into a seemingly unwinnable position, then storm back to take the match. In the finals of the 1925 Illinois State Championships, against a far inferior player, Tilden won two sets, then inexplicably dropped the next two and went down two-five in the fifth. With the scene properly set, Tilden began its climax. He poured a pitcher of ice water over his head, beckoned imperiously for a ball boy to bring him a towel, and proceeded to dismantle his supporting actor. The script read eight-six in the fifth, Tilden.

On another occasion, when he found himself winning far too easily, Tilden not only allowed his outclassed opponent back into the match but also began picking arguments with the umpire, the well-respected H. Levan Richards. "Tilden glared at linesmen after decisions that everyone could see were correct, stormed about the court, and called on heaven to witness the injustice of it all. At one point he stopped in mid-court, placed hands on hips, and shouted at the chair for all to hear, 'For heaven's sake, Lev! Are you blind?'"

"Play the game, Tilden!" The shouts and boos rained down from the stands. But Tilden continued to play the wronged crusader, strutting nobly about as if all the world were against him. After winning with great ease in the end, he shook the umpire's hand and said, "I'm sorry, Lev. I apologize. But they really deserved a show, don't you think?"

At other times, though, his anger would be genuine. And like John McEnroe fifty years later, Tilden discovered that instead of stifling his anger he could harness it—let it blow but in the right direction, like combusting rocket fuel. And woe betide the player who got on his wrong side. He would transform instantly from the effeminate prima donna, complaining with hands on hips, to the aggressor, the deployer of power tennis of a force never before seen. George Lott once made the mistake of quick-serving Tilden (serving before he was ready) to get himself to match point in a best-of-three match. Tilden, enraged, stormed back to take the match. Another time, when Lott was again way up in a match, he decided to enjoy it too early. "Come on, Tillie," he taunted across the net when Tilden was taking his time. Lott didn't win another game.

If you got Tilden mad enough, or when he was feeling particularly theatrical, he would pull his five-ball trick. Serving for the match, he would hold five balls comfortably in his left hand, toss one, and hit his famous cannonball for an ace. He would then do the same thing three more times. After the fourth ace, he would toss the fifth ball into the stands and trot to the net to shake hands. No wonder one writer extolled "the grand, almost regal manner with which Tilden is wont to destroy his opponents."

Tilden was indeed the king of tennis from 1920 on, and his insistence on being treated as such exacerbated his troubles with the USLTA. As it was until the advent of open tennis in 1968, tennis in Tilden's day was mostly amateur; that is, the tournaments offered no prize money. In fact, however, many of the top players did quite all right for themselves with under-the-table guarantees, inflated "expenses," and valuable perks. Don Budge always claimed that he never received anything more than modest reimbursements for expenses. If so, then he was one of very few champions not to get what he could out of the "shamateurism" system. George Lott, for instance, wrote without shame of routinely filing reimbursement requests for double the actual expenses, and of agreeing to play in a particular tournament only after an offer of $350 (for a fifty-dollar train fare) plus hotel and meals. Bobby Riggs remembered being paid $500 cash plus expenses to play in a small tournament in Wisconsin in 1937. Other times, when expenses couldn't be justified, a tournament director would bet a player a hundred bucks that he couldn't jump over the net. And even Budge had his job as a packing clerk for Wilson, a position that probably didn't require too many hours in the office. L. B. Iceley, the president of Wilson (who was later best man at Budge's wedding), gave Riggs a job too, for $200 a week, for "theoretically working," as Riggs put it.

But no man ever played the expenses game like Big Bill Tilden. If a tournament wanted the best player in the world, it had to pay for him, with lodging at the very finest hotel, meals fit for a prince, and other exorbitant "expenses." Tournament directors also often had to make room in their draws for a few of Tilden's protégés.

It had begun in 1921, the year after Tilden became world champion and brought home the Davis Cup. That spring the USLTA offered him a thousand dollars in expenses for his European trip. Tilden just laughed: a thousand dollars for three weeks in Paris and four in London, not to mention boat fare? Not when, as he wrote, "I felt it beneath the dignity of the United States to have its champion travel in any way except first class." That meant, of course, a full suite at Paris's and London's most exclusive hotels. While playing an exhibition at the White House, Tilden had no qualms about discussing his predicament with President Harding. Soon afterward the USLTA bigwigs agreed to Tilden's demands.

What could they do? They needed Tilden, so he generally got what he wanted. They were already in debt to him for having brought the Davis Cup back home after seven years on foreign shores, and Big Bill kept redoubling the amount due year after year. Since the Davis Cup is decided by the best three out of five matches, one great player can win it almost on his own by taking two singles matches and the doubles. Of course this puts extreme pressure on that linchpin, as Tilden confessed. Nonetheless, from 1920 to 1926, Tilden was an unassailable force, dominating the Challenge Rounds and keeping the Cup in the United States.

In 1925 France's "Four Musketeers"—Henri Cochet, René Lacoste, Jean Borotra, and Jacques Brugnon—arrived in Philadelphia to begin their crusade to bring down Big Bill and take the Cup. In the first match Tilden, ill with ptomaine poisoning and wilting in the extreme heat, was losing to Borotra 6-4, 0-6, 6-2, 6-5, with Borotra serving for the match. Tilden poured a jug of ice water over his head, took the set 9-7, and proceeded to drop-shot and lob the exhausted Borotra into submission, 6-4 in the fifth set. Tilden also beat Lacoste, "le Crocodile," the statuesque, brilliant son of one of France's greatest automobile magnates, who would later become even more famous for his clothing line than for his tennis, in a long five-setter. But it was clear that the young Frenchmen were going to pose a strong challenge for years to come.

The next year the Americans beat the French again, but Lacoste managed to topple Tilden in the final match. The Cup had already been decided and Tilden was half-lame with a recurring knee injury— he really should have defaulted—and still it took Lacoste four sets, two of them eight-six. But the French had finally beaten him: the king had been brought down! They celebrated almost as though they had won

the Cup. Then in 1927 they came to Philadelphia with a vengeance—
and a plan to depose the thirty-four-year-old monarch.

Both Tilden and the French knew that the American had to win all
three of his matches, as Johnston was by now well past his peak and
possibly already weak with the tuberculosis that would kill him at the
age of fifty-one. They also knew that Tilden would have to conserve
his strength in the Philadelphia heat. So, like picadors in the bull ring,
they set out to wear him down. In the first match Cochet, the diminutive, lithe "stylist supreme" from Lyon, who along with Lacoste would
dominate tennis for the next few years, stretched him to four tough
sets. The next day, in the doubles, Borotra and Brugnon lobbed Big
Bill mercilessly, bringing him to net and then forcing him back to the
baseline, giving him the lion's share of the work in a strenuous five-set
match. Tilden and his partner Frank Hunter won, but the picadors
had done their job. On the final day Tilden had nothing left in him. A
well-rested twenty-three-year-old Lacoste chased every ball down and
put it back in play, running the older man all over the court; it was over
in four sets. The standing-room-only crowd of more than fifteen
thousand saturating the wooden stands at Germantown was stunned.
Even here at his home club, no one had ever liked Tilden all that much,
but they had grown accustomed to his winning face. Now that he had
lost, they finally gave him the ovation he had never had at home. They
stood and cheered as he walked, head bowed, off the court. Tilden
looked up and for a moment seemed as if he didn't know how to re-
spond. Then, paradoxically, he clasped his hands together above his
head, like a boxing champion, and brought another wave of cheers
around him.

When Cochet beat Johnston in the final match and tossed his
racket thirty feet into the air, Tilden and Lacoste, who had been
watching together, merely turned and shook hands. It had taken all
four Musketeers and three years, but at long last France had taken the
Cup away from Big Bill. Back in March, President Calvin Coolidge
himself had conducted the draw for the 1927 tournament, pulling the
names of nations out of the historic trophy. But now the Frenchmen
would be taking it home with them. Cochet's wife couldn't stop crying;
in Paris the streets filled with people crying *"Victoire!"* In the Louvre a
special place was designated to exhibit the Cup. "How did we finally

beat Tilden?" Cochet mused many years later. "We were younger, and ahh, we had Tilden to learn from."

Big Bill was thirty-four years old. Most tennis players were long gone from the scene by that age, already years into their "real" careers as stockbrokers, lawyers, or businessmen. But Tilden was still the greatest player in the world. He had been given many offers to turn professional; the year before a Florida concern had offered him $5,000 a month to teach tennis and give exhibitions, but he was never even tempted. He placed teaching pros even lower in the social hierarchy than professional players. And a professional tennis tour did not yet exist. Promoters were trying to create one, but they needed Tilden to make it viable, and Tilden assured the press that he would never play professionally.

At times recently, however, his interest in tennis had seemed to be flagging. "It's silly for a big crowd to enthuse over two men batting tennis balls at each other," he told a reporter in an off-guard moment. "It disturbs my sense of balance. I am getting sick of it. My position in sport means very little to me." What had always been most important to him was art—in particular, the theater and writing. His room at the Algonquin in New York was cluttered with a writer's detritus: books, manuscripts, notebooks, pencils, and cigarettes. His "most constant companion" was Samuel Merwin, a respected if modest-selling author of the time. ("It disgusts me when people rush forward to greet me and don't know who Sam is. I'd give the last string in my pet racket to write a single short story as good as any Sam has turned out by the dozen!")

He also courted Hollywood royalty as his friends: Douglas Fairbanks and Mary Pickford, Charlie Chaplin, Greta Garbo, and above all Tallulah Bankhead, his favorite London nightlife cohort. Ted Tinling remembered The Bankhead, as Tilden liked to call her, "chewing a pink rose down to the thorns" at Wimbledon in 1928 as she watched Tilden play a nerve-wracking five-setter. She was also "*en rapport*, if you will excuse the euphemism," with his doubles partner Frank Hunter that summer, which drove Tilden up the wall, as he felt Hunter should be spending more of his leisure time on the practice court. He'd roll his eyes and crow, "That girl would sleep with a *swan*."

At the same time Tilden was forever implying romantic relationships between himself and actresses such as Peggy Wood and Marjorie Daw, which somehow never quite managed to reach the serious stage. He was genuinely fond of these women, but it was the theater he was really in love with.

In 1926 Tilden had managed (by putting up a lot of his own money) to secure his first Broadway role. It was in a forgettable melodrama, and the critics had more fun than the audience: "Tilden keeps his amateur standing," intoned the cleverest of them. Another paper headlined its theater review, TILDEN STILL TENNIS CHAMP. The show flopped, and for the first time since 1919, Tilden seemed to show imperfection on the tennis court as well. He lost several matches over the winter, dropped that dead rubber to Lacoste, and then, inconceivably by this point, lost at Forest Hills. "Black Thursday," they called it, as Tilden, Johnston, and the great veteran Dick Williams all lost in the quarterfinals to the French Musketeers Cochet, Borotra, and Lacoste. True, Tilden's knee was still killing him, but even if the crowd had known that, they would still have been shocked to see him go down eight-six in the fifth set to Cochet. Big Bill's streak of six straight U.S. titles was over, and he missed the finals for the first time since 1917.

Even the week before his loss, however, talking to a reporter, Tilden was more excited about his upcoming return to the Broadway stage. This time it was a comedy, an "elementary school entertainment," according to the *New York Times*, in which Tilden "strikes a good many poses and manages to play about half of his scenes directly to the audience." One can imagine Tilden's sideways smirk to the gallery when his character, a wealthy heir impersonating a chauffeur impersonating a writer, is asked if he ever fancies a game of tennis.

This show too was a dismal failure, but not before Tilden burned a chunk of his personal fortune trying to keep it going. And on the tennis court the losses to Lacoste and Cochet proved the beginning of the end for Tilden. He would not win a major tournament in 1926, 1927, or 1928. Yet he remained Big Bill, the biggest name in tennis, even if he was no longer world champion. And in 1927, though the Frenchmen finally wrested the Davis Cup from him and also beat him in each of the three major tournaments he played, those losses produced some of his most memorable matches.

In May, at the French Championships, he revenged himself on Cochet in straight sets in the semifinals, but then lost an excruciating match in the finals to Lacoste. At Wimbledon he lost, unfathomably, in the semifinals to Cochet after leading 6-2, 6-4, 5-1. Some people, remembering the Tilden of old, speculated that he had noticed the King of Spain entering the Royal Box at five-one in the third and wanted to give him a bit of a show but, after giving away a set, was unable to regain his form. If so, then Tilden learned the hard way that the days of playing cat and mouse with his opponents were over. George Lott, for one, saw this as a turning point in Tilden's career: "His belief in his own invincibility was strongly shaken."

The Myth of Tilden was crumbling. A couple months later the Musketeers carried out their successful siege of thirty-four-year-old Big Bill in the Davis Cup at Germantown, and the week after that the young Lacoste took him down in the finals of Forest Hills, 11-9, 6-3, 11-9. Tilden sometimes remembered that as the best match he ever played; in fact, he had played much of his greatest tennis that year, but he had lost everything. And then a few months later Mike Myrick and the USLTA finally decided that they didn't need Tilden anymore. The next summer, just before the 1928 Davis Cup matches in Paris, Big Bill Tilden was banned from amateur tennis.

They had been dying to stick it to Tilden for years. Even before he was a top player, when he was covering tennis for the *Evening Ledger*, he was constantly criticizing the tennis establishment. Once he became world champion, he was absolutely insufferable. He would show up uninvited at the annual USLTA meetings, telling them how they should rank players and how they should amend the rules. Just that February he had paid his own way to the annual meeting in Chicago to argue against a proposed new rule banning glaring at officials on court. "Tilden rose," reported the *New York Times*, "with some choice remarks and some very impressive glaring, and the rule against 'dirty looks' was voted down.'" But the major source of friction over the years had not been Tilden's facial expressions or his meddling in officialdom, but rather his pen.

Somehow the USLTA's image of an amateur tennis player could not include writing about the sport for pay. Tilden had been a tennis journalist before he was a top player, and as a superstar he commanded top fees from newspapers and magazines. The USLTA had been living with this uncomfortably for years, but in 1924 it finally decided to put its foot down and ruled that no players might write about tennis for pay. Defiantly, Tilden announced, "I cannot give up my profession," and furthermore, since the rules committee had deemed him a bad influence, "I cannot, with self-respect, represent this country on the Davis Cup or Olympic teams." (Tennis, which had been an Olympic sport since the modern games began in 1896, was discontinued after the 1924 games and not reinstated until 1988.) He did skip the Athens games, but by the time of the Davis Cup in September, public pressure and the support of his fellow players, the press, and the newly formed Bill Tilden Fair Play Society had convinced the USLTA to amend its rule. Henceforth only current coverage of an event in which the player was entered would be banned. Tilden easily got around this restriction by writing long columns that were then enclosed in quotation marks and presented to newspaper readers as "interviews." The USLTA didn't take kindly to this evasion and warned Tilden to cut it out, and Tilden calmly ignored them. And they laid off him—until four years later, when his armor started to crack, and the Davis Cup was lost anyway.

In July 1928 Tilden was in Paris as top player and captain of the Davis Cup team, to try to win the Cup back from the French. Just as the draw was about to be made for the Interzone Final against Italy, the chairman of the Davis Cup Committee, Joseph Wear, announced that he had received a radiogram from New York while onboard his ship. To his great regret and shame, and against his wishes and advice, the USLTA had banned Tilden from all amateur tennis for violating the "Amateur Writer Rule": one of his articles about Wimbledon that year, syndicated in hundreds of newspapers, had appeared in one of them less than the requisite forty-eight hours after Tilden had been eliminated from the tournament.

Transatlantic furor ensued. The French had just built a brand-new stadium, named for their flying ace from the Great War, Roland Garros, specifically to accommodate the hordes they expected for their first Cup defense. All tickets to the Challenge Round had been long sold out, in anticipation of the arrival of "Beeg Beel." As soon as Tilden's ban was announced, demands for refunds poured in by the thousands. Lacoste announced he would not defend his U.S. title and even stated that it was pointless to defend the Cup if Tilden were not playing. In the United States the news dominated front-page headlines, and the press and public alike were giving the USLTA hell. Finally the U.S. ambassador to France, Myron Herrick (not to be confused with the USLTA's Mike Myrick), stepped in. Herrick, a man beloved by the French for refusing to quit Paris as the Germans approached in 1914, and who, according to fellow Ohioan James Thurber, "wore amiability like a gay cockade" and had "one of the most effective handshakes in Ohio history," made a plea in the strongest terms, in the name of American-French relations. President Coolidge himself may have put in a phone call as well.

The USLTA relented. The United States had by now defeated Italy, and "in the interest of international good feeling," Tilden was reinstated to the U.S. team the day before the Challenge Round. Throughout the ordeal he had presided over the controversy like a martyred emperor, giving countless press conferences, "crying passionately" at one point, "I refute all charges! We will win the Davis Cup yet! I hereby apply for the job of training American Davis Cup members for the grueling matches ahead." When his reinstatement came through, he practiced for the first time in days and went out the next afternoon to face Lacoste, who had beaten him three straight times. Lacoste was twenty-three, the undisputed world champion, playing for his home crowd on his favorite surface. Tilden was a thirty-five-year-old has-been; no one gave him a chance.

But this time the old man outsmarted the youngster. Tilden came out with an array of slices, topspins, sidespins—any spin he could think of. Then, for surprise, he'd nail a flat one to the corner, or throw in a drop shot or lob. He played everything but his own game, and everything except what Lacoste expected. He was practicing exactly what he had preached in his book *Match Play and the Spin of the Ball*, published three years before and destined to be the bible of tennis for over fifty years: "It is the love of study of tennis that has led me to the point where I never hit a shot without a conscious application of twist or the deliberate attempt to use none." Lacoste surely had read the book but was nonetheless flabbergasted: "I never knew how the ball would come off the court, he concealed it so well," the Frenchman lamented afterward. When it was over, the old man was triumphant, six-three in the fifth set. To many, it would remain his greatest victory ever. Even the French crowd was standing and cheering the American, an unprecedented tribute in Davis Cup play.

Perhaps they sensed that the Cup would remain at the Louvre anyway, that Big Bill was past the days of winning the thing single-handed. Though he managed to outlast Lacoste, he had little left for the remaining matches. He and Frank Hunter lost the doubles in five sets, and Cochet finished off Tilden on the final day in three close ones. Tilden had made the Roland Garros stadium's Davis Cup debut memorable—and a bonanza for the French—but the Cup wasn't coming home.

A few weeks later, with the Davis Cup safely over, Mike Myrick and the USLTA struck again. After a six-hour "trial," which this time the defendant wasn't able to upstage, they suspended Tilden from amateur tennis "indefinitely." It seemed now that they really wanted to be rid of this mammoth in their china shop once and for all.

The time seemed obvious for Tilden to turn pro, which is probably what they wanted, but he steadfastly refused. Pointing out that he had spent more than two thousand of his own dollars to travel with and captain the Davis Cup team, he averred, "I am far more amateur in spirit than some of the men who have run tennis for years with one eye on the gate, while exploiting me for their advancement. . . . I will have nothing to do with professional tennis. I hope everybody knows me better than that." Instead, he served out his suspension with the air of "Jeanne d'Arc about to be burned at the stake." Being forced to sit out Forest Hills, when he knew he had precious few chances left to win great titles, must have rankled. He bided his time pleasurably enough, though, at the theater, on the town, and in his rooms at the Algonquin, where he wrote his lone novel, *Glory's Net*. Although he never sat at the hotel's famed Round Table of writers, actors, and wits, which was in its final days at this time, he may well have felt inspired by the proximity of such talent. Unfortunately, Tilden was no better a novelist than he was an actor. *Glory's Net* was as hackneyed and corny as his short stories. He did manage, though, to get in his digs at the USLTA and "shamateurism." David Cooper, the greatest tennis player in the world, is saved from the disgrace of being a "tennis gigolo"—playing as an amateur while making a handsome living from a phantom job—by the love of a good woman:

> You are a great artist in your line, David. Any artist belongs to his country and to the world. . . . Now you will play as your own master. No longer will you be in a position where your whole earning power depends on tennis, and your employer is using your reputation for his own ends. You are a man, standing on your own feet, playing when and where you can, playing of your own free will for the good of your country and for the game.

Figuring one Forest Hills missed was enough punishment—and sensing that no contrite apologies were going to be forthcoming—the USLTA reinstated Tilden in February 1929, and apparently all involved had kissed and made up. Strangest of all came the announcement that Tilden would be writing a series of tennis articles for *Tennis*, the USLTA's publication, which, Tilden later sniped, "evidently feels my work will not injure *its* amateur standing—a doubtful compliment to my literary skill."

In any case, Bill Tilden was back on the amateur tennis warpath. He lost to Lacoste in Paris and to Cochet at Wimbledon, but upon his return to Forest Hills in September, he took back the title with a five-set victory over Hunter in the final. (The French Musketeers did not make the ocean voyage in 1929.) This victory seemed to recharge the old Tilden legs, for in the spring of 1930 he swept through Europe like the Hurricane Bill of old, winning everything on the Riviera and in Italy, Germany, and Austria. After eighteen straight weeks of tournament tennis ("For once Bill Tilden had his heart's desire—enough tennis," wrote one reporter), he descended on Paris, where "his personality dominated the entire meeting. The French even wanted him to win." He didn't, losing to Cochet in the final, but at Wimbledon he asserted his greatness one last time. With Lacoste ill and Cochet losing in the quarterfinals to Wilmer Allison, only one Frenchman stood in

Tilden's way. And he beat the third-seeded Jean Borotra in the semifinals in his last great victory, seven-five in the fifth set. "This was indeed a battle of giants," wrote *The New Yorker*, "and the giant of all time won." The final was easier, as he put away his countryman Allison in straight sets for his third Wimbledon crown, at age thirty-seven.

Nonetheless, despite his victory, age seemed to be weighing on Tilden. His decay was psychological more than physical, though, a wearing away of reserve and dignity more than of joints and tendons. His homosexuality, stanched by a tourniquet of repression all these years, began bleeding through; effeminate mannerisms became more pronounced. He was acting fussier than ever on court in the eastern grass-court tournaments leading up to Forest Hills. When a doubles opponent made fun of Tilden wagging his finger at his partner by doing the same to his, Tilden stomped off court and defaulted. At the Orange, New Jersey, tournament, he let the imperfect court conditions throw him completely off temper, raging at the umpire that he was "not accustomed to playing tennis in a cow pasture." The next week, at the Eastern Grass-Court Championships in Rye, New York, he was struggling valiantly on (as he saw it) with a pulled muscle in his leg, losing badly in the quarterfinals. The crowd grew restless at the poor tennis and at Tilden's constant bickering with the officials; finally a woman shouted out, "Play tennis!"

It was a catcall he'd heard hundreds of times before, from Omaha to Cleveland to Forest Hills. He had usually considered it merely a challenge to win the crowd over. But today he felt weary of it all. "I think I've had enough of this gallery," Tilden announced, gathered up his rackets, and departed.

He arrived at Forest Hills at the end of summer knowing it was his last time. They had stolen 1928 from him, but he still had one last chance to win his eighth U.S. title and break away from Richard Sears and William Larned, who had also won seven, in the old days when the champion had to play only the Challenge Round. In the semifinals, though, Tilden came up against Johnny Doeg, the tall lefty with the biggest serve in tennis. And on this day Doeg found the rest of his game working like clockwork as well. He aced Tilden twenty-eight times and won his serve at love in nine of the last sixteen games. Big Bill became dejected, even more so after falling in the second set and scraping up his leg. "After that," wrote *Time* magazine, "he hobbled around, glowering, displaying occasional samples of the brilliant game he used to exhibit consistently." He waited petulantly for the crowd to quiet down after Doeg's winners, he quarreled with the umpire and linesmen. He lost the first two sets 10-8, 6-3, and even after winning the third 6-3 continued to skulk about the court in bad temper. Finally, after yet another outburst, the twenty-two-year-old Doeg blurted out, "Oh, for God's sake, Bill, let's play tennis!" Tilden's shoulders noticeably slouched. "The fight seemed to go out of him," recalled one old friend. He managed to keep holding serve but with far more difficulty than his opponent, and Doeg finally broke him to take the set and match, 12-10.

The world Tilden had conquered was disappearing. Eleventh months before, the stock market had crashed, and the effervescent carnival of the Twenties, over which he had lorded as the king of the courts, vanished. A drought in the summer of 1930 intensified the misery for working-class America. Stocks continued to plummet, more than a thousand banks went out of business, and six million people were unemployed. Little Bill Johnston had just entered a sanatorium to try to cure the tuberculosis that would eventually kill him. Frank Hunter too had been ill of late and was turning away from tennis toward a business career. Even Lacoste, Tilden's young conqueror, had retired at twenty-five for health reasons; within a year or two the other Musketeers would be gone from amateur tennis as well.

There was nothing left for Tilden to accomplish, and he was tired of his constant feuding with the USLTA. On the last day of 1930, just a year and a half after declaring, "I will have nothing to do with professional tennis. I hope everybody knows me better than that," he announced that he had signed a contract to play a one-on-one professional tour against the current pro champion, Karel Kozeluh.

A decade after he had won his first championship, Big Bill Tilden left amateur tennis forever transformed. When he first started playing Forest Hills and other big tournaments, tennis had been a polite game played by ladies and gentlemen on country club lawns. Yes, there was an (unofficial) world championship, Wimbledon, but even that was played "in a pastoral setting" resembling "a delightful vicarage garden party." Tilden himself wrote about the game of his youth: "They played with an air of elegance—a peculiar courtly grace that seemed to rob the game of its thrills. . . . There was a sort of inhumanity about it [and] it annoyed me. . . . I believed the game deserved something more vital and fundamental."

And that is exactly what he gave it.

With his power game, his stormy demeanor, and his writings, Tilden created a science and philosophy of tennis, aimed at *winning*. "When two players start a match," he wrote in 1950, when he was fifty-seven and still winning the occasional pro match, "it is always a battle to see who will dominate the match, and who will be pushed around. One player or the other will ultimately impress his tennis personality on the other. The one who does will win, because by so doing he forces the recognition of impending defeat upon his opponent."

How often his opponents had seen their impending defeat materialize on the horizon and grow larger. For a few more years professional players would meet the same fate. But Big Bill Tilden had finally turned away from the amateur sport he had loved and dominated. Now, without glory's net to hide behind, he would, more and more, have to face himself.

SIX YEARS LATER, IN 1937—TEN YEARS SINCE BIG BILL LOST THE Davis Cup to France—Don Budge is in danger of becoming yet another American to leave the Cup in Europe. It's 8-6, 7-5 for Cramm, and two-all in the third. At the start of the third set, Budge railed against himself: "Every year, it seems, the Americans come over here, do great at Wimbledon, and then blow the Davis Cup. Shields, Wood, Allison, Ellie Vines in '32 and '33. Even old Tilden back in '30 when he won his last Wimbledon. Well, you're not going to let it happen again!"

He didn't say a word to Walter Pate when they switched sides at two-one in the third. Pate, for his part, though he was dying inside, knew better than to speak to Budge. Don had more competitive fire than anyone he'd known, and he could see it now in his eyes. Pate merely sipped his tea while Budge barely stopped to towel off on his way to the other end. But now, after Cramm has broken back with those four astonishing returns of serve, Pate wonders if his boy's come-back has been stifled already.

He doesn't have to wonder long. Cramm's lightning-quick break seems to have stunned him as much as Budge, and the American responds with a barrage of offensive service returns himself, breaking right back with four straight points. And then, after another change of sides with again nothing more than a confident nod between player and captain, Budge plays his strongest service game yet. Three straight games at love, one for Cramm and two for Budge, and the American leads four-two in the third set. The rest of the set goes quickly on serve, and when Budge delivers a service ace to win the tenth game, he has the third set six-four. As quickly as that, what looked like a certain upset for Germany has turned into a tight match. "It is characteristic of von Cramm to lose a third set after winning two," notes the *Times* man on his pad, but this is not a routine second-round four-setter. This is the world champion storming back. Has the baron let a tiger out of his cage?

As THE PLAYERS AND CAPTAINS LEFT THE COURT FOR THE CUSTOM-ary ten-minute break between the third and fourth sets (an intermission standard in tennis at that time, except at Wimbledon during the Championships), the Homburgs and "Florentine" hats floated up in a standing ovation. It felt as though tennis had never been played at quite this level before. In general, any player is happy if he can hit more winners than errors in a match, and it's rare if both players can manage it. In this match, both Budge and Cramm were hitting *twice* as many winners as errors. The American fans, of course, were delirious. All was apparently not lost. But even the British, hoping that Cramm could somehow take the Americans out of the running, thrilled to the recognition that a great battle was building. As Budge forged his third-set resurgence, the crowd seemed to have forgotten its allegiances and roared its approval.

With Fred Perry gone, the Londoners knew they would probably have little to cheer about next week, whether their team played Germany or the United States. And there had been few opportunities for gaiety in general these past few years. The Depression had laid England low just as it had America: the previous year unemployment had soared to 2.2 million. London was recovering, but things were still bad in most of the country, and the rebound down south was mostly due to rearmament. Hitler had declared his new conscription law and marched into the Rhineland, and Italy had invaded Ethiopia, prompting Foreign Secretary Anthony Eden to warn, "Eighteen years after the war we find ourselves confronted with the same problems dreadfully similar in character and portent to those of 1914." The new Conservative government responded by passing a massive rearmament bill, and factories worked around the clock turning out new battleships, destroyers, submarines, and fighter planes. Enough gas masks for every citizen were manufactured and stored in strategic places to be ready in case aircraft, such as those Italy had deployed in Africa, attacked with mustard gas.

War was in the air, but while rearmament had spurred economic recovery in the capital, England exhibited none of the nationalistic enthusiasm for conflict as had proliferated in 1914 or as could be seen in Germany today. As one historian wrote, "the nakedness of the government in foreign policy was unconcealed. The League [of Nations] was wrecked, collective security broken, France paralysed, friendship between France and England enfeebled, the aggressors triumphant. [The public had gotten] a course of sedatives and one piece of shock treatment, and became passive, acquiescing in failure and despair."

Over in America, people felt less threatened by Hitler than by the Depression. The Crash of '29 had turned millionaires into paupers, and the epidemic of bank closings in 1931 had crushed ordinary families by vaporizing their savings. Brutal droughts in the Midwest, Great Plains, and South gave "the overall economic calamity an almost biblical character." Although the sense of impending catastrophe had faded away in the past three years, "the crisis," as it was called, lingered on; people were almost used to the fact that ten million men were still out of work. And even while some attention was diverted over the ocean to the ominous international situation there, Americans had a strong feeling that they should not once again be tempted into a European war.

Millions of them had the Civil War more on their minds, as *Gone*

*With the Wind* was by far the best-selling book of 1936 and 1937. When they weren't debating who should play Scarlett in the movies, Americans were dancing to Benny Goodman, the "king" of the new "swing" sensation, and his lesser royals, such as Don Budge's favorites the Dorsey brothers. Roosevelt was back in office after a bitter campaign but a landslide reelection. During the long campaign international relations and the specter of war had hardly been an issue. A balanced budget, a sound currency, the sanctity of the Supreme Court (which had steadfastly vetoed much of the New Deal), and other domestic issues dominated the political scene.

The Roosevelt-haters—and there were millions of them—were mostly among the relatively wealthy. And, as in England, the upper class tended to be most lenient regarding Nazi Germany, admiring the economic miracle that Hitler had apparently engineered and choosing to ignore troubling "internal" issues, such as the persecution of Jews and other undesirables. During the 1930s American thinkers had shifted in attitude from Eurocentrism toward Americentrism, and now, as Europe whipped itself into a frenzied readiness for war, America experienced a growing push for isolationism. Those sympathetic to Germany, such as the German-American Bund, joined forces with right-wing politicians and businessmen and also pacifists on the Left to try to keep America out of the coming European war. Soon to be the most visible of these isolationists was the most famous American of all, Charles Lindbergh.

Lindbergh made his first visit to Nazi Germany in July 1936, borrowing a Miles Whitney Straight airplane and flying with his wife Anne from their new English home to Berlin, for the purpose of reporting on German aviation to the U.S. government. The Lindberghs were greeted at Staaken military airport by fifteen German bombers and "a phalanx of heel-clicking officers." By the time he had finished his guided tour of Berlin and various Luftwaffe installations (as well as opening day at the Berlin Olympics), Lindbergh was reporting "a spirit in Germany which I have not seen in any other country. There is certainly great ability, and I am inclined to think more intelligent leadership than is generally recognized. . . . [Hitler] must have far more character and vision than I thought . . . he is undoubtedly a great man, and I believe has done much for the German people."

While Lindbergh was hardly the only American to be sympathetic toward the Nazis, he was certainly the most prominent. But in this sympathy he and his wife would not have stuck out at all in upper-class England. At the end of 1935 they had fled hypercelebrity and death threats in America for a quieter life across the sea. They were relaxing at their country home in Kent on May 20, 1937, while the world celebrated the tenth anniversary of his historic flight from New York to Paris, and two months later when the United States battled Germany for the Davis Cup at Wimbledon.

On THE FINAL DAY OF THAT COMPETITION, ANOTHER FADING American hero, Bill Tilden, sat ringside at Centre Court cheering on his friend Gottfried against the newest American phenom, Budge. Don's coming on strong, he thought, but Gottfried's still up, two sets to one. We're in good shape.

Did he have conflicted feelings coaching another country against his homeland? Probably. But it served the USLTA right, he undoubtedly told himself. Sure, they'd wished him "every success" when he announced he was turning pro, and he'd sent a wire back, "wishing the game of amateur tennis and the United States Lawn Tennis Association all success in the future and thanking you for many courtesies to me." But the antagonism had never ceased. In 1933, when the United States sent world champ Ellsworth Vines and Wilmer Allison to Paris to try for the sixth straight year to wrest the Davis Cup free from French hands, Tilden had offered to coach the team—for free. Mike Myrick and his USLTA cronies turned him down and instead chose Mercer Beasley, a man who had never played on the heavy French clay in his life. In the Interzone Final at Roland Garros Vines and company went down four matches to one, to England's Perry and Austin.

Perhaps, Tilden mused, Myrick had been afraid of some sort of scandal involving him and an American player: the USLTA had survived ten years of having a fruit as its king and savior, and maybe Myrick and company didn't want to push their luck. Fine, he wouldn't burden them with another offer. He couldn't help but smile. Few people knew he was coaching the Germans, and fewer still outside tennis knew of his true sexual nature. Almost no one realized that Gottfried was of the same inclination. What would the folks packing these Wimbledon stands, or the millions listening to the radio broadcast, have said if they'd known the greatest secret behind the match? That the team playing for Nazi Germany, representing the highest ideals of Aryan athleticism and manliness, had a homosexual as its star and another—an American, to boot—as coach.

# "I'M PLAYING for MY LIFE"

TILDEN ROSE AND STRETCHED, decided to walk around the grounds for a few minutes. If he considered going to the locker room to see Gottfried and offer some advice, he thought better of it. His position as coach was to remain unofficial, and who knew who would be in there? Plus, he had no desire to antagonize the American boys. He knew them all, had practiced with most of them individually. Mako in particular he liked; one hell of a contract bridge player, that lad. He also had nothing against Walter Pate, though he would have preferred to be the captain himself.

Then they would have had a coach in the bargain. Hell, he could still be the number-two singles player if he had stayed amateur. Hadn't he just beaten Perry a couple of times in their pro tour stateside? Sure, Fred had run him off the court the first bunch of matches, but old Tilden wasn't through. He had come back and beaten him the last two matches. And Fred had said that he'd been even tougher to play than Elly Vines. He'd certainly given Gottfried a run for his money in some of their practice matches. He had *beaten* Gottfried in that exhibition match at Rot-Weiss four years ago. At forty-four he was a bit dinged up from over twenty years of constant tennis, but that shoulder operation six months ago had really seemed to do the trick. And overall he felt as strong physically as ever. Time takes its toll, and he couldn't play at the top level day in and day out anymore, but with a bit of rest he could give anyone trouble. Certainly he could still handle the likes of Parker and Grant.

No, you wouldn't want to still be mucking around in that amateur business. Far better to have been paid honestly these past seven years. And ah, if you were playing for or coaching the Americans, you wouldn't have had the chance to help Gottfried. And by God did he want Gottfried to win this match!

It looked good. Losing one set was no cause for panic. In fact, Budge was so good now that a straight-set victory would have been unthinkable. And even he, Tilden, in his greatest days, often dropped a set. Sometimes it was to give them a better show—he smiled—but sometimes you just had a letdown, it was only human. No, this was Gottfried's day, he was playing like a dream. There were some days when you simply could not lose.

He was outside the stadium now and ran into a reporter he knew, who asked for his impressions so far. "I've never seen two men catch fire like these two have today," Tilden told him. "This is the greatest Davis Cup match I ever have seen." On he went, ambling along the walkway beside the tea lawn. Those with only grounds passes, who had been following the match on the electric scoreboard and only hearing the cheers from within, mingled with the lucky ones just taking a break. At least half the people he passed looked up in thrilled recognition, or nudged their companion to look who was walking by. He loved every second of it, tossing off friendly smiles like flower petals. Why shouldn't they gawk? He was the best there had ever been, the greatest thing ever to happen to this sport. Let Mike Myrick come walking past him, and he'd throw him a benevolent smile too. He'd played his own sweet game and shown them all.

In the corner of his eye he caught another fan gaping up at him. But something was different and might have got Tilden's attention. A young black man, dressed in a clean but well-worn jacket and tie, was watching him with a faint smile on his face. Tilden would have smiled back and nodded. It was incongruous to see a Negro at a tennis match in the States, much less at Wimbledon. They weren't even allowed to play in USLTA tournaments. Back in '29 those two New York boys, one from City College and one from a city high school, had applied for the national junior indoor championships but were turned down. "In pursuing this policy," the USLTA had said, "we make no reflection upon the colored race, but we believe that as a practical matter, the present method of separate associations for the administration of the affairs and championships of colored and white players should be continued." Typical USLTA speciousness. You could make a killing in expense money and under-the-table payoffs, but you couldn't make a living as a journalist—it tainted the game.

This young man in the three-piece suit had light skin and a broad, handsome face. A fierce intelligence burned behind his eyes; much more than his skin made him stand out from the throngs milling about the stadium. All this may have gone through Tilden's mind in the brief moment when the two men's glances met. Then he moved on, heading back into the Centre Court stadium and to his front-row seat.

Ralph Bunche had recognized Big Bill Tilden immediately and couldn't help but smile. The moment would certainly make it into his diary entry tonight. Bunche was thirty-three years old and a professor of political science at Howard University in Washington, already making a name for himself as a brilliant thinker and writer on the issues of race and imperialism. He had been in London since February with his wife and children, studying cultural anthropology at the London School of Economics in preparation for a year in Africa researching the impact of colonial rule and Western culture on Africans.

Bunche was having a fine time in London, attending seminars, learning Swahili, and hanging out with a crowd of dynamic, revolutionary young Africans. He also spent a lot of time with Paul Robeson, then at the height of his fame as an actor and singer. Despite Robeson's mansion and chauffeur, he fit right in with the radical Africans in London: Bunche found him at the time to be an ardent Marxist (like Bunche), "anti-white and all out for USSR."

Still, Bunche had his reservations about "this staid, glum and curt, though always 'courteous' little isle." Courteous, yes, but the stench of racism was always there, under the surface, just like back home. At the cinema they had shown the newsreels of Joe Louis's June 22 knockout of the "Cinderella Man," James Braddock. Someone behind Bunche in the theater kept referring to Louis as "that darkey." Bunche finally twisted around in his seat. "Well, that 'darkey,' as you call him, gave Braddock one hell of a beating, didn't he?"

He was also a tennis fan, though well aware of the racism inherent in the game's ruling bodies. (In 1959 Bunche, by then under secretary of the United Nations and winner of the Nobel Peace Prize, would speak to the president of Forest Hills' West Side Tennis Club, site of the U.S. Championships, about a club membership for his son. Bunche was told politely that Jews and Negroes were not "invited" to be members. Bunche took this no more quietly than he had taken the racial slur in the London cinema, and within days the story was front-page news, the club president was forced to resign, and both Bunches were offered memberships. They politely declined.) And while he hadn't been able to make it to Wimbledon for the Championships, he made sure he got tickets to all three days of the U.S.-Germany Davis Cup tie. He'd loved every minute of it but particularly the stunning play between Budge and Cramm today. And then there was this unexpected sighting of the legend.

So that was Tilden. "Crowds hang around entrances to see players enter—idol worshippers," Bunche had written in his diary after the first day of play. Well, he worshipped no man, certainly not an over-privileged white one from Germantown. Still, there was something about a person who had reached such dizzying heights in any field of endeavor. In this case, he was seeing him on the other side, though, on the way down. What he saw was just a man, a somewhat rumpled man at that, in a cheap suit that looked like it hadn't been cleaned in some time. Bunche would have been surprised, he'd always read what a dapper figure Tilden cut on court. And no hat—he was about the only man on the grounds without one, as if so everyone could recognize Big Bill coming. Perhaps he felt a twinge of melancholy, a premonition of decline for the old master, for all men. He shook his head and continued on, back into the stadium, for the finale of what he would describe that night as "the most exciting athletic combat I've ever seen."

THE INTERMISSION OVER, BUDGE AND CRAMM WALK BACK ONTO Centre Court together. At 6:30 P.M. there is still plenty of midsummer sunlight, but its angle is steepening, heightening the drama of the match's final stages. The numbers on the electric scoreboard shine with a vespertine glow: 8-6, 7-5, 4-6, the German still in command. The crowd's mood, if anything, is even more anticipatory than at the match's commencement. Now they know it won't be a quick three-set repeat of the Wimbledon final. Either Cramm will finish off his masterful job, or Budge will continue his comeback, and everyone will be in for a classic five-setter.

It doesn't take long to determine which direction the match will take. The audience has hardly taken their seats before Budge makes it clear that the third set was no mere aberration. Four fine returns of serve, four quick points, and he has broken Cramm in the first game of the fourth set. They change ends, and he promptly holds serve and then breaks again. Another change, another hold: he's practically skipping from point to point, as if he can't wait to put the ball back in play. In a blistering five-minute span, the American goes up four-love with the loss of only five points. For the first time all afternoon, stunned silence follows the quick burst of applause for each Budge winner. This was what the audience feared before the match: another American steamroller. Can Cramm really feel as calm as he looks? One would think he is being trounced in a mere practice match.

IN A CORNER OF THE GRANDSTAND, ONE MAN HAD BEEN CLAPPING harder and harder throughout the match; he hardly knew for which player he was cheering. Daniel Prenn would have left work early in Kentish Town, caught the tube, and made two transfers to get down to Wimbledon. He wouldn't have bothered with the first match; he'd known Henner would take Bitsy apart. But he'd have been sure to get there before Gottfried took on Budge. He wouldn't have missed that.

He should have been playing, of course. Not in the number-one slot anymore—Gottfried was truly remarkable, and Prenn was already into his thirties. But if he'd been able to continue concentrating on tennis, he felt he would still be above Henkel. It should be Gottfried and him, still together, bringing the Davis Cup home to a democratic Germany, the Germany that had saved him from Soviet Russia. No, *defending* the Cup, for surely they would have won in '33, with both of them at their prime, after having come so close the year before. And then, with the privilege of defending it each year on the red clay at Rot-Weiss, the best surface for both Gottfried and him, they might have held off England even with Perry reaching his peak. Instead . . .

He didn't dwell on it often. After all, he was one of the lucky ones. He and Charlotte had settled down in Kensington, just five miles north of Centre Court, and with a loan from Simon Marks, the tennis-mad retail magnate, he'd started his own business: Truvox Engineering, producer of its own line of loudspeakers. He was doing all right, too, with five employees already. And now they had a baby on the way—just two months to go, in fact.

There hadn't been much time for tennis. He practiced sometimes with the English players and was always available for social doubles with Marks; it was the least he could do to let the older man show off his "ringer." But the demands of a new business and a new life made it impossible to maintain the high level of play he had once practiced. His first year here, 1934, he'd played Wimbledon but lost badly in the first round to Frank Shields, whom he had crushed in the 1932 Davis Cup. "The man without a country," as the English papers hailed him, continued to play Wimbledon each year—they were kind enough to grant him entry based on his past glory—and he'd gained back much of his form this year, beating an American and two British players before falling to Frank Parker in the fourth round. In the mixed doubles he played with the English girl Evelyn Dearman, and they made it all the way to the semis, losing a tight one to a French team, 6-2, 9-7. But he knew his best tennis days were far behind him. He was an English businessman now, soon to be a father and eventually a British citizen.

Watching his old friend and teammate on the verge of beating the world champion and bringing the Davis Cup home to Germany, Prenn would have had mixed feelings. Nothing would gall him more than to know the Davis Cup was on display under the Swastika in Berlin. But he had the warmest feelings for Gottfried, who he knew hated the Nazis as much as he did, and who was the finest of men. It was hard to root against him. He also knew of Gottfried's sexual tendencies, and he wondered how long Himmler and his gang would leave him unharmed. Perhaps a Davis Cup championship would save his friend.

Like most of the crowd by this point, Prenn found himself cheering for both men, surrendering to the balletic beauty of the contest.

One of his sisters had managed to emigrate as well and lived near him and Charlotte in London. His parents were still living peacefully in Warsaw, and his younger sister was married and living in Prague. They were lucky to be out of Germany, but their luck would hold for only another year or so.

Back in Germany, the lives of Jews were becoming darker and more tenuous every day. It had started even before Prenn had left, right after the Nazi takeover of the government. Along with the declaration that ended his tennis career came a slew of others, excluding Jews from public office, the civil service, journalism, farming, teaching, and film and theater. The next year they were banned from the stock exchange and terrorized out of practicing law or medicine. And then in September 1935 came the Nuremburg Laws, which officially took away their citizenship and forbade them from marrying or having sexual relations with Aryans.

These new laws only formalized the nightmarish situation for Jews left in Germany. Even before that many groceries wouldn't sell them food, and pharmacies wouldn't sell them medicine. Around the country signs greeted them: "Jews Strictly Forbidden in This Town"; "Jews Enter This Place at Their Own Risk"; and even "Drive Carefully! Sharp Curve! Jews: 75 Miles an Hour!"

However, despite the reporting of these and other atrocities by some foreign journalists, Nazi Germany was somehow maintaining in many people's eyes the semblance of a respectable regime. During the Berlin Olympics of 1936 Propaganda Minister Joseph Goebbels led one of his greatest campaigns to this end. The only other time Germany had had a chance to host was in 1916, and those games had been canceled due to the war. Germany had been awarded the 1936 Olympics back in 1931, before the Nazis took over, and as the games approached Goebbels seized upon the chance to show the world the New Germany.

But even while the 42-million-Reichsmark, 325-acre Olympic sports complex, including the grandiose 110,000-seat Olympic Stadium, built of natural stone, was being constructed outside Berlin, international controversy threatened to derail the Berlin Olympics. German sports had by now been purged of non-Aryan athletes, and the United States, which usually sent the largest number of athletes and won the most medals, was threatening to boycott the Olympics. The Amateur Athletic Union declared that participation meant "giving American moral and financial support to the Nazi regime, which is opposed to all that Americans hold dearest." The AAU was joined by Jewish and African American groups, religious leaders, forty-one college presidents, and a number of politicians in demanding a boycott.

If the United States did boycott, England would likely follow suit, and possibly France and Italy as well. Cash-poor Nazi Germany was desperate for the foreign currency the Olympics would bring in; a boycott would be a financial disaster as well as an embarrassment. "The German government are simply terrified," reported the British embassy in Berlin, "lest Jewish pressure may induce the U.S. government to withdraw their team and so wreck the festival, the material and propagandistic value of which, they think, can scarcely be exaggerated."

Hans von Tschammer und Osten, the Reich sports leader, invited Avery Brundage, the head of the American Olympic Committee, to Berlin, gave him the VIP treatment, and even showed him special athletic training facilities supposedly reserved for use by Jews. Brundage, who virulently opposed the boycott, ascribing it to "concerted efforts by Communists . . . and Jews," wrote home that he "liked [Tschammer] very much," and he joked with the Nazi officials that his own men's club back home in Chicago excluded Jews too. Charles Sherrill, an American member of the International Olympic Committee, was personally received by Hitler, at which time he warned the Führer that "the Jew LaGuardia" and other American Jews might succeed in getting America to boycott the games. He also suggested that Germany add a "token Jew," in the American tradition of the "token Negro," to the German team in order to placate American Jews. Eventually Tschammer announced that not only would Jews from other countries be allowed to participate, but Helene Mayer, part Jewish (though, like Prenn, completely nonobservant) and a former gold-medalist fencer, would be reinstated on the German team. And Theodor Lewald, the former head of the Olympic Committee, who had been replaced because he had a Jewish-born father, would be restored to his position.

(He became in effect nothing more than a Hitler toady and was forced to retire shortly after the Olympics.)

The American chief consul in Berlin, George Messersmith, thought it "inconceivable" that America should participate in the Nazi games; "there are many wise and well informed observers in Europe," he wrote, "who believe that the holding or non-holding of the Olympic Games in Berlin in 1936 will play an important part in determining political developments in Europe." However, Secretary of State Cordell Hull, determined to preserve German-American goodwill, ignored Messersmith's pleadings. The boycott faction looked to President Roosevelt, a famous defender of the Jews and human rights. But Roosevelt's detractors already considered him a bit too "Jew-friendly," and his advisers convinced him that the safest position for him politically was to take no sides.

Finally, on December 8, 1935, the AAU voted, by the thinnest of margins, to participate. A Swedish colleague of Brundage's on the IOC cabled him congratulations on foiling "the dirty Jews and politicians." The other countries quickly fell in line, and the Berlin Olympics were on.

Under Goebbels's direction, Berlin underwent a massive whitewashing. "Undesirables" were removed from the city streets and sent to detention centers. (The most prominent of these was the newly opened Sachsenhausen concentration camp, just thirty kilometers north of the city center in the suburb of Oranienburg, soon to become a final destination for many of Germany's homosexuals.) All of the "Jews Forbidden" and "Don't Buy from Jews" signs disappeared, replaced by countless Olympic and Swastika banners. ("One wonders," wrote the African American *New York World*, "if the next Olympics were to take place in Atlanta, Georgia, or almost any one of the states below the Mason-Dixon Line, would the 'powers that be' remove signs in the railroad stations reading, 'Whites on this side, Colored on that side'?") The virulently anti-Semitic newspaper *Der Stürmer* was removed from newsstands, and SS storm troopers were ordered to refrain from attacking or rounding up Jews for a few weeks, and to be gentle and courteous to all, which greatly amused the foreign correspondents who knew better. (As the blackshirts smiled, though, they hummed the tune of the song that had been going around the barracks: "*Wann die Olympiade ist vorbei, / schlagen wir die Juden zu Brei*" [When the Olympics are over, we'll beat the Jews to a pulp].)

The authorities also invited back to Berlin some seven thousand banned prostitutes to bring to twenty-five thousand the number ready to address the needs of Olympic visitors. Some gay bars were even allowed to temporarily reopen—as if world opinion looked favorably on such establishments—and the Berlin police were instructed to leave homosexuals, especially foreign visitors, alone for the interim. Remarkably, the great German hope in the women's high jump, Dora Ratjen, was a male transvestite—as was the Polish silver medalist in the women's 100-meter dash, Stanislawa Walasiewiczówna! Ratjen, however, failed to win a medal and was discovered and disgraced (though he did survive the Holocaust) after winning the 1938 European championship.

All the events were sold out. Not only was there no boycott, but foreign ticket sales were strong; they had soared even after Hitler invaded the Rhineland in March 1936. Leni Riefenstahl, Hitler's favorite filmmaker, who had glorified the Nazis in her brilliant but later infamous *Triumph of the Will*, captured virtually every moment of the Olympics on film and later whittled it down to the four-hour film *Olympia*, which was a powerful propaganda tool for Hitler's Germany in theaters all over the world (except for England and the United States). And although legend has it that Jesse Owens's four gold medals destroyed Hitler's dream to prove Aryan superiority, the fact is that Goebbels's Olympics were a great success. The Germans won the most medals by far, outdistancing the usual winner America by 89-56. "Germany stands far and away on top with 33 gold medals," wrote Goebbels in his diary afterward. "[We are] the premier sports nation in the world. This is wonderful!" And while visitors should have taken heed of the artillery booming dramatically in the distance during the closing ceremonies, they instead naïvely came away with an impression of Nazi Germany as the most vibrant, friendly, and salubrious of nations.

As for the famous story of Hitler snubbing Owens after his victories, the fact is that Hitler, faced with the choice of personally congratulating all the medalists, Jews and blacks included, or none of them, decided on the latter option. Owens never felt insulted by the Nazi leader and liked to tell the story, probably untrue, of Hitler acknowledging him from his box with a wave. Back home, where he faced much worse ostracism than he ever did in Berlin, Owens campaigned later that year for Republican Alf Landon against Roosevelt, calling Hitler "a man of dignity" while dismissing Roosevelt as "a socialist."

Every day of the Olympics, spectators had filed past a statue of Max Schmeling that had been hastily created and placed at the Reichssportfeld in honor of the boxer's astonishing knockout of Joe Louis at Yankee Stadium on June 16. Schmeling, Gottfried Cramm's old acquaintance from the Roxy Sportsbar, had gained superstardom in Germany when he became heavyweight champion of the world in 1930. But he had won that fight by disqualification when his opponent, Jack Sharkey, hit him below the belt, sending him to the canvas in pain. He defended his title successfully once, but in 1932 he lost it to Sharkey in a controversial split decision. ("We was robbed!" his manager Joe Jacobs famously shouted.) Since then Schmeling had remained one of the top heavyweights, but by 1936 he was considered well past his prime and lucky even to get a chance against the up-and-coming young American, Louis.

Schmeling, with the "high cheek bones of an Indian" and an "almost Neanderthal slope to his brow," was hardly the Aryan paradigm. Furthermore, his insistence on retaining Jacobs, as crass and pushy a caricature of a New York Jew as ever there was, as his manager for his many fights on U.S. soil was something of an embarrassment to the Nazis. But Schmeling, the son of a shipworker who counted many artists and intellectuals among his friends, was a skilled chameleon. When in America, he palled around with Jacobs and other prominent Jews and even accompanied his manager to synagogue. Yet he managed to pacify the Nazis and even become a favorite of Goebbels and Hitler, appearing at Nazi rallies and flashing the Nazi salute when necessary but never joining the Nazi Party. Apparently the Nazis accepted Schmeling's relationship with Jacobs as a necessary evil, the price to be paid for bringing home all those American dollars.

James Braddock was the current world heavyweight champ but was completely overshadowed in the public consciousness by Joe Louis.

Louis, twenty-two, was undefeated in twenty-six professional bouts and already was considered by many the greatest boxer ever. An enormous idol for black America, his income had risen to $400,000 in 1935, and he was still on the ascent. White crowds invariably jeered him and cheered against him wherever he went, and even now, when he faced the Nazis' man, many American whites were rooting for Schmeling. The Jewish community, however, tried to organize a boycott of the fight, not wanting to put any American money in the Nazi coffers. "While condemning Hitler," countered the black *Amsterdam News,* "let us remember that there is nothing he is now doing to the Jews that has not been done by the United States on a longer, vaster and more brutal scale to its black citizens." Ralph Bunche too was writing that year about the parallels between Nazi policies and racism at home, which he called "the great American shibboleth. . . . Racial crises threaten not only the future of the United States but the peace of the world."

Hitler may not have been much of a sports fan, but he did like boxing, which he saw as perfect training for his young Nazi fighters. "There is no sport," he wrote in *Mein Kampf,* "that cultivates a spirit of aggressiveness, that demands lightning-quick decisiveness, that develops the body to such steely smoothness [as boxing]." As such, boxing had risen to become the most popular sport in Germany, and Schmeling-Louis was the sporting event of 1936. It was broadcast live all over the country at three in the morning, and Hitler had ordered that his radio be in perfect working order so he could listen in his private railroad car en route to Munich. Schmeling's wife, the movie star Anny Ondra, listened with Goebbels and his wife (and reporters and photographers) at their home. "It is every German's obligation to stay up tonight," repeated a radio announcer throughout the evening of June 16. "Max will fight overseas with a Negro for the hegemony of the white race!"

And yet almost no one, in Germany or elsewhere, picked Schmeling to win. He was over the hill, and the Brown Bomber was unstoppable. American reporters advised him to practice his fall to the canvas, and even German papers, who described Louis as lazy and having no conception of honor, gave Schmeling little chance.

But Schmeling had discovered a weakness in Louis, a habitual dropping of the left hand that left him vulnerable to repeated right crosses. And before a screaming Yankee Stadium crowd and a world-wide radio audience of many millions, he made his observation pay off. Though Louis won the early rounds, Schmeling kept pounding away with his right, and by the twelfth round he had reduced the Bomber to a blinded, bloody mess. Finally Louis went down and could not get up.

Louis would get his revenge, knocking Schmeling out in the first round the next time they met, in 1938, but for the moment the Germans, and German sports, were on top of the world. In the dressing room Schmeling received congratulatory cables from Hitler, Göring, and Goebbels: "I know that you have fought for Germany. Your victory is a German victory. We are proud of you." He soared home in style, on the zeppelin *Hindenburg,* and was received personally in Berlin by the Führer, who watched the film of the fight with him, slapping his thigh with delight as each right cross jolted the American's face. Two months later the movie *Max Schmeling's Victory—A German Victory* was shown in English at Berlin theaters throughout the Olympics.

If SCHMELING WAS, IN THAT SUMMER OF 1936, "THE MOST FAMOUS and best loved athlete in modern German history," Gottfried von Cramm was not far behind. Ever since he won the French Championships in 1934, he had been recognized as Germany's most accomplished tennis player ever. In 1935 he led Germany to within a hair of the Davis Cup Challenge Round, and although the team lost to the United States, Cramm cemented his reputation as "the Gentleman of Wimbledon" with his famous "tipped ball" admission in the pivotal doubles match. Then in the spring of 1936, with Schmeling versus Louis still a wisp of a hope for German fans, Cramm won at Roland Garros for the second time.

The year before, he had been uncrowned in the final by Fred Perry in four sets. Perry had begun his reign over the tennis world by winning the 1934 Australian, Wimbledon, and U.S. titles, and by beating Cramm he added his only French championship to his résumé. In 1936 Cramm got his chance for revenge, as he and Perry moved through to the final with relative ease.

On an unusually cool Paris afternoon the two champions battled evenly for four sets. But as he had done so often, Cramm seemed to become fresher and stronger in the fifth set. Two years before, in the final here against Crawford, he had won nine of the last twelve games after being down match point in the fourth. In 1935, in the semifinal against Bunny Austin, he had dominated the fifth set, six-love. Now once again, even against one of the all-time greats at his absolute peak, Cramm's unceasing training paid off. "Firing a devastating attack that observing critics pronounced as almost perfect," rushing the net at every opportunity, he ran off six straight games to become French champion again, six-love in the fifth.

After the trophy ceremony, as he entered the locker room and accepted the handshakes and shouted congratulations of Kleinschroth and Henkel, he was handed a telegram: "Hearty congratulations on your victory against the strongest Europeans. I invite you to carry Germany's colors to America. Reichssportführer Tschammer und Osten."

It was a joyous conclusion to a personally tumultuous spring. On March 15, realizing that returning to Berlin to see Gottfried and to try to salvage his family's savings was no longer safe, Manasse Herbst had finally left Germany for good. Gottfried again promised to try to continue sending small amounts of money out of the savings Manasse had entrusted to him. In addition to the bits he had sent from foreign shores while playing tournaments, he had also sent some to his brother-in-law in London, and had instructed Manasse to retrieve it there. But it was getting more and more dangerous. Hitler had recently announced a new four-year economic plan, designed to ready the nation economically for war, and one of its main tenets was the stanching of currency leaving the country. "Everything in any way connected with foreign exchange is *verboten*," wrote one legal expert, "and one encounters the most bizarre difficulties. . . . Judges themselves are bewildered by the endless restrictions, laws, regulations, and decrees concerning foreign exchange." Even sports stars had to toe the line; recently the head of German boxing had had to apply for special permission to take the equivalent of ten pounds sterling out of the country.

Two days after Manasse left Berlin for the last time, Gottfried's father died. Gottfried had been on the Riviera in February, playing the circuit, and had moved on to Egypt to try the Cairo and Alexandria tournaments for the first time. There he received a telegram. His father's cancer had suddenly grown worse, and Gottfried should return home immediately. On March 17, in the hospital in Hanover, the Baron Burghard von Cramm passed away. He was sixty-two.

Gottfried's had been a charmed life in most ways, but now, at the age of twenty-six, that sheltered existence was bombarded with the first deep sadnesses and difficulties. Political pressures, partings with loved ones, the first close death. It all seemed to be happening at once, as if even the loss of his father were a consequence of the noose of fascism tightening around his homeland.

Six weeks later, in late April, Cramm was in Barcelona with the German team to play the first round of the Davis Cup against Spain. Herbst met him there, and they were able to spend several nights together in Gottfried's hotel. The German tennis squad was not expected to have any trouble with Spain, the highlight being the final appearance in the Davis Cup of forty-year-old Manual Alonso, Spain's greatest player ever. And in fact the Germans swept the first three matches on the red clay of the Real Club de Tenis de Turo easily to secure the win. However, on the night after the doubles match, as they celebrated their modest victory, Gottfried received yet another telegram. It was from Lisa, asking him for a divorce.

He could not have been surprised. She was well aware of his true proclivities, and although they were fond of each other, they both knew the marriage was a facade. He also knew she had fallen in love with the ice hockey superstar Gustav Jaenecke. Though he was an accomplished tennis player as well and had played on the Davis Cup team in '33, Jaenecke was absolutely revered on the hockey rink, where "he could shoot from any direction, and it was as if his skates were grown on his feet like the pedestal on Bismarck's statue." So she was going to leave Germany's greatest tennis player for its premier hockey star. He couldn't be bitter; he liked Gustav too and wished them well. But still the breakup was painful. He did love Lisa and wished he could have been more to her. The divorce would bring sorrow to his mother, on top of mourning for her husband. And now that all pretense of being a happily married heterosexual man would be gone, Himmler and his goons would be watching him ever more closely.

The next day he had to go back out on the clay and play a dead rubber against Enrique Maier, the current number-one Spanish player. Maier, a Barcelonan of German heritage, was a good friend of Gottfried's, and they had often played doubles together. But Gottfried had never lost to him. On this day, however, he dropped three quick sets to Maier, the Germans' only loss, in fact Cramm's only Davis Cup singles loss all year. To be told his marriage was over right in the middle of his bittersweet reunion with Manasse—who knew when they would ever see each other again?—and so soon after losing his father. . . . It was too much for the moment. He showed no emotion on the court, said not a word about it to reporters. He simply lost.

A month later, though, he had assimilated his misfortunes and come to terms with his new, more precarious existence. In Paris, at Roland Garros, he was a greater player than ever, recording his amazing six-love fifth set over Perry in the finals. And then it was on to Wimbledon, where he was seeded second and hoped finally to reach his childhood dream of becoming world champion. Only Perry had stopped him last year, and now he had finally beaten the Englishman, an important hurdle to overcome.

Cramm had some good-natured revenge over Maier in the fourth round, beat the declining Jack Crawford easily in the quarters, and outgunned Bunny Austin in a routine four-set semifinal. Perry, still solidly number one in the world despite his loss to Cramm in Paris, lost only one set in reaching the final. That was in the first set of his "masterpiece of savagery," the semifinal against the emergent young Don Budge.

Gottfried woke up that morning of his second Wimbledon final, July 3, 1936, in his ornate room at the Savoy, one of London's most opulent hotels and always Tilden's choice as well. In the adjoining room was his wife Lisa, still his friend, still willing to put up a good show for the public until the divorce came through. They breakfasted together in his room; she may have laughed and slid the *Daily Telegraph* over to him: ". . . There is also the factor that Perry is not the phlegmatic philosopher, like the German, where doubtful decisions are concerned. His democratic nature rebels inwardly against any feeling of injustice, though the linesman may not actually have erred."

Just like Bill. Perry did seem to emulate some of Tilden's on-court mannerisms, particularly his hands-on-hips glaring at officials. He also knew, like Tilden, how to work the crowd: he would wave to famous friends in the gallery, josh around with the ball boys, and even chat with folks in the box seats when he was ahead. But also, like Big Bill, he could forget the joviality when he needed to and turn on the heat of his awe-inspiring game.

It was almost noon, a cool and damp morning after a rainy night, when Gottfried and Lisa got into the limo sent from the All England Club. The weather boded well for Cramm: as the *Telegraph* had reminded him, the damp grass would not only play a little slower, it would allow him to "indulge his Continental habit of sliding for the last precious foot," as he was used to doing on clay. (Robert Twynam's assessments notwithstanding, clay-court players—even great ones— like to slide.) And maybe it would slow down the locomotive-fast Perry, who loved a nice dry grass court.

Gottfried would have been staring through droplets on the side window, musing on these thoughts, as the Bentley rolled down the Strand toward Trafalgar Square. Suddenly a black taxicab streaked onto the road in front of them without stopping. The Cramms' driver swerved left and stamped on the brakes, avoiding the taxi and coming to a stop against the curb. Gottfried and Lisa were thrown forward against the front seat. They weren't injured, but it wasn't the sort of fright one wanted on the way to play the Wimbledon final. Lisa in particular was rattled and took the rest of the ride to regain her composure.

Perry was already in the locker room when Cramm finally arrived. Gottfried greeted him and told him about the near-accident, perhaps joking about how his wife had found a way to get all the attention even when he was in the Wimbledon final. But their repartee was broken by a sudden cry from Cramm. His right thigh was cramping badly. This was what happened to his opponents in fifth sets on brutally hot days; it didn't happen to *him*, and certainly not in the locker room before the match. But perhaps the cold weather, recent tensions . . . maybe he hadn't been eating as well as he should. In any case, there he was before the biggest match of his life, writhing on the floor trying to stretch out his leg. Perry tried to help, and then a trainer came running across the locker room, got the muscle stretched out, and massaged it for a few minutes. Gottfried gave the okay, and right on schedule at two P.M. he and Perry followed Ted Tinling under the Kipling quotation that famously hangs over the entrance from the players' dressing room to Centre Court: "If you can meet with triumph and disaster and treat those two impostors just the same . . ."

The gates had been closed for two hours. The stands were packed right down to the last inch of standing room for "what was expected to be the hardest-fought final in the history of the Wimbledon tournaments." And in the very first game it appeared the promise would be fulfilled. Both players crushed the ball at full tilt, corner to corner, waiting for a short ball to attack the net. The crowd's enthusiasm, held in check for hours, came bursting out, and the umpire had to call for quiet repeatedly between points. Perry never had such a time holding serve. Nine times the score reverted to deuce, until finally, on the twenty-fourth point, Perry took the game on a ball that tipped the net and fell over. The crowd stood and cheered as the players changed ends.

But then, on his very first serve of the match, as he twisted back to deliver his famous American Twist, Cramm felt something go in his thigh. The muscle that had cramped in the locker room and then stretched every way possible in that torturous first game had finally given way. More likely the "cramp" had been a muscle strain incurred during his automobile accident, the pain masked initially by a rush of adrenaline and other hormones. Then, with another pain-numbing hormone rush—the thrill of stepping onto Centre Court for the Wimbledon final—he had ignored the injury, run hard, and torn the muscle. He managed to hold his serve, but the pain was getting worse. With each point, he was less able to run down Perry's shots. The Englishman ran out the first set six-one.

Everyone in the stadium could see something was wrong with Cramm. He refused to betray the slightest limp, but he looked pale, and by the second set he was hardly running at all. Perry even asked him what was wrong as they switched sides, but Cramm only smiled and said he was fine. Nonsense, said Perry, you're obviously hurt. Please get some treatment. I don't mind at all. No, Cramm waved him off, they should play on. "Play shall be continuous," said the rules, and that was how he would play. Several times Perry enjoined him to take a break and get treatment, but Cramm refused.

Perry didn't want to win his second Wimbledon because of an injured opponent, but he also wasn't going to take it easy on one. He knew that any player worth his salt would consider it an insult to be coddled on court, and he was certainly right in the case of Cramm. He continued to pound the ball from corner to corner, and the German merely smiled and acknowledged his appreciation of the fine strokes. The audience sat quietly in their seats, stunned in disappointment, and clapped politely after points. When it was over, 6-1, 6-1, 6-0 in forty-five minutes, they stood for the first time since the opening game and cheered their countryman for his third straight title.

Several tournament officials surrounded the peaked German at his courtside chair, and then one of them said a few words to the chair umpire. "Ladies and Gentlemen," the umpire then spoke into his microphone, "Baron von Cramm strained a muscle in a thigh in his first service of the match today. He would like you to know that he is sorry he could not play better."

As they walked off court, Perry seemed as disappointed as the spectators, a fact not lost on Cramm. "I'm afraid there was only one game for me today," he told a reporter in the dressing room. "But I am sorrier for Perry and the crowd than I am for myself." (Perry, however, had no regrets. "I was always a believer," he said, "in stamping on my opponent if I got him down. . . . If I could have beaten him six-minus-one instead of six-love, I would have done.")

A couple weeks later Cramm was back at Wimbledon, all healed, for the 1936 Davis Cup Interzone Final, this time against the Australians. Unfortunately, although Cramm was fit, Henkel had spent the intervening week in bed with the flu and was unable to make much of an impact. He defaulted after two sets to Crawford, he and Cramm lost in four sets to Crawford and McGrath, and then he lost the clincher to McGrath in four. But on the opening day Cramm delivered one of his greatest performances, for which he would long be remembered in England.

He was paired against Adrian Quist, the young South Australian who at twenty-three had just that year become national champion and had been seeded third at Wimbledon, right behind Cramm. On this stormy day, gale winds were blowing through Wimbledon, perhaps adding to Henkel's misery in his opening-match default. But Cramm and Quist, "adjusting themselves astonishingly to the violent eccentricities of the wind, at times half blinded by spirals of dust," managed to wage a "Homeric battle," "a first-class heartbreaker," spanning three hours, sixty games, and fourteen match points.

After winning the first set six-four, Quist sprained his ankle early in the second set, and it appeared he might not be able to continue. But there was Cramm, crossing the net to tend to his fallen opponent, and this time it was the German offering extra time to deal with an injury. To the crowd's relief, the Australians accepted the offer, and before too long Quist was ready to carry on. Two hours later they were deep in the fifth set. Cramm had eight match points, Quist five, but neither could quite pull it off. Finally, on his ninth, Cramm hit a twist serve that the wind transformed into an unreturnable corkscrew, and it was over, 4-6, 6-4, 4-6, 6-4, 11-9. "The spectators stood from their seats, almost in delirium from the tension." The Gentleman of Wimbledon had won them over again. One German reporter was moved to declare, "his manner is so sympathetic and his game is so good, that if Perry had to give up his title, the English would prefer it go to von Cramm. Even if he never wins Wimbledon, he would get the prize for the best tennis manners. And in this way he does his country a greater service than if he merely took Perry's crown away."

Back home, Gottfried wondered if the authorities were seeing things the same way. Two straight losses in the Wimbledon final, two years coming up short in the Interzone Final. At what point would his usefulness as a propaganda tool be outweighed by his danger as a subversive element? Though he had continued to represent the regime, at least in their eyes, he had also been edging dangerously close to overt defiance. On several occasions he had made quips to foreign reporters about the cost to the Davis Cup team of losing Prenn. And he had repeatedly refused to join the Nazi Party. Göring in particular, an avid tennis player and influential member of the Rot-Weiss Club (influential since 1933, anyway), had been imploring him to make his patriotism clear by joining the party, implying strongly that such a move might go a long way in securing his own safety. Cramm's principled obstinacy in refusing resulted in an apocryphal story that was often repeated and published in later years, in which Göring produced the mortgages, held by Jewish banks, on the various von Cramm estates and tore them into pieces. "Now you are free," he told the baron. "If this is the way the Nazis do business," Cramm is supposed to have said, "I'll *never* join the party. And if I outlive the Nazis, I'll honor those notes as best I can."

He did his best to keep his private life hidden, tried to keep a low profile. "He was always pleading," remembered one friend, "no interviews, no articles, no sensationalism of any kind!" But he was so polite that it was difficult for him to turn down journalists—and even more difficult to stop loose talk. It got back to him that Peter Herbinger had been telling people that he and Gottfried were lovers. Peter, that slender blond boy from the Barthels' tennis club. Hans Barthel, one of the teaching pros at Rot-Weiss, also ran a small private tennis club at two lovely red-clay courts behind his apartment building on Zähringerstrasse, near the Ku'damm. He had taken Gottfried over there one day to show him. Peter and his older brother often played there, and Peter had given Gottfried a ride home, zooming through Charlottenburg in his MG, scarf flying behind his head like he was a pilot in the Great War. He said he was the fashion designer Hans Gehringer's "steady friend." Hmm, Peter. One of us, and half-Jewish too. What would become of him?

CONSIDERING THE HOMOPHOBIC RAMPAGE THE NAZIS HAD BEEN on ever since taking power, it was remarkable that they let Bill Tilden even play in Germany, much less train the German team. Tilden, in between playing professional tournaments in England and France in July and August 1936, was working out with the German Davis Cup team and their official trainer, Hans Nüsslein. His life since turning pro at the start of 1931 had been a ceaseless global whirlwind of tennis. It seemed he was always playing somewhere, from Miami in the winter sun, to the Mobile Country Club in the drizzle, to Madison Square Garden, to Europe. All over the United States life savings were evanescing as banks failed, working people's salaries plummeted, and soup lines wrapped around city blocks; even Babe Ruth had to swallow a ten-thousand-dollar pay cut. But Tilden earned as much as a movie star and somehow managed to spend it just as fast.

There had been no professional tennis at all until Suzanne Lenglen was signed for $50,000 in 1926 to tour against Mary K. Browne, Tilden's old mixed-doubles partner and U.S. champ from 1912 to 1914. Tilden, however, continued to turn down exorbitant offers throughout the 1920s. It wasn't until he finally turned pro that professional men's tennis made it into the headlines.

He began by demolishing the current world pro champion, Karel Kozeluh, in a one-on-one tour. Almost fourteen thousand showed up at Madison Square Garden in February 1931 to watch thirty-seven-year-old Big Bill take on the playful, diminutive Czech, who drove opponents wild with his unerring baseline game and loved to "take the crowd into his confidence" with joking asides and bits of pantomime. But Big Bill, playing as well as ever, mopped him up there and again in sixteen straight matches from Boston to Youngstown to Chicago to Omaha to Los Angeles. He ended up winning sixty-three out of seventy-six matches, and then they headed for Europe, where they played for huge crowds in Paris, Brussels, Amsterdam, and Berlin.

His old pals Frank Hunter and Vinnie Richards were pros now too, but Tilden made mincemeat of them as well. The opinion of most observers was that Tilden was playing better than ever, and that his old legs, which had once covered a hundred yards in ten seconds, were still the quickest in tennis. "This incredible athlete's . . . youth seems to have been renewed since he turned pro," reported *The New Yorker* from the U.S. Pro Tournament at Forest Hills; "he has never played better than this summer." His off-court game was also better than ever:

> As usual when he wasn't playing, Tilden hurried busily around the grounds and clubhouse, dropping into the press tent to dash off some copy or a telegram, phoning long distance, taking some protégé out on a back court for practice, and stopping at the committee's box to bully the officials a little in his best manner, just to pass the time.

In his first six months as a pro, Tilden made more than $100,000, a fortune in Depression dollars. In addition to all those winner's checks, he was making instructional films in Hollywood and endorsing Spalding tennis shoes ($3.50 at the Spalding store on Nassau Street in New

York), Tilden Championship Tennis String, and other items. Soon the Spalding Top-Flite racket ($15 strung) that he had been using in recent years became the "Tilden Top-Flite."

But the money never lasted long. For one thing, he kept his suite at the Algonquin year round, though he was there one month at the most. And his hotel bills on the road, according to Vinnie Richards, were "staggering":

> An hour after checking in he has usually run up telephone charges of fifty to a hundred dollars, calling up people in New York, California—sometimes Europe. He eats three-dollar breakfasts and buys them for other people. He sends telegrams and cables by the ream. He will lose seventy-five dollars at an evening's bridge.

He formed a company, Tilden Tennis Tours, Inc., and led a troupe of players to every tennis corner of the country, but his business acumen never matched his tennis skills. He never had a checking account, paying players, umpires, secretaries, and other promoters in cash. And he was scrupulous, paying every dime even if the gates were disappointing. By the end of 1931 he was nearly broke.

No matter. "He was always broke," remembered Richards, "but there always seemed to be more where the last came from."

> Bill went right on playing tennis, writing articles, playing bridge, racing around the country in fast cars, and living in the style to which he was accustomed. . . . When Tilden tours he is happiest. It is his troupe. He is the star and the impresario. He is the boss and he is also the temperamental leading man. Rehearsal at ten sharp and bring two rackets.

In 1932 he toured with the top German pro, Nüsslein. Hans "Hanne" Nüsslein, only twenty-two years old and one of the top international pros, might have been one of the world's top amateur champions and a powerful Davis Cup teammate for Cramm through the mid-1930s. But when he was sixteen and the top young player at his club in Nuremburg, he picked up a few extra marks giving informal lessons to some club members. Someone from a rival club informed the German Lawn Tennis Federation, and Nüsslein was summarily banned from amateur tennis for life. Deprived of the dream of playing Wimbledon and Davis Cup, he became a coach and a professional player. Solid and steady to extremes, "a machine with a brain, and one of the best tennis players I ever saw," according to Tilden, Nüsslein went on to win the French, British, and U.S. professional titles. But in 1932 Tilden had no more trouble with him than he had with Kozeluh. In 1933 he convinced Cochet to turn pro and promptly went to Paris and clobbered him 6-3, 6-4, 6-2 in less than an hour. Then when he was in Berlin, he beat Cramm convincingly in an exhibition match at Rot-Weiss, just months before Cramm won his first French title. It was like his amateur glory years all over again.

In 1934 Ellsworth Vines signed a contract to tour against Tilden, and everyone agreed that finally the master would be brought down. After all, he was about to turn forty-one, and Vines was twenty-two, just coming into his prime. On January 10 the largest tennis crowd in American history, sixteen thousand, packed the seats and aisles of Madison Square Garden to see their first battle. Vines's performance was "far superior to his showing as an amateur," according to the *New York Times*. Tilden won 8-6, 6-3, 6-2.

Another time in Buffalo, he beat Vines in a long five-setter, including one 17-15 set. Vines barely made it back to his hotel room, where he collapsed on his bed.

> In bursts Bill, looking like he just stepped out of the barber's chair. He's had his shower . . . is all decked out in that long polo coat with a bushel of racquets under his arm. He's pulling out for Cincinnati—right then at one a.m.—with an eight-hour drive staring him in the face. His only admonition was, "Be there . . . on time, boy! We should do well in Cincinnati!" . . . and he was gone.

The grueling tour of seventy-three one-night stands finally wore the old man down, and Vines took the tour 47-26, but for one night, well rested, "the miracle man of tennis" was still the world's greatest.

Tilden spent the 1930s on the road, running from his lost parents, his lost brother, his repressed desires. Night after night, month after month, on trains and boats, driving highways and back roads, constantly promoting new tours, constantly playing tennis. Although from 1934 on he was never the tour champion, he was always the top draw. Each year new top amateurs were signed to take on him or Vines, but it was Big Bill the people really came to see. "The difficulty with this scheme," wrote one observer, "lies in the sad fact that Tilden, one day, may be altogether unable to hobble out on the court. He may even die. Nevertheless, the whole being of professional tennis is built around him at this moment, and I do not think the Garden would have been half-filled without his celebrated presence, without the oddly spectacular and, to my mind, feminine perfection of his game."

As the years went by, new box office stars such as Perry and Budge did join the pro ranks. But even as Tilden, in his mid-forties, slid further and further down the world rankings, he remained the greatest star. "All they can do is beat him," wrote Al Laney in the *Herald Tribune*. "They cannot ever be his equal."

"I am the most ardent admirer of the German people," declared Tilden as late as 1938. "I would rather play in Berlin than any city in the world." German tennis fans returned the adulation, particularly after he partnered their beloved Cilly Aussem, the beautiful and spirited German women's champion, to the French mixed-doubles title in 1930. (It was not unusual even then for mixed doubles to feature international partnerships.) After turning professional later that year, he became Aussem's coach and guided her to the French and Wimbledon singles crowns in 1931. And in late 1935 Tilden helped train the German Davis Cup team for the first time. Gottfried Cramm was happy to have his friend and mentor working with the German team, and Bill had always felt at home in Germany, where crowds thronged him wherever he went, and where he enjoyed an acceptance and even hero's idolatry that never quite happened in America.

Until recently, he'd also taken pleasure in Germany's more tolerant society; he and Gottfried spent much time together sampling the Berlin nightlife. When they had met in 1928, Cramm remembered many years later, "I was immediately accepted as an integral member of the entourage of the Berlin complement, which he, the king, assembled in all the world's tennis centers." One year early on in their friendship, when the American Davis Cup team was in town, Bill and Gottfried took Johnny Van Ryn and Wilmer Allison, soon to become the most famous American doubles team, to one of their favorite clubs for dinner. Van Ryn and Allison were twenty-four-year-old college grads, and seasoned travelers on the world tennis tour, but they "had never seen anything like this," as Van Ryn recalled. "There were all these tables, each with a telephone so you could call someone at another table. . . . You would see these fellows with lipstick on, dialing each other and going 'Woo-woo!' We were shocked."

"Berlin Bill loved," Gottfried smiled as he remembered. "Even for a few years after the Nazis took over, it was unique, cosmopolitan, tolerant—a dynamic momentum that could not be killed with one stroke. And Bill basked in the adoration, paid him more abundantly here than in any other center."

Their evenings would invariably begin in the rooftop bar at Tilden's hotel, the cosmopolitan Eden. Though Tilden was an adamant teetotaler, he was the life of the party. As his friends tossed back cocktails, he washed down the first of the evening's steaks (he might have three or so before morning) with a pot of coffee, chain-smoking cigarettes as he regaled them with his unassailable opinions on everything from modern art to the latest gossip to, of course, tennis officials.

From there they would sashay from one bistro and nightclub to another, and although Tilden only sipped ice water (in Paris in '27 they had started ordering water by saying, "I'll have a Tilden"), he and the others enjoyed "the limitless range of attractions," as Cramm tactfully put it, "which appealed to a voracious liver, as he was." Back at the Eden, Tilden would entertain the last stragglers of the night's party. The next morning, though, he would be the first one at the tennis courts, ready for exhibition matches or a few hours of practice. "Everyone assumed that Bill just didn't need any sleep at all."

It was only in Weimar Berlin that Tilden had first been able to relax, let his hair down, and experience anything close to an openly homosexual lifestyle. But by 1936, although Berlin still sported a glittering nightlife—and a few outposts of *Girlkultur*, most notably the

Suzanne Lenglen and Bill Tilden, tennis's first idols, in 1920. By 1922 Wimbledon had built a new Centre Court and grounds, on the present site, to accommodate the demand these two superstars created. *(Library of Congress)*

Tilden in his prime simply *was* tennis, hardly losing a match from 1920 to 1926. Here he is seen helping win the Davis Cup for the third straight year, in 1922. *(Library of Congress)*

Tilden always swore he would give up tennis for a life in the theater. His favorite place to play tennis was Charlie Chaplin's court in the Hollywood Hills, and Chaplin *(horizontal)* would be one of the only friends to stand by him in the end. To the right are Douglas Fairbanks, another close friend and tennis nut, and Spanish champion Manuel Alonso.

Portrait of Gottfried von Cramm. "Like a comet a new star fell from the tennis heavens," wrote one French newspaper. "If he plays tennis as well as he looks," remarked a female member of his tennis club, "he'll be world champion." *(The Granger Collection, New York)*

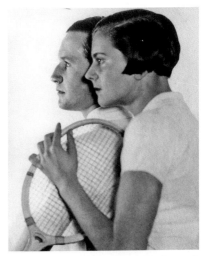

Cramm married childhood friend Lisa von Dobeneck in 1930, and soon they were the toast of Berlin, posing here for the cover of the popular weekly *Berliner Illustrirte Zeitung*. In public at least, their life and marriage seemed charmed. *(The Granger Collection, New York)*

Transvestites at the Eldorado nightclub. Berlin had been a haven for homosexuals since the eighteenth century, and in Weimar Berlin the Eldorado was a hot spot for revelers of all sorts. Cramm's relationship with a Jewish actor he met there would prove perilous to the tennis star. *(The Granger Collection, New York)*

Daniel Prenn, a Jewish refugee from Russia, was Germany's greatest player in the early 1930s. He and Cramm, playing singles and doubles, came close to bringing Germany the Davis Cup in 1932. But Hitler's rise to power meant the end of Prenn's career, and he was forced to emigrate to England. *(The Granger Collection, New York)*

The all-American redhead: early Don Budge pose, 1934, age nineteen. Unlike Tilden and Cramm, Budge grew up in modest surroundings in Oakland and learned to play on the gravel courts of a local public park. In 1935 he took the tennis world by storm, reaching the semifinals at Wimbledon in his first attempt and leading the United States to the Davis Cup Challenge Round. *(Jeff Budge)*

From the time they were sixteen, Budge and Gene Mako were best friends and doubles partners. In 1935, on their first Davis Cup trip abroad, they impressed with their tennis, their ingenuousness, and their traveling collection of jazz records. "No pair has ever played with more real rhythm." *(Jeff Budge)*

Cramm forced to grin and bear it, greeting the Führer, 1933. The ascension of the Nazis put him in a difficult place. Thousands, including friends of his, were disappearing into concentration camps. But if he were to emigrate like Prenn, or refuse to play for an evil regime, his family (including his quarter-Jewish wife) might be endangered. *(The Granger Collection, New York)*

The 1937 U.S. Davis Cup team in London, posed around their Buick. Captain Walter Pate, in a unique move, housed his team like a family in a rented apartment. *From left:* Bitsy Grant, Pate, Frank Parker, Budge, Mako, Wayne Sabin. *(Jeff Budge)*

In the 1937 Wimbledon Championships, two weeks before the Davis Cup, Cramm and Budge met in the finals, each seeking his first title. The two impeccable sportsmen met at the net afterward. *(The Granger Collection, New York)*

Two weeks later they walked back out on Centre Court to decide the Davis Cup. As though out for a friendly game, the two friends strolled toward the net, spinning a racket to see who would serve first. *(The Granger Collection, New York)*

From the very first point Budge knew he was facing a very different von Cramm than the one he'd faced in the Wimbledon final. Cramm seemed determined to make up for all his near misses at Wimbledon and in the Davis Cup. "He could, at times," said one player, "play the most brilliant tennis imaginable." *(The Granger Collection, New York)*

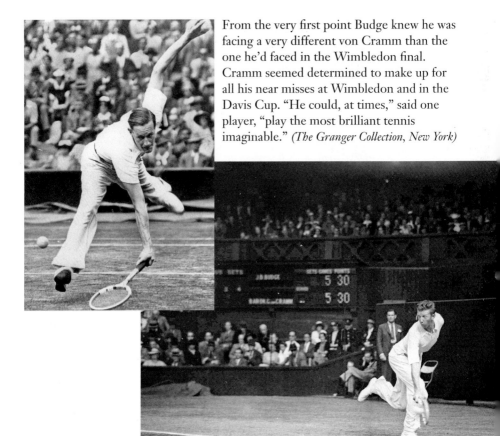

The English crowd, laid low by the Depression and the threat of war, cheered desperately for Cramm—for his charisma, his incomparable manners, and for his disappointments in the past, but also because a German victory seemed the only hope for the English team. Budge stretched for a great return, but with the first set dead even at five-five, thirty-thirty, the crowd was energized. The German had a chance! *(AP/Wide World Photos)*

Budge had greatly improved his conditioning, but Cramm was famous for his staying power. As this best-of-five match went the distance, the advantage seemed to be his. "Fifth sets are mine," he used to tell himself. But today, so much more than tennis was on his mind. *(The Granger Collection, New York)*

After he turned pro Budge flourished financially and otherwise. Gossip columns linked "the Romeo of tennis" to many prominent ladies, but none more impressive (whether the rumors were true or not) than movie star Olivia de Havilland. *(Jeff Budge)*

Tilden, forty-seven, played the part of the frail old man after losing to Budge in a 1940 match to raise money for the Finnish Relief Fund. But the next year the Old Master actually beat the world champ seven times in fifty-four matches. *(AP/Wide World Photos)*

In 1949 Tilden was sent to prison for his second stint in three years, both times for morals violations with teenage boys. At the end of the year, a few days after his release, the press almost unanimously voted him the greatest tennis player of the half-century. Nonetheless, he was ostracized from L.A.'s tennis clubs and had to scratch out a living giving lessons on public courts. *(AP/Wide World Photos)*

Cramm narrowly escaped the fate of most German homosexuals. Prisoners like these, displaying the pink triangle at the Sachsenhausen concentration camp, were singled out for the most debasing and deadly punishments. *(The Granger Collection, New York)*

German soldiers lie dead in the Russian snow. More than four million Germans—and ten million Soviet soldiers—died on the eastern front. Cramm was airlifted out with frostbite, and only 19 of his company of 120 men made it home alive. *(The Granger Collection, New York)*

After the war Cramm returned to Davis Cup play as West Germany's top player. In 1951, at age forty-two, he played his final Wimbledon and made headlines by escorting Barbara Hutton to the tournament. She finally got "her tennis player" in 1951, when they married, but it didn't last. The ill-starred heiress was one of the few friends Cramm was ultimately unable to help. *(The Granger Collection, New York)*

Resi and Haus Vaterland, remained open—the Nazis had shut down most of the gay and lesbian clubs.

The Nazi leaders were determined to rid the Third Reich of what they called "sexual Bolshevism." (Of course, the Soviets called it "fascist perversion," and Stalin had made all homosexual acts punishable with heavy prison sentences.) Ever since the murder of Röhm on the Night of the Long Knives, Germany's homosexuals had known they were under siege. Just a few months later, in October 1934, Himmler's Gestapo sent a letter to police departments all over the country demanding lists of "somehow homosexually active persons," along with their political background. Political opponents were the main targets at first, and if they didn't show up on these lists, a street hustler could always be bribed to testify against them. Furthermore, with the ironically named Law Against Insidious Slander of December 1934, they began encouraging private citizens to denounce others as homosexuals (or political undesirables). More new laws soon allowed the police to take into custody, for an indeterminate length of time, anyone they determined was an enemy of state, including "anti-community minded" people who threatened the "moral fiber" of German youths.

In 1936 Himmler, in a rare speech, crowed, "As National Socialists we are not afraid to fight against this plague within our own ranks. Just as we have readopted the ancient Germanic approach to the question of marriage between alien races, so, too, in our judgment of homosexuality—a symptom of racial degeneracy destructive to our race—we have returned to the guiding Nordic principle that degenerates should be exterminated." The previous year Paragraph 175, the 1871 antihomosexual law, had been broadened. Before, only "actions resembling coitus" had been punishable, but now anything from mutual masturbation down to the merest kiss or touch could be interpreted by the courts as "criminally indecent activity between men" and punished by incarceration. And in 1936 the Gestapo established the Federal Security Department for Combating Abortion and Homosexuality. Gottfried and his friends watched in horror as the numbers of gay men—or at least those denounced as homosexual—disappearing from the streets into prison or, more and more often, to concentration camps, swelled: nine hundred in 1934, more than two thousand in 1935, perhaps nine thousand in 1936. . . .

As the witch hunt reached its peak, denunciations came pouring in. Street hustlers were recruited to inform on their clients and to spy actively on well-known homosexual meeting places, such as the Alexanderplatz train station. But thousands of other denunciations were unsolicited. Jealous girlfriends, feuding neighbors, and business rivals were among the thousands of ordinary Germans who took advantage of the terror to settle scores. Evidence was gravy. A doctor was sentenced to prison after a neighbor reported him letting a young man into his apartment and then drawing the curtains. A senior employee at the Siemens company was accused by a messenger boy of flirting with him; sent to prison for "attempted seduction," he was then transferred to a concentration camp, where he died. All that was needed to get rid of a rival was an anonymous note to the Gestapo; Himmler's henchmen were all too happy to add to their growing lists.

So far they had left Gottfried alone. Again, he had to wonder if it was only his success on the tennis court that had kept him safe. Two French championships in three years, and he and his teammates had been so close these last two years to finally taking the Davis Cup. Certainly they were on the verge.

Word had gotten back to him that Göring was personally protecting him from persecution. It was true that that ridiculous rotund peacock, that "primitive, bounding creature with the limitless appetites of the true parvenu," was perfectly willing to put his own personal tastes above Nazi ideology, whether it be decking himself out in outrageous priceless costumes or gorging himself on luxuries of which princes could only dream. Look at Gustaf Gründgens, one of Germany's greatest actors and an old friend of Göring's wife, the actress Emmy Sonneman. Through her he had become Göring's favorite, sort of his pet thespian. As a result Gründgens, whose numerous homosexual affairs were well known, appeared to be above the law, and Göring had even appointed him director of the State Theater. (Klaus Mann, son of Thomas Mann, had just published his novel *Mephisto*, a thinly disguised portrait of Gründgens, his former colleague and brother-in-law. Klaus, half-Jewish and homosexual, had left for Amsterdam and been stripped of his citizenship in 1933 and was now moving to the

United States.) It was well known that the Gestapo, in a presumed nod to Göring, was not to arrest homosexuals in the theater or other arts without first running it by Himmler.

Göring was similarly attached to athletes and in particular was a tennis fan, so perhaps the rumors were true. But how long would Göring put up with Cramm's refusal to join the party? If he didn't win Wimbledon or the Davis Cup, Göring might quickly lose interest in him. And Himmler's interest he didn't want. The Gestapo chief hated aristocrats almost as much as he hated homosexuals; he dreamed of executing them all and replacing them with a "new nobility" gleaned from his elite black-shirted SS men. Princes were no better than Jews, he said. He would hang all the royals of Prussia and Bavaria in front of the Imperial Palace in Berlin before a cheering crowd of workers. It would be simple to indict them on various charges: espionage and treason, if not sexual perversion. No doubt most of them were guilty anyway. And it was well known that Hitler despised and feared the aristocracy too. "The von Cramms were staunch Hanoverians . . . and monarchist," wrote a friend of Gottfried and his brothers. "They incorporated just about everything the Nazis hated most." Never mind Gottfried's sexuality and his having married a partial Jew.

Well, if Göring wanted to protect him, that was his business. At least Gottfried would never be like Gründgens, selling his soul to the Nazis for the privilege and damnation of being one of their inner circle. It was bad enough that he had to watch the fat fool lord it over his beloved Rot-Weiss Club, bad enough he had to salute him with an outstretched arm and "Heil Hitler!" as he had had to do to the dictator himself when he was presented to him a couple of years ago. But he would never be Göring's pet tennis player.

In April 1937 Gottfried finally heard the knocks on the door. Two Gestapo agents came for him and took him back to their infamous headquarters on Prinz-Albrecht Strasse. There he was questioned for hours regarding a denunciation that had come in. A street hustler in Hanover had signed a statement. He said that often when Cramm was back home in the Hanover area, he would help the tennis star "search for a suitable young man."

Cramm hotly denied the accusation and demanded to be given the satisfaction of confronting his accuser face to face. That would not be necessary, he was told. In any case, there were a number of other "pieces of evidence" in his file. Surely he couldn't deny them all. What other evidence? he asked but was ignored. This is the first I've ever been told of any "denunciations," he said. The two officials looked at each other. One left and shortly came back, whispering something to the other. Well, he said, apparently this is the first time we've had you in for a visit. I had thought otherwise. In any case, you are free to go for the time being, Herr Baron.

Gottfried certainly knew where he stood, if he hadn't before. The next month, in Paris, the German Lawn Tennis Federation ordered him to play only doubles in the French Championships, the tournament that had brought him his greatest fame. It was doubtful that the federation had really made this decision—to give him rest, as they said. Policy regarding German athletes was being debated at the highest levels of the Nazi hierarchy. That same spring of 1937 Max Schmeling sailed to New York to follow up his knockout of Joe Louis with a championship bout against titleholder James Braddock. But although he had agreed to fight Schmeling, Braddock wanted Joe Louis instead. When the champ didn't show up for what was later pegged "the phantom fight," the Germans were livid. "With the Führer this afternoon," wrote Goebbels in his diary when Braddock threatened to be a no-show. "Question if we, ourselves, in the event that Braddock chickens out, should declare Schmeling world champion. I say yes to it. The Americans are the most corrupt people on earth." Whether or not Goebbels was pulling the strings of the tennis authorities, Cramm, the defending champion of France, sat in Paris and watched as his doubles partner, Henkel, won the singles. Even a champion could be expendable.

He did as he was told, made no complaints. His divorce proceedings with Lisa were coming through their final rounds in the courts; by the time the tournament ended, he was officially a single man. Although it was in one sense a relief, this final legal parting from Lisa caused enough stress that he might have been almost glad he wasn't playing the singles. He did play the French doubles with Henkel, and they won the championship. And then in June, in the Davis Cup, they easily beat the Italians in Milan and the Belgians back home to reach the finals of the European Zone. Then it was time for Wimbledon.

Once again, it was a relief to be back in London. Not that England was particularly a haven for homosexuals—they had their own laws, as did the United States—but at least there weren't spies and denouncers on every corner. And Gottfried had good friends here and was treated like a true champion. In public he dined with the German players, often with foreign players as well, and of course Bill Tilden was in town and seemingly omnipresent. Cramm also was seen at All England Club events and even government receptions. One evening at the German Embassy there was a painfully awkward scene that he must have enjoyed in retrospect: a prominent Englishman, chatting with Cramm, Ribbentrop, and a few others, cheerfully praised Gottfried as "Germany's best ambassador."

Somehow, despite his divorce, the growing threat of imprisonment, and a bustling social life in London, once the Wimbledon fortnight began Cramm was able to concentrate on his game. He played some of his finest tennis ever, blazing through to the final. Just as he had last year, he took out Crawford in the quarterfinals and Austin in the semis. Crawford, thought to be well past his prime, stormed back to take the third and fourth sets, but fifth sets belonged to Cramm, and he put the Australian away quickly. The English spectators had been behind Cramm all tournament, and even in the semifinal against Austin, once it became clear the Englishman had no chance, they began cheering Cramm once again, hoping that this year the Gentleman of Wimbledon could finally be the champion.

At least one other American too, besides Tilden, was cheering on the German. Barbara Hutton, the twenty-four-year-old Woolworth heiress and leading lady of the gossip pages, was at Wimbledon all week and attended the finals with her second of seven eventual husbands, Count Curt von Haugwitz-Reventlow. Reventlow, a German-born Danish nobleman who had fought for Germany in the Great War, was, like Cramm, tall and handsome with chiseled features, fluent in five languages, and an accomplished athlete. (He was an expert skier and mountain climber.) But though he had swept Hutton off her feet in 1935, Reventlow had already fallen out of favor. Among other faults, he could never compete in her mind with the charms of Gottfried Cramm.

Gottfried and Barbara had met earlier that year, at the Gezirah Sporting Club in Cairo. Hutton "had a craze for tennis" as a young woman, and although she never became very good, she used a bit of her $50 million inheritance at age twenty-one to practice every day with professionals. When she met Cramm and saw him play, she fell for everything about him: his graceful game, his sophisticated handsomeness, his gentle chivalry. "I loved you the first time I laid eyes on your face," she wrote him later that year. She was married, of course, and whether she saw it or not, Gottfried certainly couldn't love her back in the same way; but they did commence a romance of sorts, in letters and finally that summer at parties at her London mansion, where he was made the guest of honor.

Almost every time Gottfried won a point in the finals against Budge, but especially after his more delicate drop shots and imperious passing shots, Barbara would clap boisterously, attracting looks from nearby spectators, while Reventlow fumed. He kept quiet until they were safely in their Rolls after the match, and then he laid into her with a violent tirade that lasted all the way home. They would divorce the next year, but Hutton would hang on to the man she called "my tennis player" for twenty more years.

In that championship match, of course, Cramm faced the new Don Budge of 1937, whose complete game now seemed unstoppable. Though Cramm jumped out to a great start, firing "jeweled strokes" corner to corner, Budge stormed right back to win in three straight sets. "Both played shots of blinding speed and of the richest blend," and Cramm almost made a comeback in the third set with a salvo of "splendid saving strokes," but the outcome was never really in doubt. The German was the runner-up for the third straight year, and Budge was champion, 6-3, 6-4, 6-2.

Cramm showed no disappointment beneath his gallant smile as he congratulated Budge at the net. He had finally played up to expectations in the finals, but all he had to show for it was a straight-set loss for the third year in a row. He refused to play the part of the tragic loser. "I was quite satisfied with my form today," he told a reporter. "But what can one do against such perfect tennis?"

Cramm hadn't seen Manasse Herbst in a year, since their rendezvous in Barcelona. Now, in London, he was spending much of his time with another young actor. Possibly via Teddy Tinling, whose fashion business "almost owed its survival" during the Depression to the costume demands of big West End productions, he had met Geoffrey Nares, an "elf-like" twenty-year-old fledgling actor and stage designer with a perfectly formed baby face and "dark, melting" brown eyes. The son of one of England's most beloved stage and film actors, Owen Nares, Geoffrey had recently completed a yearlong run at the Globe Theatre in Dodie Smith's *Call It a Day*, in which he played opposite his father in father-son roles.

Owen Nares was surely pleased to see one of his two sons following his path into the theater, especially Geoffrey, who had always seemed so "sad, striving, and rudderless." But any such pride was subsumed in fiery rage at Geoffrey's "unmanly" ways. Sniggers at the theater about Geoffrey and "his tennis champion" must have riled the famous actor, and he issued his son stern warnings about the family name and so on. Geoffrey paid him no mind and, after the older generation retired for the night, drove off to meet Gottfried again.

From friends, or perhaps from Christopher Isherwood himself, who was back in London, they may have heard of the trial of Isherwood's longtime German boyfriend Heinz Neddermeyer, which concluded just as Wimbledon was getting under way. Christopher and Heinz had been wandering about Europe ever since the Nazi takeover in 1933, and Christopher had been desperately trying to get Heinz through the treacherous Nazi emigration nets. A Belgian lawyer had advised that Heinz needed to travel briefly to Trier, the German city closest to the border, to secure emigration papers. In Trier, just as Heinz and the lawyer left the visa office, papers in hand, the Gestapo stopped them and took Heinz away.

This was in May. Now, just a month later, Heinz had been convicted of "mutual onanism" with "the English citizen Ischervood [sic], who unfortunately cannot be brought to justice." Christopher lamented into his diary how Heinz's lawyer had convinced him to confess to a lesser crime than actual coitus: *eine ausgesprochene Sucht zur wechselseitigen Onanie:* " 'a pronounced addiction to reciprocal onanism.' This was the name which their love was to dare to speak, in the face of its enemies!"

Isherwood had secured a good German lawyer, and Heinz got off relatively easy: six months in prison, to be followed by a year of labor service for the state and two years in the army. So at least arrest didn't mean certain death in the camps—not yet, anyway, if you had the right connections. Gottfried must have shuddered as he remembered his hours in the Gestapo interrogation room in April. They had been surprised that he hadn't been there before. Surely they planned to bring him back.

And then, in the Wimbledon locker room before the deciding fifth match against Budge in the Davis Cup, a telephone may have rung. Or not; no one will ever know for sure. Budge, in his later years, loved to tell the story: he and Gottfried were being led from the dressing rooms toward Centre Court by Teddy Tinling, whose immediate concern was getting Budge and Cramm out there quickly, so as not to keep the royals waiting. As Tinling led them along, a telephone rang somewhere. They paid no attention, but just as they were about to pass under the Kipling verse and out onto the court, a locker room attendant came running up. "Mr. von Cramm, long distance for you, sir." Tinling, who had each man by one arm, was having none of it: "Come on, you can't keep Queen Mary waiting."

"But it might be an emergency," said Cramm. Why else would someone phone him just as he was about to begin the most important match of his life? Tinling grumbled but let go, and Cramm walked over to the telephone. "Yes, hello, this is Gottfried Cramm." Then, a few seconds later, *"Ja, mein Führer."* Another pause, followed by *"Ja, mein Führer,"* and the same pattern repeated again. He spoke firmly and respectfully, but without emotion, and he said almost nothing else. A few minutes later he rejoined Tinling and Budge by the door. "Excuse me, gentlemen," he said. "It was Hitler. He wanted to wish me luck." Tinling handed him back his passel of rackets and opened the door, and they stepped onto Centre Court, engulfed by the rising cheers of fourteen thousand.

Cramm always denied the story; a "fairy tale," he called it. Historians find it highly unlikely, and there is no evidence it ever happened. For Gottfried, what did it matter? Whether it happened or not, his situation was the same. According to the German tennis writer Ulrich Kaiser, "it was made clear to him [after his loss in the 1937 Wimbledon final] that his last chance was now the Davis Cup." Even if Hitler had called him, it would have felt like a dream, just one part of this faintly tinged nightmare—no fairy tale—that had been dissolving his life for four years. Hitler didn't phone athletes, but then good German citizens couldn't disappear like fog, for no good reason; it could not be true that so many of the brightest, the finest people of the Fatherland could be driven out by the basest, the lowest criminal element. The past four years couldn't have happened, could they?

O~N A TENNIS COURT, THOUGH, LIFE REMAINED THE SAME. INSIDE~ the dependable white rectangle, everything made sense. So here it is again, the perfect tennis of Don Budge. Gottfried's down four-love in the fourth set of the deciding match of the Interzone Final, after being on the verge of victory. What can one do against such tennis? Play perfect tennis of one's own, and Cramm has done just that in the first two sets, even so just squeaking by, 8-6, 7-5. Then he dropped that close one in the third, but now the Budge juggernaut is rolling. There is no way Cramm is going to break Budge three times in one set, he knows, and that is what he would have to do to win the fourth. He decides to conserve his energy for the fifth set. He puts up little resistance on Budge's next two service games, wins his own without too much exertion, and concedes the set six-two.

Walter Pate has been sipping tea since the beginning of the third set. When Budge takes the fourth to even the match at two sets apiece, Alistair Cooke notes, Pate begins to enjoy his tea. It may be the opinion of Pate, the American team, and the majority of those watching from the stands or listening to the radio, that the German is finished. Budge has surged back into his Wimbledon form, where no man alive could stop him. And what's more, the baron looks beat. He was barely moving for balls near the end of the set.

But Budge knows better. Cramm trains harder than anyone, and it has paid off time and time again in five-set matches. He even told Budge once that anytime a match goes five sets, he figures he has a three-to-one advantage in the fifth. Rather than relax and enjoy his own tea, Budge steels himself for the inevitable Cramm fifth-set surge.

In the stands, though, Bill Tilden is worried. He wonders if the lethargy his friend is displaying is more than savvy strategy. He has seemed thin and drawn, in Tilden's opinion, for months, showing signs of great stress. Tilden knows, of course, about the divorce, but also that marital problems are the least Gottfried has to worry about. In Paris he told Tilden that after Roland Garros, Wimbledon, and the Davis Cup, he was planning an eight-month trip to play the American and Australian championships, among many other tournaments. Tilden spoke up. "You shouldn't play all that tennis this year, Gottfried. You need a rest. Take six months off after the Davis Cup."

Cramm just stared back at him "with the strangest expression in his eyes." "You don't understand, Bill," he said. "I'm playing for my life."

Startled, thinking he must be joking, Tilden smiled. "I mean it," said Gottfried. "The Nazis know how I feel about them. And they know about *me*." He shot Tilden a look. "They won't touch me as long as I'm number one in Germany and winning. But I must win. I can't lose, and I can't quit."

# NO MAN LIVING or DEAD

On June 6, 1937, six weeks be-fore the Budge-Cramm epic, when the American team boarded the SS *Columbus* (a German ship, as it happened) for the crossing to England, Walter Pate lined up his boys on deck for the photographers and newsreel cameras. All were in jacket and tie, except for Mako in his open-necked shirt, holding a couple of jazz records. Just a week earlier the team had wrapped up the American Zone championship with a 5-0 revenge victory over Australia. (Australia, which by default was in the American Zone, had squelched the Americans' Cup hopes the year be-fore, 3-2.) Pate announced that his players would be competing in the Queen's Club warm-up tournament and then of course Wimbledon before the Interzone Final. However, he made clear, "Our one objec-tive on this trip is to bring back the Cup. Everything else will be sec-ondary. It would be nice if one of the boys could win the British championship, but if I feel that any of them is jeopardizing our chances of winning the Cup by playing at Wimbledon, that the strain is taking too much out of him, I will urge him to drop out."

Five days later, on the other side of the Atlantic, the American contingent—Budge, Mako, Frank Parker, Bitsy Grant, and Wayne Sabin, along with Pate—settled in to their quarters, a rented apart-ment at Fulham overlooking the Thames, only three miles from the

All England Club, for a six-week stay. This was a new arrangement, brainstormed by Pate. He felt that living together as one close group, almost like a family, would heighten their team spirit. "We lived together, ate together, and planned together," Pate recalled later. "The sole idea was to let nothing interfere with the training program." They even steered clear of the theaters and cinemas. Every night after dinner, before going back to the flat, they stopped off at the nearby Hurlingham Club's long, undulating eighteen-hole putting course. "Putting became just as much a part of the routine as eating, and we rarely missed an evening."

Earlier team captains had sometimes had trouble keeping their boys in line when they stayed at London hotels; it was too easy for the players to sneak back in the early morning hours after a night on the town. One former player used to drag his comrades to the London dog races, and Frank Shields "used to stay up all night drinking and chasing dames." Shields was in Hollywood now, and the impish, irrepressible gambler Bobby Riggs, who had been practicing with the team back home, hadn't made the travel squad for England. Riggs, nineteen, had started the year as the number-four ranked American and would be number two by the end of the summer, but he was more or less despised by Perry Jones, the czar of Southern California tennis. Effeminate and fastidious, with no apparent sense of humor at all, Perry had no use for the wise-cracking iconoclast Riggs, and he had enormous sway with the USLTA.

So although he had beaten both Parker and Grant in the Davis Cup squad practices and was ranked far ahead of Sabin, Bobby Riggs was pulling big under-the-table bucks playing stateside instead of getting his teammates into trouble in London. But Pate still wasn't taking any chances, even though he really didn't have to worry about the extracurricular activity of this year's team, including his star. Don Budge had dated a few young women at home by now, but none seriously, and he wasn't very interested in "chasing dames." "I was more dedicated to tennis," he said. "I wanted to be the best player in the world, and so everything I did was predicated by the question, 'Is this good for your tennis?'" Sure, he and Mako loved to go out and hear jazz, but even if Pate hadn't been watching over them, they wouldn't have stayed out late enough to ruin their practice schedule. "In 1937 Don spent his life with me," said Mako. They lived together for the better part of the year, double-dated, sought out jazz clubs together, and played lots of two-on-two basketball. ("We took on two of the best players in the country and beat them," said Mako, who later played semipro basketball.) In London, though, it was just tennis.

After Budge dismantled Cramm in the Wimbledon final, the Americans, having already won their Davis Cup zone back home, continued their quiet domestic life in Fulham. The German team headed straight for the boat train, traveling back to Berlin and the Rot-Weiss Club for the European Zone finals against Czechoslovakia. Their old rival Roderich Menzel was facing them again, along with the Slovakian Jew Ladislav Hecht. The following year Hecht would escape the German invasion of Czechoslovakia by three days, fleeing to the United States. But now he strode right into the belly of the beast on the quixotic quest of trying to stop the powerful German tennis duo. On the first day, as he went up against the Roland Garros champion, Henkel, he couldn't help but notice the ominous motley smattering of green, brown, and black—the uniforms of the various military units in attendance—commingling with the bright colors of summer dresses and hats. Before the largest tennis crowd in Berlin since the 1929 Interzone Final against Tilden's U.S. team, Henkel proved too powerful for Hecht. The Slovak served at five-four in the second set and was up five-one in the third, but each time Henkel came storming back with his power baseline game and won 6-1, 7-5, 7-5.

The crowd rose and cheered as their champion, Gottfried von Cramm, walked on court for the more anticipated match of the day against Menzel. But Cramm was in a funk. Maybe it was the rush home to play a match that felt anticlimactic so soon after the Wimbledon final, or maybe it was the settling disappointment of that crushing loss to Budge—three straight years the Wimbledon bridesmaid. The pressure to win the Davis Cup that had thickened around his shoulders after Wimbledon certainly didn't help, and then there was the return to the omnipresent Swastikas, storm troopers, and oppression, the gloomy foreboding of his closest friends, after the freedom of London. He felt heavy in his legs, sick to his stomach. The crowd sensed it immediately and sat stunned as the steady but unspectacular Menzel took the first two sets easily and led four-two, thirty-love in the third.

Then Cramm shook it all off. What was he doing? This was his club, his red clay, his calling. Somehow, on court he had always been able to forget his personal problems and the tragic course of events in his country. Playing tennis was like a drug that brought on optimism, even cheerfulness in the darkest times. It had taken longer today, almost too long, but now Gottfried started hitting the ball with his characteristic power and depth. As though he had jettisoned leg weights, he began sprinting like his old self across the dirt surface. He won four straight points to escape that seventh game and went on to run out the rest of the set, six-four.

Heinrich Kleinschroth, worried that his star player and friend had appendicitis or some other serious ailment, had already called a physician to be ready in the locker room. During the ten-minute break after the third set, the doctor examined Cramm and found him fit. An hour ago you would have had a more interesting examination, Gottfried may have told him. I'm all right now. He returned to the court without stretching the intermission a second and proceeded to dismantle the flabbergasted Menzel. His peerless kicker serve was launching off the clay for aces, and his relentless ground strokes had Menzel running a track meet all over the court. The Czech tried to slow the game back down and was roundly booed by the crowd for stalling, but the match was no longer in doubt: Cramm swept the last two sets 6-3, 6-2.

Cramm and Henkel won the doubles easily the next day to clinch victory. Cramm did play the first singles match the final day, sweeping aside Hecht with little trouble, but after that the Germans stuck in Hans Denker to play the final match while Cramm and Henkel left to catch the night train to The Hook of Holland. There they got the ferry to Harwich and the train back to London, back to the Savoy. This allowed them a few days of practice, getting used to the grass again, for the Interzone Final against the United States. And there was no question in anyone's mind by then: the Interzone champ would be the winner of the Cup.

"Cable stories aver," wrote *American Lawn Tennis*, "that while Germany is availing itself of the services of a coach, Hans Nüsslein, the American leader and players have no need of such aid." Bill Tilden must have smirked when he saw that. Tilden had been training the

German team off and on for a year and a half, along with his friend and
pro competitor Nüsslein. Bill had been in Europe since the spring,
working with Cramm and company in between playing an exhausting
schedule of professional matches. In fact, both he and Nüsslein had
just gotten back from Cologne, where they had been contesting the
Bonnardel Cup, the professional international team competition of
the day, intended to be analogous to the amateur Davis Cup. Tilden,
at forty-four, had beaten the twenty-seven-year-old Nüsslein to put
the Americans in the final round just as Cramm and Henkel had done
the same for the German Davis Cup team in Berlin.

Tilden could understand why the Germans wouldn't want to publicize having an American coach, but he found it amusing that the
Americans pretended to have no need. Even when Tilden was still the
team's star, they had hired Karel Kozeluh as coach—although in fact
(Bill smiled again) Karel had functioned as no more than his assistant.
In 1934, after years of turning down Tilden's offers to train the team
for free, the USLTA had even hired Nüsslein as coach! Bill had to
admit, he had taken some guilty pleasure in the Americans' loss to England that year. Even last year and this year Kozeluh had helped work
out the American team in its May practices back home.

But the United States had taken no coach to England, and no one
was second-guessing that decision. This year's team was tightly knit, fo-
cused, disciplined. And independent. "Why would we need a coach?"
Gene Mako said. "We were the best players in the world, what would we
need a coach for?" Walter Pate seemed to agree. "Can you imagine anybody coaching Budge?" he asked rhetorically at practice one morning
after the kid had smoked a crosscourt backhand better than any man
had ever hit one.

The team liked to have three to five short practice sessions a day, of
less than an hour each. Much of it consisted of practice sets, directed
by Pate. About the only thing Pate could do at practice, though, was tell
whom to play against whom. Usually Cramm and Henkel were on another court with Kleinschroth and Nüsslein, sometimes even the adja-
cent court (as Tilden kept a low profile, often watching both teams from
a nearby seat). And on more than one occasion the Americans even
practiced with the Germans. "Sure, we practiced with the Germans
when we felt like it," said Mako. "Cramm and Henkel, Kleinschroth

and Tilden, and we were all good friends. We saw them every day in London."

After a full day of practice sessions, Pate would take his team to "the best restaurants" and have hearty meals such as steak and mashed potatoes to get their weight back after all that tennis. Sometimes they dined with Cramm and Tilden, or even with the other Germans as well, but most nights it was just themselves and often Paul Lukas, Budge and Mako's actor friend. Then a round of miniature golf to aid digestion and back to the apartment. Breakfast was at eight A.M. prompt.

Cramm, on the other hand, was back in the London swing. Tennis came first, of course, and as always he was the first on the practice courts and the last to leave. When he did leave, however, he enjoyed a social life almost as demanding. There was Geoffrey Nares, still infuriating his father and sneaking off to meet Gottfried after his busy days designing the scenery for the new J. B. Priestley play at the Duchess Theatre. There were receptions of various kinds, orchestrated by Ambassador Ribbentrop. Cramm couldn't stand the shallow, self-important jackass; as Robert Vansittart, the head of the British diplomatic service, put it, "To [Ribbentrop] one has to listen without much chance of interruption . . . for he is guided by his command of English." But Gottfried was at home mingling with the crust of British society, and he dutifully played his role. To Ribbentrop he was a walking advertisement for Nazi Germany, but in his own mind he was representing the dignity of the German people, a quality that would long survive its current distortion.

Barbara Hutton, too, was still in town. Her husband, Curt Reventlow, had been livid at Barbara's obstreperous Centre Court cheers for her hero at the Wimbledon final. He saved his scathing rebuke for the ride home, and when her personal chauffeur defended her, Reventlow retaliated by firing him the next day. By this point Barbara could hardly stand to be in the same room as her husband, a fact she made no effort to hide. On the contrary, she made a show of displaying her infatuation with Cramm, showering him with invitations to her magnificent new neo-Georgian mansion, Winfield House. Set among twelve acres in Regent's Park, it was the largest private estate in

London—after Buckingham Palace, that is. Gottfried—who had helped Barbara design the property's red-clay tennis courts—commanded the spotlight at her dinner parties there, where she scarcely took her eyes off him. Though he was used to adulation, hers must have made him feel at least a bit awkward, as it clearly did nothing to assuage Reventlow's rage. But she was bent on divorce by this point, despite her husband's reluctance. (Many millions of dollars were on the line, so for Reventlow "hatred between spouses was no reason for separation.")

Reventlow's lone, if small, victory that week was getting Barbara out of town before Cramm took to Centre Court again. She accompanied her husband to Venice just before the Interzone Final began, but not without securing Gottfried's promise that he would join her there in a few weeks and take part in Princess Jane Campbell San Faustino's charity tennis tournament.

The Americans were heavy favorites to beat Germany in the Interzone Final and go on to win back the Davis Cup. After all, Budge had just beaten Cramm easily in the Wimbledon final and would surely have no problem with Henkel either. The Wimbledon-champion doubles team of Budge and Mako would provide the third point if necessary. And for insurance they had Frankie Parker, who had already beaten Henkel in the quarterfinals of Wimbledon and taken a set off Budge in the semis.

Some called Frank Parker a "tennis robot" because of his placid expression and steady, unspectacular strokes. But at Wimbledon he caused much comment with his "short shorts" and collarless white T-shirts. Their own Bunny Austin had invented tennis shorts, but Bunny's came down near the knee, while Parker's almost indecently reminded one of briefs. And his love life, were it not for the moment still secret, would quickly have shed him his reputation for dispassion.

It was the unlikeliest of destinies that had brought Frank Parker to Wimbledon at all. Don Budge and Alice Marble had emerged from the middle class and the public parks, but Parker (born Franciszek Andrezej Paikowski in Milwaukee) was probably the first champion to come from what he called "the low, low class. My mother took in washing. I worked as a ball boy for the Town club in Milwaukee and would make a dollar a week at five cents a set. Mercer Beasley, who was the pro at the club, allowed me to hit with some of his pupils and he saw something in me that made him think I might become a champion."

Beasley and his wife Audrey all but adopted Parker, taking him with them when Beasley became tennis coach at Tulane University and then at the prestigious Lawrenceville School near Princeton, New Jersey. In fact, they wanted to adopt him, but his mother would not allow that. But Beasley had been right about the boy, and he developed quickly. At the age of fifteen, while a student at Lawrenceville, he was national boys champion (under fifteen); the next year, at sixteen, he won the national juniors (under eighteen); and when he was seventeen, he was the eighth-ranked man in the country. The same age as Budge and Mako, he was rated ahead of both of them as the trio reached adulthood.

By this time he found himself irredeemably in love with Audrey Beasley, over twenty years his senior and his virtual foster mother. Belying his on-court image as an automaton, he gave in to his passion completely, and it was returned. The Beasleys' marriage had been lifeless for years, so Parker couldn't be accused of stealing her away, but Mercer Beasley might not have seen it that way. He had all but adopted the boy, been a mentor and father figure, given him the best personal coaching all these years, turned him into a champion. One can only imagine the scenes that played out later that year, when the three of them were sharing a house in Bermuda, and Frank and Audrey, "discovered," finally confessed to Mercer. Only one thing was clear: there was nothing Frank could do about it. They were in love, and that was it. Fifty years later, long after she was gone, Frank still called her "the love of my life." Mercer never accused her publicly, for she, in Parker's words, "had the goods on him." What dark secret Mercer Beasley held was never revealed. In 1938, when Parker was twenty-two, the Beasleys quietly divorced, and Frank and Audrey were married.

In the summer of 1937, though, all was still concealed, and Parker was in England alone with the Davis Cup team. Twenty-one years old, almost as handsome as that other Frank, Shields, he had had a marvelous Wimbledon in his debut there, reaching the semifinals. In the fourth round he had faced Daniel Prenn, who was himself having his finest showing since emigrating to England four years earlier. Busy building a new life in a new country, Prenn had lost in the first round at Wimbledon his first three years as an English resident. This year, however, he had found his old form and run through the first three rounds in straight sets. And against Parker, after losing a close six-four first set, he proceeded to run off five straight games in the second. But Parker, "without a change in expression or his methodical attitude," took the next seven and the match 6-4, 7-5, 6-2. Then, in a quarter-final portentous for the upcoming Davis Cup matches, he upset the third-seeded Henner Henkel in five sets. It was almost an easy straight-set win, before Henkel came back from two sets down and two-four in the third, only to lose six-two in the fifth. Walter Pate and the USLTA had to be feeling confident about the Interzone Final now.

Pate spent much of his time after Wimbledon furrowing his brows, trying to decide whether to name Bitsy Grant or Frank Parker as the number-two singles player. Two days before the draw Grant actually took a set off of Budge, and then played Parker to a dead standoff, both men holding their serve until practice ended. Each seemed to be playing the best of his life. On July 15, though, the day before the draw was announced, Budge took Bitsy apart in two quick sets. Of course, everyone agreed that Budge might do that to anyone in the world on a given day. Pate, pacing around the practice courts, "merely continued to shake his head and look mysterious," when asked what his decision would be. Meanwhile both Germans were looking strong. Cramm and Henkel played a practice set on Centre Court while the Americans looked on, waiting for their turn. It was eight-all when they ran out of time, and the American team just shook their heads, agreeing out loud that Henner Henkel had the biggest serve in tennis.

On July 16, the day before the first matches, Walter Pate announced his lineup: Budge at number one, of course, and Budge and Mako in the doubles, and at number-two singles . . . Bitsy Grant. Bryan Morel Grant Jr., a twenty-six-year-old from Atlanta, was the oldest member of the team and also, at five foot four, 120 pounds, the smallest. He was a perennial U.S. top-tenner throughout the 1930s and a solid bet to reach the quarters or semis of the major tournaments. Frank Shields used to make fun of him, saying "the little shaver" was playing sneaky by hiding behind the net, and it was said that once, in an inebriated

state, he held Bitsy upside down out of a London hotel room window
with one hand. But Grant got him back on the tennis court often
enough. Allison Danzig called Bitsy "the greatest tennis competitor
the world has ever seen. . . . On second thought, you can strike out the
'tennis.' For sheer fight and bull-dog tenacity in hanging on against
overwhelming force, I never saw his superior in any game."

However, Grant had gone out rather meekly in the Wimbledon
quarterfinals against Austin, Bunny crushing Bitsy in straight sets. And
Parker seemed to have really come into his own with his convincing
dismantling of Henkel. Neither man was expected to have a chance
against Cramm, but surely Parker was the better bet against Henkel.
The strange decision "evoked quite a lot of comment from the English
wiseacres on the spot" and in fact had most in the tennis world
scratching their heads. "Why did U.S. choose Grant over Parker?"
wondered Ralph Bunche in his diary. The journalist Al Laney was convinced that the decision had come from New York, where the USLTA
wanted to pacify some influential southern tennis officials. "I did not
think it the correct selection," he wrote later, "but I do know that all
who saw the series can be grateful for the error." For without it, Budge
versus Cramm might have been a dead rubber, quickly forgotten.


Aʟ Lᴀɴᴇʏ ᴡᴀs ᴀ ꜰᴏʀᴛʏ-ᴏɴᴇ-ʏᴇᴀʀ-ᴏʟᴅ sᴘᴏʀᴛsᴡʀɪᴛᴇʀ ᴡʜᴏ ʜᴀᴅ
fallen in love with the game of tennis as a schoolboy in 1914. More
specifically, he had fallen for the dashing power game of the California
Comet, Maurice "Red Mac" McLoughlin, whom he had the good luck
on a holiday to watch in the Davis Cup Challenge Round at Forest
Hills. This was the year that Germany lost to Australia in Philadelphia
on the day war was declared; during the Challenge Round, Laney read
in the paper that the ship of the German players had been captured,
and the players Froitzheim and Kreuzer interned by the British. Then
McLoughlin overpowered the legendary Australian, Norman Brookes,
and made tennis front-page news for the first time. Laney was hooked,
and he became not only an avid fan but one of the two leading American tennis writers (along with Allison Danzig of the *Times*) for the next
fifty years.

After McLoughlin faded, Laney became one of the many adoring fans of Little Bill Johnston, and he rooted with clenched fists for Little Bill to take revenge on the man who had unseated him—Big Bill Tilden. But after becoming the *Herald Tribune*'s tennis man in 1924 and covering Big Bill's exploits throughout the rest of the 1920s, he underwent a conversion and ever after proselytized to his readers regarding the unequaled brilliance of Tilden. Now there was Budge, and although he would never quite replace Tilden atop Laney's pantheon of tennis greats, Laney was thrilled to be in London to watch the kid, as Laney expected, bring the Cup home.

Laney was the quiet sort, more comfortable alone in front of a typewriter than making speeches or having any sort of attention thrust upon him. So he was put "in a state of mild shock" when he arrived at the *Herald Tribune*'s London office in Bush House to find a note from his friend and colleague, John Tunis, who was to broadcast the matches on NBC. "Taken ill," said the note, "too sick to broadcast, sailing for home, and hope you don't mind but I told them you'd take my place." Laney walked slowly up Haymarket toward Broadcasting House to meet with the woman from the BBC who was coordinating the broadcasts, all the way composing his speech declining the job. After listening patiently, she informed him that she had never heard such "utter rot"; his friend Mr. Tunis had said he would do it, and that was that. He was about to protest more stringently when she told him that there were to be only three fifteen-minute broadcasts each day, one of them a scripted summary of the day's matches to be read on air at midnight London time. For this minor commitment he would be paid $500. Laney just nodded.

On Saturday, the day of the first singles matches, Laney headed out to Wimbledon in the morning for a meeting with Colonel R. H. Brand. Ten years earlier, when the BBC broached the subject of broadcasting the Championships for the first time, the All England Club agreed, provided the BBC commentator be accompanied in the booth by their own steadfast Colonel Brand, "to ensure the new-fangled gimmick would not lower the tone." By all accounts, the long-retired colonel's commentary did not elaborate much further than "Forehand! Recovery. Backhand! Recovery. Smash! Oh, well done, sir!" But he had been part of the BBC's Wimbledon broadcasts ever since, and Laney had asked if he could buy him a drink and elicit some advice in this new venture. Brand "was a bluff and quite friendly man with a don't-mind-if-I-do personality," Laney later wrote, "who was willing to have me buy him any number of spots and splashes, but he did not communicate much of the technique of describing a tennis match. . . . The most I could get out of him was 'Nothing to it, old boy. You'll do well. Don't worry.' "

Laney was more nervous than any of the players when he climbed into the claustrophobic little "commentary hut," about the size of a Spitfire cockpit, on the south end of Centre Court for the first match: Grant vs. Cramm. The booth originally had no ventilation, so that the broadcasters' voices didn't disturb nearby ticket-holders, but by 1937 there was one inch separating the front glass from the desk, so that notes could be passed in and out. He settled himself in, squeezed his head into the uncomfortable headphones, and waited.

Cramm had already held serve for the first game when Laney finally heard the words, *The National Broadcasting Company has prepared a special shortwave broadcast of the all-important Davis Cup Interzone Final tennis matches between the United States and Germany. We take you now to Wimbledon, England.* Laney took a breath and jumped right in. "Hello, Americans. This is Al Laney speaking from Centre Court, Wimbledon. The first match has just begun between Grant and von Cramm. . . ."

With such a promising match-up between two powerful teams, featuring the great Budge and Cramm, the All England Club had for the first time scheduled a non-Challenge round on Centre Court instead of Court Number One. As the two matches were expected to be cursory on this first day, and the skies were threatening, the stands were not packed. But even so, between ten and twelve thousand spectators showed up, more than justifying the decision, and the rain held off.

From the beginning, Bitsy Grant, playing in shorts as Austin and Parker had at Wimbledon, pulled out his entire arsenal of slices, chops, topspins, and sidespins, "while flitting about the court all the time and retrieving the most impossible-looking shots," to little avail. No one could accuse "the little shaver" of going in without a plan. Time and time again he drop-shotted Cramm and, when the German came roaring in, sent a deep lob over his head. But Cramm "could put a lob out of its misery from any part of the court," and all too often Laney's commentary repeated itself: "Grant throws it short, Cramm shoots deep, Grant lobs, and Cramm kills it." In fact, Cramm was seizing the net whether Grant invited him in or not, putting away his volleys and smashes seemingly at will. "Cramm is tall, blond, and very handsome," reported Laney, "and most delightful to watch. His play is all fire, vigor, intense concentration. Grant on the other hand is a little man—that's why they call him Bitsy—the smallest Davis Cup player ever seen, and also the toughest. . . . Lots of passing shots for Grant, but Cramm's attack is relentless."

After what seemed like hours, the handwritten note finally came sliding under Laney's window: *15 minutes are up. Sign off.* "This is the first game of the second set. Cramm won the first set six-three. That will be all for now. We return you to America." Orchestral music came through the headphones as he slid them off with a sigh. Well, that wasn't so bad. He extricated himself from the "hut" and hurried to the press box to watch the rest, but for Bitsy Grant there was no escape: 6-3, 6-4, 6-2 for Germany, as expected. "I did my best," Bitsy wrote in a letter the next day, "but he was just too classy for me."

After a short break Don Budge and Henner Henkel took the court, with the tables turned. Now it was Germany's turn to try to pull off a near-impossible upset. "Budge is inimitable," Colonel Brand was telling his listeners during the break. "His performance at the Championships here was absolutely unmatchable. He hits with incredible speed. His service is simply amazing, untakable, reminiscent of Bill Tilden's old cannonball. . . . He has improved beyond what one could imagine possible."

If anyone other than Cramm had a chance against him, though, it was probably Henkel. The third seed at Wimbledon after winning in France, Henkel possessed the kind of power game that just might, on a great day, catch Budge off guard. Especially on the grass, which was playing even faster than normal after some dry weather and an army's worth of footsteps from the recent tournament.

Henkel's first serve, which all the players agreed was the only one in the world faster than Budge's, was a physiological marvel. He would simply bring his racket straight up behind his ear like a shortstop making a quick throw to first—"a backswing that he could uncoil easily within the walls of a phone booth"—and then let it rip like a slingshot.

The solidly built six-footer liked to keep his blond hair neatly combed straight back from his forehead and kept a comb handy, "wielding it on occasion at the umpire's chair." Budge called him the strongest player he ever saw, "and certainly the one with the most incredible appetite." He would devour two or three dozen oysters in a few minutes, then swallow a chocolate sundae as another appetizer, before moving on to a plate of spaghetti "and finally something really substantial."

Unfortunately, when this man of power and appetite missed his feared first serve, he was in trouble. For while Cramm's second serve was even more imposing than his first, Henkel's second serve was "a little cream puff," according to Budge: "It was hard to believe that a man of such strength and with such a hard first serve could hit such a dainty little second serve." Colonel Brand agreed: "Henkel's second service is a lamentable, high-bounding ball, not heavily cut, and Budge can do whatever he likes with it."

On this day the match seemed decided even before the players reached their chairs. Budge, though outwardly modest as always, couldn't help but glow with confidence after his magnificent Wimbledon and a strong week of practice. This was his match to orchestrate, and he stopped Henkel even before they reached the squadron of photographers posted around the umpire's chair to spin his racket for the choice of serve. He won the toss and almost everything that followed. The crowd, buoyed by Cramm's easy opening victory, roared when Henkel redirected one of Budge's cannonballs for a service-return winner, but Budge held on for that game anyway, and soon his "dazzling form reduced Henkel almost to a state of impotence." Even the German's heaviest artillery—that imposing first serve—fell before the Budge arsenal, which seemed to have no weakness. Every facet was clicking in perfect order, just as he had left off at Wimbledon. He "pasted unmercifully" Henkel's second-serve offerings, and late in the match "regaled us with service aces and stop volleys in rich profusion very much like a conjurer producing rabbits out of a hat." Cramm had beaten Grant in only an hour and ten minutes, but Budge was best in this regard as well, allowing Henkel only fifty minutes on the Centre Court stage before escorting him back to the dressing rooms.

It was a sobering fifty minutes for German tennis fans and equally encouraging for the Americans. "Even though Cramm played wonderfully," Laney told the folks at home in his evening recap, "if it comes down to the last match between Budge and Cramm, we can be absolutely confident that the match is ours, because there doesn't seem to be any chance at all that Budge can be beaten."

Matches were never held on Sundays at Wimbledon, even for the Davis Cup, so after a relaxing day off, the teams and spectators—largely the same people each day—reconvened on Monday, on a hot and thundery afternoon that again remained dry despite ominous skies. Budge and Mako, Cramm and Henkel walked back out onto Centre Court to play the critical doubles match. Two weeks earlier, on the same court, the German team had won the first two sets in the Wimbledon semifinal before Budge and Mako stormed back. These were without question the two best teams in the world. And with everyone expecting Germany and the United States to split the last two singles matches, the doubles might very well be the deciding contest.

Unfortunately for the Americans, Don Budge was not quite the invincible fortress he appeared to be when he was in the groove. And this morning his right shoulder had finally given in to the weeks and months of constant ball-battering and greeted him with a steady throbbing soreness. When they walked on court to warm up, he turned to Mako and said, "Listen, Gene, do you mind taking most of the lobs today? Just call me off of anything you can reach, and I'll get out of the way." Mako said, "Sure," and they proceeded to warm up.

It was remarkable evidence of Budge's confidence in his partner. For Mako had suffered such a devastating injury the year before that he was the last person one would expect to be given the responsibility for hitting overheads. In 1934 Fred Perry had called the eighteen-year-old Mako "a prospective world champion . . . his service is one of the world's fastest, and his ground shots match it in power." Even as a sixteen-year-old in Los Angeles, he had been chosen to take part in a serving contest with Tilden, Vines, and a few others, using a pre-radar ballistic speedometer; and Mako, like the others, had clocked in at over 150 miles per hour.

But during a match at Forest Hills in 1934, as he stretched to deliver a booming cannonball serve, he felt something tear in his shoulder. He was able to keep playing, but there was a persistent soreness in his arm. And then in London in 1936 he was practicing with Bitsy Grant at the Queen's Club; the grass was a bit slick from recent rain, and he slipped while running for a shot. As he tried to right himself, he suddenly "heard something pop" in his chest, up near the shoulder. This time the pain was so intense that he had to stop playing immediately and sought out a specialist in London. The news was not good. All they could tell him was that "virtually every muscle from his arm to his chest had been torn to pieces," the damage was irreparable, and he would have to quit serious tennis for good.

A disconsolate Mako sailed back home alone after defaulting at Wimbledon. Doctors in New York offered no consolation: his tennis days were over. But when Budge arrived home after his close semifinal loss to Perry, he somehow convinced Mako that he could keep playing, even without a serve. "Guys were used to me hitting my serve a hundred fifty miles an hour, and the next time they saw me it was more like thirty-five or forty. I would never have played if Don and I hadn't been such good friends and he hadn't been so loyal."

Somehow, within a couple of weeks Mako was back on the court playing great doubles, and only six weeks after the injury he and Budge won the U.S. National Doubles at Longwood. In the finals they beat Allison and Van Ryn, the formerly acknowledged world's number-one doubles team—*for the eleventh time in a row* (including twice after Mako's injury). What's more, Mako teamed with Alice Marble to win the mixed-doubles title the same day, beating his buddy Budge and Sarah Palfrey Fabyan.

"I really don't know how I did it," said Mako. "Hell, I couldn't serve at all, it was almost a sidearm delivery. It was a pain in the ass for me because I had to come in and hit tough low volleys," since the opponents had no trouble hitting their returns down low at his feet. "But mentally I was tough and knew what to do. And we won all our big tournaments after the injury, with me playing like a little old lady."

Budge could easily have expressed his sympathy after the injury and found another partner. Pate and others wanted to try him with Allison or Van Ryn for the Davis Cup. But he would hear nothing of it. No one else, he knew, had the racket skills or the mental game of Mako:

He has so many surprises up his sleeve, he acts with such light-ning quickness at the net, and has so much confidence in doing the unexpected and daring, that the opponents are on tenter-hooks as to what he is going to pull off next. His drop volleys, dink shots, and use of angles and lobbing, combined [perfectly] with my power and straighter hitting.... Each of us could sense almost instinctively what was in the other's mind and so we moved as a unit in carrying out attacking operations or falling into a defensive formation.

Even so, after his injury he might have seemed an odd choice as the man to take all the overheads. But Budge was hurting, too, and hadn't been feeling right on overheads all week—the only hint of a weakness in his game. And Mako sounded like he'd be confident with no arm at all: "I still had a strong hand and a strong wrist, and I could just angle the overheads off for winners. I could play for six months and never miss one. So hell no, I didn't mind taking 'em."

From the very beginning, it was obvious to all that something was wrong with Budge's shoulder. It's common practice in doubles to take something off the first serve and spin it in like a second serve, because this allows more time to get to net. But Budge was not in the habit of trading power for strategy, and it was shocking to see him serving barely harder than Mako. "For a long time Budge was as likely to make a loose shot as a murderous one, and his serving at half-speed may not have been wholly tactical," noted one reporter, who went on to add, "Budge, far from dominating, was being audibly 'nursed' by Mako."

Fans had long speculated on what Budge and Mako said to each other as they paced the baseline between points, as they were in the habit of doing, shoulder to shoulder, jabbering away. It looked to some like they were quarreling, to others like they were plotting strategy. "Nothing could be farther from the truth," said Mako at the time. "We just talk, hardly ever about tennis. We talk about what we'll do after the game, whether we'd like to have a speedboat, should girls smoke, and so forth. Sometimes we talk animated, but it's just talk." That may have been true in the second round at Seabright, but not today. Not with the Davis Cup on the line. Clearly James Thurber was correct today when he referred to "Mako's muttered pep talks." Don was aching and off his game, and Gene was trying to keep the world's greatest player from blowing everything. With Mako serving at four-three, ad-in, a game point to make it five-three, Budge got an easy lob and hit his overhead a foot past the baseline. That's all right, Mako murmured to his friend, we'll get another. But they didn't. The Germans took four straight games from two-four and won the first set six-four.

Budge had double-faulted in the final game of that set, and his wounded serve was broken again in the second set to let Henkel serve at five-three. Though "no pair has ever played with more real rhythm," wrote one observer, "no more jittery bugs ever existed than Budge and Mako." And now they were really at it, crisscrossing the court like bumblebees, exhorting each other. Goddamnit, said Mako, we are not giving these guys a two-set lead again!

In a parallel situation to that of the Americans, Henkel had been the surprise mainstay of his team. Cramm, though not injured, was flagging a bit, just like Budge. He seemed to be "always in trouble" with his volleys and had been double-faulting just as much as his counterpart, doing so at four-all in the first when he struggled to hold serve. Now, though, it was Henkel's turn to buckle. With a chance to hold serve for a two-set lead, he not only kept missing his first serve but was called twice for foot faults, and the Americans broke easily for four-five. Mako held, and then they broke Cramm, who not only double-faulted to lose the game but also hit his partner in the head with an overhead. Budge managed to hold his serve, thanks to several fine smashes from Mako, and the match was even.

The third set was on service with Mako serving at four-five, when he and Budge suddenly found themselves down thirty-forty, set point. Mako hit one of his side-armed spinners off to Henkel's backhand and came scurrying in to net. Henkel had won the first set with a sliced crosscourt backhand return of Budge's serve, and now he tried to do the same with Mako's. Mako stopped just inside the service line, realizing he wasn't going to reach Henkel's angled return, and his shoulders began to slouch at the loss of the set. But the ball landed one inch wide of the sideline. Deuce.

A minute later it was ad-out, another set point for the Germans. This time Mako did reach the return and hit one of his beautiful touch volleys, surprising Cramm by going at him, or rather by him, a perfectly placed finesse shot that landed in the middle of the doubles alley. Deuce again, and this time Mako managed to serve it out to "deuce" the set at five-all. Then they broke Henkel at six-all, and Mako served out the set eight-six, for a two-sets-to-one lead.

The four players retired to the dressing rooms for the ten-minute intermission. Cramm and Henkel must have felt they should have been shaking hands at the net already. They'd won the first, been up five-three in the second, and had set points in the third. Instead, they were losing. Mako and Budge, for their part, instead of being thrilled at their lucky escape, were simmering. They'd blown the first set and then had to dig themselves out of deep trouble in the next two. "God-*damnit*," Mako repeated his refrain as they changed out of their sweat-drenched shirts, "we are *not* going to get off to a bad start in the fourth!"

Before they could get some sweat into their new clothes, they were serving at one-four. From one-all the Germans had knocked off twelve straight points. Once again the Americans had to pull themselves out of a hole, and once again they did. Budge finally seemed to shake himself out of his trance and began punishing the ball as he had in singles. He joined Mako in a series of brilliant volleys, including several that came off of blindingly fast smashes by Henkel. Again and again they returned the Germans' serves, unthinkably, with deep lobs to the baseline that allowed them to counterattack and take the net. The crowd, after two hours of sitting in the sultry, overcast afternoon, came to life, and several times were reprimanded by the umpire for cheering miraculous gets in the middle of long points.

Cramm and Henkel fought for their lives, but nothing could stop the Americans now, with Budge coming alive. They answered the Germans' string of twelve points with a run of the final five games. Budge had had it with saving his shoulder, as *The Times* noted: "One will long remember Budge in the last game of all, bracing himself for the service and crashing down two aces for the match."

After an ulcer-inducing cascade of tight moments for Walter Pate, he finally burst out of his chair by the umpire's stand with an exultant

smile as Budge fired his final ace past Henkel's backhand side. The
pressure was off his choice of Grant over Parker. Now even if Bitsy did
lose to Henkel, Budge would clinch victory in the final match. After
all, he had routed Cramm at Wimbledon, and the baron wasn't anywhere near his top form today. Budge over Cramm was a sure thing,
wasn't it?

As the players put their blazers back on and prepared to leave the
court, and the crowd paid tumultuous homage to "one of the most
glorious doubles matches in Davis Cup history," Don Budge let the
applause wash over him, rubbing his right shoulder absentmindedly
through his coat. *Maybe Bitsy will upset Henner,* he told himself, *and I
can take it easy against Gottfried*—or better yet, let Frankie play. If not,
that's okay. There'll be plenty of opportunities to rest the shoulder
after tomorrow.

A<small>ND</small> <small>THEN</small> <small>IT</small> <small>WAS</small> T<small>UESDAY</small>, J<small>ULY</small> 20, <small>AND</small> <small>THE</small> <small>STANDS</small> <small>WERE</small>
packed right down to the last corner of standing room, with thousands
more who hadn't arrived early enough following along on the electric
scoreboard outside Centre Court. In the Royal Box, Sir Milsom Rees,
laryngologist to the royal family, sat solicitously by the queen. Hans
von Tschammer und Osten traded pleasantries with several Conservative MPs, including Thomas Mackay Cooper, the solicitor general for
Scotland, and Sir Samuel Hoare, recently the foreign secretary. (When
he resigned that position after public uproar following his proposal to
cede much of Ethiopia to Mussolini, the joke on the street was, "No
more coals to Newcastle, no more Hoares to Paris.")

Without a drop of rain since the Championships, Centre Court
was playing faster than ever; the brown patches behind the baselines
and just inside the service lines, which endured the most footwork,
were as hard as solid earth: "cement with fuzz on it," as one player put
it. It wasn't of much concern to Robert Twynam and his fellow
groundsmen. "These are not ornamental lawns," he once said. "This is
a true hard surface for lawn tennis. This is hard-growing grass." Usually of more concern in the damp English climate was the opposite:
that too much rain would render the courts soggy. Years later Twynam
would recall a night when he left the courts uncovered and a storm

threatened to ruin them. "I got down on me knees and prayed, I did. I got down on me knees and prayed." This week, though, was probably one of those occasions when he would request the opposite. As usual, he would delay his supplication until about ten-thirty at night, "when everyone's gone home from the boozer. A drop of rain, no more—just to give it a drink, just to cool the grass." But in this case no refreshment had been forthcoming.

In the first match on Tuesday poor Bitsy Grant faced not only the powerful Henkel but the disapproving eyes of all those who thought Parker should have been chosen instead of him and who waited expectantly for him to fall on his face and prove them right. Also aligned against him were the fervent hopes of the German and British fans and the desire of all except the most die-hard American supporters— and possibly even some of them—that the final match, between Budge and Cramm, the two greatest players on earth, be for all the marbles. Everyone loves a dramatic showdown, and so everyone was hoping Henkel and Grant would do their part to ensure a fitting end to this Interzone Final.

Bitsy did his best to disappoint them. After falling behind five-one in the first set, his slices and chops finally began to undermine Henkel's power game, and he broke him back twice, saving four set points, to even the set at five-all. But then he faltered for just a moment, and the set was gone, seven-five. Undaunted, he came right back and took the second, six-two, covering the court like a paranoid squirrel: *"Comme il court!"* (How he runs!) a Frenchman in the stands cried, letting his admiration join the international cacophony. For a brief time it looked as though Grant might make the Budge-Cramm match moot after all. But then Heinrich Kleinschroth, during a change of sides, whispered a few crucial words to Henkel—You're being too defensive, playing his game instead of yours. Get to net!—and his man responded with a flurry of aggressive play that took the final two sets, 6-3, 6-4. "Grant wagged his head," noted Laney, "tossed his racket into the air, and acknowledged defeat."

Laney was as glad as anyone for Grant's loss, as he had been one of those who took issue in print with Pate's decision. He had broadcast another fifteen minutes at the start of the match before retiring to the familiar comfort of the press box. Now, with a half-hour interval between matches announced, he made his way down under the stands back toward the broadcasting booth. He was surprised to hear "as much German spoken around me as English." The first two days of doing radio had gone all right, and he was feeling more confident as he squeezed into the "hut" and looked over his notes.

Earlier, in the press box, he had heard the news that Marconi was dead, and he may have wondered if this was a bad omen for his up-coming broadcast. A heart attack at sixty-three, just as he was about to leave for an audience with his fellow fascist Mussolini. Well, I almost had a heart attack myself in that little cubbyhole on Saturday, and it would have been his fault. It was only forty years since the young Italian had made his very first transmissions, right here in England. Then came the first transatlantic transmissions, in the early years of the new century. The 1920s had brought the first commercial broadcasts, and in 1927 Wimbledon had finally allowed the BBC to build its little four-by-seven-foot booth in the hallowed stadium. And now this, thought Laney: I have to describe one of the most important matches in history to all the folks back home—*as it happens!* Well, thank God it's only fifteen minutes.

Finally the moment arrived. Budge and Cramm were on the court, chatting like practice partners, spinning Gottfried's Maxply, warming up with smooth, strong, flawless strokes. The venerable old stadium seemed swollen to the breaking point; could even more spectators have squeezed in since the first match? The Royal Box was almost as packed. The moment was perfect: almost five P.M. on a picturesque summer afternoon, the clouds and humidity of yesterday having given way to a deep cerulean sky. Electric expectancy cutting through the warm still air. A white ball tossed nine feet above the grass, the crack as the catgut launched it. Release.

Laney related the opening games with as much enthusiasm as any spectator. Both men were all over the court, getting to net whenever they could and firing off enough aces to stay on serve through the first half of the set. At one point listeners in America heard an ominous rumbling noise come through their radio speakers. Laney didn't hear it, but then a hand appeared, stuffing a paper under the glass: "Stop rattling those papers. Sounds like thunder over the air!" He had been nervously handling the notes about the two players that he had written to help himself fill any dead time. Now all he could do was stare at the top page; he didn't dare turn it over. The match was so engrossing from the very start, however, that he soon found he didn't need his notes. He was surprised when another message came under the glass: "New York says continue for another 15 minutes." He hadn't realized he was near the end of his time.

When Cramm won the first set eight-six, Laney was stunned, and more so when another note came through: "New York says continue." With no time to get nervous, and no commercials, he just kept talking. "I do not know how I managed at all," he said later. "I may have been a little hysterical myself." Then, with Budge serving at five-six, forty-love in the second set, Cramm came back with fearless attacks on the net, finally hitting that winning volley that gave him a two-set lead. While practically shouting into his microphone, Laney looked out to the side to try to get his technician's attention, but all he could see was the man's arm and hand, slipping yet another message through: "New York says continue to end. Programs canceled." Now his heart was really pumping. He'd been sure they'd let him crawl back to the press box after this set. He was limp with exhaustion and crushed with disappointment at the Germans' imminent victory. It occurred to him, though, that if Cramm won, NBC would certainly cancel next week's Challenge Round broadcast. He'd be out five hundred bucks, but, despite his love of American tennis, "it seemed almost worth it at the moment."

But then Budge began his long slow climb back, winning the third set by one service break and then dominating the fourth. Finally the match was even. One set would decide, for all intents and purposes, whether the United States or Nazi Germany would win the Davis Cup. Al Laney had been yabbering away for two hours now without a break. Even when the players had their ten-minute intermission before the fourth set, he had to keep talking, recounting what had happened and offering his prognostications for the rest of the match. Now he pronounced that Budge would surely take the fifth set. But he wasn't so certain. It seemed to him that Cramm had lost that fourth set a little too easily, and he silently guessed that the German was probably "saving his strength for the vital fifth set, to which he appeared to be looking all through the fourth."

• | •

Don Budge agrees. As Cramm collects the balls from the ball boys and prepares to serve, Budge gazes carefully across the net at his opponent. Though he knows something of the pressures Cramm is under, he can't believe that the easy fourth set was anything but a strategic move. He can practically hear Gottfried talking to himself: *Fifth sets are mine! A three-to-one advantage.*

Budge may well smile as he silently rejoins: Well, Gottfried, you'd better think again. There's no way you have a three-to-one physical advantage on me. Maybe a year ago. Definitely, a year ago. But not now.

He blew a chance for early greatness the year before, losing that Forest Hills final to Fred Perry, ten-eight in the fifth, after two weeks of late-night milkshakes. Perry gave him an easy fourth set in that one too, six-one, before fighting back in the fifth. And then Budge served for the championship at five-three but was too exhausted to finish it off.

Well, that's history. He vowed to get into world-class shape, and he's done it. In 1937 no one except Cramm can match his endurance. No, Gottfried is going to have to do more than outlast his opponent this time. If he wants the fifth today, thinks Budge, he's going to have to take it from me.

The black hands on the old white clock in the northeast corner of the stadium show just a bit before seven P.M. Still two hours to sunset, but the sun is low now: as the deciding set begins, "long shadows streaked the Centre Court, and each point was punctuated by sighs, groans and cheers from the crowd." The first three games go on serve, and then Cramm seems to realize that Budge isn't going to fade away in the fifth, that he's going to have to do something more than outlast him. When the American makes a couple of errors in his service game to go down one-two, love-thirty—normally no cause for alarm for someone with Budge's cannonball to bail him out—Cramm makes his move. He creeps in closer and closer and does the unthinkable, taking Budge's cannonball serve on the rise and rushing the net. The speed of the serves are such that the returns look like half-volleys. Budge is stunned, blocking one back for an easy Cramm volley and missing the next to lose his serve. Three-one, Germany.

Cramm stands at attention at the baseline, waiting only for his opponent's nod that he is ready. Then, before the gallery can assimilate his sudden shocking feat, he is firing a quartet of world-beating serves himself. First "a low sizzler," hissing with so much sidespin that it barely leaves the grass, skidding wide past Budge's forehand for an ace. He takes a few steps to his left, lines up his stance, and this time hits his specialty, an American Twist that leaps high from the grass to Budge's backhand side. Budge lunges after it, shouting "Oh baby!" even as he just manages to graze the ball with his racket. The crowd loves it, rising and cheering both the impossible serve and the gymnastic effort to retrieve it. Cramm moves to forty-love on a routine baseline point, then steps to the line and launches one more perfect ace, this time right down the center of the court. The sound reverberates like a gunshot through the silent cavern before the outbreak of thunderous applause, "an almost overwhelming ovation," according to one English reporter. "They not only admired the winning strokes of the German, all achieved under ruthless pressure, but his emotional control, his quiet poise and delightful fighting spirit, had captured their hearts." Thoughtfully—almost regretfully, it seems to some—Cramm knocks the other ball he's been holding over to the ball boy and walks toward the chairs. Almost there, he's almost there.

Budge, stunned by Cramm's daring recapture of the momentum, walks toward the chairs, wondering, Is he really this invincible in the fifth set? Am I going to go down just like all the others? Walter Pate, who has tried not to betray his emotions during the two-and-a-half-hour roller-coaster ride, is wringing his hands. To one observer it appears "his hands [are] clasped and his eyes turned heavenwards." Budge, as he approaches, holds out an arm for his towel. But Pate, covered in nervous perspiration, is busy using it on himself. Finally he tosses Budge the towel, afraid to say a word, at this climactic juncture, that might tip things the wrong way.

Sensing Pate's discomfiture, Budge feels he should say something. "Don't worry, Cap," he tries to sound confident, encouraging his captain like a man on the gallows comforting his lawyer. He doesn't have to remind Pate that he and Mako lost that awful and decisive doubles match to the Australians in Philly last year after being up four-one in the fifth set themselves. And of course yesterday they did the same thing to the Germans in the fourth set. "Look, I'm only down one break. And I feel great, not tired at all. I'll win this thing if it kills me."

Up in the stands Bill Tilden can contain himself no more. For the past hour he's been writhing in his seat as Budge has lifted his game to new levels and pounded away at Cramm's lead. Now, finally, somehow, Gottfried has found new reserves of power to stanch the onslaught. He's going to win this thing after all!

Tilden raises his tall lanky frame and turns around. A few rows back are Henner Henkel and other members of the German contingent. Hundreds of fans in the vicinity recognize the greatest player of all time as he gets Henkel's attention and makes an O with his thumb and forefinger, gesturing "it's in the bag."

Budge's Hollywood friends Paul Lukas, Jack Benny, and Ed Sullivan are sitting right between Tilden and Henkel. They've been annoyed all along that the famous American player is obviously rooting for the German. Now Ed Sullivan is furious. "Why, you dirty son of a bitch!" he hisses as he jumps to his feet, pulling off his coat. Before he can start climbing over seats to get to the traitor, however, Lukas and Benny get their arms around him and urge him back into his seat. Tilden merely throws him a contented smile and sits back down to enjoy the great match's denouement.

Budge and Cramm, aware only of some slight disturbance in the stands, switch sides and take the court. Budge has the serve, and true to his claim, he plays with full power and confidence, winning the game with four straight points. On one of them, as if to underscore his undauntedness, he truncates a long baseline rally with a drop shot, cut with backspin, that flutters just over the net and dies on the grass.

He finishes off the game at the net, and as he walks slowly back to the baseline to return serve, he tells himself he has to make something happen: Cramm only has to hold his serve two more times, and it's over. You need some luck, but you've got to make yourself lucky! *You've got to take a chance, try something new*. Without figuring out the odds, without really debating whether it is the most sensible thing to do, he makes a decision. There isn't much he can do on Cramm's powerful first serves except try to get them back and then play the points as best he can. But if Gottfried misses any first serves—and admittedly, he isn't missing many today—if he has to hit a second serve, Budge will move in close, take it on the rise, and charge the net—just as Cramm has done to him.

On the last point of Budge's service game, one of Cramm's gut strings snapped as he attempted a passing shot, the popping sound, like that of a toy popgun, echoing up to the stadium rafters. Without emotion he walked to the side to select a new racket from his pile, exchanging no more than a nod with Kleinschroth. No great matter, but he would have preferred not to have to take a new one right before serving. Racket-stringing is still more of an art than calibrated machine work. The stringers at Wimbledon are the best, but still there is variability. You tell them you want it "tight, but not board tight," and hope for the best.

Budge walks to the corner of the court, "wiping his nose, his eyeballs thumping," to wait for Cramm. A small group of Germans in the stands near him are cheering in unison, *"Deutschland! Deutschland!"* Cramm comes back on court, and Budge studies him for a moment. Is it his imagination, or is Gottfried a bit edgy? He seems overly anxious to get the balls from the ball boys. After all, it is the biggest moment of his career. All he has to do is hold his serve twice—eight easy points on his own serve—and the Davis Cup will certainly go to Germany for the first time ever. But will the pressure get to him? Will he finally give Budge an opening?

Sure enough, on the very first point Cramm rushes his serve, striking the ball a microsecond early in his swing, just enough to send it two inches long. Budge nods imperceptibly and, just as Cramm tosses the ball for his second serve, takes two quick steps closer to the net. When Cramm delivers his famous kick spin second serve to the backhand, a shot that normally bounces up high and wide, forcing a defensive return, Budge is in close to pick it up on the rise and hit a hard sliced return deep to Cramm's backhand. He follows it into the net and picks off the passing shot for a volley winner. Love-fifteen.

The second point is almost an exact replay. First serve long, second serve returned with a deep chip, followed by a volley winner. Love-thirty. Cramm does manage to regain his composure enough to fire one cannonball for a service winner. But then, incredibly, twice more in a row, he misses his serve just inches long, and Budge is able to attack the second serve and win the game.

Budge looks "crazy and inspired," notes Alistair Cooke. "He was up at the net almost as von Cramm was swinging his racket high for his rhythmical serve. Time and again, von Cramm's crafty passing shots were cut off by tremendous volleys, and before the crowd could sit down and let its nerves simmer, von Cramm had miraculously retrieved a placed volley and Budge had reached it again and scored a point." "At this critical moment," Laney will write, "when even one mistake might bring defeat, his aim was sure, his nerve steady, and he was at his wonderful best." "His shots took on new velocity and accuracy," agrees another reporter. "His recoveries bordered on the miraculous."

Even so, Budge's break back required Cramm's missed first serves and two passing shots that sailed just beyond the baseline. Was the new racket strung looser than the other? Or did Cramm finally give an inch to the gravitas of the moment—or to the pressure of Budge's attack? In any case, the match is as good as even, back on serve at three-four, and as he switches sides, Budge smiles ever so slightly at Pate, who looks like he's just received a presidential pardon.

Cramm regains his composure and retakes the offensive, earning two break points in the very next game, but on each of them "he failed on his backhand to return a 'snorter' hurled at him by the champion." On the first Cramm appears to hit a sure winner crosscourt to Budge's forehand side, but the American somehow runs it down and sends it humming straight down the line for a winner of his own. Then he finishes off his comeback with his third ace of the game, and it's four-all in the fifth.

By now most of the audience seem to have forgotten whose victory seemed so crucial to them two hours ago. The British, who were hoping against hope to play Germany in the Challenge Round, are completely won over by Budge's comeback. They "thundered for 'the Red-Headed Terror,'" James Thurber will write home. "The cheering watchers, whose sympathy had been with von Cramm, had taken Budge and his unwavering calm to their hearts."

And on they play, holding serve as the midsummer sun falls behind the stadium, leaving the entire court in shadow:

The match now turned into a perfect exhibition game, each man sure-footed, playing his favorite strokes in his own time, and the two white figures began to set the rhythms of something that looked more like ballet than a game where you hit a ball. . . . People stopped asking other people to sit down. The umpire gave up stopping the game to beg for silence during the rallies.

On several occasions the crowd rewards a particularly brilliant point with an entire minute of applause.

Cramm is now charging the net at every opportunity, at the same time keeping his shots so deep that Budge finds himself forever trapped behind the baseline. "The mark of aristocracy in the tennis stroke," the baron is fond of saying, "the mark of quality, is neither force nor rotation. It is depth!" Anyone who has played him at his best knows the onslaught of ground stroke after ground stroke landing within a foot of the baseline like a barrage of leaden bombs, pinning one helplessly in the backcourt.

Budge makes another bold decision. Just as he determined to take Cramm's second serves early and come to net, so he now vows he is going to get to net on these long points no matter what. He begins to move forward just as Cramm is hitting his deep drives and intercept them in midcourt, hitting volleys from "no-man's-land" on his way in. "I made my own opportunities," he will say afterward, "even if I did have to forget about correct position in the court and take desperate chances."

From four-all, two long deuced games ensue, "in which winners [are] hit off balls that themselves appeared to be certain winners." Cramm, serving with new balls, quickly goes up forty-fifteen, but Budge gets back to deuce and then has two break points, two chances to serve for the match at five-four. But the German saves them both, one with an ace, and then wins the game with another ace that raises a puff of chalk from the sideline. Budge takes a tough service game of his own for five-all, but Cramm shoots right back in front with a love game on his serve, featuring three gorgeous volley winners.

As the players change ends, the crowd on its feet, the unlighted stadium like an intimate hideaway in the falling dusk, Budge raises some nervous laughter and scattered applause in the stands as he pours another jug of ice water over his head. He takes his towel from Pate, dries his face, strides back on court, and wins another love game on serve. Six-all.

The level of play is almost hard to believe. James Thurber has "the impression of passing shots cut off by finishing volleys which in turn were whisked back. The chalk lines were hit two or three times in some of the rallies. An inspired brilliance, amounting almost to physical genius, rode on the two racquets." Walter Pate will declare years later, "No man, living or dead, could have beaten either man that day." And then, just as it seems that this unforgettable set, this perfect match, might go on forever, each player refusing to allow his serve to be broken until the deepening dusk finally forces a halt for the day, Budge makes his move. In a flurry of aggressive precision, he turns the four straight points he has just won into eight. Continuing to storm the net, he forces three Cramm errors, and on the one point when the German manages to get to net first, Budge responds with "a glorious backhand pass" that leaves Cramm lunging in vain. In a matter of two minutes the match has been transformed from an unending masterpiece, like an extra-innings pitchers' duel, into a sure thing. Don Budge is serving for the match at seven-six.

Both men walk more slowly this time, it seems, toward their chairs, as though they both sense that this might be the last change of ends. The feverish staccato rantings of the German radio announcer, which during Cramm's great charge were uncontainable by the glass of his booth, have subsided. Now it's Al Laney's effusions that cause nearby spectators to look around. The German fans are no longer chanting; now the Americans in the gallery become boisterous, jackets long torn off, standing in their shirtsleeves and shouting themselves hoarse.

BILL TILDEN COULD BARELY STAY IN HIS SEAT HIMSELF. LIKE everyone else, he'd truly thought Cramm had this one. Now Budge seemed to have it in hand. But of course it was only one break, Gottfried might well break back, we've all come back from worse than this.

What else was giving Tilden the jitters, what other ghosts haunting his mind as he watched this tennis match on a fine summer day? He'd blown almost all of the $500,000 he earned in his first six years as a pro—a gargantuan sum in Depression dollars. Just a year later he would be holed up in London again, unable to return home. The Algonquin Hotel was seeking $2,239 in back rent, the U.S. government even more in back taxes—Big Bill apparently had been busy touring every April 15. His old rival and doubles partner Vinnie Richards, now a professional tennis tour promoter, came to his aid. He paid off the Algonquin, traveled to Washington and negotiated a deal with the government whereby Tilden would have to pay only a fraction of what he owed, and then sailed to London. Advancing Bill a few thousand dollars against his guarantee for the next tour, he encouraged him to come on home. A week after that Tilden cabled him that he was out of cash again.

Where did it all go? Big Bill was simply unable to live a life more thrifty than that of royalty. "He traveled like a goddamn Indian prince," Laney wrote. He still stayed at the finest hotels, ate at the best restaurants, and picked up the check for everyone with him. His Algonquin bill was constantly accruing even while he spent most of the year on tour. And then there were the boys. The Rot-Weiss Club's phalanx of cherubic ball boys had always been as much an attraction to him as its world-class clay courts. Back home he usually traveled with his own "personal ball boy," often a German lad, always nicknamed "Fritzi," whom he'd brought to the States. The two of them rode alone in Tilden's big blue Buick or shared a train compartment. In a typical occurrence one of these young men, who was living with Tilden at the Algonquin, visited all the finest Madison Avenue shops, charging clothes, jewelry, and other items to Tilden's account. Another time, on the road, Tilden came into the hotel lobby and told one of the other players, "Fritzi did the cutest thing this morning. Before I woke up, he took four hundred dollars and went out and bought himself a watch."

But the money was trivial. He could always make more cash. He was Big Bill Tilden! His face adorned Camel cigarette ads and sporting-goods ads in all the finest magazines. He was getting $5,000 a year from Spalding for the use of his name on its rackets and another $1,500 for sponsoring its tennis shoe, $1,000 for endorsing Armour catgut strings, $7,500 for his newspaper writing. And he was still the biggest draw in tennis, whether he won or lost. Why, he'd just beaten the great Fred Perry, who was at his peak, the same age as Gottfried, two matches in a row in April! No, money could never be a serious problem for Tilden. Unless . : .

Unless the public found out what he really was. He'd been less circumspect the past year or so, letting his guard down too often. Should never have let everyone see how distraught he was when Fritzi locked him out of the train compartment. There was more than one midwestern American town that he wouldn't be playing in again. Even dear old cousin Twin had warned him. Auntie had died, and Twin had moved to Yorkshire, England, where her parents had come from. Earlier this summer Tilden had made the three-hour trip from London to visit her. It had been years since she'd seen Junior, and she was startled at the changes. "He was starting to walk like a real fruit," George Lott remembered later; some instructional films Tilden made in Hollywood even drew snickers from audiences because of his feminine bearing. Twin tried to tell him, over tea and sandwiches, as obliquely as she could, that he should be a bit more discreet.

Junior didn't take the advice well. He fixed her with his famous glare, the one that had withered linesmen and ball boys for decades, and marched straight out of her cottage and back to London. He never again spoke to the last family member who truly loved him.

The public would understand, though, wouldn't they? There had always been great men who were "somewhat away from the normal." He was merely the latest in a long line of men of exceptional achievement who had required relationships of a different sort. Oscar Wilde, for instance, his favorite example. What a kinship he felt with him. Ah, if only he could have traded his athletic genius for one great run on Broadway! Wilde had ended badly, of course: prison and exile. But that was the nineteenth century. The present was a more enlightened age. More and more it seemed ridiculous to have to hide his true nature. It wasn't a question of degeneracy; at most a mild psychological "illness." Lord knew he'd been under pressures and emotional strains for decades that would have driven most men mad. People would understand.


BUDGE AND CRAMM HAVE TAKEN AN UNUSUALLY LONG TIME AT their chairs, sipping tea, toweling off, pondering the moment. Not a word is exchanged with the captains, other than a perfunctory "Well done" or "That's all right." They both seem to be finally feeling the effects of the marathon match as they walk slowly to their respective sides for the fourteenth game of the fifth set. Budge needs only to hold his serve to virtually give America the Cup. He accepts a few balls from the ball boy and gets into position to serve—then stops. For just a moment his entire body seems to relax like that of a soldier having a last cigarette before the attack. Then he is back at attention, catching Cramm's nod of readiness, tossing up the first ball.

The serve travels straight into the bottom of the net. It is the first time he has succumbed to his nerves in the entire match, and he shakes it off. That's as much choking as there's gonna be, he scolds himself. Cramm comes to net on the second serve and puts away an overhead smash, but Budge retaliates on the next point with a brilliant passing shot. Three points later he has worked himself to match point. Hardly a soul in the stadium, whatever their nationality, doubts that this great match and the Interzone Final have finally come to an end. A baseline rally ensues, each player waiting for a vulnerable short ball that never comes. Cramm finally sees an opening where no one else does and obviates his net-rushing plans with an outright forehand winner. Deuce.

Now Budge has a chance to come in, but he plays it safe, staying back, and Cramm, as cool as if it's the first point of the match, hits a bold approach shot, takes the net, and puts away a flawless stretching volley. But on break point Budge's cannonball comes through for a saving ace. At deuce Cramm forces his way to the net yet again and this time puts away an overhead smash for a second break point. Again, he is one point away from tying the match at seven-all. And this time Budge's serve falters; he misses the first and puts the second in safe and short to the German's backhand. Gottfried rotates his shoulders and sweeps his racket through the ball with perfect fluidity, ready to advance forward for another volley. But the ball hits the top of the net. The crowd groans; Cramm merely turns and walks back to the baseline. Deuce again.

A Budge ace gives him a second match point. But again Cramm saves it, this time hitting a rock-solid forehand return of serve with unthinkable sangfroid for a clean winner down the line. The stands shake with applause and cheers. The men from the press are scribbling madly: "Cramm has saved these match points with some of the most wonderful shots ever seen on a tennis court!" and "I cannot recall any effort quite so heroic and sustained with such gorgeous shots." *What is he thinking?* Budge must be railing. How can he do that on match point? Right, he's not thinking at all. He's in that special place; I've been there, too. I've been there *in this match.* Anyway, he's not going to make it easy for me, that's for sure.

Indeed, Cramm is beyond conscious thought. He isn't thinking of Budge, or Hitler or Himmler, or Tschammer und Osten up there in the box. He isn't thinking of the Gestapo's fat "von Cramm" file, with detailed descriptions of his comings and goings at those questionable underground clubs off the Kurfürstendamm. He is just *in* the moment, racing back and forth across the manicured turf like a boy chasing a balloon, his strokes as natural to him as eating and breathing. It's the greatest match of his life, and he is far beyond worrying about politics and police, winning and losing. He is playing tennis.

Twice in a row at deuce Budge hits overhead smashes to give him match points number three and four. But on both occasions his greatest stroke, his backhand, lets him down with balls that just miss. "Ouch," *American Lawn Tennis*'s Ned Potter actually jots in his notebook. "Oh . . . oh . . . oh . . ." Several reporters in the press box turn to each other and agree: if Budge loses his serve after all this, he's finished. How could anyone overcome that kind of emotional disappointment?

It is already the longest game of the match by far, sixteen points, and they're back to deuce. Now Budge gains the advantage once again when another unconscious Cramm backhand launched toward the baseline sails a few inches past it. Match point for the fifth time.

The spectators are beside themselves, looking left and right, silently congratulating one another on being present to witness this match. How long can the set go on? How long can this *game* go on? But as the players get ready once again, all conversation ceases. It sounds as if all respiration has ceased: Walter Pate will long remember the seeming vacuum of sound in the packed stadium.

For the two hundred and thirty-third time that afternoon, Don Budge tosses the ball above his head and hits his famous serve. Exhausted as he is, he goes for one of his cannonball aces, and it crashes beautifully right on target. There is a gasp from the stands as Cramm somehow lunges and not only returns it but gets it back deep. They exchange several crosscourt ground strokes, keeping them hard and deep so neither can attack. Finally Budge gets a backhand he thinks he can do something with and hits it hard down the line, intending to disrupt the rhythm of the point and take the offensive. However, it doesn't land as deep as he hoped, and instead Cramm takes it on the rise with his forehand, driving it deep to the opposite corner and charging the net, as he has done so successfully all afternoon. The crowd rises to its feet as one as Cramm sweeps forward.

Immediately Budge sprints to his right, all the way across the court at full speed. Cramm's shot is all but unreturnable. As Budge nears it, far off court on his forehand side, and lunges to intercept it, he loses balance and realizes he is going to fall. This is going to be his last shot; all he can do is go for a big passing shot and hope for the best. The German is at net, edging over to his left, the only side Budge will be able to hit to from his position. Budge takes a powerful swipe at the ball and tumbles forward onto the grass.

Bill Tilden knows just what he is feeling, for he described it in the opening sentence of his famous book: "There is no sensation in the sporting world so thoroughly enjoyable to me as that when I meet a tennis ball just right in the very middle of my racquet and smack it, just right, where my opponent should be but is not."

In fact, Cramm *is* where he should be, but it doesn't matter against a perfect shot. All he can do is watch as the ball rockets past him, out of reach, way out of the court but angled so sharply that it bounces just in the corner for an outright winner.

For a second the gallery can't believe the match is over. Then it explodes. The match has been "something so close to art," in James Thurber's view, "that at the end it was more as if a concert had ended than a tennis match. The shouts of 'Bravo!' when it was over came out of an emotion usually reserved for something more important." Alistair Cooke agrees: "And then a British crowd forgot its nature. It stood on benches . . . and must have been aware that the deep kind of roar they were making does not belong on any tennis court. It has belonged outside Buckingham Palace the night war was declared." Ned Potter simply puts down some shorthand in his notebook: "B fh pass lovely 7:23pm."

From where he lies sprawled on the ground, Budge at first can't tell if the ball was in or out. But even before he sees the linesman's call, he "could hear the cheers begin to swell. They were different cheers." Budge has won. The United States has won. Slowly, incredulously, the American lifts himself up off the grass and jogs toward the net, where Cramm has had to wait patiently for what seemed an unbearably long time. It feels like slow motion to Budge, and he has no desire to speed up the film. Applause falls on him like a refreshing mist. There at the net stands his vanquished friend, the most gracious sportsmanlike smile masking what must be turmoil underneath. Three Wimbledon finals in a row lost, and now the Davis Cup, which he was within a whisker of bringing home to Germany. But then Budge realizes that the smile is not a mask. Cramm is genuinely happy. Happy for his friend, glad for the fans who have watched such a fine match, at peace with himself. He seems to have absorbed into his being the Centre Court inscription, meeting triumph and disaster and treating those two imposters just the same. *Gottfried*, Budge thinks, *you certainly have got more out of the game than any player who has won everything.*

As he approaches, Budge moves to hug Cramm, but the German stops him by clasping his hand. "Don," he says, eloquent as an ambassador, "this was absolutely the finest match I have ever played in my life. I'm very happy I could have played it against you, whom I like so much. Congratulations." And with that their arms are around each other, as the crowd, still on their feet, cheers and cheers.

# MIRACLES of REDEMPTION

A YEAR LATER GOTTFRIED CRAMM was in prison. Bill Tilden was back in Europe, playing constantly and avoiding his creditors back home. And Don Budge was one tournament away from achieving tennis's first Grand Slam.

As expected, the American-German Interzone Final had decided the Davis Cup. Four days after Budge and Cramm's classic battle, the Americans took on Great Britain and easily defeated them, 4-1, reclaiming the Cup for the first time since 1926. English tennis fans were so resigned to this eventuality that they didn't even fill Centre Court for the Challenge Round. Fifteen thousand had stuffed the place for the Interzone Final, with a sizable throng left over to roam the grounds; but only about half that number came each day to watch their own team take on the United States.

Those who came saw Bunny Austin beat Frank Parker on the first day, in a match that looked like a snapshot from the future: the sun-tanned Parker in his short shorts, the Englishman in his own long shorts, sporting a "new fangled racket" of his own design, the Hazell Streamline, whose tripartite throat gave it the appearance of being oversize. But after Budge took out the big young lefty Charles Hare in straight sets (despite an unexpected 15-13 struggle in the first set), and then he and Mako won the doubles, Parker made up for being left out of the Interzone Final by providing the winning margin. He beat Hare easily, and the Cup was won. Budge beat Austin in the dead rubber, in which they joked with each other, swapped rackets for a while, and drank tea together during some of the changeovers. When Princess Helena Victoria presented the Cup to the victors, James Thurber noted that Budge "was given the most tremendous cheer of the day by a gallery whose hearts he had completely won. He was a heroic figure throughout Wimbledon and the Cup matches, and although ice never once formed on his wings, he deserved a Broadway shower of streamers as much as Lindbergh."

And that's just what he got. After five days of Ping-Pong and sun on the SS *Manhattan*, with the Davis Cup on display in the library, the team reached New York Harbor on August 5. There they were greeted by a group of luminaries including Dwight Davis and Holcombe Ward themselves, the originators of the Davis Cup. Then the players and captain, along with their Cup, rode on the top of a double-decker sightseeing bus down Fifth Avenue, while the Seventy-first Regiment Band played ahead of them and confetti and ticker tape fell on their shoulders.

A FEW WEEKS LATER GOTTFRIED CRAMM MADE HIS FIRST AND only visit to America, in the company of Henkel, Kleinschroth, and Germany's leading woman player, Marlies Horn. (Alfred Hitchcock, who was preparing to shoot his new film *The Lady Vanishes*, starring U.S. Davis Cup mascot Paul Lukas, disembarked the *Queen Mary* with them in New York on August 23.) *Time* magazine, introducing Cramm, their cover boy, to the American public, noted he was "equally amiable" speaking French, Italian, or English. "He likes dancing, field hockey, swimming, hiking, the cinema, Wagner, and after tournaments, night clubs and champagne."

Disregarding Tilden's advice to take a break from the rigors of touring, Gottfried had been happy to leave his troubles at home, embarking on an eight-month tour of America, Japan, and Australia. Life seemed much freer abroad, with no Gestapo agents following him, no ex-lovers needing his covert aid, and less pressure, it seemed, to win. (Shortly after the Davis Cup, he had lost in an early round of the

German Championships, dropping a rare fifth set. Henkel had run off with the title, in perfect harmony with the Nazi sports authorities' designs for the succession of power.) The only people hounding him and Henkel were friendly reporters, to whom Gottfried happily tossed characteristically modest bons mots: "For three years Tilden has been saying that I am the best amateur. It is the only time I have known him to be wrong."

Upon their arrival in New York, the Germans headed straight to Penn Station for the train to Boston. There, at the Longwood Cricket Club, Cramm and Henkel finally got revenge on Budge and Mako, surprising the Americans in the finals of the national doubles in straight sets. Then back to New York for the singles at Forest Hills. The American fans, who had been eager to finally see the famous German player, took Cramm to heart. "Gottfried's popularity was so great," Henkel wrote home, "that the last days he was constantly accompanied by two Pinkerton detectives [for] protection against the autograph hounds, and to enable him to go into the clubhouse unmolested."

His greatest fan had bodyguards of her own. Barbara Hutton was there in the front row every day Cramm played. She sat next to Curt Reventlow, still her husband, who fumed right through his gray morning coat and top hat; but she was really there with Gottfried, far more elegant on court in his white flannels and tailored ground strokes. "Her eyes were on Cramm from the minute she came in, as they changed ends, all the time," recalled another occupant of the box. "She was as taken by him as any person I've ever seen. She never said a word to anyone. I looked for an opportunity to say hello to her, but her gaze never wavered."

In the finals it was Budge and Cramm again, each looking for his first U.S. title. And again it went five sets, but this time Budge went on a rampage, launching a nearly flawless attack, and it was over quickly, six-one in the fifth. No one doubted that Cramm was the second best in the world again this year, but Don Budge was without doubt the world champion.

Apparently Gottfried had not been completely able to escape his troubles. At times throughout the tournament he had seemed oddly lackadaisical, losing two sets each to Bitsy Grant and Bobby Riggs before staging comebacks. At least one reporter found that although "from what we have seen of von Cramm in America we are able to recognize a great player . . . it is within bounds to say that he has not been at his peak since he almost beat Budge at Wimbledon. His malady is diagnosed as much more mental than physical. . . ."

He didn't linger in New York. On the very night of the Forest Hills final the German contingent boarded the *20th Century Limited* for the overnight trip to Chicago. After they played exhibitions there, the Santa Fe Railway's diesel-powered *Super Chief* pulled them across the Great Plains and Rockies, all the way to Los Angeles in only forty hours. There they met Budge, Mako, and the rest of the West Coast tennis world for the Pacific Southwest tournament at the Los Angeles Tennis Club. This was the showcase of western tennis, the most important hard-court tournament, and a favorite of the tennis-loving Hollywood crowd.

This year the Hollywood set had a surprise planned. Their crowd, which included a number of prominent Jews, were outraged at the sanctioned anti-Semitism raging in Nazi Germany, and also at the willingness of mainstream America to overlook it. So when Hitler's tennis star, Gottfried von Cramm, made his first appearance on the LATC's Center Court, a vast majority of the box seat occupants were going to stand and walk out in protest. On September 20 Cramm walked out onto the gray cement court for his California debut, against a young San Franciscan named Modeste Alloo. A bright smile lit his face as he walked toward the umpire's chair, gazing up around him at the crowd and the crisp blue sky. Applause rang out from the upper reaches of the stadium; the German seemed to have won over a new audience even before he began playing. The Hollywood royalty in their boxes shifted their weight, looked around at one another, and rested in their seats again. No one walked. If there was such thing as the opposite of a Nazi, they knew they had just seen it. "When I saw that man," Groucho Marx told Budge later, "I just felt instant shame at what I was supposed to do." A few months later Groucho and his friends would feel great relief that they had not snubbed Gottfried von Cramm.

Although he had rarely played on hard courts before, Cramm reached the finals of the Pacific Southwest, where he lost to Budge in four sets, and he won the mixed doubles with Helen Wills Moody, the great ex-champion, who at thirty-two was no longer playing competitive singles (though she would make a comeback the next year and win Wimbledon). Then it was up to the Berkeley Tennis Club for the Pacific Coast Championships, where Cramm disappointed the promoters, who were banking on another Budge-Cramm final, by falling to Bobby Riggs in the semis.

On October 7 Budge drove over from Oakland to the San Francisco Pier to wish Cramm, Henkel, Kleinschroth, and Horn bon voyage. He posed for a few pictures with them on the Japanese liner *Taiyo Maru* and then waved as they sailed through the Golden Gate and on to Japan. There, as they toured the country and dominated the few tournaments they played, Gottfried apparently began to feel more relaxed and started to speak freely. Asked to give a speech in Tokyo, he spoke about German-Japanese relations, conspicuously failing to mention even once Hitler or the Nazis.

In December they sailed on to Australia, where they met Budge and Mako. They celebrated Christmas with their American friends and played a series of exhibition matches. Gottfried was playing beautifully, and he beat Budge twice, including a thrilling 4-6, 10-8, 12-10 battle in a triangular team competition between Germany, the United States, and Australia.

This was a free and easy time for Gottfried. He played tennis, soaked in the sun, and saw the country. He and Henkel caused a minor stir by sunbathing in illegal topless bathing trunks at the beach in Glenelg. In Melbourne he flirted with Charles Buttrose, the journalist assigned to ghostwrite his stories for the Melbourne *Sun-Pictorial*. Buttrose was impressed with Cramm's intelligence and sophistication but less pleased "when after having caressed my right kneecap he suggested that we take it beyond journalism and into more intimate fields." Australia felt like another world from Nazi Germany. They couldn't follow him down here, could they?

In fact, there were many ears Down Under sympathetic to the Nazi regime, including a small but active subset of the local German community called the National Socialist Organization of Foreign Germans. One way or another, word was getting back to the Gestapo of certain loose statements coming from Cramm concerning his own government. He had decried the loss of Daniel Prenn to the Davis

Cup team. He had complained that mandatory military service was undermining the development of young tennis players. He had referred to the Führer as "a housepainter"!

Perhaps, as Tilden guessed, Gottfried wasn't feeling as carefree as he looked and was finally beginning to crack under the constant threat of persecution: "I think he had reached the point where he almost wished something would happen to relieve the strain of holding himself in. More and more openly he spoke out against Hitler."

Warnings were reaching him. After a newspaper reported that Cramm and the other Germans had gone to see the antiwar film *The Road Back*, an English adaptation of Erich Maria Remarque's novel, which had been banned by the Nazis, a letter arrived at their hotel. A Dr. Cahn, a former Hamburg journalist and now a podiatrist in Melbourne, warned the German players that they would now be in danger should they return to Germany: "Perhaps the time has come for you too to flee German soil." Another acquaintance told Gottfried that he would surely be on the Gestapo's blacklist, and would probably be arrested, for the public comments he had made. To both of these warnings Cramm merely laughed and shrugged his shoulders, as if such a fate could not befall him, or if it did, it was all the same to him.

By the time everyone made it to Adelaide for the Australian Championships, Cramm's game was showing signs of cracking as well. He was in nowhere as good form as he had been in the exhibitions, and he went down in the semifinals in straight sets to the young Australian John Bromwich, who lost even quicker in the finals to Budge.

Cramm and Henkel also lost the doubles final in straight sets, to Bromwich and Adrian Quist. The only good news for Gottfried in his final days in Australia was a letter that found its way to him from Paris. It was from Manasse Herbst, who wrote that he had been unable to find work in Lisbon and was now living in the French capital with his brother. Well, at least he was safe, thank God. It would be good to be back in Paris, just a few months from now, to see Manasse, to be back on the red clay of Roland Garros. Don said he was going to play there for the first time, so finally he would have a chance to face Budge on his favorite surface. Ah, Paris in May.

But Gottfried would not see Paris for a long time. On March 4, 1938, after three weeks at sea and a train ride from Naples, he and his companions arrived at Munich; they had spent two hundred days abroad. The next day they split up, each to his own home. They had planned to reconvene in Berlin in a few days for an official reception by Reichssportführer Tschammer und Osten but were told the event had been canceled for indeterminate reasons. Gottfried traveled with his mother, who had met him in Munich, back to Brüggen for a joyful homecoming with the rest of the family.

There, the next evening, as all the Cramm brothers sat around the castle salon after dinner with their mother, wives, children, and friends, there came again the insistent knocks on the door. A servant announced that two men from the government were here to ask Gottfried about his trip. With an ironic smile he left his family. When he finally returned, after quite a time, there was no point in continuing the facade. "I'm afraid I'm under arrest," he announced. He was given a short time to pack, and then the Gestapo agents took him away in their black Mercedes. "To Berlin" was all they would tell his hysterical mother.

They didn't know whom they were brushing off. Jutta von Cramm was by all accounts a force to be reckoned with. The very next morning she followed them to Berlin, set up camp in a friend's home, and set about finding her son. She finally found him in a cell at the Gestapo's Prinz-Albrecht Strasse headquarters—the most feared address in Berlin. But only after weeks did she learn that he was being held for suspected "moral delinquency"—which could mean only one thing. And this time when she visited him, she found he had taken a turn for the worse. He seemed to have suffered a nervous breakdown: "[His brother] Adalbert and I visited Gottfried, the entire surroundings were abominable. But I remained calm, and he was also able to. He looked bad, had bedbugs and very cold hands, and said he awaited our orders but intended to kill himself. I was able to hug him and strengthen him, and we had a good talk."

For the next six weeks she hardly rested for meals as she exhausted every influential contact the family had. She went to Prince Bernhard zur Lippe, a distant relative who had just visited Brüggen and who had been a member of the SS; but he had fallen out of favor with Hitler recently by marrying into the Dutch royal family. King Gustav of Sweden, Gottfried's old tennis friend, was receptive to her entreaties, but he too had little influence in the Third Reich. She hired one of the most famous lawyers in Berlin, Carl Langbehn. Langbehn, thirty-six, though a member of the Nazi Party, was by now a fervent opponent of the regime. He also had good connections with Himmler, as their daughters were school friends. Langbehn was able to use this connection once, later in 1938, to free his old law professor from a concentration camp. Sadly, though, it would not be enough to save his own skin just six years later.

Jutta didn't write to Don Budge, but Budge did his best to help his friend anyway. He got a group of twenty-five sports figures in California to sign an open letter to the German government demanding Cramm's immediate release. They called him "the ideal sportsman, a perfect gentleman and decency personified. . . . No country could have wished for a finer representative—no sport for a more creditable exponent." They also complained of the "dark secrecy" behind the case and insisted the charges were "mere subterfuges." The letter was signed by Budge, Joe DiMaggio, Alice Marble, Little Bill Johnston, Helen Wills Moody, and others. (Conspicuously missing was the name of Bill Tilden, but then Big Bill was on the road as always, this time to Ireland for a tour with Henri Cochet, and Budge likely never asked him to sign.)

The Americans' demands probably had as little effect as the efforts of Prince Bernhard and King Gustav. But on April 13 Jutta finally secured an audience with Göring himself. What did Gottfried expect? the corpulent sybarite may well have asked her from behind his ornate desk. I warned him many times, gave him every opportunity to secure his safety. But he spurned my protection, spoke out of line once too often. Pity: if only he had won that match against the Americans, I could probably have kept Himmler off his back. Imagine the Davis Cup on display at Rot-Weiss! But no matter, my dear lady. A great spirit must be given a little leeway. Personally I'd like to see him back on the team for 1939. I will make sure the punishment is relatively lenient. You need not worry.

Along with virtually every other aspect of public life, the Nazis had transformed Germany's judicial system. Upon taking power Hitler had appointed as secretary of state of the German Ministry of Justice one Roland Freisler, a lawyer and judge who before 1933 had done time in prison for aiding and abetting fraudulent bankruptcy, perjury, and general fraud. Now he was in utter control of every aspect of the judicial system, and those who had previously tried and condemned him— those who hadn't been sent to concentration camps, that is—were forced to stand and applaud his every contemptible speech. Under Freisler, judges now held total power over the fate of their defendants. In his words, the judges were "completely independent, no longer the slave of paragraphs in law books, or of misguided public opinion." They handed down sentences as they personally saw fit, like "an absolute king, accountable only for the welfare of the State."

Judge Spohner, who handled Cramm's case and in fact heard almost exclusively "Paragraph 175" cases, was no different. And he was famous for his decrees not being appealed. The reason, he willingly revealed, was that after sentencing he dispatched a subordinate to make clear to the defendant that an appeal would lead only to a harsher sentence. "Well, my good sir," he told a reporter with a laugh, "if the case were appealed, it probably would be reassigned to me, which would mean new and much more cautious proceedings. You know that in sexual offenses it is impossible to check details, and securing proof is difficult business and a nuisance. [I] make it clear that it would be best to accept the verdict without challenge."

Langbehn, Cramm's lawyer, devised a crafty strategy to minimize the damage. In his first days in prison, distraught, Gottfried had confessed to sexual relations with Herbst from early 1931 well into 1936. There was no point in retracting the confession completely; they had made it clear that if he refused to confess, they would punish him with a stay at a concentration camp. However, Langbehn wanted him to declare that he had mistaken the dates due to his state of nervous collapse. He would insist at the trial that he and Herbst gone no further than *gegenseitigen Onanieverkehr* (mutual masturbation), and that they had ceased even that transgression by the beginning of 1935, when the Nazi broadening of Paragraph 175 made *all* homosexual activity punishable by law.

But Cramm was charged not only with homosexual offenses but also with *Devisensvergehens* (foreign-exchange transgression), an equally serious crime. In the cash-desperate Third Reich, citizens incurred stiff penalties for so much as forgetting to take off their wedding rings before leaving the country. And the Gestapo had discovered that Cramm had funneled some 20,000 Reichsmarks abroad to Herbst over the past few years.

There was only one way out of this, Langbehn told him. Herbst was safe in Paris, and he wasn't coming back while these murderers were in power. Cramm must tell them that Herbst blackmailed him, that he threatened to tell them everything if Cramm didn't send him the money. Manasse would understand. He would want Gottfried to do it.

On a Saturday, May 14, 1938, in the gloomy old Moabit courthouse on Lehrterstrasse, closed to both press and public, Judge Spohner heard the evidence against Gottfried von Cramm. As he had been coached, Cramm admitted to the affair with Herbst—up to a point. For good measure, the Gestapo had thrown in a denunciation by the notorious Otto Schmidt, a street hustler whom, when he wasn't blackmailing gay men on his own, the Gestapo paid to testify against accused homosexuals. But Cramm swore, as he had from his earliest interrogations, that Schmidt's testimony—that he had seen Cramm disappear into the Hotel Bavaria for a couple hours with a young male streetwalker—was an utter fabrication.

At the end of the day, in an unusual gesture, possibly due to the international interest in the case, Spohner allowed the small crowd of reporters, family, and friends who had gathered in the hallways into the courtroom to hear his verdict.

The court accepted the defense regarding the currency transgressions. It was certainly believable that a Jew would blackmail anyone for 20,000 Reichsmarks given the chance. But Spohner rejected the defendant's claim that he had ceased relations with the Jew Herbst beginning in 1935; and he further refused to accept Langbehn's argument that one could not be punished for violations that occurred before the new Nazi laws made them illegal or on foreign soil. Von Cramm was found guilty of the Paragraph 175 transgressions.

As regarded sentencing, the court considered it in von Cramm's favor that it was his first conviction, that he had rendered distinguished service to German sports, and that "his partner, a Galician Jew, was not particularly in need or worthy of protection." On the other hand, Spohner pontificated, it was to the baron's great shame that he had brought disgrace on such a fine family and on the very institution, German sport, that he had helped to glorify.

But perhaps Göring had kept his promise to Jutta von Cramm. For after going on and on about Gottfried's weak character and moral delinquency, Spohner pronounced an unusually light sentence: one year here in Moabit prison, minus the two months already spent in confinement.

So here he would stay, in this dreary hundred-year-old dungeon, a ten-minute drive from his apartment. The guards took him back to his new home: four walls, a bed, a wooden stool, and in the corner a humiliating excuse for a toilet. For exercise, instead of striking tennis balls with perfection on the groomed clay courts at Rot-Weiss, he spent an hour a day walking in a circle around the courtyard with the other prisoners. Many of Cramm's three thousand fellow prisoners—Jews, political prisoners, and other homosexuals—were beaten mercilessly, and some were even killed with random violence; but Cramm apparently settled into a relatively bearable existence. He was given jobs as an office clerk or kitchen help. While most prisoners were denied books or newspapers, Cramm was permitted, presumably while working in the office, to listen on the radio as Australia destroyed Germany's new Davis Cup team in the Interzone Final in Boston.

It was a miracle they had gotten there at all. To replace Cramm, the German Lawn Tennis Federation had taken advantage of the *Anschluss* with Austria. Just days after Cramm had been arrested in March, Hitler's troops marched into Vienna, and Austria joined the Third Reich without so much as a whimper of protest. Hitler not only annexed his home country, but the Davis Cup team annexed Georg von Metaxa, Austria's number-one player. Never mind the Davis Cup rule that a player must sit out for three years before playing for a different country. The Davis Cup nations fell over themselves to oblige Germany and amend Regulation 33:

> If a player shall have represented a Nation and such Nation shall be absorbed, in whole or in part, by another Nation, he shall, if belonging to the whole or part absorbed, be deemed for the purpose of these Regulations not to have previously represented any Nation.

Poland was the only country to protest, but it was ignored, and before long the Davis Cup would be the least of its concerns. Of course Metaxa was no Cramm, and in the European Zone final against Yugoslavia in July at Rot-Weiss, after Henkel had lost in a stunning upset to Franjo Puncec, the new German barely squeaked by unknown Josip Palada, 12-10 in the fifth set. It then took another five-set win by Henkel and Metaxa in the doubles to advance.

In Boston, against Australia, the absence of Cramm was fatal. The Germans lost in five quick matches to John Bromwich and Adrian Quist. Henkel and Metaxa were particularly downtrodden in the final two singles matches, for that morning they had received a cable from Berlin ordering the team home immediately "for a rest." It sounded like a punishment for losing so badly, but it might also have been Germany retaliating for Don Budge's announcement that as a direct consequence of the jailing of Gottfried Cramm, he would not be playing in Germany that summer as he'd planned. Or maybe the government didn't want its team to be in the United States just as Hitler was ordering a mobilization of the armed forces and planning his takeover of the Sudetenland. In any case, Henkel and Metaxa were forced to default in the national doubles at Longwood and also miss Forest Hills and a planned California trip. Perhaps Cramm heard this news on the radio as he worked in the Moabit office and smiled grimly as he filed more prison sentences.

As he followed Budge's easy victories in the French, Wimbledon, and U.S. championships, he smiled more easily, genuinely happy for his friend's success. But again he must have felt great frustration. How he would have loved to be able to provide some tougher competition— particularly on the clay at Roland Garros, where they had never met. But he had to be satisfied with reading about the major tournaments in the German newspapers, which never mentioned the name von Cramm.

On Sunday, October 16, 1938, a large automobile pulled up before the gates of the Moabit prison, and Gottfried von Cramm quickly slipped in. Almost five months before his sentence was due to end, he was being released "for good behavior" on two years' parole, "during which he must prove worthy of this act of mercy." His brother Adalbert sat behind the wheel, and together they sped back to Brüggen, where the family was finally able to celebrate Gottfried's return for good.

Cramm knew he had gotten off easy. Nineteen thirty-eight was the peak of the antihomosexual terror: the Gestapo in Berlin alone had thirty-five officers working exclusively on Paragraph 175 cases. Homosexuals had been disappearing from the Berlin streets by the thousands, and most who went to prison, when their sentence was up, were transferred to Sachsenhausen or other concentration camps. Just this April, while Gottfried was awaiting trial, the Gestapo had announced that any man convicted of "gross indecency" with another man could be sent directly to the camps.

There homosexuals, along with Jews, suffered the most humiliating and deadliest treatments of all the inmates. Identified by the pink triangles on their uniforms, they were often singled out for the *Strafkompanie* (punishment company), work detail so brutal and unceasing that it was nearly the equivalent of a death sentence. They were called in front of the camp to be savagely beaten. At night, clothed only in thin nightshirts in the frozen winter, they were ordered to keep their hands outside the covers "to keep them from masturbating." Violators were taken outside in the snow, had buckets of cold water dumped on them, and were left standing there for an hour. Few survived.

The litany of tortures designed for the men with the pink triangles, as well as for the general inmate population, goes on and on. But for homosexuals, persecution continued long after the end of the war. Richard Gabler, the last Nazi head of antihomosexual operations in the Berlin criminal police, was not only still at work in 1946 but was promoted to head of the entire vice squad. The courts of the Allied Occupation decided that the concentration camps did not count as lawful incarceration, and homosexuals liberated from the camps were sent back to regular prisons to finish their sentences. For legally speaking, they were still criminals. The Nazi enhancements to Paragraph 175 were still on the books in West Germany until 1969, and the law itself was not revoked until 1994.

"I have gone to see von Cramm," Henner Henkel told a French journalist in October 1938, "and I have found him in perfect physical condition. His desire is to compete in the next Davis Cup campaign if possible." The very same day, however, Erich Schönborn, the head of the German Lawn Tennis Federation, was thinking along other lines: "Since the return of the Sudetenland to the Reich, we can count on Roderich Menzel, who ought to be our number one."

"—but von Cramm?" ventured a reporter.

"I do not know whether he will play Davis Cup. At the moment we can count on Menzel, Henkel, and von Metaxa. Quite a trio, in fact." He may have thought he'd have Bunny Austin playing for Germany before long. Clearly, though, even Göring wasn't going to be able to get a convicted homosexual back on the Davis Cup team.

Instead Cramm accepted an invitation from his friend King Gustav, who had just turned eighty, to come live in Sweden, work with the Swedish team, and perhaps even play for them. Then in early 1939 he was back in what had become a second home, Cairo, practicing in the heat as usual, preparing for another season of tennis. He played some tournaments in Egypt and then, back in Stockholm in May, played for Sweden in an unofficial team competition against the United States (winning both his matches). Thus he refuted radio sportscaster Bill Stern, a notorious rumor-monger who had informed his listeners not long before that "a squad of Nazis led by Max Schmeling had cut off the feet of Gottfried von Cramm in a concentration camp."

In June he was back in London, hoping to make his Wimbledon comeback. But, still blacklisted by his own country, he had no choice but to apply as an individual (national tennis federations normally entered their players), and "a Wimbledon committee made up of viscounts and wing-commanders and right honourables" decided they could not admit a player who had been convicted of a morals charge.

The Queen's Club, which held the biggest pre-Wimbledon tune-up tournament, after a heated debate did allow Cramm to play, and he took full advantage of his opportunity. In the quarterfinals he easily beat Elwood Cooke, who would get to the finals of Wimbledon in a couple weeks. And then in the semifinals came the big match against Bobby Riggs. With Budge gone professional, the twenty-one-year-old Riggs had risen to the top of the American ranks and was widely expected to win Wimbledon. Whoever won this semifinal at Queen's was sure to win the final against Ghaus Mohammed of India, so to many this match was no less than "the unofficial world's championship."

"Rushing to the club from the reception at Guildhall to King George and Queen Elizabeth," Cramm ran onto the court and ran away with the match. He completely overwhelmed Riggs 6-0, 6-1. Tilden and Budge, who were in England for the beginning of a European pro tour and had both been happy to see Gottfried again, watched the match together in courtside seats. At the end of the match, which took all of half an hour, Tilden shook his head in admiration. "Von Cramm is undoubtedly the finest amateur in the world today," he said once again. This time he was finally right. Though noticeably thinner and paler than when English tennis fans had last seen him two years before, Cramm "was in ruthless trim," reported *The Times*. "There was not an ace for which he did not strive to the limit of his flashing strokes. . . . The conclusion was that von Cramm, were he in the Wimbledon field, would take on the invincibility of a Budge."

Riggs went on to win Wimbledon, despite some lowering of expectations after the loss to Cramm. But then perhaps lowered expectations were exactly what Riggs wanted. In small tournaments in the States, he often would throw the opening games, or even a set, until his brother in the stands gave him the signal that he had succeeded in taking a few bets. Then Bobby would take over the match. But his reputation as a hustler first became a legend that week in London, when he bet on himself to win the Wimbledon singles, doubles, and mixed doubles. He pulled off the trifecta and raked in 20,000 pounds—$100,000 at that time, a veritable fortune. Surely the crushing loss to Cramm at the Queen's Club had raised the betting line against him. (To be more accurate, the legend grew over the succeeding decades. Much like Budge's story of the Hitler phone call, Riggs didn't tell the story this way until many years later. According to his biographer, Tom Lecompte, it is more likely that he *tried* to place such a bet but was only allowed to bet on himself winning the singles, which netted him forty pounds. But as with Budge's story, Riggs's embellishment was so often repeated that it became established "history.")

Even allowing for his chicanery, though, most experts agreed that 1939 was Gottfried von Cramm's best chance to finally win Wimbledon. One reporter claimed that his play at Queen's could have been equaled only by "a Perry or a Budge at their best." "If ever a player looked as though he could go on and win the Wimbledon championship," wrote

*The Times,* "it was von Cramm." Yet when Wimbledon rolled around, that same paper had not a word to say about his shameful exclusion from tennis's greatest showcase. Instead they remarked admiringly how German tennis officials "have always found someone to step into the breach when men like Prenn and Gottfried von Cramm dropped out."

At least England allowed him into the country. Cramm had planned on returning to the United States in August and playing Forest Hills. But when he applied for a visa with the American Consulate in Berlin, he was automatically rejected due to his conviction of "moral turpitude."

He had been telling some reporters that he was considering living in the United States instead of Sweden, and even that he might consider "a good professional offer" if it came his way (and in fact promoter Jack Harris was planning to make one). But all that was rendered moot not only by the visa rejection but by the eruption of war. At the beginning of September, when Hitler invaded Poland and a new world war began, Cramm knew exactly what he must do. Although he could easily have become a Swedish citizen and remained there, he did not. In a letter to Tilden, he wrote, "No matter what my views or feelings toward the present government, Germany is my homeland and I could not look myself in the face if I did not return."

Normally a man of his background would have been given a commission as an officer in the Wehrmacht. But his criminal record precluded that, and he was drafted as a private in May 1940. He spent a year and a half on peaceful duty in occupied Utrecht, Holland. But the last day of 1941 found him with his regiment on a transport train rolling eastward, toward the Russian front. From Smolensk they were flown to the fighting stage, and they leaped from the plane into hell on earth. After six months of murderous, pillaging invasion into the heart of Russia, the Wehrmacht had finally ground to a frozen halt nineteen miles from Moscow, blocked at last by Soviet forces and the historically indomitable Russian winter. Hitler's army was now in full retreat and suffering the vengeful counterattack of the Red Army. Cramm was assigned to a six-man machine-gun group. Lying in the snow in their thin coats, they tried to keep the guns operating in the bitter cold, vainly resisting the brutal Soviet onslaught.

After three weeks of this horror, Cramm's life was saved by a blessing in disguise: frostbite overcame both his legs, rendering him useless. A Junkers 52 aircraft carried him off from the airport he and his comrades had been trying to defend, and he ended up in the military hospital in Warsaw. Of the 120 men in his company, 19 eventually came straggling back to Germany.

By the time Cramm recovered from his injuries a few months later, he was a civilian. Somewhat mysteriously, and despite the fact that he had been awarded the Iron Cross for bravery, he was given a dishonorable discharge from the Wehrmacht. Probably it was part of a growing movement within the Nazi Party to remove the aristocracy from positions of influence, culminating with the "Princes Decree" of May 1943, which removed all royalty from the government, party, and armed forces.

It was too late for two of the Cramm brothers. Adalbert had died of pneumonia in the service in 1940, and Berno went missing in action around the time of Gottfried's injuries. Gottfried went home to Bodenburg and helped to run the family estates. He also spent much time during the rest of the war in Berlin and Stockholm. He was still helping to train Sweden's young tennis players, including Lennart Bergelin, the future coach of Björn Borg. But he was also carrying messages from the growing Resistance in Berlin to the outside world via neutral Sweden. When in Berlin he lived in the home of family friends, the Gersdorffs, which was a prominent meeting place of the Resistance. Also living there was Marie Vassiltchikov, a displaced Russian princess who was intimate friends with many Resistance figures. Here Gottfried got to know these people too, and he pledged to do what he could to help undermine the Nazi machine. Upon each return from Sweden, he was interrogated by the Gestapo, but apparently they were unable to find any evidence with which to charge him.

On July 20, 1944, a Resistance plot to assassinate Hitler was put into action. Count Claus von Stauffenberg, a high-ranking officer who had lost an eye and one hand in Africa the year before, attended a military briefing at Hitler's *Wolfsschanze* (Wolf's Lair) headquarters in East Prussia. In his briefcase were two small bombs. He set off the timed detonator with a pencil, placed his briefcase under the conference table near the Führer, and soon excused himself to take a phone call. Unfortunately, another officer found the satchel to be in his way and moved it to the other side of a heavy wooden table support. When the bombs went off, destroying most of the room and killing four people, Hitler, though bruised and shaken, suffered only minor injuries.

Enraged, he ordered bloodthirsty vengeance. Anyone remotely connected with the plot must be rounded up and "hanged like cattle." He meant it. Among the more than two hundred people executed— from a pool of five thousand detainees in a mad, wrathful roundup of anyone generally suspected to be an enemy of the Reich—many suffered torturous deaths, strung up with piano wire from slaughterhouse meathooks.

Cramm and Missy Vassiltchikov had forged "an intense friendship" as together they lived through the nightmarish bombing of Berlin, which reduced his beloved city to "hillocks of rubble," the blazing infernos from the fire bombs making the outdoors warmer in winter than the cold houses with no heating fuel. Now they suffered together at the reports of the arrests, perfunctory trials, and horrid executions of their friends, including Carl Langbehn, the lawyer who had defended Cramm in his 1938 trial. Somehow the Gestapo's indiscriminate net of terror passed them by. Upon returning from Bodenburg in August, he told Missy, "I don't want to hear what is happening to them. All I want to know is whether any of them will survive and get out, who is still free, and when they intend to try again. For if so, they can count on me!" He asked her to arrange a meeting between him and Alex Werth, one of the undiscovered conspirators, but nothing came of it.

Cramm spent the last few months of the war at Bodenburg and was there when the last German soldiers came through, heading east for the final defense of Berlin. The war was over. Two of his brothers were dead; most of the brave members of the Resistance he had known in Berlin during the war had been executed. Kai Lund, his old doubles partner, came home missing an arm and a leg, and Henner Henkel had disappeared into the black hole that was the Battle of Stalingrad. Geoffrey Nares, of happier days in London, was dead too. He had joined the 12th Royal Lancers and became captain of an armored car in Egypt in 1941 and 1942. He had proved "a most courageous and intelligent officer," but just before the Battle of El Alamein he'd come down with sandfly fever and died of a brain tumor in the hospital in Cairo. Since his affair with Gottfried, Geoffrey had vanished from his famous father's biography in *Who's Who*. His valor in the desert was not enough to reinstate him.

Manasse Herbst, at least, was safe in the United States. Like Daniel Prenn, he had had to escape two cataclysms and had made it out of France before the Wehrmacht marched in. Herbst would marry, and he and his wife would visit Gottfried in Germany twice after the war. Cramm had helped save him and his family by allowing them to get out of Germany with their savings, and Langbehn had been right: if being accused of blackmail saved Gottfried years of prison time or worse, Herbst was happy to have been the temporary scapegoat.

Gottfried's ex-wife Lisa had married Gustav Jaenecke in 1940, and both had survived the war. Gottfried remained their good friend and even waded with them through their ruined apartment, which had been hit in the Allied bombing raids, helping to set things right. A few years later she and Jaenecke also divorced, and Lisa married a third time, to a Dr. Wolfgang Ammann, and this marriage lasted for the rest of a long lifetime. Whenever Gottfried was in Munich, he visited them at their beautiful lakeside home on the Ammersee.

In 1946, as Germany dug itself out of the rubble, Cramm got right back to tennis. He and a few others undertook to rebuild the Rot-Weiss Club, which had been badly damaged in the bombing of Berlin, and within three years there was a new clubhouse and a new Center Court stadium and the club was once again hosting the national championships. In 1947 and 1948, now in his late thirties, Gottfried von Cramm was once again the number-one German tennis player and was named "Athlete of the Year" by the German sportswriters. Though the Nazis had defamed him with their prosecution and prison sentence, the taint hadn't stuck. Many people felt, or at least proclaimed, that it had been a trumped-up charge with political grounds; and those who knew the truth didn't seem to mind. "Gottfried was a very private man," said Ladislav Hecht, the Jewish Slovakian player who escaped the Nazis and played as an American after the war. "We knew he was homosexual. He always seemed to have an entourage of young men around him. But none of us ever gave it much thought. Gottfried was such a kind man, a gentleman in every sense."

At the age of forty he was training as hard as ever, working out for hours in the baking heat of Cairo's Gezirah Tennis Club, running far younger players into the clay. He practiced often there with the future world champion Jaroslav Drobny, who had fled Czechoslovakia and become an Egyptian citizen, and beat Drobny in the Alexandria tournament in 1949. Two years later Cramm experienced for the second time Germany's reinstatement in international tennis after a world war, and he led the Davis Cup team again after a fourteen-year absence. Almost single-handedly he led Germany to the 1951 European Zone final, winning all three of his matches in three straight 3-2 victories.

That same year Cramm appeared at Wimbledon for the first time since his famous match with Budge. He drew his friend Drobny, the number-two seed, in the first round, and the All England Club scheduled Cramm's comeback appearance as the tournament opener on Centre Court. As the Gentleman of Wimbledon, almost forty-two, stepped onto the hallowed grass, as dashing as ever in his now-anachronistic long white slacks, the sellout crowd rose in a standing ovation. He fought hard and produced some of his brilliant tennis of old, but he lost to Drobny, who would soon be a Wimbledon champion, 9-7, 6-4, 6-4. Another standing ovation escorted him as he left Centre Court for the last time.

He played his final Davis Cup tie in 1953, in another farewell appearance, at Roland Garros stadium in Paris, the scene of his two greatest championships. Nearing the age of forty-four, he won one match, lost two tough five-setters, and waved good-bye to the Parisian crowd and to Davis Cup tennis.

On his postwar visits to Wimbledon, as a player and later as a spectator, Cramm often saw his old partner Daniel Prenn. A Jewish refugee, a clay-court specialist in the land of lawn tennis, Prenn had made good in England. In 1938, knowing his friend was in a Nazi prison suffering the fate that he himself had escaped, Prenn played his next-to-last summer of serious tennis. He entered the singles, doubles, and mixed doubles at Wimbledon. Although his best result was reaching the third round in the mixed, he played a highly competitive first-round match in singles, winning the first two sets against another Englishman and succumbing only six-four in the fifth set. If he had won, in the second round he would have faced the number-four seed: Henner Henkel.

After losing in the first round again in 1939, he finally turned completely from tennis to business. He brought Truvox Engineering through the war years, wondering all through the Battle of Britain, as the bombs rained down on London's rooftops and on Centre Court, whether he would have to make a third escape—or if a third escape would even be possible. By war's end his mother and sister Tamara had disappeared into the unfathomable hell of the Holocaust. (His father had died of pleurisy at the beginning of the war.) But he had his son Oliver now, and his sister Betty, or "Bobka," was thriving in London as well, working for the BBC World Service. He turned his back on the past and poured all his energy into the future.

Truvox became a runaway success. In 1950 Prenn's first major acquisition of another loudspeaker company ended the era he later would describe as "before my first Rolls." He sent his son to Oxford and hobnobbed with the queen as they watched his racehorses gallop. Though he didn't play tennis anymore, his son Oliver became Junior Wimbledon Champion in 1955 and played on the international circuit for a few years before joining the family business. Prenn later had another son, John, who in 1981 became world champion in rackets (a sport similar to squash but played with a harder ball on a larger court).

Over the years Cramm and others tried to get Prenn to return to Berlin and the Rot-Weiss Club for various events, but he refused. Finally in 1984 the president of the Rot-Weiss Club, Wolfgang Hofer, won him over, and the eighty-year-old Prenn did pay a visit, watched some tennis on the courts he had once ruled, and palled around with Hanne Nüsslein and Fred Perry. He loved seeing the old club, and old friends again, and he had done so in the nick of time, for not long afterward he began to recede into the fog of Alzheimer's disease. The Jew born in Vilnius who fled the Russian Revolution, the German tennis champion who escaped the Nazis, died just before his eighty-seventh birthday, in 1991, a wealthy English gentleman.

Even more sensational to the Wimbledon crowd in 1951 than Gottfried von Cramm's comeback on Centre Court was his activity off the court. Every day the papers ran photos of him and his daily escort, Barbara Hutton. The heiress's fascination with "her tennis player" had not abated at all since 1937. Even the day before she married her third husband, movie star Cary Grant, in 1942, a gossip column was reporting that she had recently been making "secret transatlantic telephone calls to a certain 'German Baron'" with whom she was "apparently deeply in love." Indeed, she had been placing "radio-telephone calls" to Gottfried at Bodenburg from a hotel in Mexico City. And even while married to Grant, she sent Cramm love poems extolling his "honey hued" hair and his eyes like "green lakes in the snow"; even while traveling during the war, he had carried with him a red leather picture frame she'd sent with three photos of her. She drove Grant and two successive husbands to distraction with her obsession for Cramm, even telephoning him for hours while on honeymoons with others. When she was sick or depressed, it was Gottfried she called for. On her thirty-ninth birthday, in 1951, when she was in the midst of substance addiction and deep depression, Cramm invited her to Cologne for a month. Finally in 1955 she got her man. He joined her in Tangier for a vacation, from where she wrote a friend that they were engaged: "Imagine! After all these years. 18 to be exact."

According to Cramm's friends, he didn't really want to marry her but thought he could help her by doing so. After the war he had set up three of his former machine-gun-group comrades, who fled eastern Germany with nothing but the clothes they wore, in business and hired the other one as his chauffeur. Later, he helped East German tennis players to seek asylum in the West, paying many of the expenses himself. When Kai Lund came back from the war maimed, Gottfried bought him a small hotel near Baden-Baden to run. Now perhaps he could help his friend, the "poor little rich girl" who had turned a life of unimaginable wealth and privilege into one of addiction and depression and who was convinced that only her tennis champion could save her.

For her part, she must have thought she could right the one thing she could see wrong with him. They were married on November 8, 1955, in Versailles, but almost from the beginning the marriage felt wrong to both of them. He could never be more than a close friend to her and not even as close a friend as she wanted. She expected Gottfried to go gallivanting around the world with her, living the life of the idle superrich. But he had started his own cotton-importing company in Hamburg in 1951 and also was still very much involved in German tennis. Also, to the dismay of both, the United States still would not allow Cramm into the country. Like the All England Club, the U.S.

government considered a conviction a conviction, no matter that it came from the notoriously corrupt Nazi courts. And those guilty of "moral turpitude"—that is to say, homosexuals—were explicitly unwelcome in the United States.

As a result, husband and wife spent much of their time apart, and even when they were together, the fairy-tale ending seemed to be dissolving. He was uncomfortable with her heavy drinking and dissolute lifestyle, and she became more and more enraged at his preference for young men over her. They parted for good after little more than a year, though the divorce was not finalized until 1959. Through the years she would still occasionally call on Gottfried for emotional support, and as late as 1974 he flew to Madrid to see her. But Barbara Hutton was one person he was ultimately unable to help. She died of a heart attack in 1979, at the age of sixty-six, after years of drug abuse, alcoholism, anorexia, and depression.

After splitting with her in 1957, Cramm went back to his life in Germany and also continued to spend much of each year in Egypt. He had amassed so many friends and contacts there over time that he was able to forge a very successful business importing cotton from Egypt, and later from Sudan and Iran as well, to West Germany. He also still enjoyed playing tennis and socializing in Cairo, Alexandria, and Khartoum. And just as he had been Paris's favorite foreign champion, so too, according to Dick Savitt, a tennis great of the 1950s, "I don't think I've ever seen a man more revered in a foreign country than the baron was in Egypt."

On November 9, 1976, he was in Alexandria on business. When he was finished meeting with his business associates, they offered him their car and driver to take him back to Cairo. Cramm accepted and joined the driver in the front seat, as always. Call me Gottfried, he'd say, and carry on a pleasant conversation instead of sitting in the back like a baron.

The 130-mile road was straight as a sideline, one lane each way, with few intersections. You could drive for miles without seeing another car. They were only 20 miles from Cairo when a military truck coming toward them suddenly swerved into their lane, out of control. Cramm's driver had no chance to avoid the collision and died instantly. Gottfried, whom no one could remember ever being ill, hated hospitals and had sworn he would not die in one. He did not, passing away in the ambulance on the way.

Gottfried Cramm had never betrayed the slightest melancholy or resentment over having lost his greatest chances in tennis to nefarious imprisonment or prejudiced exclusion. When fifteen hundred Allied planes were thundering overhead, turning Berlin to fire and deafening noise, he was in a chaotic underground shelter, calmly reading Schopenhauer. If he was aware of his situation in the ambulance, about to die of a car crash after surviving Nazi persecution and the Russian front, he probably accepted his fate with the same serenity. "Gottfried was amazing," recalled his friend Wolfgang Hofer. "He seemed absolutely untouched by the war. He never talked about the horrors of the Russian winter. He never talked about being in jail." Wherever he went, as a socialite, a businessman, or an ambassador of German tennis (and president of the Rot-Weiss Club from 1966 to 1975), he mesmerized with his elegance, his charm, his joie de vivre.

And of course with his tennis. "Chamber music with white balls" was how a German music critic put it in the 1940s. With his back straight, knees bent, he swept his long, luxurious strokes through a tennis ball with perfect timing, dispatching it so deep into the court. Even in later years, playing socially, the tennis baron showed this "mark of aristocracy in the tennis stroke." "His shots came just a few centimeters above the net," recalled one player, "and with such length, like magic. Even then he could open the court, make it wider and wider." As wide as the world itself.

FOR BIG BILL TILDEN, THAT SUMMER OF 1937, WHEN HE WATCHED Gottfried come so close to tennis's greatest heights, marked the approximate beginning of the end. Since he had turned professional in 1930, he had been pro tennis's biggest attraction. But his extravagant lifestyle had eaten through his prodigious earnings, and by the time Vinnie Richards bailed him out of debt in '38, he was a sad shadow of his old self.

Still, he never stopped playing tennis. He set out on yet another pro tour in 1939, at the age of forty-six, with Don Budge, Ellsworth Vines, and a few others. They planned an extended European and

South Seas tour and kicked it off indoors in May at the Wembley
Arena, near London. Al Laney was there:

> Tilden came to play Budge, the greatest player of the day, for
> the first time, with the air of a master about to give a lesson to a
> promising pupil. He strode majestically onto the court and
> made you feel, in spite of yourself, a bit sorry for Budge. . . .
> When it was over [6-2, 6-2 Budge], he strode off the court as
> if he were the victor. . . . [And then] he was out there giving
> twenty years to Vines and beating him.

He even beat Budge in a later match. Overall, he finished behind the
younger players, but on a given night the old man could still beat anyone.
"I have never seen such scenes," wrote another reporter. "The crowd,
spellbound, rose to the great master and gave him a great ovation."
"They shouted and stamped on the floor," wrote Laney, "and told him
there was no one like him and never had been." Budge, ever the gallant
sportsman, said Tilden had taught him a lesson, playing "the greatest
tennis I have ever seen." Tilden, for his part, humbly acknowledged that
he had caught the champ on an off day.

They were still playing in England when war broke out. Everyone,
it seemed, even the children playing in the streets, had gas masks either in hand or hanging around the neck. Young men were literally leaving the stands to go join their regiments, and on one occasion Tilden
and Budge looked up from their match to see a sky full of "barrage bal-
loons" dragging steel cables, designed to wreak havoc on low-altitude
bombing raids.

The rest of the tour was canceled, and the troupe boarded the SS
*Washington* and made it safely to New York. Around this time Tilden
moved to Los Angeles, where he could play outdoors all year and rub
elbows with the Hollywood crowd he so adored. In addition to Tallulah Bankhead and Greta Garbo, Tilden had been friends with tennis
nuts Charlie Chaplin and Douglas Fairbanks since the 1920s. His favorite place to play was Chaplin's home court on Summit Drive, high
in the hills over Sunset Boulevard. Every Sunday Tilden would be part
of what Chaplin called "the Big Tea," a tennis party featuring "the most
extraordinary mixed bag of players and kibitzers": Garbo, Bankhead,

Fairbanks, and also Joseph Cotten, Spencer Tracy, Olivia de Havilland, and others, including of course Errol Flynn, the champion of the stars. James Thurber also enjoyed exercising his slapstick brand of tennis on Chaplin's court when he went out to Los Angeles to collaborate on a play in the summer of 1939. Chaplin "plays tennis left-handed," he wrote home, "but not like Johnny Doeg."

In 1941 the forty-eight-year-old Tilden signed up for one last one-on-one pro tour, against the world's best, Don Budge. From January to May they crisscrossed the country with Alice Marble and Mary Hardwick, playing singles and mixed doubles. Crowds thronged to the indoor arenas to get a look at the mythical Big Bill, and he didn't let them down, either with his tennis or his theatricality. "He still sinks his fangs into offending ball boys, linesmen, and umpires," reported *Newsweek* from the tour, and as Budge remembered, "Every night something would happen, and you'd sit back and say, 'I wonder how he's going to get out of this.'" On one occasion, after a linesman made some questionable calls *in Tilden's favor,* he approached the umpire and loudly demanded he replace the offending servant. From that point on the crowd booed him incessantly, even during points. Finally Big Bill stopped play and borrowed the umpire's microphone.

> Ladies and gentlemen, I believe you will observe the British way of letting a man defend himself before you condemn him. It is you, not I, who suffer the most from these bad calls. Mr. Budge is now the greatest player in the game, and you have paid good money to watch me try to put up a match against him. If I am to be disturbed by bad calls, I cannot play my best, and if you razz me or boo me during a point, you will only make it more difficult for me. Please boo me all you will between points. I have endured that all my life and am quite used to it. But if you wish to obtain the most for your money, hold off while I try to play the best player in the world. Thank you.

They played on in absolute silence.

After all, Tilden was playing more than a mere game. He never forgot what his friend, the famous opera singer Mary Garden, had told him long ago: "You're a tennis artist, Bill, and artists always know better than anyone else when they're right. If you believe in a certain way to play, you play that way no matter what anyone tells you. Once you lose faith in your own artistic judgment, you're lost."

Despite his public modesty, though, Tilden was no pushover for the twenty-five-year-old Budge. There were many close matches, and he even managed to defeat the champion seven times in fifty-four matches. "Don didn't seem that impressed," Gene Mako recalled. "I said to him, 'Now think about it: you're the greatest player in the world, maybe the greatest ever, and you can't beat a forty-eight-year-old every time?' It's unbelievable. Unbelievable. If you ask me for amazing sports stories, I tell you Tilden in his late forties, early fifties."

When the United States entered the war and professional tennis dried up for the interim, Tilden did his part for the war effort by making appearances all over the country to help sell war bonds and by organizing a sort of tennis-vaudeville act to play Red Cross benefits at California navy bases, Marine camps, and hospitals. He and a local pro would play a match, followed by a women's match between his protégées Gloria Butler and Gussy Moran (later known as "Gorgeous Gussy" of Ted Tinling–designed panty fame). Then Tilden and the other man would come out in drag as Misses Wilhelmina Shovelshoot and Sophie Smearone and challenge the others to a ladies' doubles match.

Otherwise, Tilden was still cutting a fine figure as he turned fifty in 1943. He had welcomed the advent of tennis shorts and himself favored particularly short ones, along with robin's-egg-blue tennis shirts under his classic Tilden sweater. "God, those legs," Gussy Moran remembered. "Fantastic. Grable should have had them." According to Butler, Tilden's outfits were effective enough on a couple occasions to land him back in his hotel room with a gay GI.

The war ended, and Tilden kept right on playing. In a 1946 tour, at the age of fifty-three, he had wins over Fred Perry and Bobby Riggs. Mako remembered winning several very tight matches against Tilden on that tour before they met in the semifinals of the final tournament, in Palm Springs. Mako had been rusty at the start of the tour, because he had been playing semipro basketball and hadn't played serious tennis for years. But by now he felt he was playing as well as he ever had. "And Bill and I are trying like sons of bitches cause it's fifty bucks for third place. He beat me six-two, six-one. And Bill and I were very good friends, so when we go to net I say 'You son of a gun, you can still play, can't you?' And he just smiles and says, 'Sometimes. Sometimes.'"

Well into his fifties, Tilden routinely got to the quarterfinals of the pro tournaments and occasionally upset a top player. In 1946 he beat Frank Parker, the reigning Forest Hills champ, in a practice match at Charlie Chaplin's court. And on tour with the pros he several times took a one- or two-set lead over world number one Bobby Riggs before finally giving out. It was commonly said that at fifty-three Big Bill Tilden was still the best in the world for one set.

On and on he played. When he wasn't on tour or playing an exhibition, he was at the L.A. Tennis Club or at his friends' private courts, scrounging up games. "If you came to Bill while he was playing bridge at the L.A. Tennis Club," said Mako, "and said 'Hey, how about a couple sets of singles,' it didn't matter how many sets he had played that day, he'd say 'Get dressed, get dressed.'" One day on tour Budge asked him, "Bill, what will you do when you can't play tennis anymore?" "Hmmph," came the reply. "Kill myself."

Active as ever, a wonder for his age on the court, Tilden seemed poised to take a leading role in the management of the emergent pro game. In fact, he was still the biggest draw in tennis. A decent-size crowd would pay to see Riggs and Budge, but they came in throngs to get a glimpse of the Old Master.

Off the court, however, something seemed to be going wrong. Tilden had always been phobic about allowing anyone to see him unclothed and would never shower in the locker room when anyone was around. Now, though, he seemed to be abandoning the practice of bathing at all. Or of doing laundry: he dressed in dirty pants and a ragged old sweater, was often unshaven in public, and smelled bad. The cramped apartments he lived in were putrid jungles of dirty clothes, rackets, bills, and manuscripts. "It was obvious to me that he was a sick man," said one old friend who visited him, "and I left with a saddened heart."

He also was increasingly letting down his guard regarding his homosexuality. He spoke freely to other players of being "different," often embarrassing them. Not that he would allow himself to accept his sexuality completely and pursue real relationships. "Ashamed of himself," wrote Frank Deford, "there was seldom any joy for the man. It's quite likely that in his whole life Tilden never spent a night alone with an adult—man or woman." Instead, he intermittently pursued furtive bouts of "fooling around," as he put it, with teenage boys. And he began taking less care to hide his activities.

On a Saturday night, November 23, 1946, two Beverly Hills policeman saw Tilden's Packard weaving erratically down Sunset Boulevard, driven by a young male, a much older man next to him with his arm around him. When they stopped the car, Tilden and the boy switched places, but the officers noted that the boy's fly was completely unbuttoned. They took Tilden to the station and booked him.

He could have gotten off. The boy, whom he had met the week before and had seen several times since, was a sexually precocious, troubled youth who knew exactly what he was doing. His parents did not want him testifying in court, and Tilden's lawyer begged him to plead not guilty. But Big Bill Tilden did not accept points that were not rightly his. A true sportsman would admit his guilt and take his punishment like a man. Furthermore, Tilden was convinced that no court would put the greatest tennis player of all time in jail. He pleaded guilty: "I sincerely regret my actions and desire that the court have faith enough in me to permit me to prove that this does not reflect my true nature and my better self. . . . I can only reiterate my deep regret, humiliation and shame. I have learned my lesson and will never forget it."

Unfortunately, Tilden's "sportsmanship" was as subjective in court as on the court. Though he admitted his guilt, he angered Judge A. A. Scott, well known for his intolerance for "moral turpitude" to begin with, by insisting repeatedly, with obvious disingenuousness, that this was the first time in many years that he had committed such offenses. After moralizing on Tilden's activities in much the same manner as Gottfried von Cramm's Nazi judge had done nine years before, Judge Scott laid down the sentence: five years' probation, beginning with nine months at the Castaic Honor Farm, a minimum-security facility some seventy miles north of Los Angeles.

Prison. Tilden's face was ashen; he appeared "near collapse . . . absolutely in shock." He had lost plenty of matches before but almost always when his opponent was simply younger and stronger. Never before had his genius for strategy let him down like this.

But Tilden weathered his incarceration well. He worked in the kitchen, as Cramm had done during his sentence, and updated his autobiography. After only seven and a half months he was released early. He returned to his life in Los Angeles, but that life was different now. A convicted pederast, he found, was not welcome in much of society. The greatest player of all time was barred from the tennis clubs—even the Los Angeles Tennis Club, where he had played so often and happily whiled away the hours at the bridge table. The "dictator" of Southern California tennis, Perry Jones, that "prim and prissy bachelor, often rumored to be a homosexual himself," who had kept Bobby Riggs off the 1937 Davis Cup team, had never much liked Tilden either. And now he had the perfect excuse to make him persona non grata.

With the country clubs off limits and lucrative exhibition matches no longer viable, Tilden took to giving lessons on the private courts of Chaplin and his fellow Hollywood bigwigs Joseph Cotten and David Selznick. These and just a few other friends stood by Tilden, but most others felt they couldn't afford to be seen with him. For a while he took a job teaching at the Château Elysées, a rundown hotel up in the Hollywood Hills, where he breakfasted on cold cereal in his room. Otherwise he inhabited a series of cheap apartments in Hollywood or West Los Angeles. Packing never took long. "In all the years I knew Tilden," said Bobby Riggs, "the only property he ever owned was an automobile, four or five rackets, some kind of blazer, a pair of slacks, and a few sweaters."

The closest people to Tilden in these years were his final young protégé, Arthur Anderson, and the boy's mother, Marrion. "Only when Big Bill discusses the kids and their ambitions," went a magazine profile back in 1926, "does a slight suggestion of sentiment creep into his quick, assured tones. 'Wish I'd had someone to give me a few pointers,' he says a little wistfully. 'My way would have been easier. I have always had to go it alone.'" Tilden became something of a father figure to Anderson, whose own father, an alcoholic, had abandoned the family. They met in 1940, and by 1946, while touring with Budge and other pros, Tilden was signing his letters "home" to Arthur, "Your Old Man, Bill." The Andersons were the closest thing to family Tilden had had since he left Auntie and Twin's house. He even moved into their house for two extended stays. As with his other tennis protégés, Tilden never made any sexual overtures to Anderson.

After his imprisonment, the Andersons stuck by Tilden more than anyone. As part of his probation rules, he wasn't supposed to be alone with any minors, but Arthur was so much like family that when it came to him, Tilden disregarded this humiliating proviso.

When the police knocked on his door on the afternoon of January 31, 1949, though, they were only tangentially interested to find him alone with Arthur, in violation of his parole. They were there with a warrant for his arrest. A man resembling Tilden had picked up a sixteen-year-old hitchhiker and repeatedly tried to fondle his genitals. The boy, who had been molested by drivers before, had written down the license plate number—Tilden's—and had positively described the offending right hand as missing half of its middle finger. This time Tilden wanted to fight the charge, but the boy was willing to testify, and he had no alibi. On his fifty-sixth birthday, "stooped and graying," he was sentenced to another year at the county farm.

Ten months later, just before Christmas, they let him out early again. He was taken down to L.A. and released from the county jail. No friends or relatives, not even the Andersons, were there to meet him. No one noticed at all save one young Hemingway from the AP who happened to be there:

J. F. Grover, jailer, said, "Well, here's Big Bill Tilden again." "Yeah," said the former champion. "Here's Tilden again." And he walked out of the jail and into the rain.

A few days later the Associated Press released a poll naming Bill Tilden the greatest tennis player of the half century. Tilden received 310 votes. Jack Kramer and Don Budge were second and third, with 32 and 31 votes each. Nevertheless, back "home" in another rented apartment in Hollywood after a second conviction, Tilden found himself almost completely ostracized from the tennis world. There were no more endorsements; racket companies recalled their Tilden models from the shelves. Old friends would look the other way when they saw him coming. "I loved Bill . . . [but] we stopped inviting him to our home," said Ellsworth Vines's wife Verle. "It was difficult to have [a social pariah] in your home for dinner. . . . I was such a snob and so wrong."

He was grateful for any tennis students he could find, and he taught them on the shabbiest public courts. (In *Lolita* Nabokov has Humbert buy Lolita tennis lessons in Los Angeles with Ned Litam, "a wrinkled old-timer with a harem of ball boys; he looked an awful wreck off the court, but now and then . . . he would put out as it were an exquisite spring blossom of a stroke . . . [with] that divine delicacy of absolute power." Ned Litam spelled backward is Ma Tilden, a pseudonym Tilden sometimes used for his fiction.) Tilden would drop by the courts at the Beverly Wilshire Hotel, one of the few respectable places that would have him, and the greatest player ever would ask if anyone needed a fourth for doubles. "I'll play tennis with anyone who wants to play," he'd say. His clothes were so soiled and malodorous that the pro there would give him some fresh ones before sending him out on the court.

And still the old man could play. In the 1951 International Pro Championships in Cleveland, the fifty-eight-year-old Tilden beat former Davis Cupper Wayne Sabin, thirty-five, before succumbing to eventual champion Frank Kovacs in a competitive match. Two years later, just after Tilden turned sixty, the Beverly Wilshire was hosting a pro tournament of its own. Tilden was invited to play, and he jumped at the chance, convincing Vinnie Richards to come out west and join him, and selling boxes of seats to his Hollywood pals. But the week before, the Wilshire decided it couldn't afford to have an infamous pervert headlining its event. In Tinseltown, of all places, the public had protested with bags of letters. Frank Feltrop, the hotel's club pro, had to give Bill the bad news:

> My God, that was the saddest thing I ever had to do in my life. They didn't even want him ever again to set foot on the place, but I couldn't tell him that, I just couldn't. I just told him that they wouldn't let him play in the tournament. And right there, I think he knew he didn't have a hell of a lot to live for anymore. He said, "But, Frank, Vinnie's coming out, all the old gang."
>
> "I'm sorry, Bill, I'm sorry."

"I've sold all these tickets to my friends. Joe Cotten, David Selznick. This is their chance to see me play again."

I just said, "I told you, I'm sorry. I can't do anything."

"I'll sue you then, I'll sue the hotel," he said all of a sudden. Oh, he still had a crust on him, an unbelievable hide.

I said, "Come on, Bill, it's your arm that's been hurting, isn't it? You can't play with that arm, can you?" And then he dropped his head and nodded and said, Yes, he would go along and say his arm was hurting, and after that he just turned and walked away. He must have been down to about one-fifty then, and he was all bent over, so his bald spot in back was showing. Jesus, it was awful. The poor old son of a bitch.

Apparently, they weren't so puritanical in Cleveland, though, for he was invited back to play in the International Pro tournament. The hell with the Beverly Wilshire. The only thing was, he didn't have the money to get to Cleveland. But just as in the days when he was running his tours, cash flow was nothing to worry about, and Big Bill was happiest when he had some tennis to organize.

He wrote immediately to Richards, who was now a VP at Dunlop: "Vinnie, could you please send me a couple of dozen balls and a racket or two? If I had them I think I could get some lessons to give. I need the money badly." Then he left a note at the office of one of his students, offering a special deal of forty lessons for two hundred dollars if he could pay it all in advance: "I am in real need of money, therefore this offer." He had convinced a few local pros to accompany him to Texas for some exhibitions, and then up to Cleveland for the tournament. It would be like the old days: Tilden Tours, Inc.

The Andersons invited Bill to dinner on June 5, the night before he was to leave for Texas. That day he played five sets on Charlie Chaplin's court, with Arthur Anderson and some others, and also gave a couple of lessons. He had been suffering from a cold for weeks, and at times he would have to walk back and lean on the fence until a long hacking cough spent itself. After the tennis, he drove back to his little apartment near Hollywood and Vine to get ready for dinner.

When he didn't show up, Arthur Anderson drove over to the apartment and found him lying on his bed, dead of a heart attack at sixty.

"Our greatest athlete in any sport" was worth eighty-eight dollars in cash when he died, plus the remaining trophies that he hadn't yet pawned. Big Bill was all dressed, shoes on, hair combed. On the floor was his bag, packed with clothes and rackets, ready for another tour.

A COUPLE WEEKS LATER, AT THE TOURNAMENT IN CLEVELAND, thirty-eight-year-old Don Budge lost a tough four-set final to the newest young world-beater, Pancho Gonzalez. Budge was near the end of a long professional career that, though successful, had been hampered by bad luck and injury. When Jack Kramer won Wimbledon in 1947 beneath "a background of avalanched rubble and twisted girders" where bombs had destroyed part of the Centre Court roof, he was led up to the Royal Box to meet the king and queen. "Whatever happened to that redheaded young man?" asked the queen. But no true tennis fan would have had to ask.

Budge's Wimbledon and Davis Cup successes of 1937 had been the springboard to an even greater year in 1938—one of the greatest performances of all time. At the end of 1937 he became the first (and still only) tennis player to receive the Sullivan Award as America's top amateur athlete, and a promoter offered him $75,000 to turn pro. But Budge had promised to defend the Davis Cup at least one year after bringing it home, and so he turned down that small fortune, even knowing that if he suffered a poor year or injury, the offer might never come again.

He also had an idea to try to achieve something that had never been done. He confided to Gene Mako that he was going to try to be the first to win all four major championships in one year. Few non-Australians even played all four at that time, due to the long boat ride necessary to get Down Under. Davis Cup qualification matches also often made it difficult to get to Paris in May. But now that the United States had the Cup, they wouldn't have to play until the Challenge Round in July. So Budge asked Mako to accompany him to Australia and said that if he won there, he intended to go to Europe early to play at Roland Garros for the first time.

"Budge is the world champion," the *Sydney Mail* introduced him to its readers in December 1937. "He is also a very fine sportsman. His main subject of discourse is the fine sportsmanship of his chief rival, Gottfried Cramm." Cramm defeated his friend twice in warm-up events, causing many in the Australian press to doubt Budge's chances of winning even the first major title of the year, but when the national championships began at Adelaide, Budge was ready.

The Australian championship was considered a major title due to that country's prominence in world tennis, but in fact only thirty-three men were in the draw that year—and twenty-nine of them were Australian. Even so, seven of the world's top ten were there, including the top three of Budge, Cramm, and Henkel. And Budge tore through the tournament without losing a single set. Cramm's loss in the semis to Bromwich robbed the tournament of a dramatic rematch, and Budge took the finals easily.

The anticipated doubles rematch between the Americans and Germans also failed to materialize when Budge and Mako, after taking the first two sets, were upset in the semifinals by Bromwich and Quist. Budge and Mako had also been aiming for a Grand Slam in doubles, but Gene told a friend later that they had been "too busy chasing girls in Australia." Considering Budge's domination in singles, it may have been mostly Mako who was concentrating on the social life: in a photo of the top players in suits and ties at a public event, Mako is seen "with the inevitable Victrola record" in hand.

There were those who thought that the slow clay in Paris would finally stop the Budge onslaught, but his game was so complete now that it was supreme on any surface. And once again, the field was not nearly as strong as it might have been. Cramm, the world's finest clay-courter (aside from perhaps Budge, who was relatively untested on the surface), was scrubbing pots in prison. Germany kept its other players at home too, including Henkel, the defending champion. And the Australians Quist, Bromwich, and Crawford didn't make it to Europe at all that summer. A stomach virus was Budge's toughest opponent, causing him to lose a few sets to far inferior opponents, but from the quarterfinals on he was doing whatever he pleased on the clay, even rushing the net after his service returns. He crushed Cramm's old rival Roderich Menzel, the only real threat, in the finals, to become the first American champion of France.

Budge had been introduced to the great cellist Pablo Casals just before the tournament, and Casals came to watch all his matches. When Budge won, Casals gave a private concert in his honor. A few friends had dinner in Casals's magnificent Paris apartment, the Eiffel Tower and Paris skyline glowing outside the picture window, and then they settled onto big cushions on the floor of his atelier. "This concert is for my good friend, Don Budge," said Casals, and then proceeded to play, with piano accompaniment, for two hours.

If Budge had wanted to take the pressure off by keeping his quest for the Grand Slam secret, he had failed, for the newspapers were talking about it even before he sailed for France. Now that he had two out of four titles and no close rival, the slam was the only drama left in the men's draw at Wimbledon. And it wasn't much drama, as Budge, a "sure thing" at unprecedented 1-5 odds, won even more easily than he had in 1937. Bunny Austin, who took out Henkel in the semifinals, could provide little competition in the finals. It was over in sixty-six minutes, 6-1, 6-0, 6-3. Budge finished his European jaunt by again winning the doubles with Mako and the mixed with Alice Marble for a second straight Wimbledon triple crown.

Back home, he led the U.S. Davis Cup team in defending the Cup successfully against the Australians, and then it was time for the final leg of the Grand Slam, at Forest Hills. Cramm was still in jail, and the Germans kept Henkel home again too. But at least the Australians were present for this one, having just finished playing the Davis Cup in Philadelphia, as were the other top Americans—Bobby Riggs, Joseph Hunt, Sidney Wood, and Parker and Grant—whom the USLTA hadn't deemed fit enough to send to Wimbledon. Amazingly, Budge's opponent in the finals was his buddy Mako, who, though unseeded, had gone on a tear. Throwing in his side-armed slice serves and "running around the court like a son of a bitch," as he put it, he became the first unseeded man ever to reach the finals, losing only one set along the way.

It didn't look like Mako had much of a chance of stopping Budge's Grand Slam, but the weather almost did. On the day of the semifinals a rare hurricane approached New York and rained out play. Later dubbed the Great Hurricane of '38, or "the Long Island Express," the five-hundred-mile-wide storm wreaked havoc on New York City and Long Island and postponed the semifinals for six days.

Six days is a long time to sit around waiting to play a monumental match. Mako was facing another uphill battle against Bromwich, and although Budge was a big favorite against Sidney Wood, being so tantalizingly close to the Grand Slam was agonizing. Budge and Mako had been rooming together at the Madison Hotel on Madison and 27th Street for a month, and by the second night of the rainout, they decided it was pointless to sit around listening to records, playing drums on the tabletops, and hoping for a break in the weather. During the days they would practice on the indoor courts at the Brooklyn Heights Casino, and at night they'd take dates, or just each other, to hear some jazz. Tommy Dorsey at the Astor or the New Yorker; the Count Basie band, Buddy Rich with the Lou Marcella band, or Artie Shaw in the clubs on West 52nd Street. Mako was friends with most of them, and he and Budge would "buddy around together" with the jazzmen. They'd leave their friends early, though, by musicians' standards, and be back at the Madison by two A.M. for a good night's sleep.

Finally the hurricane dissipated, Mako shocked Bromwich in straight sets, and the best friends met in the finals. Mako took the only set in the tournament off Budge, but Budge won the other three easily, and the championship—and Grand Slam—was his. It must have felt somewhat anticlimactic to have won the four majors so easily after his great battles with Cramm the year before. But despite the relatively weak field in 1938, Budge's Grand Slam is the feat most often cited as evidence of his greatness. It needn't be. Everyone who played him or saw him play in the late 1930s considered his "perfect game" unbeatable. From early 1937 to late 1938 he won ninety-two matches and fourteen tournaments in a row, including all six majors he played, and he also won all ten of his Davis Cup singles matches. The press voted him the greatest American athlete, amateur or pro, in both 1937 and 1938.

When he finally turned pro after the 1938 season, he looked even stronger. He took on Ellsworth Vines, the professional champ for the past five years, and beat him in twenty-two out of thirty-nine matches. Then he defeated Fred Perry twenty-eight out of thirty-six times. He was now indisputably the world's greatest player, amateur or pro. Also the richest. In 1939 he earned somewhere between $100,000 and $150,000—at a time when a steak dinner out cost two dollars and a nice hotel room five.

After the war curtailed the 1939 European tour, and Budge and

Tilden and the others sailed home, no major pro tours were held until Budge and Tilden went on the road in 1941. But there were a handful of tournaments, and Budge was still clearly the world's best when the United States finally entered the war after Pearl Harbor. He was also a married man. Like all his Hollywood friends, Budge had dated a number of glamorous young women in the four years since he'd first reached stardom. The gossip columns, which dubbed him "the Romeo of tennis," linked him with singer Edyth Wright, actress Glen Alyn, showgirl Jean Carmen, and even Olivia de Havilland, who like her frequent costar Errol Flynn was a devotee of Hollywood's tennis parties. But in May 1941 he married eighteen-year-old Deirdre Conselman, the beautiful daughter of a prominent Hollywood screenwriter. She had to fly out to Chicago to marry him the day before the U.S. Pro Championships began there, but he made up for it by agreeing to get a nose-and-ear job. A week after plastic surgery, and the day after the wedding, Budge played his first-round match against relatively unknown John Faunce, who set out to exhaust the bridegroom with drop shots and lobs to the corners. Budge lost in straight sets.

After Pearl Harbor professional tennis ground to a halt, though they did stage a U.S. Pro Championships in 1942, at Forest Hills, and Budge beat Riggs in the finals 6-2, 6-2, 6-2. He was twenty-seven, at his very peak, but what could he do? He enlisted in the Army Air Corps. "It was kind of tough to while away the time when no one in the world could beat you," he understated later. One freezing morning in Wichita Falls, Texas, his sergeant thought he would warm the boys up with a run through the obstacle course. There was a wall you had to scale by climbing a rope, and as Budge grabbed the rope and pulled himself up, he felt something rip in his right shoulder.

His serve was never the same. When tennis resumed after the war and he went on tour with Riggs, he lost the first twelve matches and eventually lost the tour twenty-four matches to twenty-two; he also lost the U.S. Pro final to Riggs in straight sets. He lost the finals to Riggs again in 1947 in a match of great financial significance, for the winner would get to tour with the newest pro sensation, Jack Kramer, and pull in $100,000. Riggs always thought he won due to his famous clutchness when big money was at stake, but Budge was simply not the player he had been. "I don't think Bobby would have had the ability to beat Don at his best," said Kramer. "But after the war, when Don wasn't able to serve as well, Bobby was able to get to him."

"And hundreds of nights staying up drinking didn't help either," according to Gene Mako. "He was never in the same condition he had been in in the late 1930s. He and Deirdre got married and had a good time." They were living in the Bel Air section of Hollywood now, with two boys born in 1945 and 1950, and they moved in a fast crowd. "Sinatra and Bing Crosby were his buddies, we'd see them all the time," said his older son David. Don and Deirdre were part of a group that included Sinatra, Crosby, bandleader Les Brown, Kay Starr, and others, who called themselves the Hymnin' Hangover: after several rounds of cocktails, they'd drive around Bel Air and Beverly Hills singing Christmas carols. "Imagine hearing 'Hark the Angels Sing' and looking out the window and seeing this group."

In 1954 the Budges moved to an apartment on East 57th Street in New York City, where they entertained friends like jazz musicians Jackie Paris and Joe Johns. Dean Martin and Jerry Lewis would come up to the Budges' table at Toots Shor's or Jack Dempsey's and yuck it up. Don became head pro at the Town Tennis Club on 56th and still played pro tennis. That year, at thirty-nine, he did his own Tilden turn, touring with the much younger players Pancho Gonzalez, Frank Sedgman, and Pancho Segura. Gonzalez was the champ, but Budge won a number of matches. And in 1957, when he was forty-one, Budge had his last hurrah, beating the great serve-and-volleyer Gonzalez on a fast indoor court in Los Angeles, 6-4, 6-4. Even then his backhand was a monolith in the world of tennis. "No one," said Davis Cupper Gene Scott, "and I mean no one, ever served to Budge's backhand until he was well into his sixties."

He never complained about his injury, never even mentioned it to his sons. Friends helped him invest his early pro tennis windfalls wisely, so money was never a problem. He enjoyed teaching tennis, though, and after his playing days were over he ran a summer tennis camp in Jamaica, and then in Virginia and Maryland, for twenty years. He liked to travel, and whenever he was in Los Angeles he stayed at Gene Mako's place in Hollywood. Mako had played some pro tennis and basketball in the 1940s but didn't make much money there. During his tennis days he had sat in on the drums with jazz bands all over the world, and he made a living at it for a little while. Then he went into the tennis court construction business for fifty years. Gradually, he got involved in the art world and eventually had his own gallery. At the age of ninety he could tell you the score of every tennis match he ever played, and he was devoting himself to the preparation of a two-volume retrospective of the artwork of his father, whom he lovingly referred to as "one of the greatest unknown artists ever." Though Mako hadn't become an artist himself, he had inherited from his father what he called "the seeing hand," which was as invaluable in picking off a topspin passing shot at the net as it was in painting a perfect archway on canvas.

As for Budge, he always enjoyed his life, and although he and Deidre went their separate ways in the 1960s, his sons remember him as as great a dad as a tennis player. He remarried in 1968 and had a long happy second marriage. On December 14, 1999, Budge was driving near his home in the Pocono Mountains in eastern Pennsylvania. He lost control of his car on the wet, serpentine road and skidded into a tree. Emergency workers cut him out of the car and airlifted him to a nearby hospital. He survived for six weeks but never came home, finally succumbing in a Scranton nursing home on January 26, 2000. He was eighty-four.

In the summer of 1947 Budge had toured Germany for the first time, playing exhibition matches at American Army bases against Bobby Riggs. As he took the court in Bad Nauheim one day, he caught sight of a thin blond man with aristocratic posture half-waving to him from behind the fence. "I didn't recognize him at first," Budge said later, "but then suddenly realized it was Gottfried. He seemed embarrassed, concerned that I might not regard him as a friend anymore." He needn't have worried; Budge embraced his old friend, and before long they were playing a series of exhibition matches in Germany. "For years," said Budge, "I tried to get him into the U.S. but couldn't because of the morals conviction."

He always remembered his Davis Cup match with Cramm as his greatest moment. Number one against number two, the United States against Nazi Germany, the Davis Cup on the line, at the sport's most hallowed temple: Centre Court, Wimbledon. "I never played better," he remembered many years later, "and I never played anyone as good as Cramm that day."

He wasn't alone in his opinion. Budge and Cramm turned journalists into poets. The London *Times* called it "a match which will be forever memorable in every land where lawn tennis is played. . . . Certainly I have never seen a match that came nearer the heroic in its courage, as in its strokes, as this." And Allison Danzig wrote, "The brilliance of the tennis was almost unbelievable. . . . The gallery . . . forgot its allegiance to the Baron, looked on spellbound as the players, taking their inspiration from each other, worked miracles of redemption and riposte in rallies of breakneck pace that ranged all over the court."

The postmatch locker room was a carnival of teammates, officials, tennis personalities, and Budge's Hollywood friends, all rushing to get in their congratulations. And then there was Bill Tilden who, according to the Associated Press, had "all but cried when the fair-haired lad was beaten." In the locker room he was fully recovered, transformed back into the domineering apostle of tennis. He grasped Budge's hand in an emotional handshake and told him he had just won "the greatest tennis match ever played."

Finally, about an hour after the match, the locker room emptied out, and Budge was able to bathe and dress. Before he was driven back into London to join his teammates, he wanted to take one last look at Centre Court. It was almost nine P.M., but there was still some midsummer light left in the sky. He stepped out onto the grass and glanced up into the stands. To his surprise, there were still thousands of people there, gathered in clusters all about the stadium. Ghostly presences in the twilight, they didn't seem to be talking much to each other, or moving about. It was as if they didn't want to leave the scene of what they had just witnessed. Three years from now, "in the bright and terrible summer of 1940," Nazi warplanes would roar up the Thames, thousands at a time, and their bombs would rain down on London for almost a year. Pieces of the Royal Box would come splintering down across the service lines, and the All England Club's faultless turf would be used to raise pigs for much-needed meat. But for the moment Centre Court was a peaceful chapel, still harboring faint echoes of a great encounter.

For a long time, Budge had a recurring nightmare: in the biggest match of his life, he was forever down four games to one in the fifth set, peering across the net at the poised, implacable, seemingly invincible Gottfried Cramm. To the end of his life, he would think back on that match. Sometimes, considering the hardships his friend had had to endure afterward, he wished that he had lost it. How would both their lives have been different if he had, if his last diving forehand had missed? Still, he couldn't help but smile as he remembered that final shot.

He had taken off across the lawn as he saw Cramm's forehand head for the corner. Four or five bounding strides, then leaning, stretching for the ball, falling forward. He went for broke, not really expecting to make such a desperate shot, but when he hit it he knew he had hit it well. As an old man he would still remember the perfect feeling of that shot, right in the racket's sweet spot. Sprawled on the ground near the spectators, way out beyond the sideline, he looked up to see the ball fly past Gottfried and bounce; for a moment he had no idea if it was in or out. Then the stands erupted. The ball had touched ground a few inches from both the sideline and baseline before careening against the dark green painted wood of the backdrop and finally coming back to rest on the English grass.

When shall we three meet again?
In thunder, lightning, or in rain?

When the hurlyburly's done,
When the battle's lost and won.

That will be ere the set of sun.

—*Macbeth*

# ACKNOWLEDGMENTS

WHEN I WAS beginning my research in late 2005, the obvious first person to contact was Bud Collins, the greatest living repository of tennis knowledge. Although he probably had no idea who I was, he immediately gave me a valuable list of people to contact, along with their phone numbers. I was and am grateful, for it gave me not only the information, but also the nerve, to start calling up some of tennis's all-time greats.

Soon I found myself in Los Angeles, where Gene Mako, Jack Kramer, Robert Kelleher, and Don Budge's son David were remarkably generous with their time. Back east, Budge's other son, Jeff, also welcomed me into his home and shared not only his memories of his dad but also his sizable collection of clippings, photographs, and other memorabilia.

In Germany, Gottfried von Cramm's nephew, Burghard von Cramm, was equally hospitable, inviting me into his Hamburg home for a long interview and arranging for me to visit the von Cramm estates in Oelber, Brüggen, and Bodenburg. His cousin, Oliver von Cramm, gave me informative tours of Brüggen and Bodenburg, and Anna von Veltheim did the same at Oelber. Sports historian Heiner Gillmeister showed great interest in my book and shared his knowledge and research with me, as well as giving me valuable contacts in Berlin. There, Gottfried's old friend, Wolfgang Hofer, former president of the Rot-Weiss Club, showed me the club and granted me a long, fascinating interview. At the Blau-Weiss Club, Friedrich Plickert devoted half his day to taking me around that club, buying me lunch, and finding me research materials. At the Schwules Museum, Karl-Heinz Steinle and Andreas Sternweiler shared with me some unexpected gems from their research.

Oliver Prenn, Daniel Prenn's son, spoke with me at length on the telephone about his father. Egon Steinkamp, Derrick Kleeman, Herbert Schmidt, Ron Fimrite, Roger Angell, Dorothy "Dodo" Cheney, Dottie Knode, and Patricia Yeomans also contributed valuable phone interviews, and Mrs. Yeomans even sent me some clippings from the great old days at the LATC.

Frank Deford and Richard Evans gave crucial answers to my e-mailed questions, and Stan Hart sent a most unusual and invaluable package: the tapes of interviews he conducted with some of tennis's greatest players for his book, *Once a Champion*.

My friends Anke Finger and Gregory Lewis were great supporters of this project, and Anke provided help with German-language sources and with my research in Germany. Mike Bergman helped a bunche in L.A., and Melissa Banta did her bit at Widener. Audrey Snell, at the Wimbledon Library, made my visit a productive one and continued to answer questions for a year and a half. Similar thanks go to Mark Young and Joanie Agler at the Tennis Hall of Fame library, Susan Luchars at the USTA archives, Nancy Miller at the University of Pennsylvania Special Collections, and Bianca Welzing at the Landesarchiv in Berlin. Joanie McMasters of the Vancouver Lawn Tennis & Badminton Club let me hold on to her photographs for far too long.

I'M GRATEFUL TO Rick Horgan for jumping at my proposal the day he saw it and bringing it to Crown. He and Julian Pavia, my tag team of editors, were relentless in getting me to clarify and sharpen my focus, even when I thought (mistakenly) that I'd done all I could do. Janet Biehl too made countless improvements with her fine copyediting.

EVERY WRITER HAS an ideal reader, often imaginary, in mind when working on a book. I was lucky to have three very real ones. Albert La-Farge, my tennis-fanatic agent, was excited from my very first e-mail outlining the idea for this book and encouraged me to write the proposal. It is highly unlikely that this book would ever have existed without his early enthusiasm. My wife Mileta Roe, a professor of literature whose dream vacation would be Wimbledon during the Fortnight, as usual was my first reader. And finally there was my brother Ron, who loves books and art and is also one of the finest tennis players you're likely to run into—and one whose reputation for sportsmanship rivals even Gottfried von Cramm's. This book is dedicated to our parents but was written for him.

THERE IS ONE last debt to mention; it regards the book's structure, which came to me almost simultaneously with the initial idea. For as I contemplated the stories of Tilden, Budge, and von Cramm, and how they converged on July 20, 1937, the sown seed was instantly set upon by the germinating agent that lies deep in the mind of every tennis-loving writer. I refer, of course, to *Levels of the Game*, by John McPhee. And so, fans of that great book will understand, what other way was there to begin than with a tennis ball, expertly tossed, rising into the ether. . . .

# NOTES

vii    Thomas Carlyle, *The Life of Friedrich Schiller*, in *The Works of Thomas Carlyle* (New York: Collier, 1897), p. 275.

## FIRST SET

2    Amelia Earhart: Amelia Earhart, *Last Flight* (1937; reprint New York: Crown, 1988), pp. 129–33; and various biographies.

2–3    "considered the Government a set of idiotic ostriches . . .": Churchill quoted in "A 'Survey of the World,'" [London] *Times*, July 20, 1937, p. 16.

4    John McEnroe and Arthur Ashe: Alan Trengove, *The Story of the Davis Cup* (London: Stanley Paul, 1985), p. 2.

4    "I sometimes wonder if the Davis Cup was a good thing . . .": Davis quoted in George Lott, "Tennis Money: It Doesn't Pay to Be an Amateur," *Collier's*, September 3, 1938, p. 28.

4    "Tournament tennis is a wonderful game . . .": Tilden quoted in Trengove, *Story of Davis Cup*, p. 7.

4–5    Tilden had . . . been helping to train the German Davis Cuppers: In his autobiography Tilden wrote, "In November 1935 the German Association brought me to Germany to coach the German Davis Cup team. . . ." See William T. Tilden, *Aces, Places and Faults* (London: Hale, 1938), p. 91. This assertion, along with the story of Hitler's putative phone call (see note to page 186), has been disputed by at least one German tennis historian. Dr. Heiner Gillmeister of the University of Bonn has pointed out, "That Tilden coached the German team is very, very unlikely. I have consulted *Der Tennissport*, the relevant and official German tennis journal at that time. In all the 1937 issues preceding the Davis Cup Interzone final . . . there is no reference whatsoever to . . . Tilden coaching the German team." See Paul Fein, *Tennis Confidential* (Washington: Brassey's, 2002), p. 275. However, it would not be surprising, if the Germans *had* hired Tilden, that they would not want to publicize the fact. Don Budge and Ted Tinling both remembered Tilden coaching the Germans, and Gene Mako (Budge's doubles partner) and Wolfgang Hofer (Cramm's close friend and former president of the Rot-Weiss Tennis Club) both agreed with that, in interviews with me. What's more, on page 19 of the Rot-Weiss Tennis Club publication *Gottfried Freiherr von Cramm: Fair Play ein Leben Lang, 1909–1976* (Berlin: Rot-Weiss Tennis Club, 1977), there is a photograph of Tilden holding forth on court with the German team, with the caption, "Tilden, in between professional matches, also trained the German team." A similar photo, of Tilden clearly in a tutelary position on court with Cramm and Kleinschroth, appears in Richard Schickel, *The World of Tennis* (New York: Random House, 1975), p. 102.

5    "Tilden effected startling changes in [his] backhand": "Von Cramm's Life Story," *American Lawn Tennis*, February 20, 1938, p. 28.

5    "admitted by all to be the perfecter . . .": John Winkler, "The Iconoclast of the Courts," *New Yorker*, September 18, 1926, p. 27.

6    von Cramm . . . had reason to think . . . : William T. Tilden, *My Story: A Champion's Memoirs* (New York: Hellman, Williams & Co., 1948), p. 132.

7    The Germans' first great chance . . . : On Germany's Davis Cup adventures in 1914 see Egon Steinkamp, *Gottfried von Cramm, der Tennisbaron: Eine Biographie* (Munich: Herbig, 1990), p. 36; "Nordics at Bay—A Shock for Diehards—August, 1914," *New Yorker*, June 22, 1929, p. 44.

8    "Budge versus von Cramm was a cinch . . . for updates": "What the Doldrums Are Like," *American Lawn Tennis*, July 20, 1937, p. 15.

8    a noticeable lull in activity on the New York Stock Exchange: Don Budge, *A Tennis Memoir* (New York: Viking Press, 1969), p. 3.

9    For the first time, Centre Court was prepared . . . : "The Centre Court and No. 1," *American Lawn Tennis*, July 20, 1937, p. 15.

9    "bewildering rabbit warren of a place": Al Laney, "The Mystery of Wimbledon," in Herbert Warren Wind, ed., *The Realm of Sport* (New York: Simon and Schuster, 1966), p. 607.

9    a regiment of crisply uniformed ushers . . . : Herbert Warren Wind, "Wimbledon—Ninety-one Years Later," *New Yorker*, July 27, 1968, pp. 68–79.

9    "green and taut as a billiard table": Laney, "Mystery," p. 607.

10   a queue of some three to five thousand . . . : John R. Tunis, "A Reporter at Large: Wimbledon," *New Yorker*, July 5, 1930, p. 41.

10   They waited outside the stadium . . . : Arthur Daley, "Davis Cup Musings," *New York Times*, August 28, 1947, p. 21.

10   Both . . . were controlled by a set of buttons . . . : Tunis, "Reporter at Large: Wimbledon," p. 38.

10   "a slim, freckled youngster out of Booth Tarkington": "Budge Takes Shields," *New Yorker*, August 24, 1935, p. 31.

10   tailored gabardine white slacks: Interview with Gene Mako, Los Angeles, December 6, 2006.

10   "Budge not only wears . . .": Franklin Pierce Adams, "Rye's Semifinals—Sartorial Notes," *New Yorker*, August 21, 1937, p. 44.

11   actually made from the serosa . . . : www.itftennis.com/technical/equipment/strings/history.asp, and www.tennis-warehouse.com/LC/Naturalgut.html.

11    If you had half a finger . . . : On Cramm's loss of his finger, see Steinkamp, *Gottfried von Cramm*, p. 31; "Von Cramm's Life Story," *American Lawn Tennis*, February 20, 1938, p. 28.

11    Budge's racket: On Budge's distinctive rackets, see Mako interview December 6, 2006, and many other sources. In 1975 Budge told George Plimpton, "The only reason there are leather handles on racquets, is that years back [in the 1930s] L. B. Iceley, the president of Wilson's Sporting Goods [and best man at Budge's wedding], got up at a meeting and said, 'Hey, look here, why don't we dress up a tennis racket like a golf club and put leather handles on it and charge a dollar more.' Everybody agreed it was a fine idea. So the result is that you see players scratching up the leather to get a better grip, coming down with blisters and callouses. The consistency of leather changes; leather absorbs 87 percent of the moisture, compared to 7 percent for wood. Bill Tilden knew it was crazy. He and I were the only ones to stick to wood. He used to say, 'For God's sake, Don, you and I are the only ones left. Don't tell anyone.'" Quoted in Trent Frayne, *Famous Tennis Players* (New York: Dodd, Mead, 1977), p. 58.

11    "It's no use when Budge turns on the heat . . .": Quoted in "Newport Reflections," *New Yorker*, August 27, 1938, p. 48.

11    "you'd swear you were volleying a piano": Quoted in Neil Amdur, "Budge Backhand: The Shot for the Ages," *New York Times*, January 27, 2000, p. D8.

12    "the surface of the court has become very fast . . .": Colonel R. H. Brand, NBC radio broadcast, July 17, 1937, NBC Radio archive, Library of Congress.

12    could hear the electrically amplified voice of the umpire: Tunis, "Reporter at Large: Wimbledon," p. 38.

12    "The German's hair flashed . . .": Alistair Cooke, "German Baron v. California Truck Driver's Son: A Study in Good Ambassadorship," broadcast over WEAF, August 4, 1937, in *Vital Speeches of the Day*, vol. 3, August 15, 1937, p. 661, in E. Digby Baltzell Papers, University of Pennsylvania.

12    von Cramm had actualy been the weaker member . . . : "America Take the Lead," [London] *Times*, July 20, 1937, p. 8.

13    "Budge, like Tilden in his prime . . .": "U.S.A. and Germany All Square," [London] *Times*, July 19, 1937, p. 5.

13    "could, at times, play the most brilliant tennis imaginable . . .": John Olliff, *Olliff on Tennis* (London: Eyre and Spottiswoode, 1948), p. 121.

14    "a personal magnetism . . .": Budge, *Tennis Memoir*, p. 8.

14    "Every player could take a lesson in etiquette . . .": Franklin Pierce Adams, "The State of Doubles—Baron von Cramm," *New Yorker*, September 4, 1937, p. 44.

14    Once when called for a foot fault . . .": Rot-Weiss Club, *Gottfried Freiherr von Cramm*, p. 35.

14–15  two years before in 1935 . . . : On the 1935 "tipped ball" doubles match, see Conrad Aiken, "Yankee Luck," *New Yorker*, August 3, 1935, p. 27; George Lott, "Tight Spots in Tennis," *Atlantic*, August 1938, pp. 197–98; Tilden, *Aces, Places*, p. 94; Budge, *Tennis Memoir*, p. 47; *American Lawn Tennis*, August 5, 1935; John R. Tunis, "Raising a Racket for Germany," *Collier's*, July 10, 1937, p. 38.

15    In the locker room afterward . . . : Trengove, *Story of Davis Cup*, pp. 120–21; Don Budge, unpublished article manuscript, 1975 (courtesy of Jeff Budge).

15    He introduced himself . . . : Cramm's early biography, unless otherwise noted, is derived from Steinkamp, *Gottfried von Cramm*.

19    A lifelong bachelor . . . never got around to practicing medicine: Interview with Wolfgang Hofer, Berlin, April 6, 2007.

20    Froitzheim brought with him to Burgdorf . . . : "Von Cramm's Life Story," *American Lawn Tennis*, February 20, 1938, p. 26.

20    "Tilden simply *was* tennis in the public mind . . .": Frank Deford, *Big Bill Tilden: The Triumphs and the Tragedy* (New York: Simon and Schuster, 1976), p. 18.

20–21  Upon his arrival in Berlin . . . : "Tilden Inspects Courts at Night," *New York Times*, May 1, 1927, p. S8; "Tilden Officiates at Berlin Match," *New York Times*, May 2, 1927, p. 17.

21    The clubhouse . . . cigars and coffee . . . : Gordon Forbes, *A Handful of Summers* (London: Heinemann, 1978), p. 209.

21    "an inspiration to any tennis player": "Tilden Inspects Courts at Night," p. S8.

21    Tilden had his first glimpse . . . : "Von Cramm's Life Story," p. 26.

21    "Every year that von Cramm steps onto the Centre Court . . .": Cooke, "German Baron v. California Truck Driver's Son," p. 661.

21    some European journalists following the tennis circuit tried to expose him: Deford, *Big Bill Tilden*, pp. 211–12.

21    gay: The word *gay* was used in the 1930s but only as a code word among homosexuals. Publicly they called themselves "queer" and were often called "fairies" or "fruits" by heterosexuals. George Chauncey, *Gay New York: Gender, Urban Culture, and the Makings of the Gay Male World, 1890–1940* (New York: Basic Books, 1994), pp. 14–15. For the sake of uniformity I have used the word *gay* in today's parlance.

22    "I thought he was sexless," "He is as famous as Babe Ruth in his own country . . . ," and "soon began to speak grandiosely . . .": Deford, *Big Bill Tilden*, pp. 214, 219–21, 223.

23    "apish, but attractive": Ibid., p. 42.

23    "A tall, gaunt figure . . .": Allison Danzig, "Tilden, Autocrat of the Courts," in Wind, *Realm of Sport*, p. 602.

23    contemporaries couldn't believe it . . . : Deford, *Big Bill Tilden*, p. 41.

23    "When he came into the room it was like a bolt of electricity . . .": Ibid., p. 19.

24    Tilden taught him to turn his grip . . . : "Von Cramm's Life Story," *American Lawn Tennis*, February 20, 1938, p. 26; "Champions at Forest Hills," *Time*, September 13, 1937, p. 21; Budge, *Tennis Memoir*, p. 13.

24    Finally an agreement was reached: Steinkamp, *Gottfried von Cramm*, pp. 36, 47.

25    the Rot-Weiss members . . . : Interviews with Wolfgang Hofer and Friedrich Plickert, Berlin, April 6, 2007; Deutscher Tennis Bund, ed., *Tennis*

*in Deutschland. Von den Anfängen bis 2002* (Berlin: Duncker & Humblot, 2002), p. 64.

25    "This script, though still not completely developed . . . ," "If he plays tennis as well as he looks . . . ," and "I'll just take advantage of his weak backhand again": Paula Stuck von Reznicek, *Tennis-Faszination* (Munich: Schumacher-Gebler, 1969), pp. 39, 44, 50.

25    spending most of the money sent from Oelber . . . : "Champions at Forest Hills," *Time*, September 13, 1937, p. 20.

27    "The Germans quietly allowed their hopes . . .": "Fate and the Davis Cup," *New Yorker*, July 27, 1929, p. 38.

27    "Tennis fever" raged all over Berlin . . . : Steinkamp, *Gottfried von Cramm*, p. 52.

27    "very slender, very blond . . . If looks could kill . . .": Reznicek, *Tennis-Faszination*, p. 40.

27    "Never have I been so thrilled . . .": Steinkamp, *Gottfried von Cramm*, p. 51.

27    "Gottfried was the most fluent . . .": Rot-Weiss Club, *Gottfried Freiherr von Cramm*, p. 31.

27    "practicing like a professor of mathematics . . .": *Lawn Tennis and Badminton* 29 (April 15, 1939), p. 1132.

28    "It was a tough assignment to train with him . . .": Rot-Weiss Club, *Gottfried Freiherr von Cramm*, p. 34.

28    He would go out at night with friends . . . : Paula Stuck von Reznicek, *Gottfried von Cramm: Der Gentleman von Wimbledon* (Nuremberg: Olympia Verlag, 1949), p. 16; Hofer interview, April 6, 2007.

28    Cramm first met Max Schmeling . . . : Patrick Myler, *Ring of Hate: Joe Louis vs. Max Schmeling: The Fight of the Century* (New York: Arcade, 2005), p. 17; David Margolick, *Beyond Glory: Joe Louis vs. Max Schmeling, and a World on the Brink* (New York: Alfred A. Knopf, 2005), p. 291.

28    "a second serve followed . . .": Steinkamp, *Gottfried von Cramm*, p. 51.

29    "no matter how proud and confident you might feel . . .": Budge, *Tennis Memoir*, p. 8.

29    "Today a different Cramm stood on the grass . . .": Menzel quoted in Steinkamp, *Gottfried von Cramm*, p. 10.

29    "I'm going to have to find a way to raise my game again": Paraphrased from Budge, *Tennis Memoir*, p. 9.

30    he seems lethargic . . . : Thomas J. Hamilton, "Budge Puts Americans in Davis Cup Challenge Round by Defeating von Cramm," *New York Times*, July 21, 1937, p. 25.

30    "Though nothing about Mrs. Simpson . . .": Cecil Beaton, *The Wandering Years: Diaries, 1922–1939* (Boston: Little, Brown, 1962), p. 299.

31    "no territorial demands to make in Europe": Charles Loch Mowat, *Britain Between the Wars, 1918–1940* (Chicago: University of Chicago Press, 1955), pp. 564–65.

31    "open support of the Spanish nationalists . . .": Ibid., pp. 572–82.

31    the British government "warned" Germany . . . : Alvin C. Eurich and Elmo C. Wilson, *In 1936* (New York: Holt, 1937), p. 336.

32    "the final battle is in sight . . .": William L. Shirer, *The Rise and Fall of the Third Reich* (New York: Simon and Schuster, 1960), p. 412.

32    "a terrified waiting for war": Mowat, *Britain Between Wars*, p. 567.

32    "with a brave show of pomp": Ibid., p. 588.

32    "The town was decorated . . .": Ralph Bunche to Dr. Mordecai W. Johnson, May 22, 1937, Ralph J. Bunche Papers, Schomburg Center for Research in Black Culture, New York Public Library.

32    "happily put everything back in place": Ted Tinling, *Love and Faults: Personalities Who Have Changed the History of Tennis in My Lifetime* (New York: Crown, 1979), p. 177.

32–33 "a little sandbox of a stadium": Laney, "Mystery," p. 607.

33    "She became the rage, almost a cult . . .": Al Laney, *Covering the Court* (New York: Simon and Schuster, 1968), p. 50. Other Lenglen material comes from *Bud Collins' Modern Encyclopedia of Tennis* (Detroit: Gale Research, 1994); James Medlycott, *100 Years of the Wimbledon Tennis Championships* (New York: Crescent Books, 1977), pp. 59, 64.

33    an Elizabethan theater: John McPhee, *Wimbledon: A Celebration* (New York: Viking Press, 1972), p. 18.

33    aircraft hangar: Laney, "Mystery," p. 117.

33    "a piece of land that is revered in the game": Budge, *Tennis Memoir*, p. 3.

33    a mix of *Poa pratensis* . . . : McPhee, *Wimbledon*, pp. 114–17.

34    "It's not everyone can line a court . . ." and "What the roller does is put a polish on . . .": On Robert Twynam see McPhee, *Wimbledon*, pp. 105–07.

34    "the greatest title in modern sport": Tunis, "Reporter at Large: Wimbledon," p. 38.

35    Budge sips some tea . . . Cramm . . . pops a sugar cube . . . : *Daily Mail*, July 21, 1937, p. 14.

35    "Budge's backhand pulled . . .": Cooke, "German Baron v. California Truck Driver's Son," p. 661.

35    "begins to stroke his chin . . .": Ibid.

36    "Preparations of the armed forces for a possible war . . .": Shirer, *Rise and Fall of Third Reich*, p. 416.

36    "A new era had begun . . .": Mowat, *Britain Between Wars*, p. 567.

## SECOND SET

37    For the first time ever the Nazi flag was waving . . . : Egon Steinkamp, *Gottfried von Cramm, der Tennisbaron: Eine Biographie* (Munich: Herbig, 1990), p. 12.

37    "incompetent and lazy, vain as a peacock . . .": William L. Shirer, *The Rise and Fall of the Third Reich* (New York: Simon and Schuster, 1960), p. 410.

37–38 "When I criticized Ribbentrop's qualifications . . .": Quoted in ibid., p. 410.

38    One political cartoon that year . . . : Charles Loch Mowat, *Britain Between the Wars, 1918–1940* (Chicago: University of Chicago Press, 1955), p. 592.

38    "I beheld a man of arresting personality . . .": David Clay Large, *Nazi Games* (New York: W.W. Norton, 2007), p. 138.

38    "Guarantee us peace [as Hitler was happy to do] . . .": Mowat, *Britain Be-tween Wars*, p. 594.

39    "[Hitler] is a born leader of men . . .": Quoted in Martin Gilbert, *Lloyd George* (Englewood Cliffs, N.J.: Prentice-Hall, 1968), pp. 69–72.

39    he'd complained to one reporter . . . To another, he'd lamented . . . : Steinkamp, *Gottfried von Cramm*, p. 123.

40    "Vigilante groups . . ." and "like boats lost in a storm . . .": Quoted in Alexandra Richie, *Faust's Metropolis* (New York: Carroll and Graf, 1998), p. 19.

41    Retired generals . . . one last postage stamp . . . : Ibid., p. 321.

41    "No other nation has experienced anything comparable . . .": Sebastian Haffner, *Defying Hitler: A Memoir*, trans. Oliver Pretzel (New York: Farrar, Straus and Giroux, 2002), pp. 52–53.

41–42  "an atmosphere of light-headed youthfulness . . . a dance of despair": Richie, *Faust's Metropolis*, p. 323.

42    Haus Vaterland . . . the Resi: Mel Gordon, *Voluptuous Panic* (Venice, Calif.: Feral House, 2001), pp. 73–77.

42    "Ever since [*Girlkultur*] undressed the female body . . .": Benjamin quoted in Richie, *Faust's Metropolis*, p. 354.

42–43  Everyone was talking about the *Berliner Luft* . . . : Gordon, *Voluptuous Panic*, pp. 1, 52.

43    "Gottfried was always [out with us at night] . . .": Paula Stuck von Reznicek, *Tennis-Faszination* (Munich: Schumacher-Gebler, 1969), p. 42.

43    "Everything comes so effortlessly . . .": Quoted in Paula Stuck von Reznicek, *Gottfried von Cramm: Der Gentleman von Wimbledon* (Nuremberg: Olympia Verlag, 1949), p. 17.

43    spending a great deal of time . . . : On Gottfried and Lisa's courtship, see Steinkamp, *Gottfried von Cramm*, p. 52.

44    "You have made me completely crazy . . .": Ibid.

44    "Like a comet a new star fell from the tennis heavens . . .": Reznicek, *Tennis-Faszination*, p. 42.

45    "I would probably take the trophy . . .": Ibid.

45    "Gottfried's unspeakably gifted . . .": Reznicek, *Gottfried von Cramm*, p. 8.

45    "Combine his shots with my head . . .": Ibid.

45    "Prenn spoke with me yesterday . . .": Steinkamp, *Gottfried von Cramm*, p. 54.

46    "Following his wedding . . .": Ibid.

46    at 35 Dernburgstrasse . . . : Ibid.

47    They spent what they could on boiled horse meat . . . : Richie, *Faust's Metropolis*, pp. 390–91.

47    "throngs of people standing around [the ornamental bridges] . . .": Emily Hahn, *Times and Places* (New York: Crowell, 1970), p. 115.

47    "in order not to fall into paralysis and despair . . .": Erich Maria Remarque, *Three Comrades* (Boston: Little, Brown, & Co., 1937), pp. 318, 338.

47    "Kill the Jews!": Richie, *Faust's Metropolis*, p. 398.

47    Embittered veterans . . . ," "grim, submerged-looking Communists . . . ,"

and *"Deutschland Erwache!"*: Remarque, *Three Comrades*, p. 397; Stephen Spender, *World Within World* (1951; Berkeley: University of California Press, 1966), p. 130.

48     "It's hard to imagine now how wild it was in Berlin": Annette Eick, in *Paragraph 175*, a documentary film by Rob Epstein and Jeffrey Friedman (Channel Four Films, 2000).

48     "Berlin means Boys": Christopher Isherwood, *Christopher and His Kind* (New York: Farrar, Straus and Giroux, 1976), p. 2.

48     "a bugger's daydream": Quoted in Large, *Nazi Games*, p. 186.

48     the swanky Hollandaise . . . : Gordon, *Voluptuous Panic*, pp. 49, 100.

48     there was a club to cater to any conceivable taste, "Berlin has become the paradise of international homosexuals," and scene at the Eldorado: Ibid., pp. 51, 79, 100, 289–90.

49     Manasse Herbst: On Cramm's first meeting and early encounters with Herbst, see Gestapo files located at the Landesarchiv, Berlin. Bestand A Rep. 358-02, Nr. 21070, 98301: "Generalstaatsanwaltschaft beim Landgericht Berlin zwei Verfahren gegen Gottfried von Cramm (*1909); eines wegen Vergehens gegen §175 und eines wegen Devisenvergehens," hereafter referred to as "Landesarchiv files"; Georg Heck, interview by Dr. Andreas Sternweiler, director, Schwules Museum, Berlin; interview with Sternweiler, Berlin, April 5, 2007.

49     "It was a necessity of avant-garde fashion . . .": Richie, *Faust's Metropolis*, p. 355.

50     "In three days," he told his star pupil . . . : Steinkamp, *Gottfried von Cramm*, p. 55.

51     drop his legal studies: Ibid.

51     "I seem to recall . . .": E. C. Potter, "Early Career of von Cramm," *American Lawn Tennis*, June 20, 1934, p. 29.

51     "hitting his ground strokes with delightful freedom": *American Lawn Tennis*, July 20, 1931, p. 27.

51     His life had changed completely . . . : On playing tennis in Scandinavia, Egypt, Europe, see Steinkamp, *Gottfried von Cramm*, p. 68.

52     "Packed buses race through the streets . . .": Joseph Roth, *What I Saw: Reports from Berlin 1920–33*, trans. Michael Hofmann (London: Granta Books, 2003), p. 162.

52     "The youth of the country . . .": "Fate and the Davis Cup," *New Yorker*, July 27, 1929, p. 38.

53     "It did not occur to [the Left] that through sport . . ." Haffner, *Defying Hitler*, p. 74.

53     "Give the German nation six million bodies . . .": *Mein Kampf* quoted in William J. Baker, *Sports in the Western World* (Totowa, N.J.: Rowman and Littlefield, 1982), p. 247.

53     German POWs, who had learned it from their English guards . . . : Patrick Myler, *Ring of Hate: Joe Louis vs. Max Schmeling: The Fight of the Century* (New York: Arcade, 2005), p. 10.

55    Jews were subject to extreme restrictions: Stacy Schiff, *Véra (Mrs. Vladimir Nabokov)* (New York: Random House, 1999), p. 20.

55    "imitat[ing] . . . in foreign cities . . .": Vladimir Nabokov, *Speak, Memory* (New York: G.P. Putnam's Sons, 1966), p. 282.

55–56  The Russians in Berlin forged an émigré community . . . : Schiff, *Véra*, pp. 9–10.

56    probably the club that gave . . . Nabokov had learned . . . : Brian Boyd, *Vladimir Nabokov: The Russian Years* (Princeton: Princeton University Press, 1990), p. 259.

56    "like a slick automaton . . .": Nabokov, *Speak, Memory*, p. 283.

56    "all of us sleepless Russians wandering the streets until dawn": Schiff, *Véra*, p. 10.

56    he assimilated . . . and excelled at table tennis . . . : Steinkamp, *Gottfried von Cramm*, p. 69; telephone interview with Oliver Prenn, November 15, 2006.

56    "seemingly inexhaustible": "Fate and the Davis Cup," p. 38.

56    "the most tenacious tennist in Europe": "Davis Cup," *Time*, August 1, 1932.

56–57  "the fiercest competitor I ever saw . . .": Najuch quoted in Reznicek, *Tennis-Faszination*, p. 50.

57    the German crowd wondered whether Perry was merely "playing dead . . .": Blau-Weiss Club, *Nachrichtenblatt*, August 1932, p. 32.

57    "This day, 10 July 1932, will never be forgotten . . .": Quoted in Steinkamp, *Gottfried von Cramm*, p. 69.

57–58  "The motion of the [shoulder-to-shoulder mass of people] was so great . . .": Ibid., pp. 69–70.

58    "there was something oppressive in the air . . .": Haffner, *Defying Hitler*, p. 84.

58    "was still widely regarded as a somewhat embarrassing figure . . . the alternately shifty and staring eyes": Ibid., p. 87.

58–59  The republic was liquidated . . . : Ibid., pp. 92–93.

59    Hitler chancellor of Germany: On the first two months of Hitler's reign, see Shirer, *Rise and Fall of Third Reich*, pp. 267–78; Haffner, *Defying Hitler*, pp. 118–19; Richie, *Faust's Metropolis*, pp. 410–17.

60    Already pamphlets and posters were appearing . . . : Haffner, *Defying Hitler*, p. 141.

60    Jews were forced to sell their businesses . . . : Richie, *Faust's Metroplis*, pp. 426–28.

60    "We need waste no words here . . .": Baker, *Sports in Western World*, pp. 247–48.

60    a fervent Nazi and enthusiastically brutal SA colonel . . . : Large, *Nazi Games*, p. 67.

61    "Non-Aryan players can no longer take part . . .": "Davis Cup Squad Named by Germany," *New York Times*, April 24, 1933, p. 19, and www .jewsinsports.org/profile.asp?sport=tennis&ID=72.

61    "Last year, when Prenn beat Austin . . .": Steinkamp, *Gottfried von Cramm*, p. 70.

61    Dr. Theodor Lewald: "Nazi Ideals in Sport," [London] *Times*, April 18, 1933, p. 10.

62     "Sir,—We have read with considerable dismay . . .": "Germany and the Davis Cup," [London] *Times*, April 15, 1933, p. 11.

62     a new law allowing players from annexed countries . . . : Alan Trengove, *The Story of the Davis Cup* (London: Stanley Paul, 1985), p. 131.

62     Prenn fled yet another pogrom . . . : Oliver Prenn interview, November 15, 2006.

62–63     he was the second athlete, and the only tennis player . . . : Max Schmeling, *Max Schmeling: An Autobiography* (Chicago: Bonus Books, 1998), p. 88.

63–64     "The world I had lived in dissolved and disappeared . . .": Haffner, *Defying Hitler*, pp. 194–95.

64     "delouse" . . . "epidemic" of "unnatural lechery between men": Richard Plant, *The Pink Triangle: The Nazi War Against Homosexuals* (New York: Holt, 1986), pp. 26, 49, 91.

64–65     "Among the many evil instincts . . .": Alfred Rosenberg, in the *Völkischer Beobachter*, quoted in ibid., p. 49.

65     "Anyone who thinks of homosexual love . . .": Ibid., p. 50.

65     "belongs purely to the private domain . . .": Ibid., p. 61.

65     "had a special horror of homosexuals": Ibid., p. 72.

65     "knew what to do with homosexuals . . . the end of the Germanic world": Quoted in ibid., p. 89.

66     Kurt Hiller: Ibid., p. 107.

66     "I would like to do that very much . . .": E. C. Potter, "Early Career of von Cramm," *American Lawn Tennis*, June 20, 1934, p. 29.

67     "our greatest Davis Cup weapon" and "a sticker . . .": Ibid.

67     Jack Crawford: John R. Tunis, "Crawford Complete," *New Yorker*, July 15, 1933, p. 40, and John R. Tunis, "John B. Crawford, World Champion," *New Yorker*, September 2, 1933, p. 48; Don Budge, *A Tennis Memoir* (New York: Viking Press, 1969), p. 103.

68     On one of the hottest days . . . : On the Cramm-Crawford match, see John Olliff, *Olliff on Tennis* (London: Eyre and Spottiswoode, 1948), p. 122; John R. Tunis, "Raising a Racket for Germany," *Collier's*, July 10, 1937, p. 38; Steinkamp, *Gottfried von Cramm*, p. 73; *American Lawn Tennis*, June 20, 1934, and February 20, 1938.

68     "Only two foreigners in my observation . . .": Tunis, "Raising a Racket," p. 38.

68–69     "if Germany had put all her children . . .": Quoted in ibid.

69     A few days later in Berlin . . . : Rot-Weiss Club, *Gottfried Freiherr von Cramm*, p. 41.

69     The Nazis were already clamping down on currency . . . : Edith Roper, *Skeleton of Justice*, trans. Clara Leiser (New York: E.P. Dutton, 1941), p. 164. For an examination of travails faced by Germans due to Nazi currency restrictions, see Roper, ch. 9.

69     A few days before the Herbsts' ship sailed . . . : This episode, and others relating to Cramm's helping Herbst get his family's money out of Germany, has been pieced together from various sources, but most of the details here are from the Landesarchiv files. This episode is from Bestand A Rep. 358-02 Nr. 98301, p. 15. It is difficult sometimes to distinguish among Nazi lies,

strategic alibis of Cramm and his lawyer, and the truth. But we know from Herbst's letters to Cramm after the war that Cramm did indeed help him get his money out of the country (see Steinkamp, *Gottfried von Cramm*, p. 124), and so these details from the file would seem to be accurate.

70  "My backswing is too pronounced for grass . . .": "Von Cramm's Life Story," *American Lawn Tennis*, February 20, 1938, p. 26.

70  he had come down with a virus: Steinkamp, *Gottfried von Cramm*, p. 73.

70  The execution of Ernst Röhm . . . : On the Night of the Long Knives, see Shirer, *Rise and Fall of Third Reich*, pp. 305–12; Plant, *Pink Triangle*, pp. 54–57, Richie, *Faust's Metropolis*, pp. 418–20.

73  "A method I frequently prefer . . .": William T. Tilden, *Tennis A to Z* (London: Gollancz, 1950), p. 117.

73  whenever Cramm finally gets . . . : On Cramm's strategy and style of play, see Thomas J. Hamilton, "Budge Puts Americans in Davis Cup Challenge Round by Defeating von Cramm," *New York Times*, July 21, 1937, p. 25; interview with Jack Kramer, Los Angeles, December 6, 2006.

73  "an astonishing stop-volley from the centre of the court" and "Oh baby!": Quoted in "Champions at Forest Hills," *Time*, September 13, 1937, p. 21.

73  "improbable passing shots": Roderich Menzel quoted in Steinkamp, *Gottfried von Cramm*, p. 10.

74  "douses his head like Jeeter Lester": James Thurber, "The Greatest Match in the History of the World," *New Yorker*, July 31, 1937, p. 41.

74  "I'm supposedly number one in the world . . .": Budge, *Tennis Memoir*, p. 11.

74  "conspicuously red-headed, even among red-headed men": Fred Perry, *My Story* (London: Hutchinson & Co., 1934), p. 177.

74  "Despite his many triumphs . . .": Frank Ernest Hill, "Flashing Budge Reaches the Heights," *New York Times Magazine*, July 11, 1937, p. 9.

74  The Californian's background . . . : On Budge's early biography, see Donald Budge, *Tennis Memoir*; Herbert Warren Wind, "Budge and the Grand Slam," *New Yorker*, February 15, 1988, pp. 75–89; Budge, interview, 1975, videotape at the Tennis Hall of Fame, Newport, R.I.

77  "I played every game you could imagine . . .": Telephone interview with Gene Mako, March 27, 2006.

77  "You play there . . .": Budge, *Tennis Memoir*, p. 152.

77  "The future of American tennis . . .": Ibid., p. 36.

77  He and Mako traveled . . . : On the expenses on first trip east, see Stan Hart, *Once a Champion: Legendary Tennis Stars Revisited* (New York: Dodd, Mead, 1985), p. 140; Budge, *Tennis Memoir*, pp. 38, 41.

78  "Tom had a different kind of personality . . .": Roger McEntyre quoted in Gail Baxter, *The Berkeley Tennis Club: A History, 1906–1976*, privately published. For more on Budge and Stow that winter, see Wind, "Budge and Grand Slam," p. 78, and Budge, *Tennis Memoir*, p. 43.

79  "Budge's forehand needs work . . . than tennis anyway": Quoted in "Davis Cup," *Time*, July 29, 1935.

79  "We aren't going to win it overnight . . .": Trent Frayne, *Famous Tennis Players* (New York: Dodd, Mead, 1977), p. 62.

79      "to the considerable amusement of their fellow passengers . . .": Walter
        Schleiter, "Some Davis Cup Notes," *American Lawn Tennis*, August 20,
        1937, p. 20.

80      "Pardon me, sir . . .": Will Grimsley, *Tennis: Its History, People and Events*
        (Englewood Cliffs, N.J.: Prentice-Hall, 1971), p. 74.

80      "The King and Queen go to other events . . .": Al Laney, "The Mystery of
        Wimbledon," in Herbert Warren Wind, ed., *The Realm of Sport* (New York:
        Simon and Schuster, 1966), p. 607.

81      Budge never thought twice . . . : On Budge's putative wave to the queen,
        see Budge, *Tennis Memoir*, pp. 52–54; Laney, "Mystery," p. 608.

82      "I was heady with new success . . .": Budge, *Tennis Memoir*, p. 88.

82      clipped Oxbridge English . . . : Arthur J. Daley, "Von Cramm Here to Seek
        U.S. Title," *New York Times*, August 24, 1937, p. 16.

82      "Excuse me, Don . . .": On Budge and Cramm's first meeting and conversa-
        tion, see Budge, *Tennis Memoir*, pp. 88–90.

84      following the example of the great Tilden . . . : On Tilden throwing points
        and so on, see Paul Metzler, *Tennis Styles and Stylists* (New York: Macmillan,
        1970), p. 90; Frank Deford, *Big Bill Tilden: The Triumphs and the Tragedy*
        (New York: Simon and Schuster, 1976), p. 60; Allison Danzig, "Tilden, Au-
        tocrat of the Courts," in Wind, *Realm of Sport*, p. 604.

84      "with just the touch of a wry smile" and "I guess you do see things my way":
        Budge, *Tennis Memoir*, p. 90.

85      opened the door, and held it . . . : Alistair Cooke, "German Baron v. Cali-
        fornia Truck Driver's Son: A Study in Good Ambassadorship," broadcast
        over WEAF, August 4, 1937, in *Vital Speeches of the Day*, vol. 3, August 15,
        1937, p. 661, in E. Digby Baltzell Papers, University of Pennsylvania.

85–86   "no score could be more deceptive . . .": E. C. Potter, quoted in *American
        Lawn Tennis*, July 20, 1935, p. 17.

86      "the game between Perry and von Cramm was such super-tennis . . .":
        *American Lawn Tennis*, July 20, 1935, p. 25.

87      London protested meekly . . . : Shirer, *Rise and Fall*, p. 391.

88      "young officers stood like marble statues . . .": Ibid., p. 392; see also Richie,
        *Faust's Metropolis*, p. 435.

88      "Our racial theory regards every war . . .": Shirer, *Rise and Fall*, pp. 393–96.

88      "The speech turns out to be reasonable, straightforward, and comprehen-
        sive . . .": Ibid.

88      "the symbol of the indestructible life-force of the German nation . . .":
        Richie, *Faust's Metropolis*, pp. 434–35.

88      Herbst was back in Berlin . . . he was virtually supporting Manasse . . . :
        Landesarchiv files, Bestand A Rep. 358-02 Nr. 98301, p. 16.

89      "was infested with human bodies in various stages of nudity and solariza-
        tion . . .": Nabokov, *Speak, Memory*, pp. 303–04.

89      Every ten minutes another group of schoolchildren . . . : Haffner, *Defying
        Hitler*, p. 146.

89–90   "The swastika flags were everywhere . . .": Ibid., pp. 239, 250.

90      those in the neighboring rooms . . . : Gianni Clerici, *The Ultimate Tennis*

*Book,* trans. Richard J. Wiezell (Chicago: Follett, 1975), p. 198; and Julius Heldman, "The Budge Style," in Allison Danzig and Peter Schwed, eds., *The Fireside Book of Tennis* (New York: Simon and Schuster, 1972), p. 241.

90   "Budge's curly red hair, his bright red cheeks . . .": Clerici, *Ultimate Tennis,* p. 198.

90   "depend[ed] largely on the newest, homeliest, and youngest member of the team . . .": "Davis Cup," *Time,* July 29, 1935.

90–91   "A phlegmatic, gentle youth . . .": "Forest Hills Finale," *Time,* September 2, 1935.

91   "was dominated throughout by [Cramm's] wizardry . . .": Conrad Aiken, "Yankee Luck," *New Yorker,* August 3, 1935, p. 27.

92   "seemed to lose all interest . . .": Budge, *Tennis Memoir,* p. 48.

92   "He had defeated me soundly at Wimbledon . . .": Ibid.

93   "He attacked incessantly . . .": Ibid., p. 10.

93   "the crowd passe[d] from enthusiasm to something near hysteria": Al Laney, *Covering the Court: A Fifty-Year Love Affair with the Game of Tennis* (New York: Simon and Schuster, 1968), p. 235.

93   At five-six, Budge walks . . . : On the final game of the second set, see Budge, *Tennis Memoir,* pp. 10–11; *Lawn Tennis and Badminton,* July 24, 1937, p. 398; Hamilton, "Budge Puts Americans in Challenge Round," p. 25.

93   "dangerously deep passing shot," "with a dancelike leap," "*Furor teutonicus,*" and "Gottfried is inimitable": Rot-Weiss Club, *Gottfried Freiherr von Cramm,* pp. 10–11. *Furor Teutonicus,* Latin for "Teutonic Fury," is an expression generally attributed to the Roman poet Lucan. The term has been used since medieval times as a catchphrase for German aggression. It was also a favorite in speeches by Bismarck and Hitler (who liked quoting Bismarck).

93   "jumps to her feet . . .": *American Lawn Tennis,* August 5, 1937, p. 40.

94   "He plays just like God would play": *American Lawn Tennis,* September 20, 1937, p. 59.

## Third Set

95   "more mad than analytical": Don Budge, *A Tennis Memoir* (New York: Viking Press, 1969), p. 11.

95   the match statistics . . . : *Lawn Tennis and Badminton,* July 24, 1937, p. 398; Ted Tinling, *Love and Faults: Personalities Who Have Changed the History of Tennis in My Lifetime* (New York: Crown, 1979), p. 149.

95   "When news of the second set loss came across three thousand miles of sea . . . : Alistair Cooke, "German Baron v. California Truck Driver's Son: A Study in Good Ambassadorship," broadcast over WEAF, August 4, 1937, in *Vital Speeches of the Day,* vol. 3, August 15, 1937, pp. 661–63, in E. Digby Baltzell Papers, University of Pennsylvania.

95   "his very wide mouth wide open in an admiring grin." Al Laney, *Covering the Court: A Fifty-Year Love Affair with the Game of Tennis* (New York: Simon and Schuster, 1968), p. 236.

96      "In the face of such superlative play . . .": Walter Schleiter, "Some Davis Cup Notes," *American Lawn Tennis*, August 20, 1937, p. 20.

96      Sure enough, Cramm does not continue: . . . On the first game of the third set, see *Lawn Tennis and Badminton*, July 24, 1937, p. 398; Thomas J. Hamilton, "Budge Puts Americans in Davis Cup Challenge Round by Defeating von Cramm," *New York Times*, July 21, 1937, p. 25.

96      they take some extra time toweling themselves off . . . : Laney, *Covering the Court*, p. 236.

97      "is in fair way to become the most popular tennis idol . . .": Franklin Pierce Adams, "Rye's Semifinals—Sartorial Notes," *New Yorker*, August 21, 1937, p. 45.

97      "The Wimbledon crowd admires him . . .": Cooke, "German Baron v. California Truck Driver's Son," pp. 661–63.

97      "Don Budge is a really nice kid on top of the world . . .": *Bystander*, July 1937.

97      "Give me some Bing Crosby . . .": Don Budge, on Shell Chateau radio show, September 26, 1936, NBC Archives, Library of Congress.

97      "Budge reached real greatness in his last-day triumph . . .": Conrad Aiken, "Yankee Luck," *New Yorker*, August 3, 1935, p. 26.

97      "boredom, isolation/insulation . . . loneliness": Joseph Killorin, ed., *Selected Letters of Conrad Aiken* (New Haven: Yale University Press, 1978), pp. 203–07.

97–98   "It won't be long . . . to the corners": James Thurber, "Budge Takes Shields," *New Yorker*, August 24, 1935, p. 31.

98      "Sorry, Don . . .": Ibid.; and "Forest Hills Finale," *Time*, September 2, 1935.

98      "sprints, slides, and dives . . .": James Thurber, "Bitsy Grant's Two-Day Match," *New Yorker*, September 21, 1935, p. 42.

98      "At one of the movie theatres in Forest Hills . . .": James Thurber, "Forest Hills Notes," *New Yorker*, September 14, 1935, p. 51.

99      "How many masters of the game would love to have this weakness!" Menzel quoted in Egon Steinkamp, *Gottfried von Cramm, der Tennisbaron: Eine Biographie* (Munich: Herbig, 1990), p. 10.

99      the Interzone Final at the Germantown Cricket Club . . . : Budge, *Tennis Memoir*, pp. 60–63; Herbert Warren Wind, "Budge and the Grand Slam," *New Yorker*, February 15, 1988, p. 80; "Australia Wins Davis Cup Tie 3–2," *American Lawn Tennis*, June 20, 1936, p. 6.

100     "a battle royal, a masterpiece of savagery . . .": Conrad Aiken, "The Machine Age," *New Yorker*, July 11, 1936, p. 32.

101     "I have no doubt that Don is going to catch up with Perry . . .": Frank Everest Hill; "Flashing Budge Reaches the Heights," *New York Times Magazine*, July 11, 1937, p. 9.

101     "For wild excitement at night . . .": Budge, *Tennis Memoir*, p. 64.

102     "They tell me Budge sometimes goes in for hot dogs . . .": James Thurber, "Summer Is Ended," *New Yorker*, September 19, 1936, p. 95.

102     "all the other sweets I had refused to deny myself": Budge, *Tennis Memoir*, p. 64.

102     Saturday, September 12, arrived . . . : On the Perry-Budge U.S. final, see

Budge, *Tennis Memoir,* pp. 64–66; Allison Danzig, "13,000 at Net Finals," *New York Times,* September 13, 1936, p. S1; Thurber, "Summer Is Ended," pp. 95–97; "Forest Hills Finale," *Time,* September 21, 1936; interview with Robert Kelleher, Los Angeles, December 5, 2006.

103 "I think Gene Mako and I established a new sleep record on the train": Don Budge, on Shell Chateau radio show.

103 For starters, he immediately cut out . . . : On Budge's new training routine, see Budge, *Tennis Memoir,* pp. 66–69; Wind, "Budge and Grand Slam," p. 81.

104 Vines was coming down with the flu . . . : Ray Bowers, "History of the Pro Tennis Wars, Chapter VIII: Perry and Vines, 1937," online at www .tennisserver.com/lines/lines_04_12_03.html.

104 "I liked his hard hitting . . .": J. Donald Budge, *Budge on Tennis* (New York: Prentice-Hall, 1939), p. 51.

105 "Before the match was even over . . .": Budge, *Tennis Memoir,* p. 75; also see Budge, *Budge on Tennis,* p. 51.

105 Perry, Cramm, and Budge all wore DAKS . . . : Kelleher interview.

105 "knocking down about every fence in Oakland": Budge, *Tennis Memoir,* p. 76.

105 Stow instructed Don to think of himself as number one at all times: Ibid., p. 75.

106 "I am convinced that you are the best player in the world . . .": Wind, "Budge and Grand Slam," p. 81.

106 "he looked like Mr. Tennis . . .": Pancho Segura, in *Kings of the Court: The Ten Greatest Tennis Players of All Time,* Tennis Classics Production Company and the International Tennis Hall of Fame, VHS tape, 1997.

106 He had always favored white rackets . . . : "Forest Hills Finale."

106 "He let me play with his racket once . . .": Quoted in Trent Frayne, *Famous Tennis Players* (New York: Dodd, Mead, 1977), p. 57.

106 "I always felt that if I served a couple of double faults . . .": Wind, "Budge and Grand Slam," p. 81.

106 "Even the most meticulous foot fault judge is obliged to admit . . .": *American Lawn Tennis,* September 5, 1938, p. 40.

107 "No matter how you forced him . . .": Paul Metzler, *Tennis Styles and Stylists* (New York: Macmillan, 1970).

107 "had that extra flair, that great freedom of motion . . .": Julius Heldman quoted in Wind, "Budge and Grand Slam," p. 89.

107 He would stand closer to the net than anyone . . . : Don Budge, unpublished article manuscript, 1975 (courtesy of Jeff Budge).

107 "Nope, I couldn't serve and volley against Budge . . .": Interview with Jack Kramer, Los Angeles, December 6, 2006.

107 "He was a marvelous athlete . . .": Interview with Gene Mako, Los Angeles, December 6, 2006.

107 "At the end of a hot match . . .": Franklin Pierce Adams, "Rye's Semifinals—Sartorial Notes," *New Yorker,* August 21, 1937, p. 44.

107 not a particularly fast runner . . . : Eugene L. Scott, "Death of a Champion," *Wall Street Journal,* February 1, 2000.

107    "They all slide to a certain extent . . .": John McPhee, *Wimbledon: A Celebration* (New York: Viking Pres, 1972), p. 86.

107    "When in form . . .": Laney, *Covering the Court*, p. 234.

108    Alice Marble: Alice Marble, *Courting Danger* (New York: St. Martin's Press, 1991).

108    "It was really a lark playing with Alice . . .": Don Budge, interview, 1975, videotape at the Tennis Hall of Fame, Newport, R.I.; also see Stan Hart, *Once a Champion: Legendary Tennis Stars Revisited* (New York: Dodd, Mead, 1985), p. 143.

109    "Whereas Cramm is all elegance . . .": Laney, *Covering the Court*, p. 234.

110    "Budge seems always a bit the underdog . . .": Hill, "Flashing Budge," p. 9.

110    he couldn't help but visualize defeat . . . : Budge, *Tennis Memoir*, p. 77.

110–11  "finding a perfect touch at once" and "Thus was the cool, crisis-proof Budge revealed": A. Wallis Myers, in *Daily Telegraph*, July 3, 1937, p. 19.

111    "began to hit the ball harder and longer . . .": "America's Day at Wimbledon," [London] *Times*, July 3, 1937, p. 7.

111    "I have to report . . . that Budge's stance in the royal presence . . .": James Thurber, "Budge and Television," *New Yorker*, July 17, 1937, pp. 38–39.

111    "just remember, all you have to do is hold your serve . . .": Budge, *Tennis Memoir*, p. 78.

112    "von Cramm's stealth on the volley . . .": "America's Day at Wimbledon," p. 7.

112    "Now I was literally shaking . . .": Budge, *Tennis Memoir*, pp. 53–54.

112    "one a low forehand volley that pitched just inside the line": Myers, in *Daily Telegraph*, July 3, 1937, p. 19.

112    "I practically had to crawl to the net . . . ," and "You know, Mr. Budge . . .": Budge, *Tennis Memoir*, pp. 53–54.

112    His hopes seemed dashed . . . : On the doubles match, see "Smashing Victory Gives Budge Title," *New York Times*, July 3, 1937, p. 7.

113    "come down like the wolf . . . out of their championships": Thurber, "Budge and Television," pp. 38–39.

113–14  "I do appreciate this chance you give me . . .": "Some Remarks by the Champion," *American Lawn Tennis*, August 5, 1937, p. 6.

114    That's all right, he tells himself . . . : For descriptions of the fourth game, third set, see Budge, *Tennis Memoir*, pp. 11–12; and Hamilton, "Budge Puts Americans in Challenge Round," p. 25.

114    "screaming in delight . . . lady on my left": James Thurber, "The Greatest Match in the History of the World," *New Yorker*, July 31, 1937, p. 41.

115    "golden years . . . liquor, and party talk": Harrison Kinney, *James Thurber: His Life and Times* (New York: Holt, 1995), p. 690.

115    "nearly driving himself mad . . . ," "six feet, one-and-a-half . . . ," "He was just good enough . . . ," and "Ada has a tennis court . . . ,": Ibid., pp. 301, 675, 512, 640.

116    "of a grasshopper finally come to earth . . .": Ibid., p. 676.

116    "won the only set of tennis he'd ever won in his life": Ibid., p. 814.

116    "Went to Wimbledon three days . . .": James Thurber to Ronald and Jane Williams, July 11, 1937, in Harrison Kinney and Rosemary A. Thurber, eds., *The Thurber Letters: The Wit, Wisdom, and Surprising Life of James Thurber* (New York: Simon and Schuster, 2003), p. 241.

116    a two-year "test period" . . . : David E. Fisher and Marshall Jon Fisher, *Tube: The Invention of Television* (Washington: Counterpoint, 1996), pp. 247, 363.

116–17  "It was a cloudy day but the little miracle came off beautifully . . ." Thurber, "Budge and Television," pp. 38–39.

117    "the baseline on the primitive screens . . .": Tinling, *Love and Faults*, pp. 177–78.

117    the Berlin Olympics had been televised . . . : Fisher, *Tube*, pp. 260–61.

117    "The word is half Greek and half Latin . . .": Ibid., p. 248.

117    *automobile* and *homosexual:* In Tom Stoppard's play, *The Invention of Love*, A. E. Houseman declares, " 'Homosexuals'? Who is responsible for this barbarity? . . . It's half Greek and half Latin!"

117    "Life is no good to me . . .": James Thurber to Dr. Gordon Bruce, June 9, 1939, in *Thurber Letters*, pp. 314–15.

117    "punishment": Kinney, *James Thurber*, p. 776.

117–18  "the greatest match in the history of the world": Thurber, "Greatest Match," p. 41.

118    "I've played tennis with Paul Lukas . . .": Don Budge, on Shell Chateau radio show.

118    "The movie people seemed to look up to us . . .": Hart, *Once a Champion*, p. 154.

118    Frank Shields: William X. Shields, *Bigger than Life: The Last Great Amateur. A Biography of Francis X. Shields* (New York: Freundlich, 1986), p. 82.

118    "night-club fistionics": Ibid., p. 100.

119    "Flynn was a hell of an athlete . . .": Mako interview.

119    "had just about become an unofficial member . . .": Budge, *Tennis Memoir*, p. 6.

119    "the sleepiest of all Broadway personalities . . .": James Maguire, *Impresario: The Life and Times of Ed Sullivan* (New York: Billboard, 2006), p. 66.

121    But Gottfried Cramm had become a good friend . . . : William T. Tilden, *My Story: A Champion's Memoirs* (New York: Hellman, Williams & Co., 1948), p. 132; Budge, *Tennis Memoir*, p. 13.

121    The greatest tennis player . . . : Tilden's early biography, unless otherwise stated, is from Frank Deford, *Big Bill Tilden: The Triumphs and the Tragedy* (New York: Simon and Schuster, 1976).

121–22  "a house where there was little expression of love and gaiety" and "The impression of grief . . .": Ibid., p. 190.

123    "dolls and other girlish gifts": Grantland Rice, *The Tumult and the Shouting* (New York: Barnes, 1954), p. 158.

123–24  "At the end, May 2, 1911 . . .": Deford, *Big Bill Tilden*, p. 201.

124–25   "He suddenly was compelled . . ." and "If you had asked me around 1915–16 . . .": Carl Fischer, quoted in ibid., pp. 32, 205.

125   "Most tennis players look upon the ball . . .": William T. Tilden, *Match Play and the Spin of the Ball* (1925; reprint New York: Arno Press, 1975), p. 1.

125   "he was holding forth on the porch . . .": Vincent Richards, "The Astonishing Mr. Tilden," *Esquire*, August 1937, in Herbert Graffis, ed., *Esquire's First Sports Reader* (New York: Ayer, 1971), p. 6.

126   "the most popular tennist ever to step on a court": George Lott, "Little Bill," in Allison Danzig and Peter Schwed, eds., *The Fireside Book of Tennis* (New York: Simon and Schuster, 1972), p. 156.

126   Bill Johnston: Ibid.; *Bud Collins' Modern Encyclopedia of Tennis* (Detroit: Gale Research, 1994); Laney, *Covering the Court*, pp. 42, 70–71.

126   "In 1919 . . .": Laney, *Covering the Court*, p. 41.

126–27   "Tilden was in charge . . .": Ibid.

127   the winter of 1919–20 . . . : George Lott, "Bill Tilden as I Knew Him for 33 Years," *Tennis*, July 1970, p. 19; Richards, "Astonishing Mr. Tilden," pp. 6–7; Deford, *Big Bill Tilden*, pp. 35–6.

127   "the Valley Forge of American tennis": Deford, *Big Bill Tilden*, p. 35.

127–28   "the shot that made it impossible to keep Tilden . . ." and "the soundest and brainiest tennis . . .": "Tilden Wins Tennis Title of Britain," *New York Times*, July 4, 1920, p. 19.

128   "the most nerve-racking battle . . ." and "perhaps the greatest of all time": "Tilden Crowned King of Courts," *New York Times*, September 7, 1920, p. 23.

128–29   "He was the autocrat of the courts . . .": Allison Danzig, "Greatest Tennis Player of All Time," *New York Times*, December 22, 1963, p. 19.

129   The next year, 1922 . . . : On the 1922–24 Forest Hills tournaments, see Deford, *Big Bill Tilden*, pp. 85–7, 94, 96–7, 128; Laney, *Covering the Court*, pp. 68–72; Grantland Rice, *Tumult and Shouting*, p. 159; "Tilden for 5th Year Is Tennis Champion," *New York Times*, September 3, 1924, p. 1.

130   "My racket did slip after a few exchanges . . .": John Winkler, "The Iconoclast of the Courts," *New Yorker*, September 18, 1926, p. 29.

131   "house of prostitution on wheels": Frederick Lewis Allen, *Only Yesterday: An Informal History of the 1920's* (New York: Harper & Row, 1931), p. 100.

131   "eating three o'clock, after-dance suppers in impossible cafes . . .": F. Scott Fitzgerald, *This Side of Paradise* (New York: Scribner's, 1920), pp. 65, 188.

132   "was not only the supreme . . .": Danzig, "Greatest Tennis Player," p. 19.

132   He demanded that ball boys throw him the ball . . . : Kelleher interview.

132   put his hands on his hips . . . throw his hands up in the air . . . : Lott, "Tilden as I Knew Him," p. 5.

132   "He elevated the procedure [of glaring at linesmen] to an art . . .": Richards, "Astonishing Mr. Tilden," p. 7.

132   "went for him with clenched fists": Lott, "Tilden as I Knew Him," p. 5.

132 "carping, demanding and fault-finding . . .": Danzig, "Greatest Tennis Player," p. 34.
133 stopping play in the middle of a game . . . : John Olliff, *Olliff on Tennis* (London: Eyre and Spottiswoode, 1948), p. 77.
133 to complain of a woman in the stands . . . : Ted Tinling, *Sixty Years in Tennis* (London: Sidgwick and Jackson, 1983).
133 "Peach!": Danzig, "Greatest Tennis Player," p. 34.
133 "I never once saw him take a point . . .": Deford, *Big Bill Tilden*, p. 60.
133 "I'm not throwing anything for the gallery . . .": Winkler, "Iconoclast of the Courts," p. 27.
133 "I feel I must compensate . . .": Deford, *Big Bill Tilden*, p. 61.
133 "Ready when you're exhausted, partner!" Ibid., p. 63.
134 "Tilden glared at linesmen after decisions . . .": Laney, *Covering the Court*, p. 60.
134 "Come on, Tillie": Lott quoted in Hart, *Once a Champion*, pp. 182–83.
135 "the grand, almost regal manner . . .": Stanley K. Wilson quoted in Laney, *Covering the Court*, p. 73.
135 $350 (for a fifty-dollar train fare) plus hotel and meals: George Lott, "Tennis Money: It Doesn't Pay to Be an Amateur," *Collier's*, September 3, 1938, p. 28.
135 "theoretically working": Bobby Riggs with George McGann, *Court Hustler* (Philadelphia: Lippincott, 1973), pp. 56–57.
136 "I felt it beneath the dignity of the United States . . .": E. Digby Baltzell, *Sporting Gentlemen: Men's Tennis from the Age of Honor to the Cult of the Superstar* (New York: Free Press, 1995), pp. 180–81.
136–37 They celebrated almost as though . . . : Deford, *Big Bill Tilden*, pp. 147–48.
137 "stylist supreme": John R. Tunis, "Lucky Cochet," *New Yorker*, September 15, 1928, p. 28.
137 On the final day Tilden had nothing . . . : On France winning Davis Cup, see "Tilden and Johnston Beaten as France Wins the Davis Cup," *New York Times*, September 11, 1927, p. S1; Deford, *Big Bill Tilden*, pp. 137–55; Alan Trengove, *The Story of the Davis Cup* (London: Stanley Paul, 1985), pp. 68–95; René Lacoste, "The Quest of the Davis Cup," in Herbert Warren Wind, ed., *The Realm of Sport* (New York: Simon and Schuster, 1966), pp. 595–601; "Paris Is Jubilant over Cup Victory," *New York Times*, September 11, 1927, p. S1.
138 a Florida concern had offered him $5,000 . . . , "It's silly for a big crowd to enthuse . . . ," and "most constant companion": Winkler, "Iconoclast of the Courts," pp. 28–29.
138 "chewing a pink rose down to the thorns": Tinling, *Sixty Years in Tennis*.
138–39 "*en rapport*, if you will excuse the euphemism," "That girl would sleep with a *swan*," "Tilden keeps his amateur standing," and TILDEN STILL TENNIS CHAMP: Deford, *Big Bill Tilden*, pp. 69, 213, 130–31.
139 "elementary school entertainment . . .": "Tilden Pseudo Tramp in a New Comedy," *New York Times*, October 13, 1926, p. 20.

140    "His belief in his own invincibility was strongly shaken": Lott, "Tilden as I Knew Him," p. 10. The story of the match is from Laney, *Covering the Court*, pp. 148–51.

140    "Tilden rose . . .": "Tilden's Glare Held Responsible for Defeat of Attempt to Ban Frowning at Officials," *New York Times*, February 15, 1928, p. 17.

141    The USLTA . . . finally decided to put its foot down . . . : On the 1928 Davis Cup drama, see "Tilden Barred from Davis Cup Play," *American Lawn Tennis*, July 20, 1928, p. 252; George Lott, "Tight Spots in Tennis," *Atlantic*, August 1938, pp. 197–98; Hart, *Once a Champion*, pp. 183–84; Lott, "Tilden as I Knew Him," p. 32; "Davis Cup," *Time*, August 6, 1928; Deford, *Big Bill Tilden*, pp. 116–22.

142    "wore amiability like a gay cockade" and "one of the most effective handshakes in Ohio history": James Thurber, "Master of Ceremonies," *New Yorker*, July 21, 1928, p. 19.

142    "I refute all charges!" "Tilden Barred from Davis Cup Play," p. 252.

142–43  "It is the love of study of tennis . . .": Tilden, *Match Play and Spin of Ball*, p. 25.

143    "I am far more amateur in spirit . . .": Deford, *Big Bill Tilden*, p. 122.

143    "Jeanne d'Arc about to be burned at the stake": Lott, "Tilden as I Knew Him," p. 32.

144    "You are a great artist in your line, David": William T. Tilden, *Glory's Net* (Garden City, N.J.: Doubleday, 1930), p. 295.

144    "evidently feels my work will not injure *its* amateur standing . . .": "Tilden's Passing Shots," his column in *American Lawn Tennis*, June 20, 1929, p. 158.

144    "For once Bill Tilden had his heart's desire . . ." and "his personality dominated the entire meeting": John R. Tunis, "A Young Man from Philadelphia," *New Yorker*, June 7, 1930, p. 64.

145    "This was indeed a battle of giants . . .": John R. Tunis, "Phenomenon . . . ," *New Yorker*, July 12, 1930, p. 63.

145    "not accustomed to playing tennis in a cow pasture": Danzig, "Greatest Tennis Player," p. 34. On the rest of his "psychological decay," see Deford, *Big Bill Tilden*, p. 158.

145    The next week, at the Eastern Grass-Court Championships . . . : Danzig, "Greatest Tennis Player," p. 34; Deford, *Big Bill Tilden*, p. 158.

146    "he hobbled around, glowering . . .": "Fall of Tilden," *Time*, September 22, 1930.

146    "Oh for God's sake . . ." and "The fight . . .": Deford, *Big Bill Tilden*, p. 162.

146    Little Bill Johnston . . . Frank Hunter: Ray Bowers, "History of the Pro-Tennis Wars, Chapter III: Tilden's Year of Triumph, 1931," online at www.tennisserver.com/lines/lines_02_03_03.html; Deford, *Big Bill Tilden*, p. 158.

146    he announced that he had signed a contract . . . : "William T. Tilden, 2nd, Becomes a Professional," *American Lawn Tennis*, January 20, 1931, p. 671.

146–47   "in a pastoral setting," "a delightful vicarage garden party," and "They
         played with an air of elegance . . .": Deford, *Big Bill Tilden*, pp. 26–29,
         206.

147      "When two players start a match . . .": William T. Tilden, *Tennis A to Z*
         (London: Gollancz, 1950), p. 115.

147      "Every year, it seems . . .": Budge, *Tennis Memoir*, p. 11; also suggested in
         *Lawn Tennis and Badminton* 28 (1937), p. 364.

147      He didn't say a word to Walter Pate . . . : For third-set details, see Budge,
         *Tennis Memoir*, p. 11–12; Hamilton, "Budge Puts Americans in Challenge
         Round," p. 25.

148      "It is characteristic of von Cramm to lose a third set after winning two":
         "The Davis Cup: Germany Fight to the Last," [London] *Times*, July 21,
         1937, p. 6.

149      "Eighteen years after the war . . .": "Peace in Europe," [London] *Times*,
         February 25, 1936, p. 8.

149      "the nakedness of the government in foreign policy was unconcealed . . .":
         Charles Loch Mowat, *Britain Between the Wars, 1918–1940* (Chicago:
         University of Chicago Press, 1955), p. 557.

149      "the overall economic calamity an almost biblical character": T. H.
         Watkins, *The Great Depression* (Boston: Little, Brown & Co., 1993), p. 64.

150      "a phalanx of heel-clicking officers" and "a spirit in Germany which I
         have not seen in any other country . . .": A. Scott Berg, *Lindbergh* (New
         York: Putnam, 1998), pp. 357, 361.

151      "wishing the game of amateur tennis . . .": "Tilden Becomes a Profes-
         sional," p. 671.

## FOURTH SET

153      Hadn't he just beaten Perry . . . : On Tilden versus Perry, and Tilden's
         shoulder operation, see Ray Bowers, "History of the Pro Tennis Wars,
         Chapter VIII: Perry and Vines, 1937," online at www.tennisserver.com/
         lines/lines_04_12_03.html.

154      "I've never seen two men catch fire . . .": "Play by Play of Thrilling Budge
         Victory," *San Francisco Chronicle Sporting Green*, July 21, 1937, p. 4.

154      He'd played his own sweet game . . . : Frank Deford, in *Big Bill Tilden*, p.
         19, tells of one day when Tilden was playing "with little distinction" for
         his prep-school tennis team. "At the end of a point, which, typically,
         Tilden had violently overplayed, hitting way out, [a friend] hollered to
         him in encouragement, 'Hey, June, take it easy.'
             "Tilden stopped dead, and with what became a characteristic gesture,
         he swirled to face the boy, placing his hands on his hips and glaring at
         him. 'Deacon,' he snapped, 'I'll play my own sweet game.'
             "And so he did, every day of his life. . . ."

155      "In pursuing this policy . . .": "Moss Explains Ban on Negroes in Tennis,"
         *New York Times*, December 28, 1929, p. 16.

155      "anti-white and all out for USSR" and "this staid, glum and curt, though

always 'courteous' little isle": Ralph Bunche, diary entries, April 1937, quoted in Brian Urquhart, *Ralph Bunche: An American Odyssey* (New York: W.W. Norton, 1993), pp. 64, 67.

156    "Well, that 'darkey,' as you call him . . .": Bunche diary entry, July 7, 1937, Ralph J. Bunche Papers, UCLA Library Special Collections.

156    Bunche . . . a club membership for his son: Philip Benjamin, "Color Line Bars Bunche and Son From Forest Hills Tennis Club," *New York Times*, July 9, 1959, p. 1; "Forest Hills Invites Bunche Application; Head of Club Quits," *New York Times*, July 15, 1959, p. 1.

156    "the most exciting athletic combat I've ever seen": Bunche diary entry, July 20, 1937, Ralph J. Bunche Papers, UCLA Library Special Collections.

156–57  The intermission over . . . : On the first four games of fourth set, see Thomas J. Hamilton, "Budge Puts Americans in Davis Cup Challenge Round by Defeating von Cramm," *New York Times*, July 21, 1937, p. 25.

157    Daniel Prenn would have left work . . . : Personal information on Prenn is from telephone interviews with Oliver Prenn, November 15, 2006, May 9, 2008, and October 16, 2008, and with Derrick Kleeman, January 9, 2007.

158    "The man without a country": Egon Steinkamp, *Gottfried von Cramm, der Tennisbaron: Eine Biographie* (Munich: Herbig, 1990), p. 71.

159    "Jews Strictly Forbidden in This Town . . .": William L. Shirer, *The Rise and Fall of the Third Reich* (New York: Simon and Schuster, 1960), p. 323.

160    "giving American moral and financial support to the Nazi regime . . .": www.historyplace.com/worldwar2/triumph/tr-olympics.htm.

160    "The German government are simply terrified . . ." David Clay Large, *Nazi Games* (New York: W.W. Norton, 2007), p. 93.

160    "concerted efforts by Communists . . .": Ibid., p. 101.

160    "liked [Tschammer] very much": Brundage quoted in ibid., p. 79.

160–62  "the Jew LaGuardia," "inconceivable," "there are many wise and well informed observers in Europe . . . ," "Jew-friendly," "the dirty Jews and politicians," "One wonders . . . ," and *"Wann die Olympiade ist vorbei . . ."*: Quoted in Large, *Nazi Games*, pp. 84, 90, 96–99.

162    Dora Ratjen: Ibid., p. 237.

162    "Germany stands far and away on top with 33 gold medals . . .": Ibid., p. 238.

163    "a man of dignity . . . a socialist": Ibid., p. 233.

163    "high cheek bones of an Indian": David Margolick, *Beyond Glory: Joe Louis vs. Max Schmeling, and a World on the Brink* (New York: Alfred A. Knopf, 2005), p. 27.

164    "While condemning Hitler . . .": Ibid., p. 144.

164    "the great American shibboleth . . .": Urquhart, *Ralph Bunche*, pp. 57–58.

164    "There is no sport . . .": *Mein Kampf* quoted in Margolick, *Beyond Glory*, p. 27.

164    "It is every German's obligation to stay up tonight . . .": Margolick, *Beyond Glory*, p. 151.

165    "I know that you have fought for Germany . . ." . . . watched the film of
       the fight with him . . . : Ibid., pp. 163, 182.

165    "the most famous and best loved athlete in modern German history":
       Ibid., p. 129.

166    "Firing a devastating attack that observing critics . . .": "Baron Triumphs
       Over British Ace, 3 to 2, Driving to Love Victory in Last Set," *New York
       Times*, June 2, 1936, p. 36; also see "Perry Beaten by von Cramm," [Lon-
       don] *Times*, June 2, 1936, p. 6.

166    "Hearty congratulations on your victory . . .": Steinkamp, *Gottfried von
       Cramm*, p. 90.

166    he had also sent some to his brother-in-law, Hans von Meister . . . : Lan-
       desarchiv files, A Rep. 358-02 Nr. 98301, pp. 7, 11.

166    "Everything in any way connected with foreign exchange is *verboten* . . .":
       Edith Roper, *Skeleton of Justice*, trans. Clara Leiser (New York: E.P. Dut-
       ton, 1941), pp. 159–60.

166    the head of German boxing had had to apply . . . : Margolick, *Beyond
       Glory*, p. 211.

167    several nights together in Gottfried's hotel: Landesarchiv files, A Rep.
       358-02 Nr. 98301, p. 6.

167    Gottfried received yet another telegram: Steinkamp, *Gottfried von
       Cramm*, p. 89.

167    "he could shoot from any direction . . .": Roman Najuch quoted in Paula
       Stuck von Reznicek, *Tennis-Faszination* (Munich: Schumacher-Gebler,
       1969), p. 50.

168    "There is also the factor that Perry is not the phlegmatic philosopher . . .":
       *Daily Telegraph*, July 3, 1936, p. 21.

169    . . . even chat with folks in the box seats . . . : Julius Heldman, "The Style
       of Fred Perry," in Allison Danzig and Peter Schwed, eds., *The Fireside
       Book of Tennis* (New York: Simon and Schuster, 1972), p. 253.

169    "indulge his Continental habit . . .": *Daily Telegraph*, July 3, 1936, p. 21.

169    Suddenly a black taxicab . . . : *Daily Telegraph*, July 4, 1936, p. 13;
       Steinkamp, *Gottfried von Cramm*, p. 90.

169    His right thigh was cramping . . . : Ibid.

170    "what was expected to be the hardest-fought final . . .": W. F. Leysmith,
       "Modern Wimbledon Record Created by Perry in Taking Three Straight
       Titles," *New York Times*, July 4, 1936, p. 8.

170    the 1936 Wimbledon final . . . : *Daily Telegraph*, July 3, 1936, p. 21; Ley-
       smith, "Modern Wimbledon Record," p. 8; Steinkamp, *Gottfried von
       Cramm*, pp. 90–91; Don Budge, unpublished article manuscript, 1975
       (courtesy of Jeff Budge); Fred Perry, *Fred Perry: An Autobiography* (1984;
       reprint London: Arrow, 1985), pp. 100–101.

170    More likely the "cramp" had been a muscle strain . . . : Interview with Dr.
       Ronald Fisher, Methodist Hospital, Houston, May 18, 2008.

171    "Ladies and Gentleman . . ." and "I'm afraid there was only one
       game . . .": Leysmith, "Modern Wimbledon Record," p. 8.

172 "adjusting themselves astonishingly to the violent eccentricities...": Conrad Aiken, "Sixty Games in a Gale," *New Yorker,* August 8, 1936, p. 54.

172 "The spectators stood from their seats...": Steinkamp, *Gottfried von Cramm,* p. 92.

172 "his manner is so sympathetic and his game is so good...": Quoted in ibid.

173 "Now you are free...: For the story of Göring holding up the mortgages, see Budge, unpublished manuscript; see also Ron Fimrite, "Baron of the Court," *Sports Illustrated,* July 5, 1993.

173 "He was always pleading...": Paula Stuck von Reznicek, *Gottfried von Cramm: Der Gentleman von Wimbledon* (Nuremberg: Olympia Verlag, 1949), p. 20.

173 Peter Herbinger: Morris Gruenberg, *Berlin N-54* (Maitland, Fla.: Romex International, 217), pp. 196–99.

174 "take the crowd into his confidence": "Tennis," *Time,* October 7, 1929.

174 The opinion of most observers...: *American Lawn Tennis,* July 20, 1931, p. 22; Al Laney, *Covering the Court: A Fifty-Year Love Affair with the Game of Tennis* (New York: Simon and Schuster, 1968), p. 41.

174 "This incredible athlete's..." and "As usual when he wasn't playing...": "The Pros Hold a Tournament," *New Yorker,* July 18, 1931, p. 45.

175 "An hour after checking in...," "He was always broke...," and "Bill went right on playing tennis...": Vincent Richards, "The Astonishing Mr. Tilden," *Esquire,* August 1937, in Herbert Graffis, ed., *Esquire's First Sports Reader* (New York: Ayer, 1971), p. 8.

175 Hans "Hanne" Nüsslein: Rainer Deike, "Der verfemte Weltmeister," in Deutscher Tennis Bund, ed., *Tennis in Deutschland. Von den Anfängen bis 2002* (Berlin: Duncker & Humblot, 2002), p. 103.

176 "a machine with a brain...": See Hall of Fame website, www.tennisfame.com/famer.aspx?pgID=867&hof_id=226.

176 "far superior to his showing as an amateur": Allison Danzig, "Vines in Pro Debut Loses to Tilden," *New York Times,* January 11, 1934, p. 25.

176 "In bursts Bill, looking like he just stepped...": Grantland Rice, *The Tumult and the Shouting* (New York: Barnes, 1954), p. 160.

176 "the miracle man of tennis": Danzig, "Vines in Pro Debut," p. 25.

177 "The difficulty with this scheme...": Morris Markey, "Jeu de Paume," *New Yorker,* January 19, 1935, p. 44.

177 "All they can do is beat him...": Laney quoted in Frank Deford, *Big Bill Tilden: The Triumphs and the Tragedy* (New York: Simon and Schuster, 1976), p. 166.

177 "I am the most ardent admirer of the German people...": William T. Tilden, *Aces, Places and Faults* (London: Hale, 1938), pp. 136–37.

177–78 "I was immediately accepted as an integral member...": Deford, *Big Bill Tilden,* p. 159.

178 "had never seen anything like this...": Stan Hart, *Once a Champion:*

*Legendary Tennis Stars Revisited* (New York: Dodd, Mead, 1985), p. 442. Judging from the telephones, this club was probably the Resi (see Mel Gordon, *Voluptuous Panic* [Venice, Calif.: Feral House, 2001], pp. 228–29), even though the Resi's clientele was not predominantly homosexual. It could have also been the Femina (see www.argo.net.au/andre/osmarwhiteENFIN.htm), but this also was not a gay establishment.

178  "Berlin Bill loved . . .": Deford, *Big Bill Tilden*, p. 160.

178  "I'll have a Tilden": " 'Tilden Cocktail,' All Water, Popular on French Courts," *New York Times*, May 20, 1927, p. 21.

178  "the limitless range of attractions . . ." and "Everyone assumed that Bill just didn't need any sleep at all": Deford, *Big Bill Tilden*, pp. 44, 159–60.

179  "sexual Bolshevism" and "fascist perversion": Christopher Isherwood, *Christopher and His Kind* (New York: Farrar, Straus and Giroux, 1976), p. 334.

179–80  "somehow homosexually active persons," "anti-community minded" people who threatened the "moral fiber . . . ," "As National Socialists we are not afraid . . . ," and nine hundred in 1934 . . . : Richard Plant, *The Pink Triangle: The Nazi War Against Homosexuals* (New York: Holt, 1986), pp. 108–11, 231.

180  A doctor was sentenced to prison . . . A senior employee . . . : Geoffrey J. Giles, "Wegen der zu erwartenden hohen Strafe: Homosexuellenverfolgung in Berlin, 1933–1945," and "Homosexuelle Männer im KZ Sachsenhausen" (review), *Holocaust and Genocide Studies* 17, no. 1 (Spring 2003), p. 197.

180  "primitive, bounding creature . . .": Large, *Nazi Games*, p. 215.

181  Himmler . . . hated aristocrats . . . : Himmler mused on his grandiose plans to his personal physician, Felix Kersten, who wrote about them in his memoirs. Quoted in Plant, *Pink Triangle*, p. 97.

181  "The von Cramms were staunch Hanoverians . . .": Tatiana Metternich, *Purgatory of Fools* (New York: Quadrangle/NYT, 1976), p. 210.

181  In April 1937 . . . : On Cramm's Gestapo interrogation, see Landesarchiv files, A Rep. 358-02 Nr. 21070, p. 4. Exact conversations are imagined from descriptions of them.

182  "With the Führer this afternoon . . .": Margolick, *Beyond Glory*, p. 217.

182  His divorce proceedings with Lisa were coming through . . . : Tilden, *Aces, Places*, p. 94; confirmed in Landesarchiv files.

183  there was a painfully awkward scene . . . : Steinkamp, *Gottfried von Cramm*, p. 141.

183  Gottfried and Barbara had met earlier that year . . . : Ibid., p. 180.

183–84  "had a craze for tennis" . . . practice every day with professionals . . . : Mona Eldridge, *In Search of a Prince: My Life with Barbara Hutton* (London: Sidgwick and Jackson, 1988), p. 43.

184  "I loved you the first time I laid eyes on your face": Steinkamp, *Gottfried von Cramm*, p. 180.

184  at parties at her London mansion . . . : Eldridge, *Search of Prince*, p. 163.

184     Barbara would clap boisterously . . . : C. David Heymann, *Poor Little Rich Girl: The Life and Legend of Barbara Hutton* (New York: Random House, 1983), p. 140.

184     "jeweled strokes," "Both played shots of blinding speed . . . ," and "splendid saving strokes": A. Wallis Myers, in *Daily Telegraph*, July 3, 1937, p. 19.

184     "I was quite satisfied with my form today . . .": *Daily Mail*, July 3, 1937, p. 15.

184–85   "almost owed its survival": Ted Tinling, *Love and Faults: Personalities Who Have Changed the History of Tennis in My Lifetime* (New York: Crown, 1979), p. 177.

185     "elf-like," "dark, melting," and "sad, striving . . .": Cecil Beaton, *The Years Between: Diaries 1939–1944* (New York: Holt, Rinehart and Winston, 1965), pp. 159, 161.

185     drove off to meet Gottfried again: On Cramm and Nares, see Michael Holroyd, *Mosaic: A Family Memoir Revisited* (New York: W.W. Norton, 2004), pp. 75–76; von Cramm's testimony for 1938 trial, Landesarchiv files, A Rep. 358-02 Nr. 21070, p. 20.

185     "the English citizen Ischervood [sic] . . ." and "'a pronounced addiction to reciprocal onanism' . . .": Isherwood, *Christopher and Kind*, pp. 281, 286.

186     a telephone may have rung: On Hitler phoning the Wimbledon locker room: Don Budge told the story frequently, and consistently, to the end of his life. And he was nothing if not an honest man. His sons swear that he was not the type to tell tall tales or embellish stories. Frank Deford says that both Budge and Tinling told him the Hitler story and "didn't seem to be dissembling." However, I can find no record of the anecdote at all before 1969, when Budge (with Deford, as coauthor) published his autobiography. Why would he have waited thirty-two years to tell the story? Gene Mako, his best friend, told me he doubted the story was true; he doesn't remember anything about it from that time.

Ted Tinling kept the story alive in his own 1979 memoir but strangely told it in Budge's words, quoting from Budge's book. Why would he do that? Either he knew it wasn't true but loved the story anyway, or he believed Budge but had no memory of it himself, or had too vague a memory. Yet Deford says that Tinling told him the story in his own words.

Cramm laughed it off as "a fairy tale," and his friends and relatives, as well as German historians, swear it never happened. The historian Heiner Gillmeister, for instance, says that Rolf Goepfert—who played on the German team in 1938, attended the 1937 match, and knew Cramm well—insisted "the story was altogether invented." (See Paul Fein, *Tennis Confidential* [Washington: Brassey's, 2002], p. 274.) The denials seem almost too vehement: after all, if Hitler made the call, it wasn't Cramm's fault and in no way reflected badly on him. Yet it has become almost a point of honor among Cramm followers in Germany to insist that it never happened.

One German tennis journalist, though, Ulrich Kaiser, writes that Tinling "swore fifty years later that it had happened"—but before the Cramm-Grant match! (See Ulrich Kaiser, "Eine Freundschaft," in Deutscher Tennis Bund, *Tennis in Deutschland*, p. 152.) On the other hand, Cramm's close friend Wolfgang Hofer told me that he and Gottfried met Budge at Wimbledon after his book came out, and Budge admitted to fabricating the story. When Cramm died in 1976, though, Budge told the *Boston Globe* that he had last seen Cramm in 1947. (Yet in his 1969 book he wrote, "we still sometimes see each other.") Personal memories are indeed a shaky foundation for history.

It is far from impossible that the phone call happened. Cramm's biographer Egon Steinkamp wrote that tennis was "as important" as boxing "as a billboard of German sport." And Hitler certainly called and telegraphed Max Schmeling, had receptions for him, and even watched fight films with him. Before Schmeling's 1938 rematch with Joe Louis, Hitler cabled him: "To the next world's champion, Max Schmeling. Wishing you every success." (And Germany lost that contest too. See Margolick, *Beyond Glory*, p. 283.) Yet in the end I would have to say that it is unlikely that Hitler phoned the Wimbledon locker room on July 20, 1937.

186    "it was made clear to him . . .": Kaiser, "Eine Freundschaft," p. 152.

187    Pate begins to enjoy his tea: Alistair Cooke, "German Baron v. California Truck Driver's Son: A Study in Good Ambassadorship," broadcast over WEAF, August 4, 1937, in *Vital Speeches of the Day*, vol. 3, August 15, 1937, p. 661, in E. Digby Baltzell Papers, University of Pennsylvania.

187    He even told Budge once . . . : Budge, *Tennis Memoir*, p. 12.

188    "You shouldn't play all that tennis this year, Gottfried . . . I can't lose, and I can't quit." William T. Tilden, *My Story: A Champion's Memoirs* (New York: Hellman, Williams & Co., 1948), p. 132.

## FIFTH SET

189    "Our one objective on this trip is to bring back the Cup . . .": Allison Danzig, "Strong U.S. Team, Headed by Budge and Mako, Departs on Quest of Davis Cup," *New York Times*, June 6, 1937, p. 83.

190    "We lived together . . ." and "Putting became . . .": Alan Trengove, *The Story of the Davis Cup* (London: Stanley Paul, 1985), p. 127. On description of putting course, see Gordon Forbes, *A Handful of Summers* (London: Heinemann, 1978), p. 156.

190    "used to stay up all night drinking and chasing dames": Jack Kramer quoted in Trengove, *Story of Davis Cup*, p. 127.

190    Bobby Riggs, who had been . . . : Tom Lecompte, *The Last Sure Thing: The Life and Times of Bobby Riggs* (Easthampton, Mass.: Black Squirrel, 2003), pp. 72–74.

190    "I was more dedicated to tennis . . .": Don Budge, interview, 1975, on videotape at Tennis Hall of Fame.

191    the uniforms of the various military units . . . : E. C. Potter Jr., "Germany Is European Zone Winner," *American Lawn Tennis*, July 20, 1937, p. 14.

191    the more anticipated match of the day . . . : On the Cramm-Menzel match, see Trengove, *Story of Davis Cup*, p. 126.

192    There they got the ferry to Harwich . . . : *Lawn Tennis and Badminton* 28 (July 17, 1937), p. 358.

192    "Cable stories aver . . .": "On the Eve of Battle," *American Lawn Tennis*, July 20, 1937, p. 30.

193    they had hired Karel Kozeluh . . . : On the various international coaches, see "Without Benefit of Publicity," *New Yorker*, July 20, 1929, p. 64; John R. Tunis, "Richards versus Kozeluh," *New Yorker*, July 26, 1930, p. 45; John R. Tunis, "Rule, Britannia," *New Yorker*, July 29, 1933, p. 42; "Prospectus," *New Yorker*, June 2, 1934, p. 86; Ray Bowers, "History of the Pro Tennis Wars, Chapter VII: Awaiting Perry, 1936," online at www .tennisserver.com/lines/lines_04_07_25.html; *American Lawn Tennis*, July 20, 1937, p. 30.

193    he had taken some guilty pleasure . . . : Conrad Aiken, "Psychology and the Davis Cup," *New Yorker*, July 28, 1934, p. 28. Tilden publicly predicted the United States would lose to Australia in the Interzone Final, but they came back from two matches down to win 3-2. In the Challenge Round, however, Perry and Austin beat them convincingly.

193    "Why would we need a coach?": Interviews with Gene Mako, March 27, 2006, and December 6, 2006.

193    "Can you imagine anybody coaching Budge?": "Davis Cup Choice Dilemma to Pate," *New York Times*, July 15, 1937, p. 25.

193    Usually Cramm and Henkel were on another court . . . : Ibid.

193–94  "Sure, we practiced with the Germans when we felt like it . . .": Mako interviews.

194    After a full day . . . : Ibid.

194    his busy days designing the scenery . . . : "Mr. Priestley's New Play," [London] *Times*, July 12, 1937, p. 10.

194    "To [Ribbentrop] one has to listen without much chance of interruption . . .": David Clay Large, *Nazi Games* (New York: W.W. Norton, 2007), p. 215.

194    Reventlow retaliated by firing him the next day: C. David Heymann, *Poor Little Rich Girl: The Life and Legend of Barbara Hutton* (New York: Random House, 1983), p. 140.

194–95  who had helped Barbara design the property's red-clay tennis courts . . . : Dean Southern Jennings, *Barbara Hutton: A Candid Biography* (New York: Fell, 1968), p. 108.

195    "hatred between spouses was no reason for separation": Mona Eldridge, *In Search of a Prince: My Life with Barbara Hutton* (London: Sidgwick and Jackson, 1988), p. 163.

195    not without securing Gottfried's promise . . . : Heymann, *Poor Little Rich Girl*, p. 143.

195–96    "the low, low class . . . : Stan Hart, *Once a Champion: Legendary Tennis Stars Revisited* (New York: Dodd, Mead, 1985), p. 160.

196    Frank and Audrey, "discovered" . . . : Cynthia Beardsley, *Frank Parker: Champion in the Golden Age of Tennis* (Chicago: Havilah Press, 2002), p. 33.

196    "the love of my life": Hart, *Once a Champion*, p. 310.

196    "had the goods on him": Ibid., p. 311.

197    "without a change in expression or his methodical attitude": "Budge, Parker and Grant Advance to Quarter-Finals in Singles at Wimbledon," *New York Times*, June 26, 1937, p. 10.

197    "merely continued to shake his head . . .": "U.S. Line-Up to Remain Secret Till Draw for Davis Cup Today," *New York Times*, July 16, 1937, p. 15.

197    "the little shaver" was playing sneaky . . . : J. Donald Budge, *Budge on Tennis* (New York: Prentice-Hall, 1939), p. 59.

198    he held Bitsy upside down . . . : William X. Shields, *Bigger Than Life: The Last Great Amateur: A Biography of Francis X. Shields* (New York: Freundlich, 1986), p. 99, and various other sources.

198    "the greatest tennis competitor the world has ever seen . . .": Allison Danzig, "Brian (Bitsy) Grant," in Allison Danzig and Peter Schwed, eds., *The Fireside Book of Tennis* (New York: Simon and Schuster, 1972), p. 267.

198    "evoked quite a lot of comment . . .": "The All-Important Interzone Tie," *American Lawn Tennis*, August 5, 1937, p. 4.

198    "Why did U.S choose Grant. . . .": Ralph Bunche, diary entry, July 20, 1937, Ralph J. Bunche Papers, UCLA Library Special Collections.

198    "I did not think it the correct selection . . .": Al Laney, *Covering the Court: A Fifty-Year Love Affair with the Game of Tennis* (New York: Simon and Schuster, 1968), p. 232.

199    "in a state of mild shock": For the story of Laney broadcasting the match, see ibid., pp. 229–37.

199    "to ensure the new-fangled gimmick . . .": Frank Keating, "Sport: Radio Days," *Spectator*, June 20, 2007.

199    "Forehand! Recovery . . .": Frank Keating, "Sound and Fury of Radio Today Had Gentler Beginnings," *Guardian*, April 10, 2007.

200    "Hello, Americans . . . : All Laney quotes from the broadcast are from NBC radio broadcast, July 17, 1937, NBC Radio Archive, Library of Congress.

200    "while flitting about the court all the time . . .": "The All-Important Interzone Tie," *American Lawn Tennis*, August 5, 1937, p. 4.

200–201    "could put a lob out of its misery . . .": "U.S.A. and Germany All Square," [London] *Times*, July 19, 1937, p. 5.

201    "I did my best . . .": *American Lawn Tennis*, August 5, 1937, p. 38.

201    "Budge is inimitable . . .": All Brand quotes from NBC broadcast, between matches, July 17, 1937, NBC Radio Archive, Library of Congress.

201    Henkel's first serve . . . : Franklin Pierce Adams, "The State of Doubles—Baron von Cramm," *New Yorker*, September 4, 1937, p. 44; "U.S. Line-

Up to Remain Secret Till Draw for Davis Cup Today," New York Times, July 16, 1937, p. 15.

201–2    "a backswing . . ." "most incredible appetite," "something really substantial," and "cream puff . . .": Don Budge, *A Tennis Memoir* (New York: Viking Press, 1969), p. 47.

202    "wielding it on occasion at the umpire's chair": *American Lawn Tennis*, September 5, 1937, p. 48.

202    "dazzling form . . . ," "pasted unmercifully," and "regaled us with service aces . . .": "All-Important Interzone Tie," p. 4.

203    "Listen, Gene, do you mind . . .": Mako interview, December 6, 2006; Hart, *Once a Champion*, p. 141.

203    "a prospective world champion . . .": Fred Perry, *My Story* (London: Hutchinson & Co., 1934), p. 177.

203    serving contest . . . : Mako interview, March 27, 2006. A similar machine, called a "ballistic chronometer," once recorded Tilden's service at 163.6 miles per hour (reported in *American Lawn Tennis*, May 1933). It is generally agreed that those old speedometers must have been inaccurate. However, the balls in the 1930s were slightly smaller than those used later and had less nap on them, both of which would have allowed them to travel faster. And as Jack Kramer told me, "There were an awful lot of aces hit in those days, against good athletes, and it's not like we were standing still."

204    "heard something pop," "virtually every muscle . . . ," "Guys were used to me hitting my serve . . . ," and "I really don't know how I did it . . .": Mako interviews, March 27, 2006, and December 6, 2006.

205    "He has so many surprises . . .": Budge, *Budge on Tennis*, p. 138.

205    "I still had a strong hand and a strong wrist . . .": Mako interview, December 6, 2006.

205    "For a long time . . .": "America Take the Lead," [London] *Times*, July 20, 1937, p. 8.

205    "Nothing could be farther from the truth . . .": "Drummer," *New Yorker*, August 13, 1938, p. 11.

206    "Mako's muttered pep talks": James Thurber, "The Greatest Match in the History of the World," *New Yorker*, July 31, 1937, p. 41.

206    "no pair has ever played with more real rhythm . . .": Franklin Pierce Adams, "Developments at Rye," *New Yorker*, August 20, 1938, p. 49.

206    "always in trouble": "America Take the Lead," p. 8.

207    "God*damnit*, we are *not* going to get off to a bad start in the fourth!" Mako interview, December 6, 2006.

207    "One will long remember Budge in the last game of all . . .": "America Take the Lead," p. 8.

208    "one of the most glorious doubles matches . . .": Thomas Hamilton Jr., "Four-Set Doubles Victory Gives U.S. Davis Cup Team 2-1 Lead Over Germany," *New York Times*, July 20, 1937, p. 27. For more information on the doubles match, see A. Wallis Myers in *Daily Telegraph*, July 20, 1937, p. 20; Thurber, "Greatest Match," p. 41; "America Take the Lead," p. 8.

208    rubbing his right shoulder . . . : Thurber, "Greatest Match," p. 41.

208    *Maybe Bitsy will upset Henner* . . . : Budge, *Tennis Memoir*, p. 7.

208    thousands more who hadn't arrived early enough . . . : Arthur Daley, "Davis Cup Musings," *New York Times*, August 28, 1947, p. 21.

208    In the Royal Box . . . : The occupants are from *Lawn Tennis and Badminton*, July 24, 1937, p. 398.

208    "No more coals to Newcastle, no more Hoares to Paris": David Clay Large, *Between Two Fires: Europe's Path in the 1930s* (New York: W.W. Norton, 1990), p. 172.

208–9    "cement with fuzz on it," "These are not ornamental lawns . . . ," and "I got down on me knees and prayed . . .": John McPhee, *Wimbledon: A Celebration* (New York: Viking Press, 1972), pp. 87–88, 108–09.

209    *"Comme il court!"* Laney, *Covering the Court*, pp. 234–35.

209    You're being too defensive . . . : E. C. Potter, "On the Sixth Match Point," *American Lawn Tennis*, August 5, 1937, p. 8.

209–10    "Grant wagged his head . . . ," and "as much German spoken . . .": Laney, *Covering the Court*, pp. 234–35.

212    "long shadows streaked . . .": Walter Schleiter, "Some Davis Cup Notes," *American Lawn Tennis*, August 20, 1937, p. 20.

212    Cramm makes his move . . . the returns look like half-volleys: Thomas J. Hamilton, "Budge Puts Americans in Davis Cup Challenge Round by Defeating von Cramm," *New York Times*, July 21, 1937, p. 26; Alistair Cooke, "German Baron v. California Truck Driver's Son: A Study in Good Ambassadorship," broadcast over WEAF, August 4, 1937, in *Vital Speeches of the Day*, vol. 3, August 15, 1937, p. 661, in E. Digby Baltzell Papers, University of Pennsylvania.

212–13    his opponent's nod . . . , "a low sizzler," and "Oh baby!": Cooke, "German Baron v. California Truck Driver's Son," p. 661.

213    "an almost overwhelming ovation . . .": A. Wallis Myers, *Daily Telegraph*, July 21, 1937, p. 20.

213    Thoughtfully—almost regretfully . . . : Cooke, "German Baron v. California Truck Driver's Son," p. 661.

213    Is he really this invincible in the fifth set: Budge, *Tennis Memoir*, p. 14.

213    "his hands [are] clasped . . .": Ted Tinling, *Love and Faults: Personalities Who Have Changed the History of Tennis in My Lifetime* (New York: Crown, 1979), p. 150.

213    busy using it on himself . . . : Hamilton, "Budge Puts Americans in Challenge Round," p. 26.

213    "Don't worry, Cap . . . if it kills me": Budge, *Tennis Memoir*, p. 14; Trengove, *Story of Davis Cup*, p. 128; and many others.

214    Bill Tilden can contain himself . . . : Budge, *Tennis Memoir*, p. 14; Frank Deford, *Big Bill Tilden: The Triumphs and the Tragedy* (New York: Simon and Schuster, 1976), p. 161.

214    he truncates a long baseline rally with a drop shot . . . : A. Wallis Myers, *Daily Telegraph*, July 21, 1937, p. 20.

214    *You've got to take a chance* . . . : Budge, *Tennis Memoir*, p. 14.

215     one of Cramm's gut strings snapped . . . : A. Wallis Myers, *Daily Tele-graph*, July 21, 1937, p. 20.

215     "tight, but not board tight": Mako interview, December 6, 2006.

215–16  "wiping his nose, his eyeballs thumping," *"Deutschland! Deutschland!"* and "crazy and inspired . . .": Cooke, "German Baron v. California Truck Driver's Son," p. 661.

216     "At this critical moment . . .": Laney, *Covering the Court*, p. 237.

216     "His shots took on new velocity . . .": Arthur Daley, "Davis Cup Musings," *New York Times*, August 28, 1947, p. 21.

216     "he fail[s] on his backhand . . .": A. Wallis Myers, *Daily Telegraph*, July 21, 1937, p. 20.

216     "thundered for 'the Red-Headed Terror' . . .": Thurber, "Greatest Match," p. 41.

216–17  "The match now turned . . .": Cooke, "German Baron v. California Truck Driver's Son," p. 661.

217     an entire minute of applause: Roderich Menzel, in Egon Steinkamp, *Gott-fried von Cramm, der Tennisbaron: Eine Biographie* (Munich: Herbig, 1990), p. 11.

217     "The mark of aristocracy . . .": Cramm quoted by Sven Davidson in John Sharnik, *Remembrance of Games Past: On Tour with the Tennis Grand Masters* (New York: Macmillan, 1986), p. 304.

217     "I made my own opportunities . . .": Budge, *Budge on Tennis*, p. 50.

217     "in which winners [are] hit . . .": Laney, *Covering the Court*, p. 238.

217     Budge raises some nervous laughter . . . : A. Wallis Myers, *Daily Tele-graph*, July 21, 1937, p. 20.

218     "the impression of passing shots . . .": Thurber, "Greatest Match," p. 41.

218     "No man, living or dead . . .": Budge, *Tennis Memoir*, p. 4.

218     "a glorious backhand pass": E. C. Potter, "On the Sixth Match Point," p. 7; also described in *Daily Telegraph*, July 21, 1937, p. 20.

218     The German fans . . . : Walter Schleiter, "Davis Cup Notes," p. 20.

218     now the Americans in the gallery . . . : A. Wallis Myers, *Daily Telegraph*, July 21, 1937, p. 20.

218     He'd blown almost all the $500,000 . . . : On Richards bailing out Tilden, see Deford, *Big Bill Tilden*, p. 174.

219     "He traveled like a goddamn Indian prince": Laney quoted in ibid., p. 52.

219     In a typical occurrence . . . : George Lott, "Bill Tilden as I Knew Him for 33 Years," *Tennis*, July 1970, p. 32.

219     "Fritzi did the cutest thing this morning . . .": Tilden quoted in Deford, *Big Bill Tilden*, p. 172.

219     Camel cigarette ads . . . : On Tilden's endorsement deals, see Vincent Richards, "The Astonishing Mr. Tilden," *Esquire*, August 1937, in Herbert Graffis, ed., *Esquire's First Sports Reader* (New York: Ayer, 1971), p. 9; *American Lawn Tennis*, April 20, 1931, and June 20, 1933, ads.

220     Fritzi locked him out . . . : Deford, *Big Bill Tilden*, pp. 171–72.

220     "walk like a real fruit": Ibid., p. 224.

220    Twin tried to tell him . . . : Ibid., p. 207.

220    "somewhat away from the normal": William T. Tilden, *My Story: A Champion's Memoirs* (New York: Hellman, Williams & Co., 1948), p. 307.

220    Oscar Wilde: "One night in Japan we sat up until 3 or 4am and he was trying to explain his life to me. He felt like he was a second Oscar Wilde." Verle (Mrs. Ellsworth) Vines quoted in Samantha Stevenson, "The Days of Vines and Roses," *World Tennis*, November 1990, p. 34.

220    question of degeneracy . . . psychological "illness": Tilden, *My Story*, pp. 307–8.

221    they walk slowly . . . his entire body seems to relax . . . : Laney, *Covering the Court*, p. 239.

221    The serve travels straight into the bottom of the net: Budge, *Tennis Memoir*, p. 16.

221    choking: In a sports context, choking means succumbing to pressure and performing badly. The usage was just becoming popular in the late 1930s and made it into Park Kendall and Johnny Viney's *Army and Navy Slang* (New York: M.S. Mill, 1941).

221–22 "Cramm has saved these match points . . .": Schleiter, "Davis Cup Notes," p. 20.

222    "I cannot recall any effort . . .": A. Wallis Myers, *Daily Telegraph*, July 21, 1937, p. 20.

222    "Ouch . . .": E. C. Potter, quoted in *American Lawn Tennis*, August 5, 1937, p. 36.

222    if Budge loses his serve . . . : Paula Stuck von Reznicek, *Tennis-Faszination* (Munich: Schumacher-Gebler, 1969), p. 42; Hamilton, "Budge Puts Americans in Challenge Round," p. 26.

222    sails a few inches past it: *Lawn Tennis and Badminton*, July 24, 1937, p. 398.

222    Walter Pate will long remember . . . : Pate, introduction to *Budge on Tennis*, p. 11.

222–23 There is a gasp from the stands . . . : Ibid.; Daley, "Davis Cup Musings," p. 21.

223    The crowd rises to its feet as one . . . : Cooke, "German Baron v. California Truck Driver's Son," p. 661.

223    "There is no sensation in the sporting world . . .": William T. Tilden, *Match Play and the Spin of the Ball* (1925; reprint New York: Arno Press, 1975), p. xi.

223    "something so close to art . . .": Thurber, "Greatest Match," p. 41.

223    "And then a British crowd forgot its nature . . .": Cooke, "German Baron v. California Truck Driver's Son," p. 661.

223    "B fh pass lovely 7:23pm": E. C. Potter, quoted in *American Lawn Tennis*, August 5, 1937, p. 36.

224    "could hear the cheers begin to swell . . .": Budge, *Tennis Memoir*, p. 18.

224    *you certainly have got more out of the game . . .* : Danzig, "The Story of J. Donald Budge," in Budge, *Budge on Tennis*, p. 39.

224    "this was absolutely the finest match I have ever played . . .": Budge, *Tennis Memoir*, p. 18.

## Aftermatch

225 English tennis fans . . . didn't even fill Center Court . . . : "United States 4, Great Britain 1," *American Lawn Tennis*, August 5, 1937, pp. 9–11.

226 "was given the most tremendous cheer . . .": James Thurber, "Budge Against the World," *New Yorker*, August 7, 1937, p. 35.

226 the team reached New York . . . : On the journey home and parade, see Walter Schleiter, "Some Davis Cup Notes," *American Lawn Tennis*, August 20, 1937, p. 20; Don Budge, *A Tennis Memoir* (New York: Viking Press, 1969), p. 79; "Parade to Welcome Davis Cup Net Squad," *New York Times*, August 5, 1937, p. 15; "Davis Cup Stars Warmly Cheered as Famous Trophy Comes Home," *New York Times*, August 6, 1937, p. 12.

226–27 "equally amiable . . ." and "For three years Tilden . . .": "Champions at Forest Hills," *Time*, September 13, 1937, p. 21.

227 "Gottfried's popularity was so great . . .": Heinrich Henkel, "Our World Tour," *American Lawn Tennis*, December 20, 1937, p. 13.

227 "Her eyes were on Cramm . . .": Interview with Robert Kelleher, December 5, 2006.

227–28 "from what we have seen of von Cramm in America . . .": S. Willis Merrihew, *American Lawn Tennis*, October 20, 1937, p. 21.

228 "When I saw that man . . .": Budge, *Tennis Memoir*, p. 8.

229 On October 7 Budge drove . . . : *American Lawn Tennis*, October 20, 1937, p. 17.

229 on to Japan: On Cramm in Japan, see Egon Steinkamp, *Gottfried von Cramm, der Tennisbaron: Eine Biographie* (Munich: Herbig, 1990), p. 109; Yasushi Yasukawa to Heiner Gillmeister, May 9, 2000 (courtesy of H. Gillmeister).

229 He and Henkel caused a minor stir . . . : Alexander Goldie, *Body and Soul* (Briar Hill, Victoria, Australia: Indra, 2003), p. 85.

229 "when after having caressed . . .": Charles Buttrose, *Words and Music* (Sydney: Angus and Robertson, 1984), p. 188.

229–30 certain loose statements . . . : Steinkamp, *Gottfried von Cramm*, p. 123; Ron Fimrite, "Baron of the Court," *Sports Illustrated*, July 5, 1993.

230 "I think he had reached the point . . .": William T. Tilden, *My Story: A Champion's Memoirs* (New York: Hellman, Williams & Co., 1948), p. 132.

230 "Perhaps the time has come . . .": Steinkamp, *Gottfried von Cramm*, p. 124. The second warning was reported by Godfrey Winn in the English magazine *The Tatler*, August 1938.

230 a letter that found its way . . . : Landesarchiv files, Bestand A Rep. 358-02 Nr. 21070, p. 21.

231 "[His brother] Adalbert and I visited Gottfried . . .": Steinkamp, *Gottfried von Cramm*, p. 122.

232 Carl Langbehn: Allen Dulles papers, Seeley Mudd Manuscript Library, Princeton University, Box 37, File 1; viewable at www.fpp.co.uk/ Himmler/Langbehn/Pringsheim_020146.html.

232 "the ideal sportsman . . . ," "dark secrecy," and "mere subterfuges":

Budge, *Tennis Memoir*, p. 108; and "U.S. Sportsmen Demand Nazis Free von Cramm," *New York Times*, May 7, 1938, p. 5.

232     Jutta finally secured an audience with Göring . . . : On Göring's interventions on behalf of Cramm, see Steinkamp, *Gottfried von Cramm*, p. 122; and Heiner Gillmeister, "Von Caesarius von Heisterbach bis Gottfried von Cramm," in Hans Sarkowicz, ed., *Schneller, Hoeher, Weiter: Eine Geschichte des Sports* (Frankfurt am Main: Insel Verlag, 1996), pp. 181–203.

232     What did Gottfried expect: The characterization of Göring is from Klaus Mann, *Mephisto* (New York: Random House, 1977).

233     "completely independent . . . ," "an absolute king . . . ," and "Well, my good sir . . .": Edith Roper, *Skeleton of Justice*, trans. Clara Leiser (New York: E.P. Dutton, 1941), pp. 52, 70.

233     they had made it clear that if he refused to confess . . . : This was claimed years later by a lawyer of Cramm's, according to Manfred Herzer, "Die Strafakte Gottfried von Cramm," *Capri: Zeitschrift fur Schwule Geschichte*, no. 1 (1991), p. 13. Such coercion was a common occurrence; in some cases, the court would openly admit to this "well-intentioned advice." See Geoffrey J. Giles, "Wegen der zu erwartenden hohen Strafe: Homosexuellenverfolgung in Berlin, 1933–1945, and "Homosexuelle Männer im KZ Sachsenhausen" (review)," *Holocaust and Genocide Studies* 17, no. 1 (Spring 2003), p. 197.

233–34  forgetting to take off their wedding rings . . . : Roper, *Skeleton of Justice*, p. 159.

234     But Cramm swore . . . : Landesarchiv files, Bestand A Rep. 358-02, Nr. 21070. Cramm's denial is on p. 21. Also see Herzer, "Die Strafakte Gottfried von Cramm," pp. 13–14.

234     The court accepted the defense . . . : On Cramm's conviction, see Landesarchiv files, Bestand A Rep. 358-02, Nr. 21070, 98301; "Cramm Sentenced to a Year in Prison," *New York Times*, May 15, 1938, p. 26.

235     this dreary hundred-year-old dungeon . . . : On Moabit prison, see Marie Vassiltchikov, *Berlin Diaries, 1940–1945* (New York: Alfred A. Knopf, 1985), p. 237; Leo Stein, *I Was in Hell with Niemoeller* (New York: Revell, 1942), p. 48.

235     Cramm apparently settled . . . : On Cramm in prison, see "Von Cramm a Jail Clerk," *New York Times*, September 1, 1938, p. 11; telephone interview with Herbert Schmidt, November 27, 2007; *American Lawn Tennis*, September 20, 1938, p. 39.

235     "If a player shall have . . .": Alan Trengove, *The Story of the Davis Cup* (London: Stanley Paul, 1985), p. 131.

236     Poland was the only country to protest . . . : "Davis Cup Changes," *American Lawn Tennis*, May 20, 1938, p. 8.

236     Henkel and Metaxa were particularly downtrodden . . . : "Germany's Davis Cup Team Is Called Home After Bad Beating at Hands of Australians," *New York Times*, August 21, 1938, p. 1.

236     "for good behavior": "Von Cramm Is Released," *New York Times*, October 17, 1938, p. 4.

237     thirty-five officers . . . : Giles, "Wegen der zu erwartenden hohen Strafe," p. 197.

237     any man convicted of "gross indecency" . . . : Richard Plant, *The Pink Triangle: The Nazi War Against Homosexuals* (New York: Holt, 1986), pp. 116–17.

237     *Strafkompanie* . . . : Giles, "Wegen der zu erwartenden hohen Strafe," p. 199.

237     They were called in front of the camp . . ." Heinz Heger, *The Men with the Pink Triangle* (Boston: Alyson, 1980), p. 34.

237     Richard Gabler: Giles, "Wegen der zu erwartenden hohen Strafe," p. 201.

237     The courts of the Allied Occupation . . . : Plant, *Pink Triangle*, p. 181.

237–38     "I have gone . . . ," "Since the return . . . ," and "I do not know . . .": "Developments in Germany," *American Lawn Tennis*, November 20, 1938, p. 16.

238     "a squad of Nazis led by Max Schmeling . . .": John Lardner, "The Total Interview," *New Yorker*, November 9, 1957, p. 167.

238     "a Wimbledon committee . . .": James Thurber, "The Helens' Wimbledon," *New Yorker*, July 16, 1938, p. 38. Cramm told reporters that he had decided not to play, and the All England Club announced publicly its regret, but almost all sources, including the following, agree that Wimbledon refused his entry due to his conviction. See Ulrich Kaiser, "Der Tennis-Baron," in Deutscher Tennis Bund, ed., *Tennis in Deutschland. Von den Anfängen bis 2002* (Berlin: Duncker & Humblot, 2002), pp. 149–51; Gianni Clerici, *The Ultimate Tennis Book*, trans. Richard J. Wiezell (Chicago: Follett, 1975), p. 202; and Godfrey Winn, *Tatler* no. 1983, June 28, 1939.

238     "the unofficial world's championship": Paul Metzler, *Tennis Styles and Stylists* (New York: Macmillan, 1970), p. 133.

239     "Rushing to the club . . ." and "Von Cramm is undoubtedly . . .": "Von Cramm Beats Riggs with Loss of One Game in London Tennis Semi-Finals," *New York Times*, June 24, 1939, p. 19.

239     "was in ruthless trim . . .": "Championship of London," [London] *Times*, June 24, 1939, p. 6.

239     lowered expectations were exactly what Riggs wanted: Tom Lecompte, *The Last Sure Thing: The Life and Times of Bobby Riggs* (Easthampton, Mass.: Black Squirrel, 2003), p. 74.

239     he bet on himself winning the singles . . . : Bobby Riggs with George McGann, *Court Hustler* (Philadelphia: Lippincott, 1973), pp. 64–66; Lecompte, *Last Sure Thing*, pp. 111–17.

239     "a Perry or a Budge at their best": *Lawn Tennis and Badminton* 30 (July 1, 1939), p. 232.

239–40     "If ever a player looked . . .": "Championships of London," [London] *Times*, June 26, 1939, p. 8.

240     "have always found someone to step into the breach . . .": "British Chances in Berlin," [London] *Times*, June 3, 1939, p. 4.

240     "moral turpitude": "Von Cramm States U.S. Bars His Entry," *New York Times*, June 17, 1939, p. 5.

240     "a good professional offer": "Von Cramm Planning to Play Tennis Here," *New York Times*, March 13, 1939, p. 24.

240     promoter Jack Harris: Ray Bowers, "Forgotten Victories: History of the Pro Tennis Wars, Chapter X: Budge's Great Pro Year, 1939," online at www.tennisserver.com/lines/lines_05_11_22_html. On Cramm's plans to live in the United States and play pro, see Al Laney, *Covering the Court: A Fifty-Year Love Affair with the Game of Tennis* (New York: Simon and Schuster, 1968), pp. 227–28.

240     "No matter what my views . . .": Tilden, *My Story*, p. 133.

240     he was drafted as a private . . . : On Cramm's military service, see Steinkamp, *Gottfried von Cramm*, pp. 137–40.

241     But he was also carrying messages . . . : Tatiana Metternich, *Purgatory of Fools* (New York: Quadrangle/NYT, 1976), p. 210; Steinkamp, *Gottfried von Cramm*, p. 141.

242     "hanged like cattle": William L. Shirer, *The Rise and Fall of the Third Reich* (New York: Simon and Schuster, 1960), pp. 1389, 1391.

242     "an intense friendship": Missy Vassiltchikov quoted in Steinkamp, *Gottfried von Cramm*, p. 142.

242     "hillocks of rubble" and "I don't want to hear what is happening to them . . .": Vassiltchikov, *Berlin Diaries*, pp. 121, 170, 232.

242     "a most courageous . . .": On Geoffrey Nares in Egypt, see Michael Holroyd, *Mosaic: A Family Memoir Revisited* (New York: W.W. Norton, 2004), p. 75; Cecil Beaton, *The Years Between: Diaries 1939–1944* (New York: Holt, Rinehart and Winston, 1965), p. 159.

243     Gottfried's ex-wife Lisa . . . : Interview with Burghard von Cramm, Hamburg, April 1, 2007; Steinkamp, *Gottfried von Cramm*, p. 90.

243     "Athlete of the Year" . . . : Paula Stuck von Reznicek, *Tennis-Faszination* (Munich: Schumacher-Gebler, 1969), p. 39; Rot-Weiss Tennis Club, *Gottfried Freiherr von Cramm: Fair Play ein Leben Lang, 1909–1976* (Berlin: Rot-Weiss Tennis Club, 1977), p. 13.

243     "Gottfried was a very private man . . .": Ron Fimrite, "Baron of the Court," *Sports Illustrated*, July 5, 1993.

244     his old partner Daniel Prenn: On Prenn's business career in England, see telephone interviews with Oliver Prenn, November 15, 2006, May 9, 2008, and October 16, 2008.

245     Prenn did pay a visit . . . : Interview with Wolfgang Hofer, Berlin, April 6, 2007.

246     "secret transatlantic telephone calls . . .": Drew Pearson quoted in C. David Heymann, *Poor Little Rich Girl: The Life and Legend of Barbara Hutton* (New York: Random House, 1983), p. 187.

246     "radio-telephone calls": FBI report quoted in ibid.

246     "honey hued" . . . "green lakes in the snow": Poem dated July 22, 1943, in Cramm's papers at Bodenburg, reproduced in Steinkamp, *Gottfried von Cramm*, p. 187.

246     a red leather picture frame . . . : Vassiltchikov, *Berlin Diaries*, p. 170.

246    even telephoning him for hours while on honeymoons . . . Cramm invited her to Cologne for a month . . . "Imagine! After all these years . . .": Heymann, *Poor Little Rich Girl*, pp. 231, 248, 277.

246    he helped East German tennis players . . . : Interview with Herbert Schmidt, November 27, 2007.

246    Gottfried bought him a small hotel . . . : Hofer quoted in Fimrite, "Baron of Court."

246–47 They were married . . . :" On the Cramm-Hutton marriage, see Heymann, *Poor Little Rich Girl*, pp. 277–82; Dean Southern Jennings, *Barbara Hutton: A Candid Biography* (New York: Fell, 1968), pp. 284–86; Mona Eldridge, *In Search of a Prince: My Life with Barbara Hutton* (London: Sidgwick and Jackson, 1988), pp. 180–81. Also see Christopher Wilson, *Dancing with the Devil: The Windsors and Jimmy Donahue* (New York: St. Martin's Press, 2001), p. 232.

247    he flew to Madrid . . . : Schmidt interview.

247    "I don't think I've ever seen a man more revered . . .": Fimrite, "Baron of Court."

247    On Cramm's death, see Schmidt interview; "Von Cramm, German Tennis Star of 1930's, Dies in Car Crash at 66," *New York Times*, November 10, 1976, p. 98.

247–48 hated hospitals and had sworn . . . : Ibid.

248    calmly reading Schopenhauer: Vassiltchikov, *Berlin Diaries*, p. 172.

248    "Gottfried was amazing . . .": Fimrite, "Baron of Court."

248    "Chamber music with white balls": Paula Stuck von Reznicek, *Gottfried von Cramm: Der Gentleman von Wimbledon* (Nuremberg: Olympia Verlag, 1949), p. 45.

248    "His shots came just a few centimeters above the net . . .": Schmidt interview. For other descriptions of Cramm's game, see Paul Metzler, *Tennis Styles and Stylists* (New York: Macmillan, 1970), p. 104; John Tunis, "Raising a Racket for Germany," *Collier's*, July 10, 1937, pp. 18, 38.

249    "Tilden came to play Budge, the greatest player of the day . . .": Laney quoted in Frank Deford, *Big Bill Tilden: The Triumphs and the Tragedy* (New York: Simon and Schuster, 1976), pp. 174–75.

249    "I have never seen such scenes . . .": E. J. Gillow, "Tilden Beats Budge at Southport," *American Lawn Tennis*, September 5, 1939, p. 20.

249    "They shouted and stamped on the floor . . .": Laney quoted in Deford, *Big Bill Tilden*, pp. 174–75.

249    "the greatest tennis I have ever seen": Ray Bowers, "Chapter X: Budge's Great Pro Year, 1939."

249    Tilden, for his part, humbly acknowledged . . . : William T. Tilden, "Pro Tourists—and the War," *American Lawn Tennis*, September 20, 1939, p. 20.

249    They were still playing in England . . . low-altitude bombing raids: Ibid.

249    His favorite place to play . . . : On the scene at Chaplin's court, see Deford, *Big Bill Tilden*, p. 229.

250    "plays tennis left-handed . . .": Harrison Kinney and Rosemary A.

Thurber, ed., *The Thurber Letters: The Wit, Wisdom, and Surprising Life of James Thurber* (New York: Simon and Schuster, 2003), p. 317.

250     "He still sinks his fangs . . .": "Big Bill Tilden, the Old Man River of Tennis, Rolls Along with Youth on a 25,25-Mile Tour," *Newsweek*, January 13, 1941, p. 46.

250     "Every night something would happen . . .": Stan Hart, *Once a Champion: Legendary Tennis Stars Revisited* (New York: Dodd, Mead, 1985), p. 141.

250     "Ladies and gentlemen, I believe you will observe . . .": Deford, *Big Bill Tilden*, pp. 170–71.

250–51   "You're a tennis artist, Bill . . .": Ibid., p. 76.

251     "Don didn't seem that impressed . . .": Interview with Gene Mako, Los Angeles, December 6, 2006.

251     "God, those legs . . . ,": Deford, *Big Bill Tilden*, pp. 235, 237.

251–52   "And Bill and I are trying like sons of bitches . . .": Mako interview.

252     he several times took a one- or two-set lead . . . : Deford, *Big Bill Tilden*, p. 244.

252     "If you came to Bill while he was playing bridge . . .": Mako interview.

252     "Kill myself": Hart, *Once a Champion*, p. 149; Deford, *Big Bill Tilden*, p. 168.

252     "It was obvious to me that he was a sick man . . .": Frederick Staunton in Deford, *Big Bill Tilden*, p. 244.

253     "Ashamed of himself . . .": Ibid., p. 18.

253     "I sincerely regret my actions . . .": Ibid., p. 250.

253     "near collapse . . . absolutely in shock": Associated Press and lawyer Richard Maddox, both ibid., p. 255. For more information on the trial, see "Tilden Goes to Jail in Delinquency Case," *New York Times*, January 17, 1947, p. 31.

254     "dictator": Bob Falkenburg quoted in Hart, *Once a Champion*, p. 381.

254     "prim and prissy bachelor . . .": E. Digby Baltzell, *Sporting Gentlemen: Men's Tennis from the Age of Honor to the Cult of the Superstar* (New York: Free Press, 1995), p. 215.

254     "In all the years I knew Tilden . . .": Riggs quoted in Deford, *Big Bill Tilden*, p. 230.

254     "Only when Big Bill discusses the kids . . .": John K. Winkler, "The Iconoclast of the Courts," *New Yorker*, September 18, 1926, p. 29.

254     "Your Old Man, Bill": Tilden to Arthur Anderson, March 17, 1946, viewed online at ebay.com.

255     When the police knocked . . . : On Tilden's second arrest and conviction, see Deford, *Big Bill Tilden*, pp. 261–64; "Tilden Gets Year in Jail," *New York Times*, February 11, 1949, p. 18; "Tilden Sentenced Again," *New York Times*, February 18, 1949, p. 18.

255     "J. F. Grover, jailer . . .": "Tilden Is Released From Jail," *New York Times*, December 19, 1949, p. 44.

255     the Associated Press released a poll . . . : "The Old Master of the Tennis Courts," *New York Times*, February 4, 1950, p. 22.

255–56 "I loved Bill . . .": Samantha Stevenson, "The Days of Vines and Roses," *World Tennis*, November 1990, p. 34.

256 "a wrinkled old-timer . . .": Vladimir Nabokov, *Lolita* (1955; reprint New York: Crest, 1959), p. 148.

256 "I'll play tennis with anyone . . .": Deford, *Big Bill Tilden*, p. 267.

256–57 "My God, that was the saddest thing I ever had to do . . .": Ibid., p. 271.

257 "Vinnie, could you please send me . . .": Laney, *Covering the Court*, p. 62.

257 "I am in real need of money, therefore this offer": Deford, *Big Bill Tilden*, p. 272.

257 The Andersons invited Bill to dinner . . . : On Tilden's final day, see Deford, *Big Bill Tilden*, pp. 273–75.

257 he played five sets on Charlie Chaplin's court . . . : Hart, *Once a Champion*, p. 213.

258 "Our greatest athlete in any sport": Al Laney, quoted in Herbert Warren Wind, "Budge and the Grand Slam," *New Yorker*, February 15, 1988, p. 89.

258 "a background of avalanched rubble . . ." and "Whatever happened to that redheaded young man?": John McPhee, *Wimbledon: A Celebration* (New York: Viking Press, 1972), p. 72. This was not Queen Mary but her daughter-in-law, Queen Elizabeth—but apparently she remembered Budge too.

258–59 "Budge is the world champion . . .": *Sydney Mail*, Schools' Number, December 8, 1937, p. 32.

259 "too busy chasing girls in Australia": Telephone interview with Patricia Yeomans, December 14, 2006.

259 "with the inevitable Victrola record": Photo caption in *American Lawn Tennis*, March 20, 1938, p. 7.

260 "This concert is for my good friend, Don Budge": Budge, *Tennis Memoir*, pp. 108–9.

260 "running around the court like a son of a bitch": Mako interview.

260 a rare hurricane . . . : On Budge and Mako during 1938 rainouts, see Mako interview; "Drummer," *New Yorker*, August 13, 1938, p. 11; Budge, *Tennis Memoir*, p. 82; *New York Times* tennis coverage that week.

261 He took on Ellsworth Vines . . . : The Budge vs. Vines figures vary slightly from source to source; these are from Ray Bowers, "Chapter X: Budge's Great Pro Year, 1939."

261 In 1939 he earned . . . : Don Budge, unpublished article manuscript, 1975 (courtesy of Jeff Budge); Hart, *Once a Champion*, p. 154.

262 But in May 1941 he married . . . : On Budge's plastic surgery and wedding, see Mako interview; Robert Kelleher interview; "Budge Loses at Chicago," *New York Times*, May 28, 1941, p. 36; Ray Bowers, "A History of Pro Tennis 1926–1945, Chapter XI: America, 1940–1941," online at www.tennisserver.com/lines/lines_06_10_01.html; interview with Jeff Budge, Newport, September 19, 2008.

262 "It was kind of tough to while away the time . . .": Hart, *Once a Champion*, p. 147.

262     Riggs always thought he won due . . . : Ibid., p. 414.

262–63   "I don't think Bobby would have had the ability . . .": Interview with Jack Kramer, Los Angeles, December 6, 2006.

263     "And hundreds of nights staying up drinking . . .": Mako interview.

263     "Sinatra and Bing Crosby . . ." . . . Hymnin' Hangover: Interview with David Budge, Los Angeles, December 5, 2006.

263     they entertained friends like jazz musicians . . . : Ibid.

263     "No one . . . and I mean no one . . .": Eugene Scott, "Death of a Champion," *Wall Street Journal*, February 1, 2000.

264     "the seeing hand": St. Mary's College of Maryland, *River Gazette*, December–January 2005, p. 14.

264     "I didn't recognize him at first . . .": Budge, in conversation with Richard Evans, quoted in "Courtside: the Racquet World," a department of an unidentified magazine, E. Digby Baltzell Papers, University of Pennsylvania.

264     they were playing a series of exhibition matches . . . : Ulrich Kaiser, "Eine Freundschaft," p. 154.

264     "I tried to get him into the U.S. . . .": Hart, *Once a Champion*, p. 41; *Boston Globe*, November 10, 1976; Arthur Daley, "Over the Net at Forest Hills," *New York Times*, August 31, 1947, p. S2; Ulrich Kaiser, "Eine Freundschaft," p. 154.

264–65   "I never played better . . .": Budge, *Tennis Memoir*, p. 4.

265     "a match which will be forever memorable . . .": "The Davis Cup: Germany Fight to the Last," [London] *Times*, July 21, 1937, p. 6.

265     "The brilliance of the tennis was almost unbelievable . . .": Allison Danzig, "The Story of J. Donald Budge," in Budge, *Budge on Tennis*, p. 38.

265     "all but cried when the fair-haired lad was beaten": "July Moments," ESPN Classic, http://sports.espn.go.com/espn/classic/news/story?page= classic_july.

265     "the greatest tennis match ever played": Budge, *Tennis Memoir*, p. 18.

265     there were still thousands of people there . . . : Ibid., p. 4.

265     "in the bright and terrible summer of 1940": Lewis Eliot, quoted in epigraph to *A Summer Bright and Terrible* by David E. Fisher (Emeryville, Calif.: Shoemaker & Hoard, 2005).

265     used to raise pigs . . . : Allison Danzig, "Pigs at Fair Wimbledon," *New York Times*, December 17, 1940, p. 36.

266     he wished that he had lost it: Don Budge, interview by Egon Steinkamp, 1988, in Steinkamp, *Gottfried von Cramm*, p. 12.

266     As an old man he would still remember . . . : *Kings of the Court: The Ten Greatest Tennis Players of All Time*, Tennis Classics Production Company and the International Tennis Hall of Fame, VHS tape, 1997.

# INDEX